Disaster Risk Reduction

Methods, Approaches and Practices

Series Editor

Rajib Shaw, Keio University, Shonan Fujisawa Campus, Fujisawa, Japan

Disaster risk reduction is a process that leads to the safety of communities and nations. After the 2005 World Conference on Disaster Reduction, held in Kobe, Japan, the Hyogo Framework for Action (HFA) was adopted as a framework for risk reduction. The academic research and higher education in disaster risk reduction has made, and continues to make, a gradual shift from pure basic research to applied, implementation-oriented research. More emphasis is being given to multi-stakeholder collaboration and multi-disciplinary research. Emerging university networks in Asia, Europe, Africa, and the Americas have urged process-oriented research in the disaster risk reduction field. With this in mind, this new series will promote the output of action research on disaster risk reduction, which will be useful for a wide range of stakeholders including academicians, professionals, practitioners, and students and researchers in related fields. The series will focus on emerging needs in the risk reduction field, starting from climate change adaptation, urban ecosystem, coastal risk reduction, education for sustainable development, community-based practices, risk communication, and human security, among other areas. Through academic review, this series will encourage young researchers and practitioners to analyze field practices and link them to theory and policies with logic, data, and evidence. In this way, the series will emphasize evidence-based risk reduction methods, approaches, and practices.

All submitted proposals are carefully reviewed by the series editor.

Publication Ethics and Publication Malpractice Statement: https://www.springernature.com/gp/policies/book-publishing-policies

Ethical, Conflict-of-Interest, and Editorial Policy Statement: https://www.springer.com/us/authors-editors/journal-author/journal-author-helpdesk/before-you-start/before-you-start/1330#c14214

Yan Cui · Rajib Shaw
Editors

Disaster Law

Implications to Governance and Implementation

Springer

Editors
Yan Cui
School of Law
Gansu University of Political Science and Law
Lanzhou, Gansu, China

Rajib Shaw
Graduate School of Media and Governance
Keio University
Fujisawa, Kanagawa, Japan

ISSN 2196-4106 ISSN 2196-4114 (electronic)
Disaster Risk Reduction
ISBN 978-981-97-7373-2 ISBN 978-981-97-7374-9 (eBook)
https://doi.org/10.1007/978-981-97-7374-9

This Springer imprint is published by the registered company Springer Nature Singapore Pte Ltd.
The registered company address is: 152 Beach Road, #21-01/04 Gateway East, Singapore 189721, Singapore

Preface

In an era marked by unprecedented natural and human-induced disasters, the need for robust legal frameworks to manage these events has never been more critical. *Disaster Law: Implications to Governance and Implementation* delves into the intricate web of laws, regulations, and policies that underpin disaster management. This book seeks to provide a comprehensive understanding of how disaster law shapes and is shaped by governance structures and the practicalities of implementation on the ground.

The primary objective of this work is to explore the multifaceted nature of disaster law and its profound impact on national and international governance. By examining case studies from around the world, we aim to highlight best practices, identify gaps, and propose innovative solutions to enhance legal and institutional responses to disasters. Our analysis spans various dimensions, including disaster risk reduction, preparedness, emergency response, and recovery, reflecting the complexity and interconnectedness of contemporary disaster management.

The book comprises of 19 chapters focusing on disaster laws from different parts of the world. Each chapter is written by expert scholars or practitioners in their respective fields, who have adequate professional experience. This book is intended for a broad audience, including policymakers, legal practitioners, scholars, and students in the fields of law, public administration, environmental studies, and disaster management. It offers a critical examination of existing legal frameworks and provides actionable insights for improving the effectiveness and resilience of disaster governance.

We hope that *Disaster Law: Implications to Governance and Implementation* will serve as a valuable resource for those engaged in shaping and implementing disaster policies. By fostering a deeper understanding of the legal dimensions of disaster management, we aspire to contribute to the development of more resilient societies capable of withstanding and recovering from the myriad challenges posed by disasters.

We will be very happy if the readers find this book useful for their work.

Lanzhou, China — Yan Cui
Fujisawa, Japan — Rajib Shaw

About This Book

Disaster Law is the core of disaster risk management. The legal framework not only provides the government an instrument for taking actions before, during and after a disaster, it also helps in the recovery process. The legislative measures provide certain levels of guidance to all different stakeholders from national governments, local governments, civil societies, and more importantly citizens. The legal provision gives the people and communities certain obligations as well as responsibilities to act during or before the disasters. Over the last several years, there have been new disaster laws formulated in many countries, and revisions have been made to adjust the existing disaster laws to be more effective. While it is important to have governance provision of disaster law, the important point is its implementation.

Keeping this in mind, this book covers the broader aspects of disaster legislation, keeping in mind the governance as well as implementation aspects. The book includes in-depth reviews as well as new data, based on case studies across the globe, involving multidisciplinary research. Finally, the book suggests specific policy and action measures to enhance the implementation of disaster legislation to enhance the resilience of people and the state. Overall, this book is a valuable resource material for students, researchers, academia, policymakers, and development practitioners.

Contents

1 **Disaster Law: An Overview on Its History, Potentials and Challenges** ... 1
Rajib Shaw and Yan Cui

2 **Disaster Management Law in the European Union** ... 15
Zhiying Zhao and Rajib Shaw

3 **Disaster Management Law and Agreement in ASEAN** ... 37
Krishnakali Ghosh, Ranit Chatterjee, and Rajib Shaw

4 **Key Issues and Challenges of Disaster Law in Japan** ... 55
Ruiyan Zhao, Tomo Kawane, and Rajib Shaw

5 **Disaster Law in the United States** ... 69
Yafang Wen and Rajib Shaw

6 **Disaster Law in China** ... 89
Yan Cui, Yafang Wen, Yinan Gao, and Rajib Shaw

7 **Disaster Law in Australia** ... 109
Rong Huang and Rajib Shaw

8 **Disaster Management Law in Türkiye** ... 121
Burcak Basbug

9 **Policies and Legislation on Disaster Risk Governance and Management in Thailand** ... 133
Indrajit Pal and Nattasuda Anusonadisai Kaplin

10 **Disaster Legislation in Malaysia: A Scoping Review** ... 149
Nurfashareena Muhamad, Aida Soraya Shamsuddin, Lim Choun Sian, and Joy Jacqueline Pereira

11 **Building a Nation of Lifesavers** ... 171
How Hwa Teong and Xuan En Constance Ng

12 **Disaster Law in Indonesia** ... 183
Ariyaningsih, Riyan Benny Sukmara, Rizqi Bachtiar, Arsyad A. Iriansyah, and Rajib Shaw

13 **Disaster Legislation in the Philippines** ... 207
Ma. Theresa P. Pamaong and Rajib Shaw

14 **Disaster Law in Bangladesh: Current Scenario, Management Strategies and Challenges** ... 223
Md. Hosenuzzaman, Ummoy Sumaia Shammy, Mohammad Golam Kibria, and Md. Anwarul Abedin

15 **Disaster Management Act of India** ... 237
Sujata Saunik, Anuska Ray, and Rajib Shaw

16 **Disaster Management Law in Nepal** ... 255
Namita Poudel, Avani Dixit, Naomi Kato, and Rajib Shaw

17 **Legal and Policy Developments for Effective Disaster Management: A Review of Disaster Laws and Policies in Sri Lanka** ... 271
Deepthi Wickramasinghe, Vihanga Amarakoon, Yasaswi Madawala, and Dilisha Gunawardena

18 **Disaster Management Law in Pakistan** ... 293
Muneeb-ur Rahman, Haseeb-ur Rahman, Atta-ur Rahman, and Rajib Shaw

19 **Water Scarcity: Judicial Responses to the Disaster in Making** ... 307
Priya A. Sondhi and Anoop Kumar

Editors and Contributors

About the Editors

Yan Cui is an Associate Professor in the School of Law at Gansu University of Political Science and Law in China. She is also a Young Scientist involved in Integrated Research on Disaster Risk (IRDR). Additionally, she is a member of the Legal Talent Pool for the Gansu Provincial Government and an adjunct researcher at the Civil-Military Integration Law Research Institute, China University of Political Science and Law. Prior to this, she served as a post-doctoral research fellow and lecturer in Law at Shandong University (Weihai Campus) in China. In addition, she holds the position of Director of the Health Law Society of Hunan Province in China. Her expertise lies in international disaster law and international humanitarian law. Her research articles have been published in the Journal of Law in China and the China Military Science Journal. She has collaborated with the International Federation of Red Cross and Red Crescent Societies (IFRC) on research related to international disaster response law and disaster risk reduction law in China. Since 2018, she has been actively involved as a coach and judge in various international law moot competitions in China, including the Philip C. Jessup International Law Moot Competition, Red Cross International Humanitarian Law Moot, and International Criminal Court (ICC) Moot Competition. These competitions provide law students with a platform to learn about current global international law issues and address them at their core.

Rajib Shaw is a Professor at the Graduate School of Media and Governance of Keio University, Japan. He is the co-founder of a Delhi (India) based social entrepreneur startup Resilience Innovation Knowledge Academy (RIKA), and RIKA Institute. He is the Co-chair of the United Nations Asia Pacific Science Technology Advisory Group (AP-STAG) and was CLA for IPCC's 6th Assessment Report. Professor Shaw is the recipient of the prestigious "Pravasi Bharatiya Samman Award (PBSA)" in 2021 for his contribution to the education sector. He also received the United Nations Sasakawa Award in 2022 for his lifetime contributions to the field of disaster risk reduction. He published 79 books and over 450 research papers. More about his work can be found at: www.rajibshaw.org.

Contributors

Md. Anwarul Abedin Laboratory of Environment and Sustainable Development, Department of Soil Science, Bangladesh Agricultural University, Mymensingh, Bangladesh

Vihanga Amarakoon Department of Zoology and Environment Sciences, Faculty of Science, University of Colombo, Colombo, Sri Lanka

Ariyaningsih Graduate School of Media and Governance, Keio University, Tokyo, Japan;
Department of Urban Planning, Institut Teknologi Kalimantan, Kalimantan, Indonesia

Rizqi Bachtiar School of Politics and International Studies, University of Leeds, Leeds, UK;
Department of Governmental Science, Brawijaya University, Jawa Timur, Indonesia

Burcak Basbug Middle East Technical University, Ankara, Turkey

Ranit Chatterjee Resilience Innovation Knowledge Academy (RIKA), New Delhi, India

Yan Cui School of Law, Gansu University of Political Science and Law, Lanzhou, Gansu Province, China

Avani Dixit Graduate School of Media and Governance, Keio University, Fujisawa, Japan

Yinan Gao Graduate School of Media and Governance, Keio University, Fujisawa, Japan

Krishnakali Ghosh Resilience Innovation Knowledge Academy (RIKA), New Delhi, India

Dilisha Gunawardena Department of Zoology and Environment Sciences, Faculty of Science, University of Colombo, Colombo, Sri Lanka

Md. Hosenuzzaman Laboratory of Environment and Sustainable Development, Department of Soil Science, Bangladesh Agricultural University, Mymensingh, Bangladesh

Rong Huang Graduate School of Media and Governance, Keio University, Fujisawa, Japan

Arsyad A. Iriansyah Indonesian National Agency for Disaster Management (BNPB), Jakarta Timur, Indonesia

Nattasuda Anusonadisai Kaplin Development Planning Management and Innovation, Asian Institute of Technology, Khlong Luang, Thailand

Naomi Kato Graduate School of Media and Governance, Keio University, Fujisawa, Japan

Tomo Kawane Graduate School of Media and Governance, Keio University, Fujisawa, Japan

Mohammad Golam Kibria Laboratory of Environment and Sustainable Development, Department of Soil Science, Bangladesh Agricultural University, Mymensingh, Bangladesh

Anoop Kumar Buxar, Bihar, India

Yasaswi Madawala Department of Zoology and Environment Sciences, Faculty of Science, University of Colombo, Colombo, Sri Lanka

Nurfashareena Muhamad Southeast Asia Disaster Prevention Research Initiative (SEADPRI), Institute for Environment and Development, Universiti Kebangsaan Malaysia, Bangi, Malaysia

Xuan En Constance Ng Singapore Civil Defense, Singapore, Singapore

Indrajit Pal Disaster Preparedness, Mitigation and Management, Asian Institute of Technology, Khlong Luang, Thailand

Ma. Theresa P. Pamaong Graduate School of Media and Governance, Keio University, Fujisawa, Japan

Joy Jacqueline Pereira Southeast Asia Disaster Prevention Research Initiative (SEADPRI), Institute for Environment and Development, Universiti Kebangsaan Malaysia, Bangi, Malaysia

Namita Poudel Graduate School of Media and Governance, Keio University, Fujisawa, Japan

Atta-ur Rahman Department of Geography and Geomatics, University of Peshawar, Peshawar, Pakistan

Haseeb-ur Rahman Institute of Space Technology, Islamabad, Pakistan

Muneeb-ur Rahman Law College, University of Peshawar, Peshawar, Pakistan

Anuska Ray Graduate School of Media and Governance, Keio University, Fujisawa, Japan

Sujata Saunik Graduate School of Media and Governance, Keio University, Fujisawa, Japan

Ummoy Sumaia Shammy Department of Agro-Meteorology, Agricultural University, Mymensingh, Bangladesh

Aida Soraya Shamsuddin Southeast Asia Disaster Prevention Research Initiative (SEADPRI), Institute for Environment and Development, Universiti Kebangsaan Malaysia, Bangi, Malaysia

Rajib Shaw Graduate School of Media and Governance, Keio University, Tokyo, Fujisawa, Minato, Japan

Lim Choun Sian Southeast Asia Disaster Prevention Research Initiative (SEADPRI), Institute for Environment and Development, Universiti Kebangsaan Malaysia, Bangi, Malaysia

Priya A. Sondhi Gurjinder Vihar, Greater Noida, UP, India

Riyan Benny Sukmara Department of Civil Engineering, National Central University, Taoyuan City, Taiwan;
Department of Civil Engineering at Institut Teknologi Kalimantan, Kalimantan, Indonesia

How Hwa Teong Singapore Civil Defense, Singapore, Singapore

Yafang Wen Graduate School of Media and Governance, Keio University, Fujisawa, Japan

Deepthi Wickramasinghe Department of Zoology and Environment Sciences, Faculty of Science, University of Colombo, Colombo, Sri Lanka

Ruiyan Zhao Graduate School of Media and Governance, Keio University, Fujisawa, Japan

Zhiying Zhao Graduate School of Media and Governance, Keio University, Fujisawa, Japan

Chapter 1
Disaster Law: An Overview on Its History, Potentials and Challenges

Rajib Shaw and Yan Cui

Abstract Disaster law encompasses a multifaceted legal framework designed to mitigate, respond to, and recover from disasters. This chapter explores the evolution and principles of disaster law, focusing on its role in managing natural and human-induced disasters. Key components include legal provisions for disaster risk reduction, preparedness, emergency response, and recovery efforts. The chapter examines how disaster law establishes institutional frameworks, delineates responsibilities among governmental and non-governmental entities, and incorporates international norms and standards. It also addresses legal mechanisms for coordination, cooperation, and information sharing during disaster events, emphasizing the importance of cross-sectoral collaboration and community engagement. Roles of international frameworks like Hyogo Framework for Action (HFA) and Sendai Framework for Disaster Risk Reduction (SFDRR) are highlighted. An analysis on the potentials and challenges of legislative measures are discussed, and specific section focuses on adaptive governance, which becomes extremely relevant in the current complex global risk landscape. Ultimately, the chapter underscores the crucial role of disaster law in enhancing resilience, protecting lives and livelihoods, and fostering sustainable development in the face of increasingly complex and interconnected risks.

Keywords Disaster law · Adaptive governance · HFA · SFDRR · Complex global risk landscape

---

R. Shaw (✉)
Graduate School of Media and Governance, Keio University, 5322 Endo, Fujisawa 252-0882, Japan
e-mail: shaw@sfc.keio.ac.jp

Y. Cui
School of Law, Gansu University of Political Science and Law, Anningxilu, Lanzhou 730070, China

Y. Cui and R. Shaw (eds.), *Disaster Law*, Disaster Risk Reduction,
https://doi.org/10.1007/978-981-97-7374-9_1

2. **Enhanced Risk Assessment and Early Warning Systems**
    - **Legal Mandates for Risk Assessment**: Legislation can mandate regular risk assessments and the development of early warning systems, leading to better preparedness and timely responses to disasters.
    - **Technological Integration**: Advancements in technology, such as remote sensing, AI, and big data analytics, can be leveraged within legal frameworks to improve risk assessment and early warning capabilities.
3. **Community Resilience and Participation**
    - **Empowering Communities**: Disaster laws that promote community engagement and capacity building can lead to more resilient communities. Legal provisions for community-based DRR initiatives ensure local needs and knowledge are incorporated into disaster management plans.
    - **Public Education Campaigns**: Legally mandated public education campaigns can raise awareness about disaster risks and encourage proactive behaviors to reduce vulnerability.
4. **International Cooperation and Support**
    - **Mutual Aid Agreements**: Disaster legislation can facilitate international cooperation through mutual aid agreements, enabling resource sharing and collaborative response efforts during large-scale disasters.
    - **Adherence to International Standards**: Aligning national laws with international frameworks, such as the Sendai Framework for Disaster Risk Reduction, can enhance global coherence and effectiveness in disaster management.
5. **Sustainable Development Integration**
    - **Resilient Infrastructure**: Legal frameworks that incorporate DRR into development planning can ensure that infrastructure and development projects are resilient to disaster risks, promoting sustainable development.
    - **Climate Change Adaptation**: Integrating disaster legislation with climate change adaptation policies can address the increasing frequency and intensity of climate-related disasters, fostering long-term resilience.

Disaster governance and legislation face numerous challenges, including coordination issues, resource constraints, and public engagement barriers. However, the potentials they offer, such as strengthened institutional frameworks, enhanced risk assessment capabilities, and increased community resilience, are substantial. By addressing these challenges and leveraging the potentials, societies can significantly improve their disaster preparedness, response, and recovery efforts, ultimately reducing the impact of disasters on lives, property, and the environment.

1.1 Introduction

Disasters, induced by natural or other types of hazards, pose significant threats to human life, property, and the environment. The complexity of managing such crises necessitates a robust legal framework to ensure preparedness, response, recovery, and mitigation. It also requires a multidisciplinary approach, integrating insights from environmental science, engineering, public health, and social sciences with legal expertise. Disaster law not only outlines the roles and responsibilities of governmental agencies at local, national, and international levels but also involves non-governmental organizations, private sector stakeholders, and the public.

Disaster laws, therefore, encompass a wide range of regulations, policies, and statutes designed to minimize the impact of disasters and facilitate effective management when they occur. Disaster law is a specialized field of legal practice and scholarship that addresses the preparation, response, recovery, and mitigation of disasters. The legal frameworks surrounding disaster management are essential for ensuring effective and coordinated actions before, during, and after such events. The evolution of disaster law has been driven by the increasing recognition of the need for structured and comprehensive approaches to manage disasters. Historically, responses to disasters were largely reactive, with ad hoc measures being implemented in the wake of a catastrophe. Over time, it became clear that proactive legal and policy measures were necessary to mitigate the impacts of disasters, facilitate efficient responses, and ensure sustainable recovery and reconstruction.

The United Nations (UN) recognizes the importance of legal frameworks in disaster risk reduction (DRR) and management. Disaster law is seen as a critical component in achieving sustainable development and resilience against disasters. The UN, through various agencies and frameworks, emphasizes the role of law in mitigating disaster risks and enhancing preparedness and response capabilities. In addition to national laws and policies, international frameworks play a crucial role in shaping disaster law. Instruments such as the Sendai Framework for Disaster Risk Reduction and the principles of international humanitarian law provide guidelines and standards for effective disaster management. These frameworks emphasize the importance of preparedness, community participation, and the need for a comprehensive, all-hazards approach to disaster risk reduction.

Disaster law refers to the body of rules and principles that govern the preparation for, response to, and recovery from disasters. It encompasses a wide range of legal frameworks, including national legislation, international treaties, regulations, and policies designed to manage disaster risks and enhance resilience. Disaster law aims to provide a structured and systematic approach to addressing the legal aspects of disaster management, ensuring effective coordination, protection of human rights, and the provision of humanitarian aid (UNDRR 2015).

The importance of disaster law is underscored by the increasing frequency and intensity of disasters globally, often exacerbated by climate change. Effective legal frameworks are essential to address the multifaceted challenges posed by disasters, ensuring that societies can not only respond efficiently to crises but also build back better, enhancing resilience and reducing future risks. In summary, disaster law is a vital field that underpins the structured and effective management of disasters. By establishing clear legal frameworks and fostering international cooperation, disaster law plays a critical role in safeguarding lives, property, and the environment, ultimately contributing to the resilience and well-being of communities worldwide. This chapter provides a simple overview of disaster law with its potentials and challenges.

1.2 The Hyogo Framework for Action and Disaster Law

The Hyogo Framework for Action (HFA) 2005–2015 was a pivotal international initiative aimed at substantially reducing disaster losses by 2015. Adopted at the World Conference on Disaster Reduction in Kobe, Hyogo, Japan, the HFA provided a comprehensive blueprint for disaster risk reduction (DRR) efforts worldwide. This framework significantly influenced the development and enhancement of disaster law, guiding national and local governments in creating robust legal structures to manage disaster risks effectively (UNISDR 2005).

The HFA outlined five priority areas for action:

1. Ensure that disaster risk reduction is a national and local priority with a strong institutional basis for implementation.
2. Identify, assess, and monitor disaster risks and enhance early warning.
3. Use knowledge, innovation, and education to build a culture of safety and resilience at all levels.
4. Reduce the underlying risk factors.
5. Strengthen disaster preparedness for effective response at all levels.

These priorities underscored the need for comprehensive and integrated approaches to disaster management, embedding DRR into all aspects of governance and societal development. The HFA's impact on disaster law is profound, encouraging countries to adopt and refine legal frameworks that support the priorities outlined. Below are key areas where the HFA influenced disaster law.

The HFA emphasized the importance of establishing disaster risk reduction as a national and local priority. This led to the development of laws that created or strengthened institutions responsible for disaster management. Many countries enacted legislation to establish national disaster management agencies or authorities, tasked with coordinating DRR efforts across various sectors and levels of government. These legal frameworks provided the foundation for coherent and coordinated disaster risk governance.

Legal frameworks were influenced by the HFA's call for robust risk assessment and early warning systems. Laws were developed to mandate regular hazard and vulnerability assessments, integrating scientific and local knowledge to inform DRR strategies. Additionally, legal provisions ensured the development and maintenance of early warning systems, crucial for timely and effective disaster response. These systems were legally required to be accessible to all, ensuring that warnings reached vulnerable communities.

The HFA highlighted the need to build a culture of safety and resilience through knowledge, innovation, and education. This priority translated into laws mandating public education campaigns on disaster preparedness and risk reduction. Schools incorporated DRR into their curricula, and community training programs were legally supported to enhance public awareness and preparedness.

Addressing the underlying risk factors of disasters, such as poor land use planning and environmental degradation, was a key focus of the HFA. Legal frameworks were developed or revised to include strict building codes, land use regulations, and environmental protection laws. These laws aimed to mitigate risks associated with infrastructure development, ensuring that buildings and communities were resilient to disasters. The HFA's ten-year tenure significantly advanced the global DRR agenda, embedding DRR principles into national and local laws and policies. Its successor, the Sendai Framework for Disaster Risk Reduction 2015–2030, builds on the HFA's foundation, emphasizing an even broader and more inclusive approach to disaster risk management.

1.3 Evolution of Disaster Law in Asia

Strengthening disaster preparedness for effective response was a central tenet of the HFA. This led to the formulation of laws that established clear protocols for emergency response, including the allocation of resources, coordination mechanisms, and roles and responsibilities of various stakeholders. Legal frameworks ensured that emergency plans were regularly updated and tested through drills and simulations. Japan is one of the key countries in the world which has established its Basic Disaster Countermeasures Act back in 1961, after the major Isewan Typhoon of 1959 (CAO 1961).

The timing of HFA was also crucial, which was after the 2004 India Ocean Tsunami, which was one of the deadliest disasters in the recent past. This also prompted the establishment of legal provisions in many Asian countries (WB 2024). India established its Disaster Management Act in 2005. This act marks the formal establishment of a comprehensive legal and institutional framework for disaster management in India. It led to the creation of the National Disaster Management Authority (NDMA) and laid down policies, plans, and guidelines for disaster prevention, mitigation, and preparedness. Similarly, post the 2004 Indian Ocean tsunami, Sri Lanka enacted this law to enhance disaster preparedness and response. The act led to the formation of the Disaster Management Centre (DMC), responsible for implementing disaster risk reduction strategies. Pakistan established its Disaster Management Ordinance in 2006. This ordinance established the National Disaster Management Authority (NDMA) and provided a legal framework for disaster management across the country. It was later replaced by the National Disaster Management Act in 2010.

The Disaster Law of the People's Republic of China was enacted on October 30, 2007. This law provides a legal framework for disaster prevention, reduction, emergency response, and recovery efforts in China. It aims to improve the country's capacity to mitigate and respond to natural disasters and other emergencies. Indonesia's Disaster Management Law was also established in 2007. The law set the foundation for disaster risk management in Indonesia. It created the National Agency for Disaster Management (BNPB) and aimed to integrate disaster risk reduction into development planning. The Philippine Disaster Risk Reduction and Management Act was formed in 2010. This act is a landmark legislation that established the National Disaster Risk Reduction and Management Council (NDRRMC). It promotes a holistic, proactive, and integrated approach to disaster risk reduction and management. Bangladesh established its disaster management framework through the Disaster Management Act in 2012, which focuses on reducing disaster risks and improving resilience. The act emphasizes community participation and the integration of disaster risk reduction into national policies and planning. Vietnam had its Law on Natural Disaster Prevention and Control in 2013. Vietnam's comprehensive disaster management law focuses on disaster risk reduction, preparedness, and response. It established mechanisms for coordination and collaboration among various stakeholders at all levels.

1.4 SFDRR and Disaster Law

The Sendai Framework for Disaster Risk Reduction (SFDRR: 2015–2030) is a landmark international agreement adopted by the United Nations to guide global efforts in reducing disaster risk and enhancing resilience to disasters. While the framework itself is not a legal document, it provides essential guidelines and principles that influence the development and implementation of disaster laws worldwide. Here's how the Sendai Framework addresses key aspects relevant to disaster law (UNDRR 2015). Following are the key principles and priorities of Sendai Framework.

1. **Understanding Disaster Risk**
    - **Legal Frameworks for Risk Assessment**: The Sendai Framework emphasizes the importance of comprehensive risk assessments, which necessitate robust legal structures to support data collection, sharing, and analysis. Laws must facilitate the integration of disaster risk information into planning and decision-making processes across sectors.
2. **Strengthening Disaster Risk Governance to Manage Disaster Risk**
    - **Governance and Legal Instruments**: Effective disaster risk governance requires clear legal mandates and institutional frameworks. The Sendai Framework calls for the establishment and strengthening of national and local legal frameworks to ensure that all relevant stakeholders, including government

agencies, private sector entities, and civil society organizations, have defined roles and responsibilities in disaster risk management.
- **Policy Coherence**: It encourages the alignment of disaster risk reduction laws with other relevant legislation, such as climate change adaptation and sustainable development policies, to create a coherent and integrated approach to managing risks.

3. **Investing in Disaster Risk Reduction for Resilience**

- **Incentives and Regulations**: The framework highlights the need for legal and regulatory measures to incentivize investments in disaster risk reduction. This includes the adoption of building codes, land use planning regulations, and financial mechanisms that promote resilient infrastructure and development practices.
- **Public and Private Sector Engagement**: Legal frameworks should facilitate public–private partnerships and ensure that both sectors contribute to disaster risk reduction efforts through investments and compliance with safety standards.

4. **Enhancing Disaster Preparedness for Effective Response and to "Build Back Better" in Recovery, Rehabilitation, and Reconstruction**

- **Emergency Response Legislation**: The Sendai Framework underscores the importance of legal provisions for effective emergency response, including the establishment of clear command and control structures, resource allocation mechanisms, and coordination protocols among various agencies and organizations.
- **Recovery and Reconstruction Laws**: It advocates for laws and policies that support the principles of "Build Back Better" during the recovery and reconstruction phases. This means integrating disaster risk reduction measures into post-disaster rebuilding efforts to enhance resilience and reduce future vulnerabilities.

Legal and Policy Recommendations

- **Inclusivity and Participation**: Legal frameworks should promote inclusive decision-making processes, ensuring the participation of all stakeholders, including vulnerable groups, in disaster risk management.
- **Accountability and Transparency**: The Sendai Framework calls for laws that enforce accountability and transparency in disaster risk reduction efforts. This includes mechanisms for monitoring, evaluation, and reporting on progress.
- **Capacity Building**: It recommends legal provisions that support capacity building at all levels, enabling institutions and communities to effectively implement disaster risk reduction measures.

International Cooperation and Legal Harmonization

- **Cross-Border and Regional Cooperation**: The framework encourages countries to enter into mutual aid agreements and harmonize their disaster laws to facilitate international cooperation and assistance during disasters.
- **Adherence to International Standards**: It promotes the adoption of international guidelines and standards in national disaster risk reduction laws, ensuring consistency and enhancing global resilience.

The Sendai Framework for Disaster Risk Reduction provides a comprehensive blueprint for enhancing global disaster resilience. By advocating for strong legal and institutional frameworks, the framework influences the development and implementation of disaster laws that are critical for managing risks, responding effectively to disasters, and ensuring sustainable recovery. Its principles guide countries in creating legal structures that are inclusive, transparent, and capable of addressing the complexities of disaster risk in an increasingly interconnected world.

1.5 Key Components of Disaster Laws

The IFRC (International Federation of Red Cross 2022, 2024) and several other organizations (like ILC 2024) have done tremendous work on the legal provisions of disaster risk reduction, mitigation, and responses. Here are some of the key elements and components of disaster laws.

1. **Preparedness and Mitigation**:
    - **Risk Assessment and Planning**: Laws mandate regular risk assessments and the development of disaster preparedness plans at local, national, and international levels.
    - **Building Codes and Land Use Planning**: Regulations enforce construction standards and land use policies to mitigate potential disaster impacts.
    - **Public Awareness and Education**: Legal frameworks often include provisions for public education campaigns to raise awareness about disaster risks and preparedness measures.
2. **Emergency Response**:
    - **Coordination Mechanisms**: Disaster laws establish coordination frameworks among various governmental and non-governmental agencies to ensure a unified response.
    - **Resource Allocation**: Legal provisions determine the allocation and mobilization of resources, including funding, equipment, and personnel, during emergencies.
    - **Legal Authority and Responsibilities**: Specific laws delineate the powers and responsibilities of different authorities during a disaster, ensuring clear command and control.

3. **Recovery and Rehabilitation**:
   - **Post-Disaster Recovery Plans**: Laws require the formulation of recovery strategies to rebuild and rehabilitate affected areas, focusing on both immediate and long-term needs.
   - **Financial Assistance and Compensation**: Legal mechanisms provide financial support to disaster victims and compensation for losses, promoting equitable recovery.
   - **Psychosocial Support**: Legislation often includes provisions for mental health and psychosocial support to aid the recovery of affected individuals and communities.
4. **International Cooperation**:
   - **Mutual Aid Agreements**: Countries often enter into mutual aid agreements to facilitate cross-border assistance and resource sharing during disasters.
   - **International Guidelines and Standards**: Global frameworks, such as the Sendai Framework for Disaster Risk Reduction, guide national disaster laws and policies.
   - **Humanitarian Aid and Relief Efforts**: International laws govern the provision and coordination of humanitarian aid, ensuring it adheres to principles of neutrality, impartiality, and independence.

1.6 Challenges and Potentials of Disaster Risk Governance and Legislation

Effective disaster governance and legislation are crucial for managing and mitigating the impacts of disasters. They provide the framework within which societies can prepare for, respond to, and recover from disasters. However, implementing and maintaining effective disaster governance and legislation come with several challenges and potentials that shape their success and efficacy (IFRC 2024; UNISDR 2014).

Challenges

1. **Coordination and Integration**
   - **Inter-Agency Coordination**: Disasters require a multi-sectoral response involving various governmental and non-governmental entities. Ensuring seamless coordination among these agencies is a significant challenge due to differing mandates, resources, and capacities.
   - **Policy Integration**: Integrating disaster risk reduction (DRR) policies with other sectoral policies, such as climate change, urban development, and public health, often faces institutional and administrative hurdles.

2. **Resource Constraints**
   - **Financial Limitations**: Developing countries, in particular, face financial constraints that hinder the effective implementation of disaster management laws and policies. Budget allocations for DRR are often insufficient, affecting preparedness and response capabilities.
   - **Human Resources**: There is often a lack of adequately trained personnel to implement and enforce disaster legislation effectively. Continuous training and capacity-building efforts are essential but can be resource-intensive.
3. **Community Engagement and Awareness**
   - **Public Awareness**: Ensuring that communities understand and engage with disaster risk reduction initiatives is challenging. There can be a lack of awareness or interest in DRR measures, leading to insufficient community participation.
   - **Cultural and Social Barriers**: Cultural beliefs and social norms can influence how communities perceive and respond to disaster risks. These factors can complicate the implementation of disaster laws that require behavioral changes.
4. **Legal and Institutional Frameworks**
   - **Outdated Legislation**: In many countries, disaster laws may be outdated and not reflect current best practices or the evolving nature of risks, such as those posed by climate change.
   - **Enforcement Issues**: Even when comprehensive laws are in place, enforcement can be weak due to corruption, lack of political will, or inadequate institutional mechanisms.
5. **Data and Information Management**
   - **Data Gaps**: Accurate and timely data is crucial for effective disaster management. Many countries face challenges in collecting, managing, and utilizing data for risk assessment and decision-making.
   - **Information Sharing**: There can be barriers to effective information sharing among stakeholders, which is essential for coordinated disaster response and recovery efforts.

Potentials

1. **Strengthened Institutional Frameworks**
   - **Clear Roles and Responsibilities**: Well-defined legal frameworks can delineate the roles and responsibilities of various stakeholders, leading to more organized and effective disaster management.
   - **Establishment of Dedicated Agencies**: The creation of dedicated disaster management agencies at national and local levels can enhance focus and capacity for DRR activities.

1.6.1 *Adaptive Governance in Disaster Risk Reduction*

Adaptive governance refers to a flexible, inclusive, and dynamic approach to managing disaster risks, accommodating changing circumstances, new information, and evolving social-ecological systems. Unlike traditional governance models that often rely on rigid structures and fixed plans, adaptive governance emphasizes learning, collaboration, and responsiveness to enhance resilience and reduce disaster risks.

This is becoming especially relevant in the current world, especially to address the complex risk landscape. The WEF (2020, 2021, 2022, 2023, 2024) have shown that in the last four to five years, new risks like infectious disease, digital power concentration, digital divide, cyber security, energy prices, cost of living, and mis- and disinformation have become new risks. These risks change when we see them in 2–3 years from risk perspectives. However, if one looks at the 10 years risk scenario, environmental risks (like disasters, extreme weather, biodiversity losses, etc.) become priority risks and there are hardly any changes. Therefore, to address the new risks, and changing risk landscape in the short term, it is extremely essential that we need to focus on adaptive governance.

Key Principles of Adaptive Governance

1. **Flexibility and Responsiveness**

   - **Dynamic Policies**: Adaptive governance promotes policies that can be adjusted in response to new information or changing conditions. This flexibility ensures that disaster risk reduction (DRR) strategies remain effective and relevant.
   - **Real-Time Monitoring**: Continuous monitoring of disaster risks and impacts allows for timely adjustments to policies and practices. This responsiveness is crucial for addressing unforeseen challenges and minimizing damage.

2. **Collaborative and Inclusive Decision-Making**

   - **Stakeholder Engagement**: Engaging a wide range of stakeholders, including government agencies, local communities, businesses, and non-governmental organizations (NGOs), ensures diverse perspectives and knowledge are incorporated into decision-making processes.
   - **Public Participation**: Involving communities in the planning and implementation of DRR measures fosters local ownership and enhances the relevance and effectiveness of these measures.

3. **Learning and Adaptation**

   - **Iterative Learning**: Adaptive governance is rooted in a continuous learning process, where policies and practices are regularly evaluated and updated based on new insights and experiences.

- **Knowledge Sharing**: Effective mechanisms for knowledge sharing and dissemination are essential, allowing stakeholders to learn from each other and adopt best practices.

4. **Polycentric Governance**

- **Multiple Levels of Authority**: Adaptive governance operates through multiple, overlapping centers of decision-making authority. This polycentric approach allows for more localized and context-specific responses while maintaining coherence across different governance levels.
- **Decentralization**: Empowering local authorities and communities to make decisions enables quicker and more contextually appropriate responses to disaster risks.

Implementation of Adaptive Governance in DRR

1. **Risk Assessment and Early Warning Systems**

- **Scenario Planning**: Utilizing scenario planning and modeling to anticipate a range of potential disaster outcomes. This approach helps in developing flexible strategies that can be adapted as situations evolve.
- **Integrated Data Systems**: Developing integrated data systems that combine scientific data, local knowledge, and real-time information to improve risk assessments and early warning systems.

2. **Policy and Institutional Frameworks**

- **Legal Flexibility**: Creating legal frameworks that allow for the rapid adjustment of policies and regulations in response to new risks or changing conditions. This includes establishing mechanisms for emergency legislation.
- **Institutional Coordination**: Promoting inter-agency and cross-sectoral coordination to enhance coherence and reduce fragmentation in disaster management efforts.

3. **Community Engagement and Capacity Building**

- **Participatory Approaches**: Implementing participatory approaches that involve communities in risk assessment, planning, and decision-making processes. This engagement ensures that DRR measures are locally relevant and culturally appropriate.
- **Capacity Building**: Investing in capacity-building initiatives to enhance the skills and knowledge of local authorities, community leaders, and other stakeholders. This includes training on adaptive management practices and tools.

4. **Innovation and Technology**

- **Technological Integration**: Leveraging advanced technologies, such as geographic information systems (GIS), remote sensing, and big data analytics, to improve disaster risk assessment, monitoring, and response capabilities.

- **Innovation Hubs**: Establishing innovation hubs or incubators that foster the development and application of new technologies and approaches in DRR.

5. **Institutional and Legal Frameworks**

- **Flexible Regulations**: Developing regulations that allow for adaptive management practices, enabling authorities to modify DRR strategies based on real-time data and feedback.
- **Multi-Level Governance**: Ensuring that governance structures at local, regional, and national levels are aligned and capable of working together seamlessly. This alignment helps in implementing adaptive strategies effectively.

Adaptive governance offers a promising approach to disaster risk reduction by emphasizing flexibility, inclusiveness, and learning. By integrating these principles into DRR policies and practices, governments and communities can better navigate the complexities and uncertainties of disaster risks, enhancing resilience and reducing vulnerability. This dynamic and collaborative approach ensures that disaster management strategies remain effective in the face of evolving challenges and changing conditions.

1.7 About the Book

The book comprises of 19 chapters focusing on disaster laws from different parts of the world. Each chapter is written by expert scholars or practitioners in their respective fields, who have adequate professional experience. Apart from this overview chapter, the next two chapters focus on regional issues, one on the European Union, the other on ASEAN. These chapters also highlight the importance of regional organizations in cross-border disasters, especially the role of legislation. The next five chapters focus on Japan, USA, China, Australia, and Turkey, and highlight the historical evolution of the disaster laws in the respective countries. The next five chapters focus on examples from ASEAN region countries: Thailand, Malaysia, Singapore, Indonesia, and the Philippines. The next five examples are from the South Asian region: Bangladesh, India, Nepal, Sri Lanka, and Pakistan. The final chapter focuses on water governance.

References

CAO (2016) Cabinet Office: basic Act on disaster Management (Act No. 223 of 1961, last version, Acyt No. 47 of 2016. https://www.japaneselawtranslation.go.jp/en/laws/view/3322/en. Accessed 23 June 2023

IFRC (2022) An introduction to IFRC disaster law. https://disasterlaw.ifrc.org/sites/default/files/media/disaster_law/2022-11/20221026_IntroductionDisasterLaw.pdf. Accessed 23 June 2023

IFRC (2024) International Federation of Red Cross and Red Crescent Societies (IFRC). Guidelines for the Domestic Facilitation and Regulation of International Disaster Relief and Initial Recovery Assistance (IDRL Guidelines). IFRC Website. https://disasterlaw.ifrc.org

ILC (2024) International Law Commission (ILC). Draft Articles on the Protection of Persons in the Event of Disasters. https://legal.un.org/ilc/guide/6_3.shtml. Accessed 23 June 2023

UNDRR (2015) United Nations Office for Disaster Risk Reduction (UNDRR). Sendai Framework for Disaster Risk Reduction 2015–2030. https://www.undrr.org/publication/sendai-framework-disaster-risk-reduction-2015-2030. Accessed 23 June 2023

UNISDR (2005) Hyogo Framework for Action, United Nations International Strategies for Disaster Reduction. https://www.unisdr.org/2005/wcdr/intergover/official-doc/L-docs/Hyogo-framework-for-action-english.pdf. Accessed 23 June 2023

UNISDR (2014) Potentials and challenges in disaster risk reduction, United Nations International Strategies for Disaster Reduction. https://www.preventionweb.net/files/40967_40967progressandchallengesindisaste.pdf. Accessed 23 June 2023

WB (2024) World Bank Open Data. https://data.worldbank.org. Accessed 23 June 2023

WEF (2020) The Global Risks Report 2020, Published by World Economic Forum. https://www.weforum.org/reports/the-global-risks-report-2020/. Accessed 23 June 2024

WEF (2021) The Global Risks Report 2021, Published by World Economic Forum. https://www.weforum.org/reports/the-global-risks-report-2021/. Accessed 23 June 2024

WEF (2022) The Global Risks Report 2022, Published by World Economic Forum. https://www.weforum.org/reports/the-global-risks-report-2022/. Accessed 23 June 2024

WEF (2023) The Global Risks Report 2023, Published by World Economic Forum. https://www.weforum.org/reports/the-global-risks-report-2023/. Accessed 23 June 2024

WEF (2024) The Global Risks Report 2024, Published by World Economic Forum. https://www.weforum.org/reports/the-global-risks-report-2024/. Accessed 23 June 2024

Chapter 2
Disaster Management Law in the European Union

Zhiying Zhao and Rajib Shaw

Abstract Considering the nature of evolving trends of extreme weather conditions within the European Union, different measures have been undertaken over time within the parameters of disaster management. This chapter highlights different legislations tactics devised by the European Union that helped to reduce the devastating effects of the natural disasters. The disaster management laws by the EU were based on the need for EU members to have a response mechanism that is more coordinated in the event of emergency and disasters. Different successes and challenges have been experienced in the sectors of risk management, providing key learning outcomes for improvement in sector preparedness and response frameworks. Therefore, the chapter provides a review of the multifaceted approach by the EU in implementing the risk management frameworks with guidance from previous European Union Treaties. An overview is also provided of specific disaster events within the EU, and the resultant implications of the legislative actions—to detect future trends that will affect policy actions.

Keywords Disaster · Risks · Legislation · Preparedness · Prevention

2.1 Introduction

This chapter seeks to provide a review of Key Learnings from Disaster Management Law in European Union over time. The safe living conditions within the European Union provide habitable zones for individuals, although natural hazards and disasters triggered by human action are prone to threatening property, cultural heritage, environment, and people at large (Räsänen et al. 2020). The EU therefore devised disaster management laws to aid in curbing the associated risks through preparedness, mitigation, recovery actions, and response protocols. The laws developed by the EU have great focus on reduction and prevention strategies, since these actions will

Z. Zhao (✉) · R. Shaw
Graduate School of Media and Governance, Keio University, 5322 Endo, Fujisawa 252-0882, Japan
e-mail: zhiying_zhao1995@keio.jp

Y. Cui and R. Shaw (eds.), *Disaster Law*, Disaster Risk Reduction,
https://doi.org/10.1007/978-981-97-7374-9_2

aid in reducing the impacts associated with adverse natural and manmade disasters. The disaster management laws therefore seek to reinforce the resilience of existing ecosystems, infrastructure, economy, and the society of the EU at large to mitigate the devastating effects of adverse events toward human life and the environment.

Recent trends in climate change such as sea-level distortion, dictate that the EU is expected to have increased vulnerability and exposure to disasters resulting from extreme weather conditions (Bonazza et al. 2018). Continuing trends in development and urbanization have associated disaster risks that affect the local dwellers such as heat waves, floods, and epidemics. Functional ecosystems are the best defense against natural disasters, but consistent degradation of the environment has reduced the defensive capacities of the ecosystems both globally and in Europe (Merz et al. 2020). Also, factors such as geopolitical tensions, rising levels of instability abroad, and hostile groups' diversification have all led to increased security threats from human activities such as cybercrime, terrorism, and hybrid threats. With such a complex backdrop, it is necessary for the EU to have proper arrangements that will allow for effective preparedness, prevention, response, recovery, and mitigation strategies for disasters.

The chapter shall outline the Key Learnings over time, by analyzing the hazard and geographical vulnerability of the European Union. The EU disaster management legislations shall also be highlighted with their evolving nature. The change process led to adoption of different technologies which provided key learnings among EU members, which shall also be highlighted. The precursors leading to EU Disaster Legislation shall be highlighted in this chapter by considering items such as early responses by different member states to disasters at the individual level; limitations associated with the divided approach of tackling disasters; and increased awareness by EU members to have a coordinated response mechanism for disaster management (Etinay et al. 2018). The review also outlines the legal frameworks that provided basis for disaster response and preparedness frameworks and foundations from European Union Treaties. The chapter also highlights the different hazards as categorized by the EU Disaster Legislation which classifies them into biological, natural, and technological hazards.

The aspect of integrating risk management frameworks by the EU has also been highlighted through an indication of coordinated mitigation and preparedness strategies, and through taking a multifaceted approach to Risk Management (Solinska-Nowak et al. 2018). Key lessons and learning gained over time have also been indicated as seen from the successes and challenges associated with disaster legislation implementation; and from the resilience and adaptability seen in the face of evolving threats. The review shall also provide an examination of EU specific responses to disaster events, and the implications of the legislations on ground level so as to assess the future trends and challenges in an effort of providing policy recommendations, future directions, and lastly a conclusive summary providing insights, key findings, and role of EU Disaster Management Law in reinforcing resilience.

2.2 Historical Context and Development of Disaster Management Legislation

Early initiatives are seen from actions by the European Commission in establishment of EU Civil Protection Mechanisms that aimed to reinforce EU countries participation and cooperation in civil protection to enhance measures of disaster response, preparedness, and prevention (Andrew 2020). The mechanism aids countries across Europe and beyond, whose response capabilities might be overwhelmed in the event of an emergency. The need for having a joint response team with well-coordinated facilities from different national authorities arises from the fact that disaster can strike one or more countries simultaneously therefore a joint approach is better adapted to gather enough assistance to meet the needs of the affected groups. A more coherent and stronger response team is the result of pooling together civil protection capabilities from different EU countries and the additional participating states—ten number total.

Increased cooperation among EU member states has been experienced due to myriad high-profile disasters and crises that have driven the EU deeper into civil protection techniques and enhancement of capacities to undertake the civil protection mandate not only in Europe but globally as well (Faivre et al. 2018). The expanding role of the EU in civil protection is a reflection of the increased capacities in other faculties such as security as seen from countering cyber-attacks, fighting terrorism, and battling organized crime. The cooperative efforts by the EU are seen to be effective, although faced with challenges during trans-boundary crises that raise the question of trust between members due to the organization of the civil protection mechanisms. The complex nature of interdependent crises that start in a single country but have the potential to ravage across borders rapidly such as disease outbreaks, earthquakes, or floods—normally have devastating effects that are experienced regionally and even globally. Such events spanning several boundaries could devastate the capabilities of a single country, and the EU therefore plays a central role of pooling resources and managing crises.

The civil protection mechanism carries out activities related to disaster prevention, preparedness, response, and assistance in the event of any type of disaster (Giumelli et al. 2021). Request for assistance may be done by a member country or any other country in the world. Response mechanisms may also be activated by requesting the UN, any international organization, or accredited agencies of the same. The two main components encompassed in the mechanism protocols are the operative and prevention and preparedness components. The operative aspect for crisis response and management relies mainly on Common Emergency Communication and Information Centre (CECIS) and the Emergency Response Coordination Centre (ERCC) for operations, among other apparatus (Tocci 2020). Additionally, the prevention and preparedness sector is responsible for carrying out activities that create awareness of disasters, cooperation of cross-border functions, training and equipping of civil protection personnel, carrying out drills for response capacities of the civil protection mechanism, transfer and collaboration of experts across the borders, and development of early forecast warning systems.

2.3 Legal Foundations and Frameworks

2.3.1 European Union Treaties and Disaster Management

The commitment by the EU to provide assistance, protection, and relief to member states is underpinned by the legal foundations and frameworks of the Treaty of Lisbon, the Sendai Framework for Disaster Risk Reduction, as well as Local and regional authorities (LRAs) (Schimmelfennig 2018). Article 214 of the Lisbon Treaty (1), provides that humanitarian operations within the Union shall be carried out with regard to objectives and principles of external action by the Union. (2) The humanitarian operations for aid should be conducted in accordance with the principles of non-discrimination, neutrality, and impartiality; and with principles of international law. Article 196 of the Lisbon Treaty provides that (1) Cooperation is encouraged between the Union and member states so as to ensure improved effectiveness of systems during protection and prevention mechanisms against manmade or natural disasters (Nimark 2019). Mandate is given to the Union to promote consistent work in international civil protection; enhance effective and swift operations and cooperation between civil protection services at both the Union and National levels; and provide support and complementary actions of risk prevention and mitigation to member states at the local, national, and regional levels—as well as training and equipping personnel for civil protection during response to disasters. Section (2) of Article 196 provides that the ordinary legislative procedure shall be adopted to establish the steps necessary for the Council and European Parliament to aid in achieving the humanitarian objectives of response, rescue, and mitigation of disasters.

The Sendai Framework is characterized by the clear definition of Disaster Risk Reduction actions orientation toward; a clear distinction of global targets; shifting priority from disaster management to mitigation and management of disaster risks; and orientation toward poverty reduction and sustainable development (Goniewicz and Burkle Jr 2019). The framework establishes a more distinguished setting for implementation of strategies for risk conceptualization, reduction, and prevention at the local level. The Sendai Framework provides a holistic approach that accounts for all European Union's policies and those of civil protection, and subsequently their adoption into other sectorial policy strategies for Disaster Risk Reduction. The Sendai Action Plan as published by the European Commission therefore builds on the agreed global plan, while defining the essential procedures needed for implementing the global framework—such as accounting for existing EU instruments, policies, tools, and assessment of recent achievements in the operationalization of the disaster risk management agenda by the EU.

2.3.2 *Frameworks for Disaster Preparedness and Response by the EU*

The European Union has civil protection systems that play an important role in the achievement of targets and goals in the sector of resilience-building and disaster risk reduction (Suk et al. 2020). The process of civil protection in different organizations across Europe is seen to exist in a wide array of structures due to the involved stakeholders, existing Land Regulatory Authorities, and different governance procedures. The Union's Mechanism for operation has principles that provide a framework for management of disasters and associated risks. One of these principles is the prioritization of civil protection aspects such as facilitated coordination and strengthened cooperation—all aimed at enhancing preparedness, prevention, and response mechanisms to manmade and natural disasters. Nonetheless, the prevention area is seen to have developed less significantly as opposed to sectors of preparation, management, and response to disasters.

Secondly, priority areas are distinguished in the process of action during the event of risk management. The Union Mechanism particularly has three priority sectors for action namely preparedness, prevention, and response (Khan et al. 2018). The third principle of the Union is providing emphasis on empowerment of Local Regulatory Authorities at their level, showing their explicit role in disaster management, and the need for the important roles they play. Another objective of the Union Mechanism is ensuring progress of the undertaken humanitarian measures by assessing risk management capabilities; preparedness levels; response quality in times of disasters; and public awareness levels of the disaster. Lastly, the need for strengthened governance forms part of priorities of the Union Mechanism. This can be done through practices such as risk management planning, assessment, and capability assessment—carried out at both sub-national and national levels for purposes of preparedness and prevention. The Union Mechanism is seen to focus mainly on risk reduction and prevention measures through prevention and preparedness projects seen from the planning of response protocols during disasters.

2.4 Key Learnings: A Thematic Approach and Case Studies

2.4.1 *Prevention and Preparedness*

The European Union devises a substantive formula for disaster management that focuses not only on recovery and response but also on preparedness and prevention mechanisms. The initiatives and strategies aim to lower risks, enhance overall capacities of handling disasters, and improve resilience (Kovács and Falagara Sigala 2021). Some of the strategies for preparedness and prevention adopted by the EU are as follows: Mapping and assessment of risks practiced and encouraged by the EU since it aids in identification of potential vulnerabilities and hazards. By identifying the potential dangers, preventive measures are further developed to deal with the specific hazards as detected in the targeted zones. European Union Civil Protection Mechanism describes the other strategy used in improving the efforts of prevention and preparedness. It plays a vital role in fostering member states' cooperation and facilitating cross-border exchange of resources, best practices, and expertise. Resilience strategies by the EU involve a step by step procedure of assessing the existing essential services and crucial infrastructure; considering the areas of vulnerability, and taking necessary steps to ensure their resilience and continued functionality when disasters strike.

Research and Innovation: the constant evolution of methodologies and technologies for disaster management within the EU is a result of heavy investment in research and adoption of new innovative strategies such as risk communication techniques, monitoring devices, and warning protocols (Pridham 2019). European Forum for Civil Protection: the forum provides a platform for discussions and creating awareness of preparedness and prevention strategies. Stakeholders within the European Union are able to provide best practice procedures and share experiences gathered in the field of disaster reduction in order to improve the body of knowledge. Financial Aid: support is offered to member states in the form of money to facilitate measures for preparedness and prevention. Dedicated programs such as the EU Solidarity Corps and other sources provide funding to the states in need. Alignment with International Frameworks for Disaster Risk Reduction: ongoing efforts by different nations in the fight against natural and manmade disasters such as the Sendai Framework—previously Hyogo Framework for Action, whose four key priority agendas work toward reducing existing risks from disasters and preventing their occurrence. These priority areas include enhanced understanding of disaster risks, improved risk governance, reducing disasters' vulnerability, and improving resilience of facilities. The overall aim of these priority areas is the achievement of a significant reduction in disaster losses and risks.

2.4.2 *Case Study: Floods Directive (2007/60/EC: Assessment and Management of Flood Risks)*

The Floods Directive's objective is establishment of a framework that will manage and assess the risks of floods so as to mitigate the negative effects of flooding on economic activities, cultural heritage, human health, and the environment within the European Union (Rauter et al. 2019). The most costly, and most common natural disasters in Europe are floods, which are becoming even more frequent due to climate change and the devastating effects such as heavy economic losses and life endangerment. Floods may also be harmful when releasing underground pollutants and spreading them across the land, they also cause destruction in the wetlands by reducing biodiversity. Higher flood risks are expected to be experienced within the coming decades in Europe, but with the proper measures in play—their likelihood of occurrence can be reduced and associated impacts can be limited to a certain degree. The flood risk management must undertake an integrated approach that focuses on measures to increase resilience of the society and natural habitat to adverse weather events. In order to benefit both nature and people, flood risk management is integrated with nature restoration and protection.

The Floods Directive provided a basis for management and assessment of flood risks by all EU countries, by issuing a requirement for all states to determine all areas that could experience significant flooding; map out the anticipated magnitude of the flood and assess the human developments and assets at risk in the selected areas; lastly, carry out coordinated and adequate steps to curb the risks associated with the floods (Adamson 2018). The directive is also characterized with public involvement in the planning stages and free public accessibility of the gathered information.

Member countries of the EU are expected to have up to date Flood Risk Maps showing the potential extreme effects associated with the flooding scenarios, and Flood Hazard Maps to indicate the geographical locations that are likely to experience floods (Kapović Solomun et al. 2022). Having these maps enables each individual country to have sufficient information for compiling a risk management plan for anticipated floods. Integrated river basin management encompasses integration of flood risk management closely within the Water Framework Directive—particularly to coordinate management plans for river basins, encourage public participation, and facilitate risk management plans for floods.

2.4.3 Response and Recovery

The European Union (EU) over time has developed strategies and mechanisms well adapted to recovering from and responding to disasters. The efforts seek to deliver effective and coordinated assistance to affected areas while enhancing long-term recovery and promotion of resilience within the environment and infrastructure (Krausmann et al. 2019). First up the response strategies will be discussed as follows: Rapid mapping: technologies adopted in the process of rapid mapping by the EU enable the quick assessment of damages extended by floods. The data accumulated plays a crucial role in coordination of efforts for emergency response procedures and effective allocation of resources. Civil Protection and Humanitarian Aid: abbreviated as (ECHO), the European Civil Protection and Humanitarian Aid Operations seeks to offer support to activities linked to civil protection and humanitarian aid. ECHO provides interventions during crises, coordinated assistance, and delivery of emergency relief to the affected areas.

Emergency Response Coordination Center, also known as ERCC, defines the body which acts as the central coordinating body for the EU that responds to disasters. The body assesses and monitors emergencies as they occur, facilitating assistance deployment, while ensuring effective communication among key actors and member states (Goniewicz and Burkle Jr 2019). Medical Assistance: the affected areas can receive medical supplies and practitioners who are deployed by the EU to handle health emergencies during disasters. The medical teams can help by preventing transmission of infectious diseases and treating the injured and affected individuals in the aftermath phase of disasters. Financial Assistance: regions affected by the adverse effects of disasters are provided with funds through programs such as European Solidarity Corps and EU Solidarity Corps—funds which further help to support early efforts of recovery and cover immediate costs associated with recovery protocols. European Union Civil Protection Mechanism, also known as the UCPM, is a mechanism that enables member states to coordinate and offer assistance to needy states. The assistance can be in the form of deploying medical personnel, search and rescue teams, and other rescue efforts to offer the necessary support.

Recovery strategies by the EU include the following: Rehabilitation of Infrastructure, the process of economic recovery and achieving normalcy requires rehabilitation of vital infrastructure such as communication, energy, and transport networks—all of which the EU contributes to with regard to demand (Nimark 2019). Research and Innovation: efforts within the parameters of research and innovation go a long way in development of methodologies that improve the overall performance of recovery strategies and encourage new technology development that will improve the resilience of locals when faced with disasters in the future.

Environmental Rehabilitation: the process of ecosystems restoration during recovery of various aspects of the environment is regarded as post-disaster actions, which seek to address the challenges arising from the disaster that is crippling the environment (Khan et al. 2018). Post-disaster learning and assessment: the response and recovery efforts are scrutinized for effectiveness through assessing the occurrence of different events, the recovery efforts deployed, and success levels achieved that can produce areas for further learning to facilitate constant improvement of strategies in disaster management and risk reduction. Social Cohesion: the affected communities are encouraged to come together in solidarity supporting initiatives for increased community resilience through sharing of initiatives that help individuals find purpose and rebuild their homes and livelihoods after disaster strikes.

Financial Aid: financial tools are provided by the EU to facilitate the redevelopment of zones hit by disasters, the financial instruments are presented as loans, grants, and other forms of capital that help in economic recovery by the victim countries (Faivre et al. 2018). Capacity building: within the EU, institutions' and community's resilience are built through capacity building which includes training of community members, emergency response services, and local authority to be better equipped to respond and prepare for future disasters. Recovery Planning for long-term: countries affected by disasters are supported by the EU in development and actualization of recovery plans for the long run. The plans seek not only to build back, but to do so with resilience in mind and integrating sustainable practices of development as well. Recovery Planning for the long run: in the event of natural disasters, the EU provides support to affected member states in development and implementation of recovery plans for the long run. The plans mainly focus on restoration of essential services, reconstruction of infrastructure, and promotion of sustainable development practices.

2.4.4 Case Study: South Sudan Gets Allocated €600,000 by the EU, to Respond to the Cholera Outbreak

The cholera epidemic in Sudan experienced a spill-over that led to release of €600,000 funding to aid South Sudan in the preparedness and response to the possible outbreak of cholera (Rumunu et al. 2022). The funding was sourced from the Emergency Toolbox of the European Union—an instrument dedicated to assist vulnerable members outside the EU, specifically during sudden crises occurrence. The state of violence between the paramilitary Rapid Support Forces and Sudan Armed Forces in Sudan had a direct consequence on the cholera cases that surpassed seven thousand, and associated deaths amounting to two hundred across the nine states. Returnees and refugees, almost 1,233 surged into South Sudan daily from Sudan which was already grappled with a severe cholera outbreak. The counties hosting the returnees and refugees in the Upper Nile state were at a higher risk for exposure to another cholera outbreak, which would be strenuous on the counties that were already on the verge of decongestion due to overstretching of the health system.

South Sudan has recorded eight cholera outbreaks since 2006, making it endemic to the same—and this is a result of—poor accessibility of sanitation, water, and health services; conflict displacement, food insecurity, poor health services and access, constant floods, and poor socio-economic conditions (Somorin et al. 2021). The ongoing state of political unrest facing South Sudan only adds on to the challenges facing a vulnerable population with dire needs and grappled with myriad challenges in areas of health, socio-economic, and political well-being. Forecasts indicate that by 2024 South Sudanese estimated at 8.9 million will need humanitarian aid, internally displaced persons amounting to two million, and asylum seekers and refugees might be over 328,000 (Trithart 2019). Partners in humanitarian efforts such as World Health Organization (WHO) shall be on the receiving end of the additional funding to aid in its quest for sample collection, set up of oral rehydration points, creation of treatment centers, case management, staff training, and implementation of sanitation, control, and prevention mechanisms. Funding provided shall also aid in supplies procurement and distribution of treatment and investigation kits to cholera prone areas.

2.4.5 Solidarity and Cooperation

Solidarity and cooperation define fundamental elements that form the foundation of the EU's tactics for disaster management, showing shared commitment toward providing support and assistance to communities and member states that fall victim to disasters (Alemanno 2020). Different strategies for solidarity and cooperation are carried out by the EU with an aim to improve response facilities and enhance collective resilience efforts. Some of the strategies are described as follows: Emphasis on cooperation across borders: the EU took an initiative of encouraging member states to have increased cooperation with neighboring countries and other member states. The collaborative technique will foster a cohesive approach of tackling trans-boundary risks that may affect several locations within the same geographical scope but in different countries. Provide member states with devising and undertaking joint training and exercise sessions; efforts by the EU for solidarity among members are seen from the promotion of joint training and exercise which fosters cooperation and seeks to achieve a more effective and coordinated response mechanism in the event of a disaster.

Collaborative research and innovation practices: actions pertaining innovation and research within the EU are conducted by multiple member states who bring out experts and data collaboratively aiming to merge ideas and devise innovative solutions for recovery, preparedness, prevention, and response (Somorin et al. 2021). Humanitarian Aid and Civil Protection, also known as ECHO, is an entity in the EU that provides support to operations of civil protection while offering humanitarian aid as well. Actions of solidarity by ECHO within the EU are essential as seen in offering assistance to affected populations suffering the devastating effect of disasters and crises. European Civil Protection Forum: this is a platform that enables stakeholders within the realm of civil protection to engage in cooperative efforts and dialogue that will boost cohesion and solidarity between states. The representatives come together from international organizations, member states, the private sector, and NGOs with an aim of reinforcing the collaborative strategies while sharing experiences to facilitate improvements on action items.

Encouraged International cooperation: this is done by the EU by engaging neighboring countries with international organizations and other member states so as to facilitate cohesion and improve response mechanisms and disaster preparedness globally (Adamson 2018).

This involves having joint exercises, best practices exchange, and information sharing within both the local and international parameters. Solidarity funds and financial aid: financial assistance is provided to member states through solidarity funds by the EU such as the European Solidarity Corps, and EU Solidarity Corps. Provision of such aid facilitates collaborative efforts toward recovery efforts and emergency funding in the regions faced by disasters. Solidarity Clause: this is a clause introduced by the Lisbon Treaty, which puts great emphasis on the need for joint actions between member states who should act in solidarity to help any victim in the event of disasters without prejudice. The need for cooperation and mutual support during emergencies is underscored in this clause.

Common Security and Défense Policy (CSDP): this is a policy body entailing several initiatives and actions that seek to enhance the capacities of the EU for crisis and natural disasters' management (Tocci 2020). The procedure involves both civilian and military action to offer support and assistance in times of emergency, while facilitating a collective approach toward disaster response and security protocols. Emergency Response and Coordination Centre: denoted as the ERCC, this body is crucial in facilitating and coordinating the exchange and distribution of resources and data when emergencies occur. The ERCC ensures that responses between states are efficient and centralized so as to foster good rapport among relevant organizations and member states. EU Civil Protection Mechanism, also known as the UCPM, provides the member states and other participating states with a platform for extending cooperation and solidarity among nations. The platform facilitates distribution of expertise, resources, and assistance for members during, before, and after disasters. Needy members can request for help on this platform, while able members can be pivotal in offering support in the form of equipment, personnel, and relief items.

2.4.6 Case Study: Solidarity During Times of Covid-19 Pandemic

Solidarity principles entailed within the Lisbon Treaty, Article 2 is described as a foundational value of the European Union with high affiliation toward respecting freedom, human dignity, freedom, human rights, and democracy (Alemanno 2020). Member states share values of tolerance, pluralism, non-discrimination, solidarity, equality, and justice between men and women alike. The Covid-19 pandemic presented challenges to the EU facing its political narrative of achieving solidarity between member states in the event of crises when put under pressure. The early stages of the pandemic experienced slow response from the EU, whereas member states took separate measures in tackling the virus. Although similar—such as social distancing rules, they were adopted unilaterally. EU's actions are limited to protecting human health as priority, and some member states had national interests that saw the closing of some borders within the EU showing lack of solidarity within the initial stages of the pandemic. Arguably, solidarity existed initially and later became more apparent as seen from a shift in the Union's mechanism to start advocating for European solidarity through coordinated efforts of economic response during the outbreak of Covid-19.

The steps taken to limit the free movement of people and contain the infection rate of disease included: intra-EU exit or entry bans, border checks reintroduction, and international travel restrictions (Medeiros et al. 2021). The members of the EU took a coordinated approach that saw the Union leaders agreeing to leave internal borders open, although six states later imposed the travel bans. An act of solidarity also arises when the Commission issued member states with an advisory for introducing temporary bans on movement beyond the external borders of the EU. Member states followed the directive almost in full partiality, with restrictions on non-essential movement from third world countries to the EU. This shows how the member states are encouraged to adopt actions and policies of the Union's law, notwithstanding the non-binding nature. The Commission also provided border management guidelines, which seek to ensure Union level coordination of actions such as distribution of goods within the EU, and thorough border checks for persons. Emphasis by the Commission is placed on the principle of solidarity, and the vital role it plays in the techniques for tackling the pandemic.

The steps adopted by the Union aimed to achieve a common and coordinated approach, whereby the internal market needs and citizens' needs for public health are balanced (Goniewicz et al. 2020). These objectives are in line with the values of solidarity that dictate priority for common union goals over national objectives. The Commission further announced in 2020 November, that a branch of the Union known as European Health Union was under development with foresight of future pandemics, whereby member states' cooperation and coordination is fundamental. The Union mentioned that the Covid-19 pandemic provided learning opportunities that brought out the importance and need for member states' coordination and cooperation during crises. Solidarity is considered as one of the Commission's soft-law instruments.

A website by the EU shows the solidarity efforts during times of Covid-19 in a display of 'European solidarity in action' (Alemanno 2020). The Union projects solidarity as the process of countries offering support to each other in sectors such as protection of health workers and citizens' health, and treatment of patients during the Covid-19 pandemic. Furthermore, there exists a 'European solidarity tracker' that visualizes and determines the various categories of solidarity among both union institutions and member states. However, other than adoption of the Civil Protection Mechanism, the Commission barely elaborates the definition of solidarity, or how it can be adopted in practice. Nonetheless, solidarity is considered an ideal for coordination, mutual support, and cooperation by member states within the EU when handling practical issues such as crisis management.

2.5 Key Learnings and Lessons Over Time

The EU was faced with several challenges during the implementation process of disaster management protocols that enabled the Union to grow and develop in different ways so as to curb potential risks that may arise (Ogie et al. 2019). The sectors that realized great success levels shall each be described in this section. Additionally, different issues also arose in the process of adoption and implementation of different legislative actions within the EU. These challenges offered the EU a chance to form resilience and adapt to different situations that call for emergency response and mitigation over time through the lessons learned.

2.5.1 Governance

The Union was able to achieve good governance practices during the adoption of frameworks such as the Sendai Framework through acts like development of laws, reviewing previous actions, designating responsibilities, implementing regulations, and encouraging cooperation (Zuccaro et al. 2020). Strengthened governance was achieved that enabled the Union to have priority actions in times of disasters, which was channeled down to the national level where each country is to have an established platform for risk reduction cultured to its own demands, with a coordinated risk reduction mechanism supported by a designate agency or ministry. The countries shall be expected to implement responsibilities and roles during disaster management that are in line with the dedicated framework, risk profile, and any arising needs. The shared experience gained by the EU will aid the member states to devise a more cohesive approach to deal with trans-boundary impacts in the quest for risk assessment and mitigation. In the sector of governance, an example is seen in the case study for solidarity during times of Covid-19 whereby the governing bodies were faced with the task of having all the countries under one umbrella as the EU when responding to the issues of the pandemic. Initially, different countries undertook different measures to tackle the pandemic, showing some lack of unity (Medeiros et al. 2021). However, the EU leadership streamlined their governance tactics and had all the member states following similar legislative protocols governing management of the Covid-19 pandemic. An example of this initiative was seen in the EU Solidarity Corps that ensured joint initiatives and solidarity throughout the EU to ensure continued mutual support and cooperation in the event of emergencies.

2.5.2 *Database for Losses from Disasters*

Following up disaster and disturbance incidents systematically and gathering data from the losses associated with the disaster shall provide learning scenarios that will be instrumental in the following: determining the benefits and costs associated with disaster risk management, demonstrate the essence for private and public investment, and show the importance of having social protection and risk sharing mechanisms (Booth et al. 2020). The systematic process of undertaking studies, collecting data, and analyzing them enabled the EU to devise informed policy choices and contribute to the body of knowledge on disaster risk management enabling easier handling of future disaster cases because of the large body of reference. The EU therefore provides emphasis on the need for establishment of disaster loss databases at the national and local levels and aligns its efforts to encourage a good understanding of the same. Having the database for losses within the broader European region will put the EU in a better position for providing advice and guidelines to ensure completeness, consistency, and coherence in the recording process of loss and damage data from disaster—data which is vital in providing evidence-based actions and policies for disaster management.

The development of a functional database for disaster loss case studies will play an important role during the framework implementation's review stage—whereby progress, challenges, and achievements are compared. Within the EU, the Emergency Response Coordination Centre—also known as ERCC, facilitates the monitoring and assessment of emergencies in real time. This enables them to record and store information regarding previous disasters, enabling them to be more versed in tackling certain occurrences due to high frequency levels that increases their proficiency (Somorin et al. 2021). However, another challenge occurs in the sector of vulnerable groups such as South Sudan in the event of the Cholera outbreak. The country received

€600,000 from the EU to cater for the cholera outbreak, which helped in reducing the outbreak's adverse effects although the country had previously recorded more than eight cholera outbreaks since 2006. Additionally, this shows that the legislative causes of action are not always successful due to the conditions surrounding the member state in need. This shows that previous research is crucial, but also existing conditions need to favor the disaster reduction and mitigation procedures.

2.5.3 *Risk Assessment*

Risk assessment is considered a fundamental step in Europe since it underpins the development of local and national strategies, provided that the assessment is intended to facilitate decision making on the actions and focus required (Mysiak et al. 2018). Understanding this has led to the EU ensuring the featuring of risk assessments at the local level. An example is seen in the EU floods directive and European commission risk assessment guidelines—which have enabled countries in Europe to adopt a characteristic methodology and common consideration during assessment and management of risks. The guidelines have enabled the countries to have a coherent risk and preparedness plan that is comparable between countries. This will improve transparency and encourage cooperative efforts between European countries in the mitigation and prevention of shared risks, such as trans-boundary disasters.

The EU member states and other countries with a platform for collaborative efforts within the socio-political dimensions of disaster risk management such as poor management and reporting system of handling disasters—ultimately makes it hard for a country to provide data on risk assessment and disaster management during cohesive actions of sharing information among member states (Alemanno 2020). Economic disparities experienced in different nations put them in different levels of participation of disaster preparedness and management endeavors due to the limited budget allocation and different priorities in the selected areas. As a result, the challenge of having satisfactory expertise in risk assessment strategies still lingers due to lack of sufficient resources that ensure a country is well adapted to handle disaster as it occurs. An example is seen from the Floods Directive by the EU that requires all EU countries to determine and map out all areas vulnerable to flooding and assess the level of risks involved. Not all the member states have the capability of generating up to date flood risk maps which makes the legislative action a challenge for other countries to implement. This further calls for more collaborative efforts by the EU to ensure all countries are in a position to carry out risk assessment protocols.

2.5.4 *Peer Review*

The European Union is keen on stages of review and advocates for member states to carry out constant and deliberate reporting of framework implementation strategies through peer reviews (Albris et al. 2020). These reviews are instrumental in ensuring improvements in strategies adopted within the frameworks for disaster risk reduction. Countries across the EU are able to share learning experiences and initiate progress in implementation of risk management practices and policies within the national level. Peer reviews take advantage of the EU countries' policy exchange programs and initiate examination of performance and exchange of best practice programs within parameters of disaster risk management policies among member states. As a result, trust and mutual understanding are achieved due to the non-binding recommendations and shared experiences aimed at improvement of policies. Therefore, peer reviews are essential in ensuring an integrated approach toward merging risk prevention strategies, disaster risk reduction, response, and preparedness strategies.

2.5.5 Key Challenges

Transfer of knowledge is one of the sectors faced with challenges, specifically lack of structure and platforms that facilitate knowledge sharing and application of policies between government institutions, researchers, and citizens (Driessen et al. 2018). There is generally, a great need for researchers and scientists working on strategies for disaster risk reduction to be included in policy making within frameworks of the EU. There has been more involvement realized by the EU in creating conference events, and networks for relevant stakeholders and practitioners as well as the inception of the Disaster Risk Management Knowledge Centre. Although measures to include scientists in policy making prevails, challenges still exist in adoption of scientific and innovative technologies into actual policy and governance domains. It is necessary therefore to have mediating actors and institutions that will facilitate knowledge transfer in a manner that is more satisfying, productive, and efficient.

2.5.6 Disaster Management Expertise

The adoption of international frameworks for disaster preparedness such as the Sendai Framework for Disaster Risk Reduction presented countries battling disaster risk management with economic and social vulnerabilities and also, lack of a system for prioritizing the vulnerabilities that need to be addressed (Zuccaro et al. 2020). Another challenge associated with poor disaster management expertise is the use of traditional risk assessment techniques relying mainly on hazard data. Adoption of policies that have a background and scientific proof will be essential in the formation of risk-reducing and preventive measures such as reduced exposure to hazards—both natural and manmade. An example is Italy which was found to have a gap in the sector of tools and methodologies necessary for undertaking holistic and comprehensive risk assessments (Zuccaro et al. 2017). This provides clarification on the question of existence of disaster management knowledge—which is underpinned by the issue of lack of experts with the know-how of performing viable risk assessments that consider the dynamic paradigm of resilience and vulnerability. Therefore it is necessary to equip the workforce with disaster risk reduction education so as to have professionals skilled enough to create awareness and implement strategies within both private and public parameters.

2.5.7 *Risk Awareness*

The scientific assessment of risks provides insights on how risks impact the operations of public institutions, their perception, and to what levels are they really aware of the risk and the level of preparedness adopted. Discussions by Driessen et al. (2018) disclose that regardless of intensive research into the aspect of risk awareness and perception, many loopholes exist up to date such as lack of scientific knowledge of probability assessment of risks by individuals. It is necessary therefore to create awareness among citizens to handle probabilistic data and discern the choice of countermeasures adopted for risk mitigation. An example described by Amaratunga et al. (2017) shows how the UK committed government resources toward raising risk awareness, but when the implementers of the risk management protocols were subjected to select specific measures, they resolve to their personal risk assessment strategies. In areas such as Switzerland and Germany, different challenges are present such as existence of guidelines and tools for policy creation and implementation—but lack of good communication channels that will ensure the dissemination of information to the desired target groups.

In the modern technological environment, risk awareness within the general population is intrinsic to the innovation of new communication and media channels (Reuter et al. 2018). The media is having new roles, especially social media—which provides professionals with new ways of communication to the public and back in the event of emergencies.

2.5.8 *Adaptability and Resilience in the Face of Evolving Threats*

The history of crises that have faced the European Union shows how the gradual implementation of policies and institutional changes have enabled the Union to tackle arising future disasters with better knowledge and prowess (Kovács et al. 2021). The crises have also been evolving with some cross-border effects calling for solidarity and cooperation mechanisms to achieve proper management and containment of risks. Therefore, it is essential for the EU to evolve its disaster response and management faculties to handle incidences of a multifaceted nature with cascading effects. To deal with future challenges, the EU shall need to improve resilience to future threats by enhancing aspects such as cross-sector crisis management, loss of disaster response data, and minimal disinformation. Efforts by the EU to build resilience and adaptability are seen in the Commission's recommendations for emphasis on the need for a fully coordinated and proportionate adoption of crisis-related measures. Different crisis scenarios like Covid-19 pandemic revealed the EU's food chain vulnerability in challenging moments of severe supply (Djalante et al. 2020). The commission therefore took steps toward having a contingency plan that mitigated the food security crisis so as to ensure delivery during crises.

Another measure taken by the EU toward facing future challenges such as animal and plant health issues, inputs' shortages, and adverse weather conditions was creating the European food security crisis preparedness and response mechanism (EFSCM) and having member states offering stakeholders, representatives, and specialists of non-EU states to form an expert group that will have periodical meetings to ensure the EU is fully equipped to handle potential challenges of food supply (Etinay et al. 2018). The Commission also devised a new framework for crisis governance known as the single market emergency instrument (SMEI)—which seeks to maintain free movement of persons, goods, and services, so as to ensure critical products' availability in times when disaster strikes on a single market.

Efforts by the EU toward resilience are also seen within the physical and digital infrastructure (Andrew 2020). An example is the directive adopted by the EU on security protocols of the network and information systems (NIS), which aimed at increasing EU countries' cooperation on the critical aspects of cyber security. The directive provided that operators of essential services within critical sectors such as data centers, research labs, and hospitals had to be provided with security obligations so as to minimize loopholes and reduce attacks.

2.6 Comparative Analysis and Global Implications

2.6.1 Influence of EU Policies on Global Disaster Management Practices

Developing countries facing climatic hazards are seen to undertake different types of adaptive responses that are in line with the EU policies for disaster management such as seeking regional support especially through trans-boundary cohesion, focusing on most vulnerable sectors, and having national adaptation plans integrated with disaster risk reduction plans (Krausmann et al. 2019). The actions adopted for risk management included improving local knowledge management capacity, development of early warning systems, and enhanced technology application. One of the countries adapting to these plans is Costa Rica which chose to merge its Risk Management Policy with adaptation plans at the local level. One of the efforts is seen through capacity building for technology transfer and resilience. The country determined adverse weather conditions as one of the key threats to human safety, with continuous efforts on disaster risk management not reflecting on any successful initiatives. Therefore, the country decided to innovate national vulnerability monitoring program to increase infrastructure resilience. Another example is seen in Indonesia, whereby Disaster Management Law was developed after a tsunami caused great destruction from loss of life to damaged property and infrastructure.

The other scenario that saw the integration of DRR was in Algeria's adaptation within multiple sectors during the extreme events of floods and earthquake (Adamson 2018). Necessary measures of innovation were undertaken to foresee a multispectral approach of assessing the most vulnerable infrastructure in the event of flooding, fire, and earthquake. The Ministry of Land Use undertook urban planning that considers all the DRR actions such as GIS mapping for identification of risk prone areas and facilitating development of sensitization for risks across the zones. The Ministry of Education took measures of DRR for raising awareness on another level and ensuring proper sensitization of teachers and students to major hazards and offering national campaigns on mitigation and preparedness programs in communities and schools.

2.7 Future Directions and Policy Recommendations

Different challenges exist in the realms of policy adoption, for example in the sector for partnerships—it is important to have a holistic and transdisciplinary approach that involves policy makers, science, practitioners, and policy implementers such as communities and individual households (Pridham 2019). It is necessary to create awareness and build strong partnerships within communities that will lead to increased awareness and exchange of skills, experiences, and knowledge. In order to have successful synthesis of scientific knowledge among member states, it shall be necessary to develop transparent and concise networks for providing learning opportunities. Effectiveness of partnerships can be measured through social network analysis that monitors the partnership's growth rate, connectivity levels, and associated impacts realized on practice and policy.

Partnerships are also faced by challenges such as continuity, with regard to the projects' life cycle and learning curve, as well as rotation of policy makers (Solinska-Nowak et al. 2018). The dynamic nature of the partnerships comes with a lot of learning outcomes that call for long-term, beneficial, well-funded partnerships. The principles of risk governance should first be agreed upon by the parties, whereby science can be more easily appropriated if aspects of risk ownership and risk tolerance are clearly outlined. The public sector within the partnership parameters is faced with challenges such as timely delivery of information during crisis management and getting reliable advice and data on policy making. Both issues can be solved if the interfaces of the science-based policies are drawn from best practice, are sustainable and well defined. Communication therefore should be ready on demand and non-biased between member states under partnership and solidarity within the EU.

Innovation is needed for technological advancements in terms of equipment used in monitoring and evaluation of the disasters' occurrence and their impacts (Tocci 2020). More efforts are needed in improving satellite, airborne, and sea-borne sensors so as to realize timely and total earth observation protocols. Scientists should also be at the forefront in development of robust, cheaper, and better instruments to monitor low priority zones. It is necessary for scientists to gather people's socio-economic data to assess the resilience and vulnerability of communities, individuals, societies, and economies during disasters. Adoption of innovative technologies will foresee a 'total conversion' among authority, regulatory bodies, and citizens.

Comprehensive disaster financing strategies facilitate new technological developments that work to minimize the risks associated with natural hazards while speeding up reconstruction and recovery. Prior to adoption, technological innovations shall be subjected to testing and demonstration before the end-users by public authorities, with a concise evaluation mechanism before commissioning (Medeiros et al. 2021). Innovations' relevance is measured through policy-impact assessments, whereby viable innovations are further institutionalized at the local level. The innovative approaches do now need to all be new, however, diffusion and embedding of innovation among members of the EU is also advised. When countries form strong bonds and build trust, there will be a better environment for fostering effective emergency aid in times of disaster. Social media is another tool that can be devised to improve self-induced mobilization strategies and coordination of knowledge, efforts, and resources for disaster response and preparedness mechanisms. Successful innovation is a result of teamwork from players such as researchers, funding agencies, policy makers, and practitioners.

2.8 Conclusion

The European Union has had a history of unprecedented emergency situations from disasters, which led to the need for a comprehensive framework that will enable not only EU member states, but other nations as well—to benefit from an elaborate disaster risk response system. The EU is seen to take a multifaceted approach in using its competencies to deal with risk preparedness and management such as using financial instruments, encouraging social cohesion and solidarity, capacity building, maintenance of key infrastructure, and research and innovation practices. The strategies taken by the EU are seen to cater for both long-term development, and relief for the short term when handling issues of disaster risk management. Key themes adopted by the EU in disaster risk management are fundamental in ensuring timely delivery of aid during emergencies, and they include prevention and preparedness strategies, response and recovery strategies, solidarity and cooperation strategies.

The rate of unpredictability, intensity, and frequency of natural disasters, aggravated by the challenging facets of climate change, underpins the need for urgent adoption of a cohesive approach toward disaster risk management within the parameters of the EU. The unified approach shall involve harnessing collective strength, having unified solutions for interconnected trans-boundary challenges, undertaking economic resilience strategies, and ensuring standardization and consistency of the defined strategies of disaster risk management. The interdependence and interconnection of the disasters, and remedies throughout the world indicate the need for evolving collective strategies based on acquired experiences and learning outcomes. This will ensure resilience within the EU, coupled with robust prowess for tackling future challenges.

However, the adoption of disaster management and mitigation strategies was faced with challenges which provided learning opportunities for the EU and associated nations. The learnings provided areas for further recommendations in areas such as research and innovation, solidarity, and adoption of frameworks. The ever-changing nature of disasters and emergencies calls for resilience-building and adaptability by the EU and participants. The efforts of building resilience and adaptability have been mentioned and suggestions provided on how to ensure continuity of the same.

2.8.1 Looking Ahead: The Role of EU Disaster Law in Ensuring Resilience

Different measures were adopted by the EU regarding network and information systems protection through digital transformation as part of the cyber security strategy. The proposals were defined to correspond to the landscape of evolving threats within the parameters of digital transformation. The measures seek to enlarge the scope of rules and ensure better incident and risk management as cooperation. Another resilience strategy by the EU is seen in the protection of vital infrastructure such as transport, energy, health, and water, to be able to cope, respond, protect against, prevent, and recover from apparent risks associated with natural or manmade disasters. The critical sectors therefore are adapted for increased physical resilience and reduced vulnerabilities.

References

Adamson M (2018) Flood risk management in Europe: the EU 'Floods' directive and a case study of Ireland. Int J River Basin Manag 16(3):261–272

Albris K, Lauta KC, Raju E (2020) Strengthening governance for disaster prevention: the enhancing risk management capabilities guidelines. Int J Disaster Risk Reduct 47:101647

Alemanno A (2020) The European response to COVID-19: from regulatory emulation to regulatory coordination? Eur J Risk Regulat 11(2):307–316

Amaratunga D, Haigh R, Dias N, Hemachandra K (2017) Synthesis report of legal, policy and science approaches within the frame of disaster risk reduction (DRR) and climate change adaptation (CCA)—National Report The United Kingdom. Enhancing Synergies for Disaster Prevention in the European Union (ESPREssO), Napoli, Italy

Andrew L (2020) The vulnerability of vital systems: how'critical infrastructure'became a security problem. In: Securing 'the homeland'. Routledge, pp 17–39

Bonazza A, Maxwell I, Drdácký M, Vintzileou E, Hanus C (2018) Safeguarding cultural heritage from natural and man-made disasters: a comparative analysis of risk management in the EU

Booth L, Fleming K, Abad J, Schueller LA, Leone M, Scolobig A, Baills A (2020) Simulating synergies between climate change adaptation and disaster risk reduction stakeholders to improve management of transboundary disasters in Europe. Int J Disaster Risk Reduct 49:101668

Djalante R, Shaw R, DeWit A (2020) Building resilience against biological hazards and pandemics: COVID-19 and its implications for the Sendai framework. Progress Disaster Sci 6:100080

Driessen PP, Hegger DL, Kundzewicz ZW, Van Rijswick HF, Crabbé A, Larrue C, ... Wiering M (2018) Governance strategies for improving flood resilience in the face of climate change. Water 10(11):1595

Etinay N, Egbu C, Murray V (2018) Building urban resilience for disaster risk management and disaster risk reduction. Procedia Eng 212:575–582

Faivre N, Sgobbi A, Happaerts S, Raynal J, Schmidt L (2018) Translating the Sendai framework into action: the EU approach to ecosystem-based disaster risk reduction. Int J Disaster Risk Reduct 32:4–10

Giumelli F, Hoffmann F, Książczaková A (2021) The when, what, where and why of European Union sanctions. Eur Secur 30(1):1–23

Goniewicz K, Burkle FM Jr (2019) Challenges in implementing Sendai framework for disaster risk reduction in Poland. Int J Environ Res Public Health 16(14):2574

Goniewicz K, Khorram-Manesh A, Hertelendy AJ, Goniewicz M, Naylor K, Burkle FM Jr (2020) Current response and management decisions of the European Union to the COVID-19 outbreak: a review. Sustainability 12(9):3838

Kapović Solomun M, Ferreira CS, Zupanc V, Ristić R, Drobnjak A, Kalantari Z (2022) Flood legislation and land policy framework of EU and non-EU countries in Southern Europe. Wiley Interdiscip Rev Water 9(1):e1566

Khan Y, O'Sullivan T, Brown A, Tracey S, Gibson J, Généreux M, ... Schwartz B (2018) Public health emergency preparedness: a framework to promote resilience. BMC Public Health 18:1–16

Kovács G, Falagara Sigala I (2021) Lessons learned from humanitarian logistics to manage supply chain disruptions. J Supply Chain Manag 57(1):41–49

Krausmann E, Girgin S, Necci A (2019) Natural hazard impacts on industry and critical infrastructure: Natech risk drivers and risk management performance indicators. Int J Disaster Risk Reduct 40:101163

Medeiros E, Guillermo Ramírez M, Ocskay G, Peyrony J (2021) Covidfencing effects on cross-border deterritorialism: the case of Europe. Eur Plan Stud 29(5):962–982

Merz B, Kuhlicke C, Kunz M, Pittore M, Babeyko A, Bresch DN, ... Wurpts A (2020) Impact forecasting to support emergency management of natural hazards. Rev Geophys 58(4):e2020RG000704

Mysiak J, Castellari S, Kurnik B, Swart R, Pringle P, Schwarze R, ... van der Linden P (2018) Brief communication: strengthening coherence between climate change adaptation and disaster risk reduction. Nat Hazards Earth Syst Sci 18(11):3137–3143

Nimark A (2019) Post-Lisbon developments in EU crisis management: the integrated political crisis response (IPCR) arrangements. In: Ethics and law for chemical, biological, radiological, nuclear & explosive crises, pp 75–91

Ogie RI, Clarke RJ, Forehead H, Perez P (2019) Crowdsourced social media data for disaster management: lessons from the PetaJakarta.org project. Comput Environ Urban Syst 73:108–117

Pridham G (2019) National environmental policy-making in the European framework: Spain, Greece and Italy in comparison. In: Protecting the periphery. Routledge, pp 80–101

Räsänen A, Lein H, Bird D, Setten G (2020) Conceptualizing community in disaster risk management. Int J Disaster Risk Reduct 45:101485

Rauter M, Thaler T, Attems MS, Fuchs S (2019) Obligation or innovation: can the EU floods directive be seen as a tipping point towards more resilient flood risk management? A case study from Vorarlberg, Austria. Sustainability 11(19):5505

Reuter C, Hughes AL, Kaufhold M (2018) Social media in crisis management: an evaluation and analysis of crisis informatics research. Int J Human-Comput Interact 34(4):280–294

Rumunu J, Wamala JF, Konga SB, Igale AL, Adut AA, Lonyik SK, ... Olu OO (2022) Integrated disease surveillance and response in humanitarian context: South Sudan experience. Pan African Med J 42(Suppl 1)

Schimmelfennig F (2018) Liberal intergovernmentalism and the crises of the European Union. JCMS: J Common Market Stud 56(7):1578–1594

Solinska-Nowak A, Magnuszewski P, Curl M, French A, Keating A, Mochizuki J, ... Jarzabek L (2018) An overview of serious games for disaster risk management–Prospects and limitations for informing actions to arrest increasing risk. Int J Disaster Risk Reduct 31:1013–1029

Somorin YM, Odeyemi OA, Ateba CN (2021) Salmonella is the most common foodborne pathogen in African food exports to the European Union: analysis of the rapid alert system for food and feed (1999–2019). Food Control 123:107849

Suk JE, Vaughan EC, Cook RG, Semenza JC (2020) Natural disasters and infectious disease in Europe: a literature review to identify cascading risk pathways. Eur J Pub Health 30(5):928–935

Tocci N (2020) Resilience and the role of the European Union in the world. Contemp Secur Policy 41(2):176–194

Trithart A (2019) Stuck in crisis: the humanitarian response to Sudan's health emergency

Zuccaro G, Criscuolo A, De Gregorio D, Di Ruocco A, Gallinella F, Leone M, Martucci C (2017) Synthesis report of legal, policy and science approaches within the frame of disaster risk reduction (DRR) and climate change adaptation (CCA)—National Report Italy. Enhancing Synergies for Disaster Prevention in the European Union (ESPREssO), Napoli, Italy

Zuccaro G, Leone MF, Martucci C (2020) Future research and innovation priorities in the field of natural hazards, disaster risk reduction, disaster risk management and climate change adaptation: a shared vision from the ESPREssO project. Int J Disaster Risk Reduct 51:101783

Chapter 3
Disaster Management Law and Agreement in ASEAN

Krishnakali Ghosh, Ranit Chatterjee, and Rajib Shaw

Abstract Association of Southeast Asian Nations (ASEAN) focuses on sectors: economics, culture, research, and industry while incorporating the principles of the Sendai Framework into disaster management efforts. It promotes regional peace, mutual assistance, and collaboration with a support mechanism to respond to disasters and mitigate disaster impacts through coordinated action. During the last two decades, the initiatives under ASEAN saw a significant paradigm shift from only political and economic cooperation to greater collaboration with partners and organizations in building resilience, strengthening institutional capacities, disaster risk management, and enhancing coordination. ASEAN has established specific collective laws and policy frameworks for disaster risk management through the adoption and implementation of the AADMER by the ACDM. Although member countries have individual laws and regulations related to disaster risk management these frameworks align with AADMER and the broader ASEAN cooperation on disaster management. This chapter systematically reviews the evolution of disaster risk management laws and agreements in the region over time. This gives an overview of the various country-specific laws related to disaster management, key stakeholder mapping in the ASEAN region, and their collective agreements that have led to improved readiness to withstand disasters. A review of the disaster management law and agreements to date shall therefore offer a robust pathway to the policymakers for managing collaborative efforts and strengthening disaster management mechanisms by fostering regional cooperation and adapting to emerging threats.

Keywords ASEAN · AADMER · Disaster risk management · Disaster management law · Resilience building

K. Ghosh (✉) · R. Chatterjee
Resilience Innovation Knowledge Academy (RIKA), New Delhi, India
e-mail: krishnakali@rikaindia.com

R. Shaw
Keio University, Minato, Japan

Y. Cui and R. Shaw (eds.), *Disaster Law*, Disaster Risk Reduction,
https://doi.org/10.1007/978-981-97-7374-9_3

3.1 Introduction

As the development is progressing globally, the number of disasters is also increasing. Disasters have caused an estimated 931, 000 direct mortalities and EUR 3.87 trillion in financial losses during the last 20 years (CATDAT 2021). The nature of these disasters is such that they are not only increasing in frequency and severity, but they are also becoming one of the major challenges in the overall development of a society (IPCC 2022). Southeast Asia is particularly susceptible to significant weather variations due to its equatorial location. A collection of the world's active volcanic mountains passes through the Southeast Asian region, contributing to its abundance of active volcanoes and its reputation as among world's maximum vulnerable regions. During 2023–24, this particular region faced 1100 disasters affecting 23.1 million people, displacing 9.1 million and leading to damages worth $631.1 million (ADINet 2020) Furthermore, IPCC Report 2021 found that the region has momentous intensifications in extreme weather events, especially strong monsoons and heat waves, which are anticipated to increase with global rise in temperatures in the coming future. This establishes the need to create instruments for addressing disasters in the Southeast Asia region.

Ministers of Foreign Affairs of the Philippines, Indonesia, Thailand, Malaysia, and Singapore signed the Bangkok Declaration on August 8, 1967. This was the day that a geopolitical and economic alliance named Association of Southeast Asian Nations (ASEAN), for Southeast Asian nations, was established. The ten-member ASEAN members consisting of: Brunei Darussalam, Malaysia, Philippines, Myanmar, Cambodia, Singapore, Thailand, Indonesia, Laos, and Vietnam; have thus far committed to fostering the social, cultural, and economic advancement of its member nations as well as regional peace and stability. It has also committed to expanding avenues for amicable dispute resolution among its members. ASEAN members have set up long-term DRM systems-related laws and regulations with countries Brunei, Malaysia, and Singapore being more concerned with emergency preparedness and response; Laos, Myanmar, Cambodia, Indonesia, Thailand, Philippines, and Vietnam have comprehensive disaster risk management (DRM) arrangements such as orders, laws, decrees, and regulations. The DRM institutions are permanent in nature and conduct risk reduction, mitigation, early recovery, preparedness, and response activities. Whereas, the Philippines system is more focused on disaster risk reduction (DRR) within this second group.

As the Sendai Framework illustrates, collaboration is crucial for disaster resilience in addition to national obligations ASEAN member states have created a regional policy structure and platform for DRM in the ASEAN region. Under these, there are task forces that operationalize in addition to the national legal frameworks for disaster preparedness, mitigation, and response. Over the past twenty years, there has been a notable paradigm shift in the ASEAN initiatives, moving away from solely focusing on political and economic cooperation and toward increased collaboration with partners and organizations in the areas of risk management, building resilience, institutional strengthening, and coordination enhancement.

3.2 Historical Overview of Disasters Management in ASEAN

There has long been an understanding in Southeast Asia about the value of regional support and teamwork in disaster management. ASEAN, as evidenced by the initial Concord I (1976) and Concord II (2003), the necessity for ASEAN Member States to increase regional cooperation and provide aid as part of regional disaster management has been emphasized. In 1976 Treaty of Amity and Cooperation in Southeast Asia (TAC) was established as legally binding code for relation between states that embodies principles of sociable cooperation and peaceful coexistence between states. The 1976 Declaration on Mutual Assistance on Natural Disasters marked ASEAN's first significant move to recognize disaster management and humanitarian assistance as regional issues. The improvement of disaster-warning messaging and communication, expert interactions in disaster management, greater data interchange, and the identification of emergency relief logistical distribution networks were the four components of intra-ASEAN cooperation that were necessary for the intended development (CFE-DMHA, Hawaii 2015). Despite the noble intentions behind this initial endeavor, the working groups that were subsequently constituted were unable to effectively execute their proposals at the national level.

The perspective on security in the region was profoundly altered multiple times: by the time the Cold War ended, the financial crisis of 1997, and the growth of ASEAN to include all of its member states (Tan 2015). At the regional level of ASEAN, non-traditional security risks like financial crises, natural hazards, and environmental dangers have begun to receive increased attention. The timeline of key milestones events in the disaster management of ASEAN are shared in Fig. 3.1. To improve interoperability between military and civilian relief operations, ASEAN member states and dialogue partners were expected to work together in accordance with the recommendations outlined in the 1998 Hanoi Plan of Action. Additionally, it created a common platform for fostering collaboration by uniting several global and local organizations, such as the United Nations (UN), East Asia Summit (EAS), Asia–Pacific Conference on Military Assistance to Disaster Relief Operations (APC-MADRO), Asia–Pacific Economic Cooperation (APEC), and Asia-Europe Meeting (ASEM).

Since the 2004 Indian Ocean tsunami, Southeast Asia has made significant strides in disaster management under the direction of ASEAN. The 2005 adoption of the ASEAN Agreement on Disaster Management and Emergency Response (AADMER) by ASEAN member states established a legislative framework that outlines each state's obligations in terms of regional cooperation and disaster management. The AADMER Agreement, on 17 November 2011, led the formation of the ASEAN Coordinating Centre for Humanitarian Assistance on Disaster Management (AHA Centre) to "*facilitate cooperation and coordination among ASEAN members and with relevant United Nations and international organisations, is promoting regional collaboration*" ever since (AHA Centre 2018).

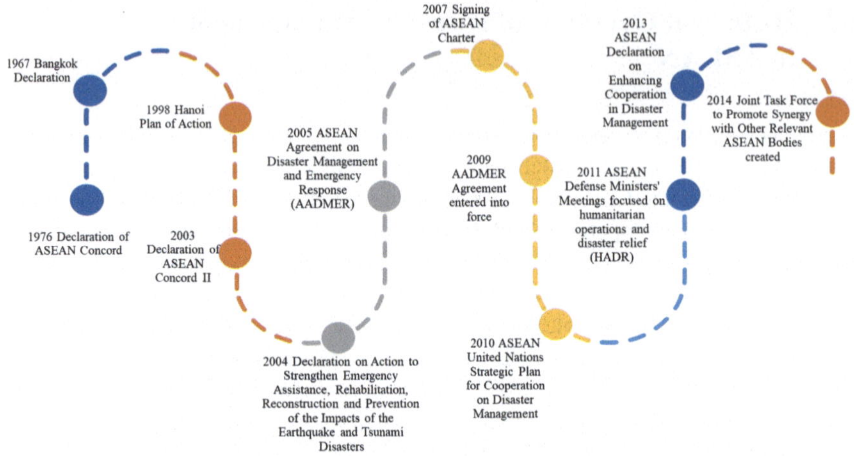

Fig. 3.1 Timeline of key milestones of disaster management in ASEAN

To take the cooperation ahead, at the 23rd ASEAN Summit in October 2013, the ASEAN Leaders adopted the ASEAN Declaration on Enhancing Cooperation in Disaster Management to foster coordination and synergy among numerous areas in firming up disaster management of the region. The Declaration, to actualize the construction of safer, more disaster-resilient communities, lower disaster losses, and cooperatively address disaster emergencies, urged for the establishment of consistent talks among pertinent ministerial bodies of the member states. In order to foster communication among the pertinent ASEAN ministerial bodies, it also mandated the creation of a Joint Task Force (JTF) and the allotment of extra joint sessions during the corresponding ministerial meetings. Further, the strategic progression for enhancing regional resilience in disaster management, during 2015–2025, was outlined in the form of the ASEAN Vision 2025 and was approved by ASEAN in 2015. "*It outlines three mutually supportive tracks to implement AADMER which are (i) institutionalization and communications; (ii) finance and resource mobilization; and (iii) partnerships and innovations*" (ASEAN 2016).

3.3 Legal Instruments and Frameworks for Disaster Management

Each of the 10 member states has a comprehensive framework of laws and policies for responding to and preparing for national disasters. These come in various forms, and not all of them are covered by a particular DRM statute. Even in cases where exist such laws, their specific goals within the nation's larger framework for risk management and development determine their breadth and amount of specificity. DRR Multi-Country Law Report identifies the "types" of DRM laws and specifies

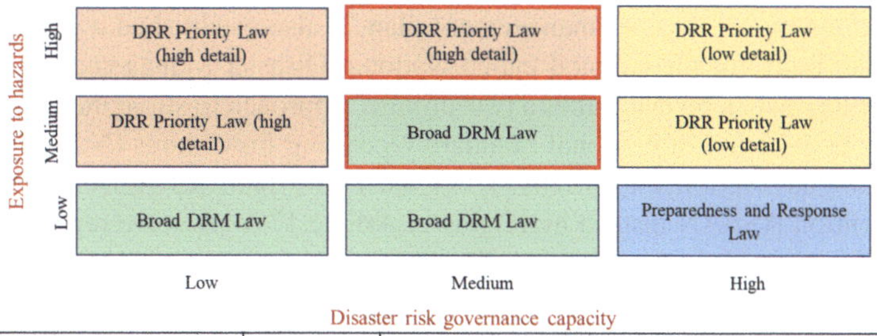

DRM Law Type	Country	Description
Broad DRM Law	Cambodia Indonesia Laos Myanmar Thailand Viet Nam	Includes full spectrum of DRM components, prevention, readiness, early warning, mitigation, emergency management and response, and early recovery. Creates specialised institutions for the coordination of DRM and at least certain local functions or structures.
DRR Priority Law (high detail)	Philippines	DRR is given particular high priority. It uses the DRM system as the primary means of establishing a disaster risk governance strategy that encompasses the entire society. Has a broad DRR mandate for the DRM institutions across sectors, including sub-national governments, civil society, and the corporate sector, and a high level of detail.
Preparedness and Response Law	Brunei Malaysia Singapore	A dedicated disaster law that emphasizes emergency planning, responding to natural hazards and some technological ones, and maybe include early warning and recovery provisions.

Fig. 3.2 DRM Law typology, suitability for ASEAN, and existing systems in different countries of ASEAN. Adapted from IFRC, UNDP DRR Multi-Country Report (2014)

where each kind of system is largely most suitable (IFRC & UNDP 2014). It affirms that DRM laws do not have to be identical in every nation because their function depends on how exposed a region is to natural hazards as well as how much of these risks are already covered by other legal frameworks in that nation. Most countries in the region would benefit from Broad DRM or DRR priority laws (IFRC 2017) Fig. 3.2 details the type of law necessary for regions like Southeast Asia which are frequently hit by disasters. The country-specific DRM legal frameworks have over the years evolved to include disaster preparedness and response to some extent which is elaborated in the following county-by-country analysis.

3.3.1 Instruments and Frameworks in Member Countries

Brunei Darussalam does not face major volcanoes, earthquakes, and typhoons, however, incidents of thunderstorms, haze, and forest fires occur with floods, landslides being the most dominant hazard. The 1984 Brunei Emergency Regulations Act conferred the power to make regulations on occasions of emergency to His Majesty the Sultan and Yang Di-Pertuan. The disaster management system is based on the Disaster Management Order 2006 (DMO) issued by the government. It identifies national bodies but does not specify sub-national structures. It established the National Disaster Council (NDC), a high-level body for planning and policy which formulates the national disaster management plan. It also established a secretariat and executing body for the Council called National Disaster Management Centre (NDMC) (IFRC 2017). NDMC takes a two-pronged approach to strengthen disaster response by preparation of National Standard Operating Procedures (NaSOP) and Strategic National Action Plan (SNAP). As the DMO predates AHA Centre, it does not mention ASEAN instead highlights in Article 17 to preserve regional and international arrangements for effective disaster management.

Cambodia made a shift from subsidiary legislation to an authoritative legislative mandate with the Law on Disaster Management (DM Law) in 2015. It officiated the National Committee for Disaster Management (NCDM) as a principal body in the Royal Government of Cambodia (RGC) for DRM. The operational roles of the Secretariat General, line government ministries, and Sub-National Committees for Disaster Management at the local level were part of the DM Law (ibid.). The Royal Decree on the role and function of NCDM highlights collaboration at the regional and international levels in disaster reduction in Article 3. Article 19 also sets out responsibilities for the local level, i.e. district and town committees for disaster management.

Indonesia faces earthquakes, volcanoes, tsunamis, flooding, and droughts. Indonesia has the Disaster Management Law 24/2007, Government Regulation PP 8/2008, Government Regulation PP21/2008 Implementation of Disaster Control, Government Regulation PP22/2008 on Disaster Aid Financing and Management, Government Regulation PP23/2008 on Participation of International Institutions and Foreign Non-Governmental Institutions in Disaster Management (IFRC 2024). The DM Law predates AADMER and offers an extensive directive to Badan Nasional Penanggulangan Bencana (BNPB) which is the national disaster management agency (IFRC 2017). Roles of BNPB are laid down under Government Regulation PP 8/2008. In accordance with the regulations, the government may designate a sensitive region as one that is off-limits to settlement and/or revoke a fractional or complete right of possession over the property. The law states that budgets for disaster management must also be set aside by regional administrations. Funding for disaster management has to be drawn from budget of national and regional government as well as communities, according to a specific regulation on "Disaster Aid Financing and Management," which also directs governments to set aside enough money for emergency response, pre-, and post-disaster phases.

Laos PDR is affected by flooding, flash floods, severe storms, and landslides. It has a series of decrees at national and sub-national levels primarily focused on providing emergency relief to meet basic needs. Prevention and mitigation are not the focus of the disaster law of the country. As of 2013, the Department of Disaster Management and Climate Change (DDMCC) under the Ministry of Natural Resources and Environment functions to address disaster risk and climate risk. National Disaster Management Office (NDMO) which is a part of the Department of Social Welfare jointly shares responsibility (IFRC 2024). The country is able to display a welcome yet robust foreign policy stance toward China in order to safeguard its interests by making use of its relationships with neighboring governments. In addition, the country has laws related to fire prevention and environmental protection (CFE-DMHA 2019).

Malaysia has several laws and protocols at the state and local levels that strengthen disaster management. The primary legislation for this is the National Security Council Act 2016. This act establishes the National Security Council (NSC), which is in control of managing disaster management efforts and implementing emergency measures. NSC has the authority to announce a state of emergency in the event of a disaster or threat to national security. Malaysia Civil Defence Force (MCDF) and the National Disaster Management Agency (NADMA) implement Community-Based Disaster Risk Reduction (CBDRR) to continue community participation. The country has a four-tier system with small units at the community or village level (IFRC 2017). The 1998 Prevention and Control of Infectious Diseases Act, 1979 Emergency (Essential Powers) Act (as amended to 2006), 1951 Civil Defence Act (Revised 1979), 1979 Emergency (Essential Powers) Act, and 1998 Fire Services Act contribute to the complete basis for disasters and emergencies management (IFRC 2024). Malaysia has used digital technology for disaster management like the kitaMATCH platform, which furnishes data on demand of relief and requirements of susceptible populations affected due to COVID-19 epidemic. It demonstrated a reduction in duplication of humanitarian operations while increasing transparency and accountability by matching the donations of donors with aid demands.

Myanmar's disaster management is based on the Disaster Management Law 2013 and the Disaster Management Rules 2015. Its objectives include regional coordination. It established the National Disaster Management Committee, the highest decision-making entity responsible for disaster management policy and coordination. The committee's role includes cooperation and coordination with international humanitarian actors at national and regional levels. Provisions for the creation of disaster management bodies and their obligations are included in the Disaster Management Law. This covers clauses about asking the armed forces for help with security in disaster-affected areas, search and rescue operations, and providing aid to victims in general. However, ASEAN is not distinctly mentioned in the laws (ibid.).

The Philippines is frequented by disasters like typhoons and in 2010 the National Disaster Risk Reduction and Management Act was passed that established a complex and multi-level DRM system. The act mandates the establishment of Local DRRM Funds by allocating at least 5% of projected revenue out of the regular sources for activities such as preparedness programs. National Disaster Risk Reduction and Management Council is responsible for policy-making, monitoring integration, evaluation, etc. (CFE-DMHA 2019). Office of Civil Defense administers the DRR in addition to national civil defense, including supporting sub-national councils. Furthermore, the laws in the Philippines guarantee women's safety and security in times of crisis, disaster, and calamity, with a particular emphasis on the possibility of sexual exploitation and other forms of gender-based violence during all phases of relief, recovery, rehabilitation, and construction. The official recognition of gender and development guides every government agency must set aside a minimum of 5% of their budget to fund gender-related programmes (UN Women 2022). This has determined the direction of the nation's deliberate attempts to integrate gender into all aspects of national development, including disaster management.

Singapore is surrounded by the most disaster-prone areas in the world. Policy framework used in Singapore has Whole of Government Integrated Risk Management approach (CFE-DMHA 2019). The legal frameworks do not have any budget allocations defined. Civil Defence Act of 2011 mandates the establishment of the Singapore Civil Defence Force (SCDF) as the primary agency responsible for disaster response. SCDF can be deployed for assistance in support of other member countries, if requested. Some other prominent legal frameworks accountable for disaster management are Fire Safety Act, Civil Defence Shelter Act, and Infectious Disease Act.

Thailand has the Department of Disaster Prevention and Mitigation (DDPM) and National Disaster Prevention and Mitigation Committee (NDPMC) as the main entities for managing disasters at a national level. These were mandated through the Disaster Prevention and Mitigation Act 2007 (IFRC 2024). Under the Act, local administrators function as DRM managers. Disaster Management Command Centres and Command Centres act as Emergency Operations Centres.

Vietnam uses inter-sectoral collaboration in the disaster prevention and control in commanding system. Several government agencies work together and have checks and balances in place, depending on the crisis. There are local flood and storm control committees at the local level. Law on Natural Disaster Prevention and Control 2013 (NDPC Law) assigns responsibilities to various departments the Vietnam Disaster Management Authority (VNDMA) housed in Agriculture and Rural Development Ministry is the key organization for DRM and the Department of Community-Based Disaster Management implements CBDRM Program in the whole country (CFE-DMHA 2019). The national level strategy for response during disasters is implemented by the National Armed Forces of Vietnam and the People's Police Force under Ministry of Public Security.

3.3.2 Instruments and Frameworks of ASEAN

ASEAN implements disaster management operations through declarations, agreements, frameworks, work plans, and terms of reference. ASEAN Leaders constituted of state heads have the chief authority to form the top policy-making entity of ASEAN followed by the ASEAN Socio-Cultural Community Council (ASCC) that works for cooperative and collaborative efforts for the delivery and realization of human development and upgradation to communities that are more resilient. The detailed institutional structure is shown in Fig. 3.3.

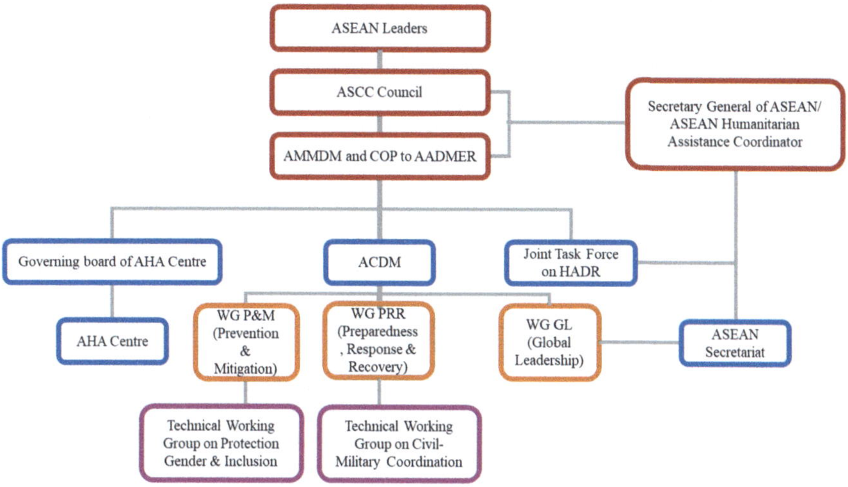

Fig. 3.3 Institutional arrangements for DRM. Modified from ASEAN (2020)

ASEAN Committee on Disaster Management (ACDM) provides guidance and supervises gratification of the goals and objectives of ASEAN. It is composed of the focal points in National Disaster Management Organizations (NDMOs) from all Member States. Working Groups under ACDM carry out decisions and initiatives implemented under respective Agreements. ASEAN Ministerial Meeting on Disaster Management (AMMDM) and the Conference of Parties (COP) are mandated to confirm the effective working of directives, orders, agreements, and other interventions related to disaster management support and cooperation in the region. The AHA Centre is the implementing center and simplifies cooperation among the states for DRM. AHA Center collaborates with UN entities (2018) establishing interoperability between UN–ASEAN more operationally relevant. Some of the key instruments functioning in the region for maintaining cooperation in disaster management are:

3.3.2.1 ASEAN Agreement on Disaster Management and Emergency Response (AADMER)

AADMER aims to "*build a region of disaster-resilient nations, mutually assisting and complementing one another, sharing a common bond in minimizing adverse effects of disasters in pursuit of safer communities and sustainable development*" (ASEAN 2022). It is the backbone and joint platform of policy for disaster management in ASEAN. A legally binding document, it became operative in 2009. It was one of the first officially binding legal document related to regional Hyogo Framework for Action (HFA) to monitor and capture information on DRR efforts from a

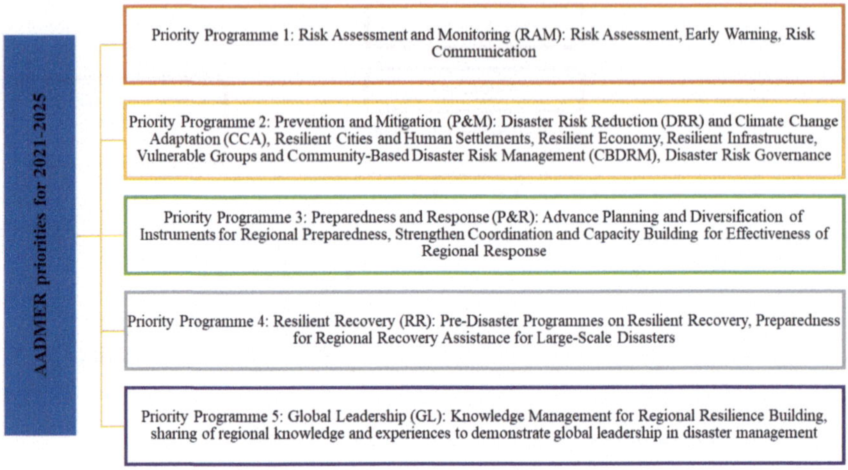

Fig. 3.4 AADMER priorities for 2021–2025

regional or sub-regional standpoint (PreventionWeb 2013). ASEAN region's priorities for disaster management were outlined in the AADMER Work Programme (AWP), which covers five years of work. ASEAN-UN Joint Strategic Plan of Action on Disaster Management IV (JSPADM) and the accompanying AWP 2021–2025 emphasize anticipatory action among its shared goals, tenets, and areas of cooperation. The AADMER priorities are mentioned in Fig. 3.4.

Through Standard Operating Procedure for Regional Standby Arrangements and coordination of Joint Disaster Relief and Emergency Response Operations, the response takes into account potential decision points prior to the occurrence of a humanitarian emergency flash point and enables response which is forecast-based, which includes financing and proactive action, according to the AWP 2021–2025.

3.3.2.2 ASEAN Agreement on Transboundary Haze Pollution

Peatland fire is one of the main causes of transboundary haze pollution in the ASEAN region. 56% of the world's tropical peatlands are found in ASEAN out of which more than 3 million hectares of peatlands in Southeast Asia were destroyed by fire in the past. Major fire and transboundary haze pollution incidents happened in ASEAN during the 1980s and 1990s. Between 1997 and 1998, one of the worst haze pollution incidents in recorded history took place with hotspots in Indonesia, Brunei Darussalam, Singapore, and Thailand. It is believed to have caused losses of above USD 9 billion in economic, social, and environmental sectors (Qadri 2001). In order to prevent and monitor transboundary haze pollution, the ASEAN member states signed a legally binding environmental pact in 2002 called the ASEAN Agreement on Transboundary Haze Pollution.

This Agreement acknowledges that coordinated national efforts and international cooperation are necessary to prevent pollution resulting from fires on land especially forest fires affecting transboundary regions. To help the Parties cooperate and coordinate in dealing with effects of such pollution that they cause, AATHP has mandated the creation of ASEAN Coordinating Centre for Transboundary Haze Pollution Control. Although, that is fruitful when it is internalized within the domestic legal system (Muhammad 2022). Members of the agreement are tasked with making sure that actions that fall within their purview do not endanger the health of the environment in other member states, outside their borders, or both. To minimize the effects of transboundary haze pollution, they are legally required to reply quickly to requests for pertinent consultations made by a State(s) that are or may be impacted.

3.3.2.3 Agreement on the Establishment of the AHA Centre

AHA Centre was formulated on a legally binding agreement made in 2011. It conducts interventions for all phases of disaster management. The AHA Centre's disaster management and emergency response responsibilities include collecting and disseminating data for monitoring, enabling emergency response and reviewing regional SOPs (ASEAN 2016). The AHA Centre regularly provides information to the public in an effort to increase knowledge of DRR. AHA Centre provides instant Flash Updates and Situation Updates during emergencies and releases weekly update on disaster when there isn't an emergency.

3.3.2.4 ASEAN Declaration on Enhancing Cooperation in Disaster Management

At the 23rd ASEAN Summit in Bandar Seri Begawan, on 9 October 2013, this declaration was adopted. It promotes collaboration, integration, and synergy among ASEAN-related mechanisms. Regular talks across ASEAN ministerial bodies are encouraged to promote disaster resilience, reduce losses, and respond to catastrophes more effectively. The declaration aims to increase dialogue among ASEAN ministerial bodies by establishing a Joint Task Force and scheduling an additional joint session during their meetings.

3.3.2.5 ASEAN Declaration on Strengthening Social Protection

Leaders of member states endorsed a proclamation aimed at improving social protection for at-risk groups during the 23rd ASEAN Summit. As coordinated and holistic methods should involve numerous stakeholders, including government and commercial organizations, the proclamation encouraged activities related to disaster management, including social safety nets for resilient recovery, prevention, and mitigation, as well as supporting multi-sectoral responsiveness to social protection during preparedness and response. ASEAN Ministerial Meeting on Social Welfare and Development and Senior Officials Meeting on Social Welfare and Development serves as the regional focal point for inter-sectoral social protection cooperation. Senior Officials Meeting on Rural Development and Poverty Eradication, ASEAN Commission on the Promotion and Protection of the Rights of Women and Children, Senior Officials' Meeting on Health Development, ACDM are the other participants in the inter-sectoral consultations (ASEAN 2013).

3.3.2.6 Declaration on Institutionalizing the Resilience of ASEAN and Its Communities and Peoples to Disasters and Climate Change

Prior to COVID-19 pandemic, political unrest at home, climate change, and economic downturns were thought to be the two main security threats confronting the region in 2019 (Tang et al. 2020). At the 26th ASEAN Summit in 2015, leaders of member states endorsed a declaration aimed at creating a future that is resilient by lowering disasters and climate risks, preventing emerging and new ones, and adapting to changing climatic conditions through physical, social, economic, cultural, and environmental actions. It recommends investing in prevention and mitigation, engaging stakeholders at multi-levels, and creating national and regional capacities to address disaster management and climate change. ACDM is leading cross-sectoral collaboration for improving resilience, with backing of Sectoral Bodies at the regional level.

3.3.2.7 ASEAN Leaders Declaration on Disaster Health Management

The leaders of the ASEAN member states jointly adopted the ASEAN Leaders Declaration on Disaster Health Management in 2017, to address the health risks associated with disasters and minimize casualties by obtaining the full sovereignty and agreement of the afflicted nations. The declaration emphasizes working together with pertinent Sectoral Bodies and associates to support the strengthening of capacity in areas like the quick deployment of medical relief on a regional and national scale, the continuation of health services and disease surveillance, the promotion of investments in infrastructure that is resilient to disasters, etc., that are pertinent to all DRM phases.

3.3.2.8 Declaration of the Special ASEAN Summit on Coronavirus Disease

For firming up cross-border cooperation related to healthcare this declaration was ratified on 14 April 2020. Seven important measures including cooperation to limit the spread of the pandemic, protection of people, safeguarding supply chains, refining multi-stakeholder, multi-sectoral approaches to efficiently address public health emergencies, jointly mitigate the socio-economic impacts, ensuring public well-being, transparent dissemination of vital health information about the pandemic. In addition, giving assistance to pandemic-affected people of member states and reallocation of existing funds for starting the COVID-19 ASEAN Response Fund were considered important.

The COVID-19 outbreak witnessed the active efforts of the ASEAN Emergency Operations Centre Network. Led by Malaysia's Ministry of Health, it offered a freely accessible platform for ASEAN member states operating in crisis and disease prevention centres to share knowledge in time. ASEAN Bio Diasporas Regional Virtual Centre which works for visualization and big data analytics contributed by releasing updated studies on national risk assessments, preparation, and response strategy (Djalante et al. 2020). Risk assessment reports with summary on deaths and active cases within ASEAN nations were shared for worldwide broadcasting of COVID-19 information.

3.3.2.9 ASEAN Declaration on Strengthening Adaptation to Drought

The drought problem is the main topic of the declaration which was formulated in 2020. This emphasizes several phases of DRM, including assessment and monitoring, resilient recovery, response, preparedness, prevention, and mitigation. Some of the holistic considerations for activities under this include a regional framework for bolstering risk assessments, adaptations and mitigation, harmonization among the Sectoral Bodies, improving research and development, and enhancing capacities by policy-making for addressing droughts.

3.3.2.10 ASEAN Regional Framework on Protection, Gender, and Inclusion in Disaster Management

It was introduced in October 2021 by the ACDM as a primary protection, gender, and inclusion strategy for all ACDM working groups of the AWP 2021–2025. Guidelines for Operationalizing document acts as a planning and prioritization toolkit to assist national disaster management actors and regional bodies working across issues on gender in disaster management. The considerations of safety, equality, access to assistance, psychological support, participation in decision-making, and empowerment are some of the areas focused by the framework.

3.4 Competence and Constraints of Disaster Laws and Agreements in ASEAN

ASEAN members have been actively fostering new relationships as well as growing and enhancing existing ones through one-on-one assistance, activities, or learning and sharing between organizations through the AHA Centre. For instance, AHA Centre has managed building the ASEAN Village at Palu City, Indonesia which offers homes to the impacted people following the earthquake and tsunami of 2018 in Central Sulawesi, with significant assistance from Brunei and the Philippines (AHA Centre 2021). There has been a rise in involvement with humanitarian agencies with due consideration to ASEAN as a viable humanitarian partner for disaster management in the area. According to a survey, it was established that more than 80% of participants felt that ASEAN has improved regional disaster management with AADMER (ASEAN 2021). Some of the prominent approaches undertaken by the ASEAN in the past are discussed below.

3.4.1 Track-Two Approach

In 2008, ASEAN was put to the test when Cyclone Nargis ravaged Myanmar. At least 130,000 people died due to this catastrophe (Petz 2014). As a result of the widespread uncertainty and the military's reluctance to allow the UN and other experienced disaster responders entry, ASEAN was able to play a crucial part in the relief effort. In this instance, ASEAN's favored approach of unofficial networking and track-two diplomacy yielded significant benefits. Amid the uncertainty, ASEAN took the initiative to remove the hurdles to trust and communication that were impeding the entry of international relief personnel and aid into the nation (Tripartite Core Group 2008; ASEAN 2010). Even though the 2005 agreement had not yet come into effect, regional response of ASEAN aligned with the goals and spirit of AADMER as majority of the member states' disaster laws include guidance on international and regional cooperation.

3.4.2 One ASEAN One Response

For boosting the pace, scope, and cohesion of reaction, the Declaration on One ASEAN One reaction was signed by ASEAN Leaders in September 2016. The experiences during the 2013 Typhoon Haiyan that occurred in Philippines served as a major inspiration for the declaration. The AHA Centre is reaffirmed in the Declaration as the main regional coordinating body for emergency response and disaster management in the ASEAN. The AHA Centre was assigned by the Leaders to operationalize One ASEAN One Response, to create the required policies, guidelines, and standards, and to fortify ties with pertinent ASEAN sectors and stakeholders.

The goal of One ASEAN One Response is to see the ASEAN Community's sectors and stakeholders united in their response to disasters, growing stronger and more cohesive over time. In terms of vision, it regards ASEAN as a community of peoples rather than merely an alliance of states (AHA Centre 2018). It advocates the principles of being inclusive, integrated, innovative, and proactive. The commitment to regional response stems from political, operational, and financial levels. It encompasses all ASEAN players, including the military, the health sector, the corporate sector, non-governmental organizations, academic institutions, and young people.

3.4.3 Interoperability and Coordination

Various sectoral bodies, diplomatic forums, and entities by which regional partners engage with ASEAN form a complex network that needs complementarity in gratifying their responsibilities. Certain obstacles have been encountered with data exchange and compatibility among ASEAN Member States and the AHA Center's Disaster Monitoring and Response Systems (ASEAN 2017). Additionally, technical support is required for data administration and sharing. It is, therefore, necessary to strengthen partnerships between agencies reporting on early warning, AHA Centre, NDMOs, and pertinent Sectoral Bodies to promote undisrupted development, upgraded knowledge sharing, interoperability of systems that issue early warnings, and strengthened operational collaborations with regional organizations working on monitoring and response to disasters.

UN–ASEAN coordination has seen a shift from internationally led to locally led interventions with the support of the AHA Centre which emphasizes the need to train stakeholders in member countries for local leadership in disaster management. Another aspect of DRM that lacks interoperability is the involvement of other sectors like civil-military coordination instruments for risk management (ASEAN 2021). Police forces in countries like Vietnam took significant roles during the COVID-19 outbreak by controlling crowds, spreading awareness, and maintaining protocols (Luong 2021). This highlights the important overlaps between the two sectors and the potential for improved coordination with the participation of these professionals in disaster management.

3.4.4 Non-interference Principle

The ASEAN members are guided by the principles of non-interference and sovereignty. The democratic and non-democratic member nations of ASEAN share separate views and do not relinquish enough powers to regional organizations, particularly ASEAN, due to their concern for maintaining state sovereignty. This state-centric method of conduct makes achieving AADMER's objectives a difficult task. Upholding the principles followed by member countries especially: respect for sovereignty, non-interference, and territorial integrity could be functionally difficult while addressing situations of transboundary impact of disasters and conflicts (Arumbinang 2021; Gerard 2014). Maintaining non-interference in the form of abstinence from criticism and views on issues that lead to humanitarian crises could be difficult for regional organizations like AHA Centres, civil organizations, joint task forces that provide consultation, and a negotiation forum for disaster management. Reluctance to share sensitive yet valuable information can delay the assistance through AADMER sectoral bodies. Through dialogs, permission for advocacy, and improved cooperation in the aspects of regional security and disaster management such issues could be addressed.

3.5 Conclusion and the Way Forward

In conclusion, the current state of disaster laws in ASEAN illustrates both the region's achievements and shortcomings in improving disaster risk reduction. Despite the notable progress made by ASEAN member nations in creating legislative frameworks, policies, and methods to mitigate risks, there are still gaps in the region's implementation, enforcement, and harmonization. Member states have a variety of national disaster laws with some countries having detailed DRR laws like the Philippines, response focused laws like Malaysia, Singapore. Countries like Cambodia, Vietnam, and Malaysia have identified organizations at different levels of government for implementation whereas Singapore has defense forces implementing disaster management interventions. Monetary allocations for disaster management capacity building, community-based disaster risk management, etc., activities have been made mandatory in only some countries like Indonesia and the Philippines whereas Singapore has no allocations defined by law. Coordination and collaboration among member nations are hindered by differences in legal systems, institutional capacities, and resource limitations.

Such issues are minimized to an extent with the existing regional agreements and frameworks which take a democratic approach. Continuous efforts are required to reinforce disaster legislation, encourage cross-border collaboration, and build resilience at all levels due to rising concerns including climate change and transboundary hazards. As ASEAN's vision progresses for a resilient ASEAN, a collaborative framework for action in sectors with direct contributions to disaster risk management and climate change such as health, planning, agriculture, economic, and welfare sectors is deemed necessary. The focus should be on the integration of local decision-making, planning, and regulations with national and regional development actions. Regional information sharing guarantees more equitable distribution of funding and maximizes resource mobilization through data-driven decision-making that fosters stakeholder trust and increases community capacity. Creation of a hub for regional information exchange that unifies governmental and non-governmental platforms must be created. At the national level, ASEAN member states may learn from successful activities and best practices from across members and globally. Going ahead, in order to attain a more comprehensive and cohesive approach to disaster management in ASEAN, instruments that strengthen persistent political dedication, funding for capacity building, and increased regional collaboration are necessary.

References

ADInet (2020) Homepage. AHA Centre Disaster Information Network. http://adinet.ahacentre.org/
AHA Centre (2018) Operationalising one ASEAN one response 2018
AHA Centre (2021) Lessons learnt on the ASEAN's recovery support of the central Sulawesi's 2018 disasters. AHA Centre 2021. https://ahacentre.org/wp-content/uploads/publications/New-Homes-of-Opportunities.pdf
Arumbinang MH (2021) Problems and Dilemmas: ASEAN commitments in disaster management. Indones Comparat Law Rev 4(1):17–25 P-ISSN: 2655-2353, E-ISSN: 2655-6545. https://doi.org/10.18196/iclr.v4i1.13219
ASEAN (2010) A humanitarian call, The ASEAN response to cyclone Nargis, Report; ASEAN Secretariat, Jakarta, p 14
ASEAN (2013) ASEAN declaration on strengthening social protection, pp 4–5. https://www.asean.org/wp-content/uploads/images/archive/23rdASEANSummit/5.%20asean%20declaration%20on%20social%20protection_final.pdf
ASEAN (2016) ASEAN vision 2025 on disaster management. https://asean.org/wpcontent/uploads/2021/01/fa-220416_DM2025_email.pdf
ASEAN (2020) ASEAN agreement on disaster management and emergency response (AADMER) work programme 2021–2025. Jakarta, ASEAN Secretariat, December 2020
ASEAN (2021) ASEAN disaster resilience outlook: preparing for a future beyond 2025. Jakarta, ASEAN Secretariat, October 2021
ASEAN (2022) ASEAN framework on anticipatory action in disaster management, Jakarta, ASEAN Secretariat, June 2022
CATDAT: CATDAT Worldwide Natural Catastrophes Loss Database v2021.04, CATDAT, Karlsruhe, Germany. http://www.risklayer.com/de/service/catdat/
CFE-DMHA (2015) ASEAN disaster management handbook, CFE-DMHA, Hawaii, p 54
CFE-DMHA (2019) ASEAN disaster management handbook, CFE-DMHA, Hawaii
Djalante R, Nurhidayah L, Van Minh H, Phuong NTN, Mahendradhata Y, Trias A, Lassa J, Miller MA (2020) COVID-19 and ASEAN responses: comparative policy analysis. Progress Disaster Sci 8:100129. https://doi.org/10.1016/j.pdisas.2020.100129. Epub 2020 Oct 22. PMID: 34173447; PMCID: PMC7577870
Gerard K (2014) ASEAN and civil society activities in 'created spaces': the limits of liberty. Pacific Rev 27(2):265–287. https://doi.org/10.1080/09512748.2014.882395
IFRC (2017) ASEAN disaster law mapping. International Federation of Red Cross and Red Crescent Societies, Geneva
IFRC (2024) Resilience Library Southeast Asia Resources. https://www.rcrc-resilience-southeastasia.org/disaster-law/disaster-law-mapping-asean-agreement-on-disaster-management-and-emergency-response/country-profiles/
IFRC & UNDP (2014) Effective law and regulation for disaster risk reduction: a multi-country report. New York. https://disasterlaw.ifrc.org/sites/default/files/media/disaster_law/2020-09/DRR%20Report%20%28full%20version%29%20final_page_LR.pdf

IPCC: Climate change 2022, impacts, adaptation and vulnerability, summary for policymakers. In: Working Group II contribution to the sixth assessment report of the intergovernmental panel on climate change. Cambridge University Press, Cambridge. https://www.ipcc.ch/report/ar6/wg2/

Luong H (2021) Contributions and responsibilities of police forces in natural disasters: a review of Vietnam's case study. https://doi.org/10.4018/978-1-7998-7210-8.ch005

Muhammad F (2022) Environmental agreement under the non-interference principle: the case of ASEAN agreement on transboundary haze pollution. Int Environ Agreem 22:139–155. https://doi.org/10.1007/s10784-021-09545-4

Petz D (2014) Strengthening regional and national capacity for disaster risk management: the case of ASEAN. Brookings Institution, Washington D.C.

PreventionWeb (2013) ASEAN Regional progress report on the implementation of the Hyogo framework for action (2011–2013). https://www.preventionweb.net/files/39137_39137aseansubregionalreport20112013.pdf

Qadri ST (2001) Fire, smoke, and haze the ASEAN response strategy. Asian Development Bank. https://www.adb.org/sites/default/files/publication/28035/fire-smoke-haze.pdf

Tan A (2015) East and South-East Asia: international relations and security perspectives. Routlege Press, p 231

Tang SM et al (2020) The state of Southeast Asia survey report: 2020. Singapore: ISEAS-Yusof Ishak Institute. https://www.iseas.edu.sg/wp-content/uploads/pdfs/TheStateofSEASurveyReport_2020.pdf

The ASEAN Secretariat (2017) Paving the way towards ASEAN resilience and joint response. Accomplishment Report AADMER Work Programme (2010–2015). July 16, 2020. https://bit.ly/3ilxHZq

Tripartite Core Group (2008) Post-Nargis joint assessment, after-action analysis, July. https://www.gfdrr.org/sites/default/files/GFDRR_Myanmar_Post-Nargis_Joint_Assessment_2008_EN.pdf

UN Women (2022) Ensuring gender responsive disaster risk reduction: good practices from ASEAN. https://wrd.unwomen.org/sites/default/files/2022-07/Good-Practices-from-ASEAN-on-Ensuring-Gender-Responsive-Disaster-Risk-Reduction.pdf

Chapter 4
Key Issues and Challenges of Disaster Law in Japan

Ruiyan Zhao, Tomo Kawane, and Rajib Shaw

Abstract This chapter delves into the evolution of Japan's disaster management framework through the lens of the Disaster Law (Basic Act on Disaster Management), which was enacted in 1961 in response to the Isewan Typhoon. It scrutinizes the impact of three pivotal disasters—the Isewan Typhoon, the Great Hanshin-Awaji Earthquake, and the Great East Japan Earthquake—on the continuous refinement of disaster policies. Following the seismic shockwaves of the 2011 Great East Japan Earthquake, this analysis uncovers the vital lessons learned from past catastrophes and their profound influence on the subsequent revisions of the Disaster Law. By examining these key historical events, this chapter illuminates the dynamic interplay between Japan's disaster response strategies and the real-world challenges posed by nature's fury, encapsulating decades of resilience-building and policy adaptation.

Keywords Disaster management framework · Basic act on disaster management · The Isewan typhoon · The Great Hanshin-Awaji earthquake · The Great East Japan earthquake

4.1 Introduction

Japan's disaster law, and in particular the Basic Act on Disaster Management (BADM), is an important aspect of the country's legal infrastructure, dictated by Japan's extreme vulnerability to natural disasters such as earthquakes, tsunamis, typhoons, volcanic eruptions, etc. The Basic Act on Disaster Management (BADM), which was enacted in 1961, is the foundation of the country's legal framework for disaster management and was born from the need to respond to the catastrophic natural disasters that have characterized the country's history.

R. Zhao · T. Kawane · R. Shaw (✉)
Graduate School of Media and Governance, Keio University, 5322 Endo, Fujisawa 252-0882, Japan
e-mail: shaw@sfc.keio.ac.jp

Y. Cui and R. Shaw (eds.), *Disaster Law*, Disaster Risk Reduction,
https://doi.org/10.1007/978-981-97-7374-9_4

The main objective of the Act is to minimize damage caused by natural disasters, safeguard the lives, property and livelihoods of citizens, and ensure national security and public welfare. To achieve this objective, the Act incorporates comprehensive measures, including regular risk assessments and the development of disaster management plans. It emphasizes the importance of disaster prevention through infrastructure development, public awareness campaigns, and community participation. In addition, the Act sets out the responsibilities of the national and local governments during emergencies, focusing on rescue, relief, and rehabilitation operations. The Act also provides guidance on the allocation of financial resources and support systems necessary for disaster management activities.

The importance of Japan's Basic Law for Disaster Management cannot be overemphasized. For a country that is frequently affected by natural disasters, it plays an important role in mitigating their impact. The system established under the Act is often regarded as a global model, providing valuable inspiration for other disaster-prone regions. By integrating disaster risk reduction into development planning and encouraging community participation, the system played an important role in building resilience to disasters. In the face of the escalating threat of climate change, it was becoming increasingly important to adapt to new disaster risks.

The Isewan Typhoon, also known as Typhoon Vera, which struck Japan in 1959, was a pivotal event that led to significant changes in Japan's approach to disaster management, ultimately culminating in the creation of the Basic Act on Disaster Management (BADM). Typhoon Vera, known for its catastrophic impact, is considered the deadliest typhoon in Japanese history. Despite being well forecast, the typhoon caused extensive damage and a high death toll, partially attributed to inadequate disaster preparedness and response mechanisms at the time. The severity of this disaster, with around 5,000 fatalities and substantial destruction, underscored the critical need for a more structured and effective disaster management system in Japan.

In response to this calamity, the Japanese government recognized the urgent necessity to reform its approach to disaster management. This led to the enactment of the Basic Act on Disaster Management in 1961, just two years after the Isewan Typhoon. The Act was designed to establish a comprehensive framework for disaster risk management, emphasizing preparedness, emergency response, and recovery. The impact of Typhoon Vera was a stark reminder of the vulnerabilities that natural disasters could exploit, particularly in a rapidly urbanizing context like post-war Japan. The BADM thus represented a significant step forward in Japan's effort to develop a more resilient approach to handling natural disasters, shaping the country's future disaster management policies and practices.

4.2 Legal Framework of Disaster Management in Japan

Japan's legal framework for disaster management is a sophisticated and comprehensive system that reflects the country's high risk of natural disasters such as earthquakes, tsunamis, and typhoons. At the heart of this framework is the Basic Act on Disaster Management (BADM), which sets the foundation for Japan's disaster management policies. Enacted to protect the lives and property of citizens and ensure national security, the BADM outlines the responsibilities of national and local governments and establishes a system for coordination between various government agencies and organizations.

The BADM mandates the creation of detailed disaster management plans at both national and local levels, emphasizing the importance of preparedness, risk assessment, and public education. It also sets guidelines for emergency response systems, including evacuation procedures, rescue operations, and the provision of medical care, as well as for recovery and reconstruction efforts post-disaster.

Supplementing the BADM are several other key laws and regulations that target specific aspects of disaster management. The Disaster Countermeasures Basic Act further solidifies basic disaster management strategies and clarifies the roles and responsibilities of citizens in these efforts. For specific natural phenomena, Japan has the Act on Special Measures for the Mitigation of and Preparedness for Earthquakes, which focuses on earthquake resilience, and the Act on the Promotion of Tsunami Countermeasures, which emphasizes tsunami warning systems and evacuation plans.

Moreover, the Fire Service Act is crucial for organizing emergency response services, especially fire departments that play a significant role during disasters. The Act on Special Measures for Large-Scale Earthquakes concentrates on urban earthquake preparedness and response. In addition, the Flood Control Act and the Forest Act, along with the Sediment Disaster Prevention Act, address risks associated with floods, forest fires, and sediment disasters.

This legal structure ensures that disaster management in Japan is well-coordinated, involving not just government agencies but also the active participation of communities and individuals. By covering a broad spectrum of potential disasters, the framework aims to protect lives, minimize damage, and enhance the nation's resilience against future catastrophes.

Japan has a range of disaster countermeasure laws designed for different types of disasters and various purposes, including disaster prevention, emergency response, and post-disaster reconstruction. Notably, for frequent occurrences like earthquakes and tsunamis, there are two comprehensive laws covering both prevention and emergency response, along with eight laws specifically addressing prevention. Laws pertaining to mudslides include preventive measures outlined in the Sand Prevention Law and the Forestry Law. Additionally, there are preventive laws related to volcanoes and blizzards. Post-disaster rehabilitation laws can be broadly categorized into measures for overall relief assistance, support for victims, disposal of disaster debris, and regulations concerning disaster rehabilitation businesses. The disaster response laws adopted in Japan are comprehensive, integrating multiple levels of government and various agencies to ensure a coordinated and effective response to disasters. The synergy and complementarity among these laws contribute to the creation of a comprehensive disaster legal framework in Japan (Cabinet Office n.d.).

4.3 Key Issues in Japanese Disaster Law

The key issues of Japan's disaster law framework relate to funding, jurisdictional complexity, and coordination challenges.

4.3.1 Funding

Adequate funding for disaster prevention, response, and recovery is essential. The legal framework must address the allocation and management of funds for these activities. For example, the Great East Japan Earthquake in 2011 required significant funds for recovery and reconstruction. Given the scale and unpredictability of such disasters, it is a challenge to ensure that these funds are adequately allocated and released in a timely manner.

The disaster relief law also suffers from the principle of benefits in kind and cash payments. The type of relief under Article 23(1) of the Disaster Relief Act provides for the 'provision or lending of funds, equipment or materials necessary for livelihood', along with the provision of accommodation facilities, food and drinking water through soup kitchens and other means. Paragraph 2 of the same law stipulates that 'rescue may be carried out by paying money to those in need of rescue (in the case of burials, to those who carry out burials), notwithstanding the provisions of the preceding paragraph, if the prefectural governor deems it necessary'. In practice, however, cash payments are not made, but in principle payments in kind. The reasons for this are: 'In times of disaster, living materials are often scarce or difficult to procure, and money is often useless for the purchase of goods'; 'In cases where money is sufficient, it is usually difficult to assume that there is social disorder that would require legal aid to preserve social order'; 'In cases of mere economic hardship, it is difficult to assume that there is a social disorder that would require legal aid to preserve social order'; 'In cases where money is sufficient, it is usually difficult to assume that there is social disorder that would require legal aid to preserve social order'. And that mere economic deprivation is of such a nature that it should be dealt with by other laws or measures. Therefore, in the case of the Unzen-Fugendake volcanic eruption disaster (1991), which was a prolonged disaster, the Disaster Relief Law alone was not enough to cope with the situation, and the Nagasaki Prefecture implemented the 'Meal Provision Project', whereby each person was provided with a daily cash allowance of 1,000 yen or breakfast, lunch, and dinner in kind, with the State providing half of the cost. Cash grants for livelihood support were also provided by Hokkaido and Tokyo in the Mount Usu eruption disaster (2000) and the Miyakejima eruption disaster (2000). During deliberations on the Miyakejima eruption disaster at the House of Representatives Special Committee on Disaster Countermeasures in November 2001, a witness, Professor Hiroi Osamu of the Institute of Socio-Information Studies at the University of Tokyo, called for a disaster relief system separate from the high hurdle of public assistance, in which those who have lost income due to disaster receive certain continuous financial payments only while they continue to live in shelters. The Institute has appealed for the implementation of a separate disaster protection system from the hardship welfare system. With the enactment of the Disaster Relief and Reconstruction Assistance Law (Law No. 66 of 1998), long-term evacuees will also receive assistance payments, but such assistance for living during evacuation is considered to be the role of the Disaster Relief Law in the first place. How to support living expenses during long-term evacuation remains a challenge.

4.3.2 Jurisdictional Complexity

Overlapping responsibilities between national and local governments lead to jurisdictional challenges. This complexity can affect the efficiency of relief and recovery operations. An example is the coordination between national and local governments during the 1995 Great Hanshin-Awaji Earthquake. The overlapping responsibilities led to delays in effective response and recovery efforts due to confusion over jurisdictional boundaries.

The complexity of jurisdiction within the framework of Japan's disaster law stems from the intricate division of responsibilities and powers between national and local governments. This complexity often manifests itself in the event of a disaster and has a significant impact on the efficiency and effectiveness of disaster management.

At the heart of this complexity lies Japan's unique administrative structure, a highly decentralized system of governance. While the central government sets overall policies and guidelines for disaster management through laws such as the Basic Act on Disaster Management (BADM), the actual implementation of these policies is the responsibility of local governments such as prefectures and municipalities.

However, this division of labor also poses challenges. In the event of a disaster, confusion may arise as to which level of government is responsible for specific tasks. For example, coordination of evacuation efforts, emergency medical services, and search-and-rescue operations may be hampered by jurisdictional uncertainty. National government agencies may have their own disaster response teams, but they must work in tandem with local authorities, leading to potential coordination problems.

In recent years, particularly in the wake of major disasters such as the Great East Japan Earthquake in 2011, the Government has been working to improve coordination and clarify responsibilities between national and local governments. Amendments to the Japan Disaster Management Law and the establishment of the Cabinet

Office have been aimed at strengthening cooperation, but Japan's inherently complex administrative structure continues to pose challenges to disaster management efforts.

In conclusion, the complexity of the jurisdictional scope of Japan's disaster law stems from a decentralized administrative system that promotes local autonomy while potentially leading to coordination challenges in the event of a disaster. Finding the right balance between local control and central coordination remains an ongoing task in Japan's efforts to improve its disaster management capacity.

4.3.3 Coordination Between Government Levels

Effective coordination between levels of government is essential for successful disaster management. The legal framework needs to facilitate such coordination to ensure rapid and effective disaster response and recovery. The need for effective coordination between national, prefectural, and local governments was highlighted during the 2011 Great East Japan Earthquake and Tsunami. The disaster required a synchronized response in terms of evacuation, rescue, and relief operations, which was extremely challenging given the different administrative systems and protocols at each level of government. The incident highlighted the importance of establishing clear and effective coordination mechanisms to manage large-scale emergency responses.

Intergovernmental coordination in Japanese disaster law presents several challenges due to the country's complex administrative structure and the division of responsibilities between national and local governments. These issues become particularly evident during large-scale disasters and can impact the overall effectiveness of disaster management efforts. One of the primary challenges is the overlap of responsibilities between national and local governments. While the national government sets overarching disaster management policies and guidelines through laws like the Basic Act on Disaster Management (BADM), local governments, including prefectures and municipalities, are responsible for implementing these policies on the ground. This division of roles can lead to confusion during disaster situations, as it may not always be clear which level of government should take the lead in specific tasks, such as evacuation, search-and-rescue operations, or medical services.

Another issue is the potential for bureaucratic hurdles and delays in decision-making and resource allocation. The multiplicity of government agencies involved in disaster management at both the national and local levels can lead to inefficiencies. Coordinating these agencies and streamlining decision-making processes is essential for a rapid and effective response to disasters.

Additionally, variations in preparedness and response capabilities among different regions can result from the flexibility afforded to local governments in developing their disaster management plans. Disasters can strike any part of Japan, and the ability to respond effectively should not be contingent on the resources and capabilities of individual localities.

Efforts have been made to address these challenges. Amendments to the BADM and the establishment of the Cabinet Office have aimed to improve coordination between national and local governments. The Cabinet Office plays a crucial role in coordinating disaster response efforts, bridging the gap between central and local authorities. However, the inherent complexities of Japan's administrative structure continue to pose challenges to intergovernmental coordination in disaster management.

In summary, the issues of intergovernmental coordination in Japanese disaster law are rooted in the division of responsibilities between national and local governments, potential bureaucratic inefficiencies, and variations in preparedness among regions. While efforts have been made to enhance coordination, finding the right balance between local autonomy and centralized coordination remains an ongoing endeavor in Japan's disaster management system.

4.4 Case Studies

4.4.1 The Isewan Typhoon

The Isewan Typhoon, also known as Typhoon Vera, struck Japan in 1959 and is considered one of the most devastating typhoons in the nation's history. This catastrophic event had a profound impact on Japan's disaster management approach and its legal framework at the time.

The governmental system for responding to large-scale disasters at the time of their occurrence has not yet been established, for example, disaster-related laws have not yet been harmonized, and the roles and responsibilities of various agencies have not been clarified. In order to improve this situation, Japan has been developing a system of governance that can operate effectively in emergency situations. To this end, Japan has established the Basic Law for Disaster Countermeasures as an overall strategy for addressing disaster-related issues, clarifying the roles and responsibilities of the Government and stakeholders (Kanbara and Shaw 2021).

At the time of the Isewan Typhoon, Japan's disaster management framework was less structured and coordinated than it is today. The country was still recovering from the aftermath of World War II, and disaster preparedness and response mechanisms were not well-developed. When Typhoon Vera made landfall, it caused widespread destruction, including flooding, landslides, and extensive damage to infrastructure and homes. The typhoon resulted in a staggering loss of life, with approximately 5,000 fatalities.

In response to the devastation caused by Typhoon Vera, the Japanese government recognized the urgent need to reform its approach to disaster management. Lessons learned from the typhoon highlighted several critical issues and legal gaps in Japan's disaster response:

Inadequate Preparedness: The typhoon exposed the lack of comprehensive disaster preparedness plans and mechanisms. The government realized the need to establish proactive measures for disaster prevention and mitigation.

Limited Coordination: The response to Typhoon Vera suffered from coordination challenges between various government agencies and local authorities. This highlighted the necessity for improved interagency coordination and communication during disasters.

Insufficient Infrastructure Resilience: The typhoon's impact on infrastructure, including flood control systems and buildings, revealed weaknesses in the resilience of these structures to extreme weather events. There was a need to establish regulations and standards for building infrastructure that could withstand natural disasters.

Inadequate Early Warning Systems: The limited early warning systems in place at the time contributed to a lack of timely information for residents in affected areas. The government recognized the importance of developing and implementing advanced warning systems.

In the aftermath of the Isewan Typhoon, Japan embarked on a journey to strengthen its disaster management capabilities. This led to the establishment of the Basic Act on Disaster Management (BADM) in 1961, just two years after the typhoon. The BADM aimed to create a comprehensive framework for disaster risk management, emphasizing preparedness, emergency response, and recovery. It addressed many of the identified legal gaps and lessons learned from the Isewan Typhoon by laying the foundation for a more organized and coordinated disaster management approach (Yoshida et al. 2021).

In conclusion, the Isewan Typhoon was a turning point in Japan's disaster management history. The legal framework at the time was ill-prepared for such a disaster, leading to significant loss of life and extensive damage. However, the lessons learned from this tragic event prompted the Japanese government to enact the BADM and address critical legal gaps, ultimately shaping the country's future disaster management policies and practices.

4.4.2 The Great Hanshin-Awaji Earthquake

The Great Hanshin-Awaji Earthquake, also known as the Kobe Earthquake, struck on January 17, 1995, in the Hyogo Prefecture of Japan. It was a devastating earthquake with a magnitude of 6.9, and its impact was felt not only in terms of the significant loss of life but also in terms of the widespread destruction it caused. This earthquake was a pivotal event in Japanese history that led to a reevaluation of the country's disaster management framework and response.

At the time of the earthquake, Japan had a legal framework in place for disaster management, but the scale and severity of the disaster exposed several weaknesses in the system. One of the notable issues was the slow and somewhat disorganized response to the disaster. Coordination between various government agencies, both at the national and local levels, faced challenges, resulting in delays in delivering aid and assistance to affected areas.

In the aftermath of the Great Hanshin-Awaji Earthquake, several lessons were learned, and critical legal gaps were identified:

Coordination and Communication: The earthquake revealed the need for improved coordination and communication mechanisms between different levels of government and among various agencies. The legal framework lacked clear guidelines on how these entities should collaborate during a disaster.

Rescue and Relief Operations: The legal framework did not provide a well-defined structure for organizing and executing rescue and relief operations. This led to difficulties in efficiently deploying resources and personnel to affected areas.

Public Awareness and Preparedness: The earthquake highlighted the importance of public awareness and preparedness. Many citizens were unprepared for the disaster, and there was a lack of public education and training programs outlined in the existing legal framework.

Infrastructure and Building Standards: The earthquake exposed vulnerabilities in building standards and the need for stricter regulations to ensure earthquake-resistant construction. While some laws existed, they needed to be reinforced and updated.

In response to these lessons and identified legal gaps, Japan initiated a series of reforms and amendments to its disaster management laws. The Basic Act on Disaster Management (BADM) was revised to strengthen coordination mechanisms, clarify the roles and responsibilities of various agencies, and emphasize the importance of public education and training in disaster preparedness. Additionally, building standards and earthquake-resistant construction regulations were reinforced and updated (Sakamoto 2017).

The Great Hanshin-Awaji Earthquake was a tragic event, but it served as a catalyst for significant improvements in Japan's disaster management legal framework. The lessons learned and the subsequent legal reforms have contributed to a more resilient and prepared Japan when facing future disasters.

4.4.3 The Great East Japan Earthquake

The Great East Japan Earthquake, which occurred on March 11, 2011, was a catastrophic event that not only tested Japan's disaster resilience but also highlighted both the strengths and weaknesses of the Japanese legal framework for disaster management at the time. The earthquake, followed by a massive tsunami and nuclear accidents at the Fukushima Daiichi Nuclear Power Plant, resulted in unprecedented devastation.

In response to the disaster, Japan activated its disaster management mechanisms, including the provisions of the Basic Act on Disaster Management (BADM). The central government, in coordination with local authorities, initiated a large-scale emergency response, including search-and-rescue operations, evacuation efforts, and the provision of medical and humanitarian assistance. The Self-Defense Forces were mobilized to provide crucial support in the affected regions.

However, despite the overall effectiveness of the response, several challenges and legal gaps became evident. One of the most significant issues was the extent of the disaster itself, which exceeded the scenarios anticipated in disaster management plans. The scale of destruction and the simultaneous occurrence of multiple crises, including the nuclear accident, strained the capacity of the disaster management system. This raised questions about whether Japan's legal framework adequately accounted for such extreme scenarios.

Additionally, the disaster exposed coordination challenges between national and local governments. The overlapping responsibilities and jurisdictional complexities occasionally led to delays in decision-making and resource allocation. The need for a more streamlined and efficient coordination mechanism became apparent.

Furthermore, the Fukushima Daiichi nuclear accident revealed gaps in the legal framework regarding nuclear emergencies. Japan had to rely on ad-hoc measures and international assistance to manage the nuclear crisis, highlighting the need for comprehensive legislation and protocols specifically addressing nuclear disasters.

In the aftermath of the Great East Japan Earthquake, Japan conducted a thorough review of its disaster management system and identified several lessons learned. These lessons included the importance of improving intergovernmental coordination, enhancing the flexibility of disaster response plans, strengthening nuclear disaster preparedness, and bolstering public awareness and education on disaster resilience.

Subsequently, Japan introduced legislative amendments and reforms to address these issues. The creation of the Cabinet Office and the passage of the Act on Special Measures for the Reconstruction and Revitalization of Fukushima were notable steps taken to enhance disaster response and recovery capabilities (Norio et al. 2011).

In summary, the Great East Japan Earthquake served as a pivotal event that prompted a reevaluation of Japan's legal framework for disaster management. While the response demonstrated the system's resilience, it also revealed areas for improvement, leading to legal reforms and a renewed commitment to disaster preparedness and resilience.

4.5 Challenges in Implementation

The practical challenges in implementing disaster law in Japan are multifaceted and encompass various aspects, including the roles of local governments, resource allocation, and public participation.

Local governments play a pivotal role in disaster management, as they are responsible for implementing disaster preparedness, response, and recovery efforts at the community level. However, this decentralization of responsibilities can lead to disparities in capabilities and resources among different localities. Some regions may have more robust disaster management infrastructure and funding, while others may struggle to adequately prepare for or respond to disasters. This discrepancy in resources can result in unequal outcomes when disasters occur, potentially leaving vulnerable communities at a disadvantage.

Resource allocation is another significant challenge. While Japan invests heavily in disaster preparedness and mitigation measures, the allocation of resources can be complex. Determining how to distribute funds, personnel, and equipment effectively during a disaster can be a logistical challenge, especially when multiple regions are affected simultaneously. The allocation of resources must be equitable and based on risk assessment and need, which requires meticulous planning and coordination.

Public participation is crucial for successful disaster management, but it can be challenging to achieve. While Japan places a strong emphasis on public education and awareness campaigns, ensuring active participation from citizens in disaster preparedness and response activities remains a continuous effort. Many individuals may not be fully engaged in disaster drills or may not have access to necessary information and resources. Engaging diverse communities and ensuring that vulnerable populations are included in disaster planning and response efforts are ongoing challenges.

In summary, the practical challenges in implementing disaster law in Japan revolve around local government disparities, resource allocation complexities, and the need for effective public participation. Addressing these challenges requires a combination of policies, resources, and community engagement efforts to ensure that all regions and citizens are adequately prepared for and can respond to disasters effectively.

4.6 Recommendations for Improvement

Given Japan's vulnerability to natural disasters and the changing nature of these challenges, disaster law reform in Japan is a crucial endeavor. In order to improve disaster resilience and response, there are a number of considerations and recommendations that we can explore for future policy development and law revision.

Strengthening centralized coordination: Enhancing coordination and cooperation between national and local governments is essential. Establishing a centralized body with the authority to coordinate disaster response at all levels of government can help streamline decision-making and resource allocation.

Risk-based resource allocation: Develop a more data-driven, risk-based approach to resource allocation. Resources should be allocated in proportion to the level of risk faced by each region, ensuring that vulnerable areas receive adequate support.

Community engagement and education: Invest in public education and community engagement programmed that empower individuals and communities to play an active role in disaster preparedness and response. These programmed should be inclusive and accessible to all segments of society.

Inclusion and Vulnerable Groups: Prioritize the inclusion of vulnerable groups, such as older people, people with disabilities, and people with reduced mobility, in disaster planning and response. Adapt policies and resources to meet their specific needs and challenges.

Technological Advances: Embrace technological advances in early warning systems, data analysis, and communication during disasters. Adopting state-of-the-art technology can significantly reduce response times and improve response efficiency.

Review and update legal frameworks: Regularly review and update existing disaster laws to reflect changing risks and challenges. Consider revisions to clarify roles and responsibilities, strengthen coordination mechanisms, and adapt to emerging threats.

International cooperation: Promote international cooperation in disaster management. Japan can learn from and share experiences with other countries facing similar risks, leading to a more comprehensive global approach to disaster resilience.

Research and Development: Invest in research and development to innovate strategies for disaster prevention and response. Encourage interdisciplinary research that combines insights from various fields such as science, engineering, social science, and public health.

Infrastructure Resilience: Implement stricter building codes and infrastructure standards that prioritize resilience to earthquakes, tsunamis, and other natural disasters. Retrofitting and strengthening of existing infrastructure should also be encouraged.

Public–Private Partnerships: Explore opportunities for public–private partnerships in disaster preparedness and response. Private sector involvement can bring additional resources and expertise to disaster management efforts.

Long-term Recovery and Reconstruction: Develop a comprehensive long-term recovery and reconstruction plan that extends beyond immediate relief efforts. Ensure that affected communities are supported in rebuilding their lives and infrastructure.

Climate Change Adaptation Legislation: Consider introducing climate change adaptation-specific legislation to mitigate the impacts of climate-related disasters, such as flooding and the increase in extreme weather events.

In conclusion, disaster law reform in Japan should be a dynamic and continuous process to address changing disaster risks. The recommendations prioritize coordination, risk-based resource allocation, community participation, technological advancement, and adaptation to ensure that Japan remains resilient in the face of disasters.

4.7 Conclusion

This chapter provides an overview of the main issues and challenges of disaster law in Japan. The need for a centralized approach to disaster management that addresses jurisdictional complexities and funding challenges is highlighted. Risk-based resource allocation strategies and stronger community participation, including the inclusion of vulnerable groups in disaster planning and response, are advocated. The importance of adapting to technological advances, updating legal frameworks and international cooperation, especially in the context of climate change, was also emphasized. This chapter highlights the need to maintain a dynamic and responsive legal framework to ensure resilience and effective disaster management, given the frequency of natural disasters in Japan.

References

Cabinet Office . (n.d.). Disaster law system. In Japan Meteorological Agency. 内閣府 (n.d.) 災害法体系について. In 気象庁. https://www.jma.go.jp/jma/kishou/intro/gyomu/wxad/kensyu/h29/pdf/2-2-2.pdf

Current Status and Issues of Systems for Supporting Livelihoods of Disaster Victims -Responses and Issues in the Great East Japan Earthquake 被災者生活支援に関する制度の現状と課題 —東日本大震災における対応と課題— https://dl.ndl.go.jp/view/download/digidepo_3050449_po_0712.pdf?contentNo=1

Kanbara K, Shaw R (2021) Disaster risk reduction regime in Japan: an analysis in the perspective of open data, Open Governance. Sustainability 14:19. https://doi.org/10.3390/su14010019

Major amendments to the Basic Law on Disaster Countermeasures from its enactment to the present 災害対策基本法の制定から現在までの主な改正の経緯について. https://www.fdma.go.jp/publication/ugoki/items/rei_0404_04.pdf

Norio O, Ye T, Kajitani Y, Shi P, Tatano H (2011) The 2011 eastern Japan great earthquake disaster: overview and comments. Int J Disaster Risk Sci 2:34–42

Overview of the Disaster Countermeasures Basic Law. (n.d.). Newton Consulting, Inc. 災害対策基本法概観 (n.d.) ニュートン・コンサルティング株式会社. https://www.newton-consulting.co.jp/bcmnavi/column/20121218_disaster-measure-law.html

Sakamoto M (2017) Crisis management in Japan: lessons from the Great Hanshin-Awaji Earthquake of 1995 and the Great East Japan Earthquake of 2011. In: Crisis and emergency management. Routledge, pp 597–632

Yoshida M, Sawano T, Senoo Y, Ozaki A, Nishikawa Y, Zhao T, ... Tsubokura M (2021) Importance of individualized disaster preparedness for hospitalized or institutionalized patients: lessons learned from the legal revisions made to the Basic Act on Disaster Management in Japan following the Fukushima nuclear disaster. J Global Health 11

Chapter 5
Disaster Law in the United States

Yafang Wen and Rajib Shaw

Abstract In comparison to other countries in the world, the disaster law of the United States has several distinctive characteristics, including an early start time, a rapid development process, and a variety of content aspects. As early as 1803, Congress passed the first separate disaster law. From the 1950s to the 1970s, disaster law in the United States reached a peak of development, and the Stafford Act of 1988 outlines many modern society's federal disaster relief efforts. There is no doubt that the United States is the leader in disaster law in the world, from early information prediction to post-disaster recovery has a special team responsible for it. In this chapter, we will focus on the development path of disaster law in the United States, the social drivers of disaster law updates, the implementation system of act and the current challenge, and direction for the future.

Keywords Characteristics of American disaster law · Disaster law · Implementation system of disaster response · The United States · Stafford act

5.1 Introduction

The United States is one of the most disaster-prone countries in the world due to its vast territory and complex and diverse environment. In 2005, the United States was hit by Hurricane Katrina, one of the most catastrophic disasters in American history (Brunkard et al. 2008). Similarly, Hurricane Sandy in 2012 caused huge damage to the East Coast of the United States (Casey-Lockyer et al. 2013). In addition to hazards caused by natural and other force majeure, man-made hazards cannot be ignored. On September 11, 2001, the 911 terrorist attacks occurred in the United States that shocked the world. The incident had a very serious impact on the United States, including huge casualties, huge economic losses, and social panic (Rose and Blomberg 2010). Due to the increasing frequency of extreme weather events caused

Y. Wen (✉) · R. Shaw
Graduate School of Media and Governance, Keio University, 5322 Endo, Fujisawa 252-0882, Japan
e-mail: wen.yafang.study@keio.jp

Y. Cui and R. Shaw (eds.), *Disaster Law*, Disaster Risk Reduction,
https://doi.org/10.1007/978-981-97-7374-9_5

by global climate change, the world has become more turbulent, and the risk of disaster has increased. It is urgent and imperative to improve the country's disaster response. Although disasters are difficult to prevent totally, improving the ability to prevent disasters can reduce their effects significantly (Twigg 2004).

Disaster-related laws are one of the key issues related to mitigate the disaster risk. A complete disaster law can improve the country's resilience to disasters, reduce losses caused by disasters, and restore order to people's lives during a short period (Lauta 2014). In addition, compared with other countries in the world, American disaster laws are quite sound. Understanding the disaster laws of the United States can enhance the understanding of disaster laws in other countries, especially developing countries, make up for shortcomings in the country's disaster laws, and enhance legislation. Improve legal procedures and promote national disaster laws to better protect citizens' lives, health, and property safety. Therefore, this chapter will give a comprehensive and systematic explanation of the U.S. disaster law, which is mainly divided into the following parts: first, sort out the development history of the U.S. disaster law, secondly, summarize and analyze the characteristics of the U.S. disaster law, and try to understand the promotion bill of renewed social dynamics. At the same time, the bill's implementation process needs to be elaborated on. Finally, we will sort out possible current problems with U.S. disaster law and make suggestions for future development directions.

5.2 The History of the U.S. Disaster Law

The development history of disaster law in the United States can be compared with that of disaster law in other countries as a result of its early start, rapid development, and complete development. From 1803 to 1950, the U.S. Congress passed 128 separate bills intended to provide disaster assistance. As there is no comprehensive disaster law, Congress must pass a separate law each time a disaster occurs, which is extremely cumbersome (Moss 1999). In the 1930s, the federal government had no formal disaster response framework for assisting state and local governments. Due to the occurrence of floods and huge economic problems in the country, the United States launched the first formal federal government assistance program for local governments in the New Deal in 1933 (Hunter 2010).

It was not until 1950 that Congress passed the Federal Disaster Relief Act, officially granting the federal government the authority to respond to major disasters. At the same time, the Federal Disaster Relief Act provides that if a governor requests federal assistance after a disaster, the president can grant the request by declaring a major disaster. It is worth mentioning that in this bill, the federal government only repairs damage to public infrastructure, but does not mention providing assistance to individuals and families.

Throughout the 1960s and 1970s, the U.S. Congress continued to amend the Disaster Act and expanded the federal government's disaster responsibilities. This stage is a process in which the U.S. Congress continues to explore the role of the federal government in disaster laws. Additionally, the federal government made significant progress in reducing community disasters in 1968. The National Flood Insurance Act was signed into law, which put individuals and families on responsibility for disaster recovery and no longer relied too much on the federal government. However, there are many immature practices, leading to problems such as an unclear and uncoordinated scope of federal government responsibilities (Comerio et al. 1998).

Many of the problems left over from this legislation period erupted during several major disasters in the 1970s. As a result of Hurricane Agnes, which struck Florida and other areas in 1972, 122 people were killed and $17.5 billion was lost (Schroeder 2018). Because the Disaster Relief Act did not fully leverage the federal government's role in this disaster. Accordingly, Congress amended the Disaster Relief Act in 1974, allowing the federal government for the first time to provide direct assistance to individuals and families affected by disasters (Disaster Relief Act Amendments of 1974). It is unfortunate that the famous Three Mile Island nuclear leak occurred in 1979. Even though there were no serious casualties, post-disaster cleanup work lasted until December 1993, costing about $1 billion (Hindmarsh 2013). Following the incident, Carter, then President of the United States, signed Executive Order 12148, revising federal disaster relief once again. Under the act, the Federal Emergency Management Agency (FEMA) was established to coordinate federal disaster relief activities and establish ten regional offices throughout the country. This act establishes the Federal Emergency Management Agency, which combines emergency response agencies under the executive branch into one unified entity to coordinate federal disaster relief activities nationwide without interference from the Cabinet (Executive Order No. 12148 1979).

It is evident that the Stafford Act plays a significant role in U.S. disaster law. This act amended the Disaster Relief Act of 1974 and was signed into law on November 23, 1988, marking the formation of modern disaster law in the United States. Consequently, federal assistance to disasters is no longer restricted by the cause of the disaster, while at the same time, it stipulates the requirements for apportioning aid funds. In addition, the federal government provides assistance funds to states and localities to administer public assistance programs. However, the bill still adheres to the principle of giving full play to local strengths. When state and regional forces are unable to respond to disasters, the federal government will provide assistance (Moss 1999).

Developed in 1992, the Federal Response Plan (FRP) describes how the federal government mobilizes aid resources and conducts rescue activities. The program involves 27 federal agencies and departments providing supplemental assistance through personnel support, technical support, and equipment support (Roth and Gaffney 1996). A significant role is played by the Federal Emergency Management Agency in the coordination and leadership of rescue operations. In 2003, FEMA was merged into the Department of Emergency Management Preparedness and Response (DEMPAR) and the Department of Homeland Security (DHS), the same year that the National Response Plan (NRP) was enacted (Adamski et al. 2006). The invasion of Hurricane Katrina in 2005 demonstrated the imperfections of U.S. disaster laws, including poor handling of flood disasters, exacerbating social inequality, and an unclear division of responsibilities between the federal government and states (Gauna 2005). Because the National Response Plan did not play a full role in this disaster, the National Response Framework (NRF) was proposed in 2008 to replace the NRP. During emergencies and disasters, the framework provides for the leadership of federal officials, including the President and the Secretary of National Security. Additionally, it emphasizes cooperation between the federal government, states, and regions, as well as between different departments of the federal government (Bea 2005). Due to Hurricane Sandy in 2012, the U.S. Congress passed two disaster-related legislation in 2013, the Disaster Relief Appropriations Act of 2013 and the Sandy Recovery Improvement Act of 2013. The law changes the process for providing disaster assistance to individuals (Brown et al. 2013).

Generally speaking, disaster laws in the United States consist of the Stafford Act and its related amendments. It involves multiple administrative agencies, including the federal government, the Federal Emergency Management Agency, and state governments (Rivera and Miller 2006). Compared with other countries, American disaster law has a long development history, a relatively complete system, and strong flexibility. The following content examines the disaster response process under American disaster law.

5.3 The Implementation Progress of Disaster Response

The American disaster response system stipulates that before certain disasters that can be monitored occur, such as hurricanes or heavy rains, the advance element of the Emergency Response Team, called the ERT-A, will be dispatched to potential disasters. The disaster-stricken areas carried out initial response work and installed communication equipment to ensure smooth rescue work. The ERT-A team is composed of Federal Emergency Management Agency program support staff and representatives of emergency support functions (ESF) and is led by FEMA leadership (Bahari et al. 2011). There is a need for a discussion of the functions of emergency support in this context. According to the Federal Response Plan (FRP), the federal government will provide assistance to states and local governments in 12 major areas: Transportation, Communications, Public Works and Engineering, Firefighting, Information and Planning, Mass Care, Resource Support, Health and Medical Services, Urban Search and Rescue, Hazardous and Material, Flood and Energy. Each field will be managed by a main agency, and there are about 17 related assistance and support agencies. They play a role in disaster reduction in different fields and provide assistance to disaster areas (Kapucu 2006; Torsell and Jordan 2009).

The situations mentioned above usually occur under predictable disasters, but there are still many disasters we cannot predict, such as earthquakes, volcanic eruptions, and tsunamis. When an area is suddenly overtaken by fire, the first persons responsible are local officials, who are asked to declare a state of emergency in accordance with the local emergency operations plan. In fact, local officials are at the forefront of the entire disaster response process (Emergency 2002). With the growth and intensification of disasters, local authorities must determine whether the local rescue forces will be able to respond to the disaster on their own. In the event that local officials believe federal assistance is needed, they should provide details regarding the type of disaster and the current impact of the disaster, as well as clearly stating the type of assistance needed. The provision of assistance, including medical assistance or evacuation of residents (Schroeder 2018).

In an early disaster report, if state authorities determine that the disaster is too severe to exceed state and local capacity, the state can request the emergency management agency and regional officials to join the preliminary damage assessment. There are ten emergency management agencies at the regional level, each responsible for a specific state. The main purpose of the preliminary damage assessment (PDA) is to estimate the losses caused by the current disaster, predict the possible subsequent problems and the needs of affected individuals and families, and evaluate whether the disaster requires application for assistance from the federal government (FEMA 2022). Collect relevant evidence for applying for assistance, determine the type and level of the disaster, and what assistance the plan hopes to receive. The more serious the disaster and the greater the losses, the less evidence is required; conversely, if the disaster is not too serious, the state needs to provide more details in the preliminary damage assessment. There is ample evidence that states are ill-equipped to respond to disasters. At the same time, preliminary damage assessments are required to provide federal disaster management agencies with local information so that relief efforts can be carried out. A disaster assessment is not only used to request presidential declarations for assistance but will also be used throughout the entire rescue process to provide the necessary real-time information to ensure the smooth progress of subsequent rescue operations (FEMA 2003).

After the PDA team completes the initial assessment and determines the damage that the disaster has caused and the possible subsequent impacts, the governor will decide whether to apply for assistance from the federal government. There are the following requirements for applying for assistance. The first is that the State must have implemented its State Emergency Operations Plan. Secondly, the requested information must include information about the disaster area required by law, including information that has been invested in rescue work or is about to be put into rescue work. The nature and quantity of local and state resources. Third, the application must satisfy the cost-sharing provisions of the Stafford Act. Fourth, applications for federal disaster assistance must be made within 30 days of the disaster (McCarthy 2011; Stafford et al. 2013).

The governor should proactively apply for what kind of rescue activities are needed based on the PDA. In fact, the federal government's basic relief activities fall into three categories: assistance to individuals and businesses, public assistance, and hazard mitigation assistance (Kreiser et al. 2018).

(1) Assistance to individuals and businesses: assistance measures for individuals, families, and businesses, which usually include disaster housing, unemployment

benefits, personal and family assistance, legal services, low-interest loans for small businesses, and other welfare measures.

(2) Public assistance: Provides financial assistance and technical support to state or local, private, or non-profit organizations for the repair and replacement of damaged public facilities.

(3) Hazard mitigation assistance: Permanently eliminate or reduce the potential risks to residents' lives and property caused by a specific disaster in the area. Additionally, the assistance will only become effective if one or both of the other two assistances are approved.

When the governor applies for federal assistance from the president, he must first submit the application information to the FEMA Regional Director in his region. After his evaluation of the disaster information and supplementary suggestions, he will then forward it to the FEMA Director in Washington, D.C. for review, who will complete it, opinion, and submit it to the President. Generally speaking, there are three criteria when proposing approval opinions. The first is to consider the type and extent of the disaster. The second is to consider the impact of the disaster on individuals, families, and the state. The third is to measure what resources does the state currently have and can use to mitigate the disaster. The president has the final say on whether to approve a governor's request for federal aid (FEMA 2003). If the President agrees to the Governor's request for federal aid, the President will decide to declare disaster, and appoint the Federal Coordinating Officer (FCO). The federal and state governments will cooperate to establish a Disaster Field Office and sign an agreement to conduct disaster assistance conferences (Stafford et al. 2013).

Generally speaking, the disaster assistance system in the United States is very complete, well-organized, and responds to the entire disaster process. Throughout the decision-making process, the governor is the first person responsible for disasters, shouldering important responsibilities such as judging the disaster situation and proposing federal assistance to the president (Smith et al. 2018). Secondly, the federal emergency management agencies from bottom to top have responsible persons who provide opinions on whether federal assistance is needed for disasters, which to a certain extent ensures the objectivity of the president's judgment. Several characteristics can be found in American disaster law, which we will discuss in the following section (Waugh Jr and Streib 2006).

5.4 The Characteristics of American Disaster Law

The Stafford Act and some disaster amendment bills are the most significant disaster laws in the United States, which play an important role in responding to disasters and reducing disaster losses. This study summarizes the characteristics of modern American disaster law: the public–private partnership model has powerful functions; local and state governments are the first persons responsible after disasters; a bottom-up disaster assistance system; comprehensive assistance objects.

5.4.1 *Private Enterprise and Public–Private Partnerships Play an Important Role*

American private companies that play a significant role in post-disaster recovery can be divided into two categories (Chandra et al. 2016). For-profit private enterprises are the first type, company's normal operation provides assistance funds for post-disaster recovery and ensures the safety of residents in the disaster area. Income plays a crucial role. The second type is non-profit private enterprises, generally non-profit charitable institutions, which raise funds from enterprises and individuals to assist in disaster reconstruction (Gotham and Cheek 2017).

Private-sector assistance in disasters is reflected in the entire disaster process, starting at the preparation stage. Several private companies will invest in, provide technical assistance, or take other measures to improve local resilience. Through its foundation, Office Depot provides emergency preparedness education to small businesses. Walmart Inc., which promotes resilience on a technical level, uses its website to promote employee preparedness and post area-specific tips and shelter or disaster information (Chandra et al. 2016).

While state and local governments, the federal government, and other government organizations all conduct disaster relief efforts when disasters strike, private companies increasingly play an important role in disaster response and recovery, by providing goods and services, and in logistics and play a role in supporting activities (FEMA 2011). In 2012, to support areas affected by Hurricane Sandy, the federal government provided approximately $60 billion, private corporations donated $141 million, and non-profits raised more than $500 million for distribution to affected Sandy residents and communities. As of December 2012, approximately 90 organizations had raised more than $400 million in response to Hurricane Sandy's devastation. Two-thirds of business assistance comes from direct donations to organizations such as the American Red Cross and Feeding America (Charities Bureau 2014).

The American disaster law system fully reflects the public–private partnership model. Government departments can consider certain private-sector partners formal partners. Private-sector consultants, specifically from business, can be quickly hired for project-oriented purposes and dismissed once the project is complete. Assist the government in saving human resources and improving the entire disaster management process (Chandra et al. 2016).

5.4.2 *Give Full Play to the Role of Local and State Governments*

According to the Stafford Act, the autonomy of the states and local governments is fully recognized in the United States. They have considerable rights when responding to disasters, but they also bear the most significant responsibility for disaster assistance. Each state has its own laws that stipulate disaster response systems and principles, designate relevant agencies for disaster response, and the process for applying for federal assistance (Becker 2009).

Based on the preliminary disaster assessment, the governor can judge whether it is necessary to apply for a presidential disaster declaration; if the governor believes that existing resources can cope with the disaster and there is no need to apply for federal assistance, he can mobilize state resources for disaster assistance. In addition, according to the principles of American disaster law, the federal government's disaster assistance does not replace state and local governments, but only serves as a supplement. State and local governments continue to be the main focus of disaster assistance (Wolensky and Wolensky 1991; Crow and Albright 2019).

5.4.3 The Assistance Service is Comprehensive

According to the Stafford Act, the federal government provides three types of assistance following a disaster. The first is individual assistance, the second is public assistance, and the third is hazard mitigation assistance. In general, individuals, families, and small businesses are essentially the hardest-hit groups, so the federal government's assistance is also very comprehensive (Olshansky and Johnson 2014).

The most basic assistance is food. The Food and Nutrition Service is an agency under the U.S. Department of Agriculture (USDA), primarily responsible for food coupons and food commodities after disasters. Residents who are in need can apply for food stamps from the agency and obtain food through the Disaster Food Stamp Program. In addition, individuals can also apply for food assistance through organizations such as the American Red Cross and the Second Harvest Food Bank Network (Billings et al. 2022). Housing is a major issue that needs to be addressed as soon as possible after a disaster. The federal government can provide housing repair and reconstruction funds for residents who request for post-disaster housing subsidies (Davlasheridze and Miao 2021).

In addition, the federal government will provide extremely low-interest post-disaster loans to individuals, families, and small businesses to help affected people return to normal life as soon as possible. Assistance for unemployed residents is also available, and the federal government can provide relief benefits and reemployment services to unemployed residents (Twigg 2004). Individuals and families can receive property damage assistance from the federal government and private companies designated as partners by some states, which includes clothing, home appliances, private vehicles, etc. In addition, legal aid and post-disaster psychological counseling, as well as special assistance for veterans can be applied for (FEMA 2003).

5.4.4 *Bottom-Up Disaster Response System*

Although the Stafford Act grants the president the power to declare a disaster, the disaster assistance system does not begin with the president. It is a bottom-up process that starts with the state and local governments and is passed down layer by layer. The governor will determine whether the state can be relied upon to respond to the disaster based on the disaster assessment (Stafford et al. 2013). On this basis, the governor will submit an application to the regional federal emergency management agency, including information on the assistance to be applied for and the disaster situation. Regional FEMA directors will make judgments and provide recommendations to their superior, the FEMA director. After considering the recommendations of the governor and regional FEMA director, the FEMA director will submit his or her own recommendations to the president, who will make the final decision (Rivera and Miller 2006).

The bottom-up aid process is very effective because grassroots governments have a better understanding of disaster situations, are able to provide more accurate disaster response, and may be able to apply for appropriate federal assistance. At the same time, it can also greatly alleviate the pressure on the federal government for aid, save time and manpower, and improve disaster response speed and quality.

5.5 The Challenge of American Disaster Law

The American Congress passed the Stafford Act in 1988, 45 years ago. Congress has revised the Disaster Act several times to better protect society and residents from disasters. In recent years, with global climate change, the frequency of extreme weather has increased, and every major disaster still brings serious losses to the United States (Bhola et al. 2023). Additionally, in the immediate aftermath of a disaster, it is imperative to ensure that the disaster law protects the rights of all residents, mobilizes social resources in an efficient manner, and is able to return life to normal as soon as possible. A sound legal system can, to a large extent, contribute to the reduction of social problems and the orderly functioning of society. Accordingly, this section will discuss some of the challenges currently facing American disaster law, mainly three aspects: inequality in housing assistance; shortage and unreasonable allocation of assistance funds; and cumbersome application processes for assistance.

5.5.1 *The Inequality in Housing Assistance*

The most affected individuals and families in disasters are individuals and families, particularly those from poor backgrounds. Due to the limited number of rescue forces and resources available during an emergency, personal interests become irrelevant in the face of the interests of the entire community. In this case, personal interests will be ignored (Gould 2009). Under the Stafford Act, survivors whose homes have been severely damaged can apply for assistance from the federal government, and those who are successful will receive rental funding assistance from the Federal Emergency Management Agency and other housing subsidies following a disaster (Pierre and Stephenson 2007). However, the number of survivors who successfully receive post-disaster housing assistance is far fewer than those who actually need it. When scholars consider the reasons for this phenomenon, they consider the shortcomings of the Stafford Act itself, namely, this part of housing assistance is discretionary and not mandatory by the Federal Emergency Management Agency, which prevents judicial agencies from intervening to safeguard the rights and interests of survivors who do not receive assistance (Stafford et al. 2013). The harm caused by disasters to poor groups is huge, and the refusal of federal emergency management agencies to help these disaster-stricken groups makes it even worse. Failure to protect disaster victims' legitimate rights and interests will widen the gap between the rich and the poor in society, increase inequality, and further lead to serious social problems (Rando 2021).

In addition, renters' interests are not as well protected as those of homeowners when it comes to housing assistance (Mickelson et al. 2019). Disaster-affected tenants are eligible for up to 18 months of rental assistance, but they may face increased risks from rental shortages and rising rental prices (Liu 2006; Ross 2013). During the post-disaster recovery process, tenants have received less assistance than homeowners. As a result of Hurricane Sandy, tenants in New York and New Jersey suffered heavy losses, but received inadequate compensation compared to their losses (Fair Share Housing Center 2014).

5.5.2 Inadequate Funding and Unfair Distribution

The post-disaster response is based on adequate aid funds and a reasonable allocation of resources (Schroeder 2018). The Federal Emergency Management Agency and the Office of Management and Budget did not include large disasters that could cost more than $5 million in their estimates of disaster aid spending for the coming year. Disaster relief funds are activated only when minor disasters occur. Typically, an emergency supplemental appropriation is required when a large-scale disaster occurs. When Hurricane Harvey hit the Texas Gulf Coast in 2017, early disaster damage estimates severely underestimated the actual damage caused by the disaster. Moreover, disasters are not just the physical damage to houses and property caused by the storm, but also the subsequent shutdown of businesses, unemployment of workers and other issues that will also result in huge losses. The lack of disaster loss estimates will result in insufficient disaster fund storage, which will negatively affect rescue efforts in the event of a disaster (Schroeder 2018).

Furthermore, there is a strong relationship between post-disaster financial allocation and social vulnerability. Many scholars believe that equitable post-disaster assistance is one of the critical features of a successful disaster response (Finucane et al. 2020; Watts et al. 2015; Farber 2007). According to some scholars, those groups with a higher level of social vulnerability were unequally affected by the aftermath of the disaster recovery process, as well as the allocation of federal recovery funds, both of which were inequitable. A serious impact was made on the overall recovery process following a disaster and exacerbated the vulnerability of vulnerable groups (Muñoz and Tate 2016). These vulnerable groups may include the elderly, female-headed households, ethnic minorities, and low-income households (Bolin 2007). Also, during the post-disaster recovery process, race is also a factor to be taken into consideration. Due to factors such as language and social discrimination, African Americans, Latinos, and Hispanics in particular suffer greater losses, have fewer opportunities to receive adequate federal assistance, and wait longer to receive aid. A process exacerbated by this increases the vulnerability of these vulnerable groups and makes post-disaster recovery more difficult (Finch et al. 2010). Billings found that applicants from low-income areas were less likely to receive FEMA assistance after controlling for flood insurance, property values, and property damage after Hurricane Harvey (Billings et al. 2022). Overall, low-income groups are hardest hit by disasters but receive relatively small federal aid (Drakes et al. 2021). An overall analysis of federal aid shows that federal aid allocation is linked to economic losses, and economic losses are positively correlated with income, meaning that aid tends to be allocated to households with higher incomes and increased home values (Hoopes Halpin 2013). In fact, this method of distributing disaster aid is more beneficial to groups with higher incomes. The total value of their property holdings is higher, and therefore they will incur more property losses as a result. Since low-income groups have less property, they will naturally accumulate less property losses (Wilson et al. 2021).

5.5.3 Applying for Federal Aid is Cumbersome

The U.S. disaster assistance system relies heavily on individual strength, which requires giving full play to the strength of individuals, families, and communities. In order to receive housing, loans, and other assistance after a disaster, disaster-affected individuals must apply on their own. There has been significant physical and emotional damage to the victims of a recent disaster, and they must still complete the application paperwork for federal assistance after experiencing such a disaster. The entire application process is very cumbersome and time-consuming. For example, if disaster-stricken residents want to be eligible for federal subsidies, if the homeowner does not have insurance, they need to make an appointment in advance with a FEMA inspector to inspect the homeowner's property. After about ten days of review, the homeowner will get the final result. If the application is successful, he will receive a remittance or check directly; if the application is unsuccessful, he will receive a rejection letter. Even if disaster-stricken people who apply for assistance apply in the normal order, they are very likely to be rejected by the Federal Emergency

Management Agency, because FEMA has discretionary power to make decisions (Wilson et al. 2021).

It is very difficult for people who have experienced severe disasters to fill out complicated and cumbersome application documents. This situation is particularly serious for low-income groups. Many scholars believe that low-income groups have barriers to properly completing the aid application process (Kaiser Family Foundation and Episcopal Health Foundation 2017; Mickelson et al. 2019; American Flood Coalition 2020). Low-income groups lack convenient transportation, fluent communication skills, and necessary paperwork, so the process of applying for assistance is difficult and quite time-consuming and energy-consuming (Sloan and Fowler 2015).

5.6 The Future Development Direction

5.6.1 Focus on Inequalities in Bills

The distribution of post-disaster assistance in the United States has been extensively studied by scholars. Disaster Act and believe that there are flaws in the equal distribution of post-disaster assistance resources, especially for disadvantaged groups such as low-income areas, African Americans, Hispanics, and the elderly, female-headed households (Emrich et al. 2022; Willison et al. 2019). These vulnerable groups in society are often the hardest hit by disasters and have difficulty applying for federal aid (Bankoff et al. 2004). It takes too long to apply for aid, and they are also denied aid because the property lost does not meet the standards (Wilson et al. 2021). Therefore, this study believes that reducing inequity in post-disaster assistance will alleviate social conflicts and improve disaster laws.

In the context of disasters, Rawl proposed that distributive justice refers to the equitable distribution of social risks, impacts, benefits, and outcomes. Disaster justice, then, is meant to help the most vulnerable groups in society (those who, for whatever social and economic reasons, are more vulnerable and less resilient when disasters strike) bear the heavy burden of disaster impacts (Bullard 2005). Groups with a high degree of social vulnerability should be provided with special assistance based on their actual circumstances, including streamlining the application processes and reducing paperwork for federal aid; adjusting the evaluation criteria for disaster compensation objects; and examining whether it is unfair to rely solely on a federal discretionary ruling to determine eligibility for aid.

5.6.2 Focus on Academic Research on Disaster Law

A majority of academic research is based on data and empirical analysis, is highly reliable and valid, and contributes substantially to the improvement and development of disaster law. Academic research also provides significant insight into cutting-edge social issues, allowing disaster law to closely follow the trajectory of social development. Christopher T. Emrich believes that the research about assessing FEMA's recovery assistance fund allocation may contribute to improving how the FEMA recovery programs operate (Emrich et al. 2022).

In addition, some information includes knowledge from non-profits working directly with disaster survivors, rapid post-disaster survey findings (Kaiser Family Foundation Episcopal Health Foundation 2017), and investigative reports. By combining the information presented above with academic research, we are able to provide stronger evidence as to what the current shortcomings in disaster law are and what should be done to improve them in the future. A better understanding of and development of disaster laws will enhance society's resilience to disasters, promote residents' return to normal life more quickly, and reduce social conflicts and problems.

5.6.3 Focus on Global Climate Change

Global climate change has been proven to be a fact and the species and environmental changes caused by climate change also affect human life. Additionally, extreme weather events are becoming more frequent, posing a major threat to human life. The risk of disasters caused by climate change will become greater and greater in the future, and humans will bear more losses as a result (Parmesan et al. 2022). Disasters in the United States have diverse characteristics, mainly floods, storms, and wildfires. Between 1980 and 2021, the United States spent a staggering amount on disaster secondary costs, with $2 trillion in losses and 15,347 disaster-related deaths occurring during this period (Bhola et al. 2023).

Scholar Vijai Bhola pointed out in his research that over the past 41 years, carbon dioxide levels, temperatures, and the number of large disasters in the United States have all increased, and there is a strong correlation between the three. Keeping up with the massive losses suffered by the United States in disasters requires the attention of U.S. authorities, focusing on disaster risk reduction and controlling disaster costs (Bhola et al. 2023). Despite the fact that disaster law cannot directly impact climate change (Schroeder 2018), resilience to disasters can be enhanced and disaster costs can be reduced by increasing the budget for disaster assistance funds and strengthening legal provisions regarding carbon dioxide emissions. Paying attention to the improvement of disaster laws can improve the entire society's resistance to disasters, reduce direct economic losses caused by disasters, and reduce casualties. At the same time, the improvement of disaster assistance can provide timely living and medical supplies to disaster victims, help disaster-stricken people quickly restore normal life order, and reduce the occurrence of social deviance.

5.7 Discussion

This chapter focuses on disaster law development in the United States from the 1950s to the present. The current disaster law in the United States consists of the Stafford Act and related amendments. It was not until 1950 that Congress passed the Federal Disaster Relief Act, which empowered the federal government to provide disaster relief. From the 1960s to the 1970s, the Disaster Act was rapidly supplemented and developed, and federal power was expanded. There are, however, many loopholes in the development of disaster law as well. Disaster response systems in the United States were unable to reduce losses caused by disasters during several disasters in the 1970s. The Stafford Act of 1988 is the symbol of modern disaster law in the United States and has been revised many times and continues to this day.

Secondly, this chapter also discusses the characteristics of American disaster law, including the important role of public–private cooperation in the disaster response system; giving full play to the role of state and local governments in disaster assistance; disaster assistance services are comprehensive and diverse; disaster response systems are initiated from the bottom up. It is worth mentioning that the bottom-up disaster response system also reflects the relationship between national, state, and local governments. The first person responsible post disaster is the governor. The governor needs to evaluate the disaster situation provided by the federal emergency response team and local governments and decide whether to request federal assistance from the state. In the process of applying for federal assistance, the governor must first apply to FEMA's regional leaders, then report to FEMA's director, and finally submit your opinions to the president, who has the final authority to announce the provision of federal assistance. State and local governments are the first responders in the entire process and have the clearest grasp of the entire disaster situation. Whether they can receive timely assistance also depends on state and local governments' response speed. Among them, local governments must cooperate with the state to provide accurate information about disaster areas to ensure sufficient evidence to apply for federal assistance. The President exercises final declaration authority on behalf of the country and will consider applications submitted by state and local governments as well as FEMA's recommendations. Therefore, the U.S. disaster response system operates from the bottom up and is assisted by the independent agency FEMA. This ensures the timeliness of the process and disaster assistance decisions' fairness and completeness.

Thirdly, this study also analyzes shortcomings in the U.S. disaster law system, such as inequities in housing assistance; inequities in the distribution of post-disaster relief funds and shortages in disaster budgets; and the very complicated application process for disaster assistance. Finally, this study proposes the future development direction of disaster law in the United States, which should focus on the equality of disaster law and protect vulnerable groups in society; focus on academic research related to disaster law and promote the development of disaster law; emphasize on disaster law's response to climate change and improve response resilience to future disaster risks.

5.8 Conclusion

Due to factors such as global warming and world turmoil, disasters have become more frequent and can have a significant impact on human life, health, and the economy as a whole. Disaster laws must be continuously improved according to social development, and it is one of the critical components of social resilience. Although disaster laws cannot directly hinder the occurrence of disasters, they can provide welfare to individuals, reduce the harm of disasters to individuals, and improve individuals' resilience in the face of disasters. At the same time, the stability of both personal and economic conditions also reduces the occurrence of social problems and enables society to continue to operate stable. In light of this, society must take the current disaster law seriously. The United States has vast territory and complex terrain, being one of the countries with frequent disasters in the world, and it attaches significant importance to disaster law improvement. In comparison with other countries around the world, the Stafford Act in the United States is relatively comprehensive and stable compared to other countries. Therefore, this study of the U.S. Disaster Act can promote its own development and may provide ideas for other countries to improve disaster laws.

Acknowledgements The first author is thankful to Japan Science and Technology (JST) for the scholarship supporting Ph.D. research.

References

Adamski T, Kline B, Tyrrell T (2006) FEMA reorganization and the response to hurricane disaster relief. Perspect Public Affairs 3:3–36. https://citeseerx.ist.psu.edu/document?repid=rep1&type=pdf&doi=1cee03ed7759a85200e68c2eb71062134ba1bef7

American Flood Coalition (2020) Turning the tide: opportunities to build social equity through federal flood disaster policy. https://assets.floodcoalition.org/2020/08/e77e13287e90914325f82c7063666448-American-Flood-Coalition-Turning-the-Tide-Toward-Equity-8.3.2020.pdf

Bahari A, Binti Hassan H, Ahmad R (2011) Emergency preparedness amongst emergency response team in managing accidents at the workplace. http://dspace.unimap.edu.my/bitstream/handle/123456789/7455/Emergency%20preparedness.pdf?sequence=1

Bankoff G, Frerks G, Hilhorst T, Hilhorst D (eds) (2004) Mapping vulnerability: disasters, development, and people. Routledge. https://www.researchgate.net/profile/Greg-Bankoff/publication/40125800_Mapping_Vulnerability_Disasters_Development_and_People/links/560d081608ae73e7a6a31a78/Mapping-Vulnerability-Disasters-Development-and-People.pdf

Bea K (2005) Federal Stafford Act disaster assistance: presidential declarations, eligible activities, and funding. https://biotech.law.lsu.edu/blaw/crs/RL33053_20100316.pdf

Becker C (2009) Disaster recovery: a local government responsibility. Public Manag 91(2):6–12. https://icma.org/sites/default/files/4718_.pdf

Bhola V, Hertelendy A, Hart A, Adnan SB, Ciottone G (2023) Escalating costs of billion-dollar disasters in the US: climate change necessitates disaster risk reduction. J Clim Change Health 10:100201. https://doi.org/10.1016/j.joclim.2022.100201

Billings SB, Gallagher EA, Ricketts L (2022) Let the rich be flooded: the distribution of financial aid and distress after hurricane harvey. J Financ Econ 146(2):797–819. https://doi.org/10.1016/j.jfineco.2021.11.006

Bolin B (2007). A history of the science and politics of climate change: the role of the intergovernmental panel on climate change. https://doi.org/10.1017/CBO9780511721731

Brown JT, Liu EC, McCarthy FX (2013) Analysis of the Sandy recovery improvement act of 2013. Congressional Research Service, Washington, DC, pp 7–5700. https://superstormresearchlab.org/wp-content/uploads/2013/07/r42991.pdf

Brunkard J, Namulanda G, Ratard R (2008) Hurricane katrina deaths, louisiana, 2005. Disaster Med Public Health Prep 2(4):215–223. https://doi.org/10.1097/DMP.0b013e31818aaf55. [Opensinanewwindow]

Bullard RD (ed) (2005) The quest for environmental justice: human rights and the politics of pollution, vol 19. Sierra Club Books, San Francisco, pp 32–33. https://doi.org/10.1093/envhis/12.2.421

Casey-Lockyer M, Heick RJ, Mertzlufft CE, Yard EE, Wolkin AF, Noe RS, Murti M (2013) Deaths associated with hurricane sandy—October–november 2012. Morbidity and Mortality Weekly Report 62(20):393. https://www.ncbi.nlm.nih.gov/pmc/articles/PMC4604935/

Chandra A, Moen S, Sellers C (2016) What role does the private sector have in supporting disaster recovery, and what challenges does it face in doing so? Rand Corporation, Santa Monica, CA. Available at: https://preparecenter.org/wp-content/sites/default/files/role_of_private_sector_in_supporting_disaster_recovery.pdf

Charities Bureau (2014) Charitable response to hurricane sandy. https://ag.ny.gov/sites/default/files/reports/Hurricane_Sandy_2014_Report.pdf

Comerio R, Pinto VEF, Vaamonde G (1998) Influence of water activity on Penicillium citrinum growth and kinetics of citrinin accumulation in wheat. Int J Food Microbiol 42(3):219–223. https://doi.org/10.1016/S0168-1605(98)00081-6

Crow DA, Albright EA (2019) Intergovernmental relationships after disaster: state and local government learning during flood recovery in Colorado. J Environ Plann Policy Manag 21(3):257–274. https://doi.org/10.1080/1523908X.2019.1623660

Davlasheridze M, Miao Q (2021) Natural disasters, public housing, and the role of disaster aid. J Reg Sci 61(5):1113–1135. https://doi.org/10.1111/jors.12534

Drakes O, Tate E, Rainey J, Brody S (2021) Social vulnerability and short-term disaster assistance in the United States. Int J Disaster Risk Reduct 53:102010. https://doi.org/10.1016/j.ijdrr.2020.102010

Emergency R (2002) Federal Emergency Management Agency. https://nrt.org/sites/2/files/FRERP1996.pdf

Emrich CT, Aksha SK, Zhou Y (2022) Assessing distributive inequities in FEMA's disaster recovery assistance fund allocation. Int J Disaster Risk Reduct 74:102855. https://doi.org/10.1016/j.ijdrr.2022.102855

Executive Order 12148—Federal emergency management (1979). https://www.archives.gov/federal-register/codification/executive-order/12148.html

Fair Share Housing Center (2014) The state of sandy recovery. Fair Share Housing Center. https://www.hcdnnj.org/assets/documents/report%20state%20of%20sandy.pdf. Accessed 19 March 2021

Farber DA (2007) Disaster law and inequality. Law Ineq 25:297. https://heinonline.org/HOL/Page?handle=hein.journals/lieq25&div=13&g_sent=1&casa_token=1h7_BLpsVhAAAAAA:BgleCQh_2KUt_p5rAmdBPQaRRcmaUiSgRh2wR6kdV9j5C-qCxnPvKviTHVN6MNfJ-0S5Qbcr&collection=journals

FEMA (2003) A citizen's guide to disaster assistance. Independent Study IS-7 September 2003. https://training.fema.gov/emiweb/downloads/is7complete.pdf

FEMA (2011) National disaster recovery framework. Strengthening Disaster Recovery for the Nation. https://www.fema.gov/pdf/recoveryframework/ndrf.pdf

FEMA (2022) FEMA preliminary damage assessment guide. https://www.fema.gov/sites/default/files/2020-07/fema_preliminary-disaster-assessment_guide.pdf
Finch C, Emrich CT, Cutter SL (2010) Disaster disparities and differential recovery in New Orleans. Popul Environ 31:179–202. https://doi.org/10.1007/s11111-009-0099-8
Finucane ML, Acosta J, Wicker A, Whipkey K (2020). Short-term solutions to a long-term challenge: Rethinking disaster recovery planning to reduce vulnerabilities and inequities. Int J Environ Res Public Health 17(2):482. https://doi.org/10.3390/ijerph17020482
Gauna E (2005) The Aftermath of Hurricane Katrina, an unnatural disaster. Center for Progressive Reform (512), 1. https://digitalrepository.unm.edu/law_facultyscholarship/469
Gotham KF, Cheek W (2017) Post-disaster recovery and rebuilding. In: The SAGE handbook of the 21st century City, London, pp 279–297. http://digital.casalini.it/9781473987104
Gould CW (2009) The right to housing recovery after natural disasters. Harv Hum Rts J 22:169. https://heinonline.org/HOL/Page?handle=hein.journals/hhrj22&div=14&g_sent=1&casa_token=HV0cRbwzFhwAAAAA:H6HQugcptlhef1swR8fhOB4TjkDKEeDo8F00THPT4q2z0UBJiSS3IScu1bPHbGGeXv1sDEGl&collection=journals
Hindmarsh R (2013) Nuclear disaster at Fukushima Daiichi. Social, political and environmental issues, New York, 209. https://www.researchgate.net/profile/Richard-Hindmarsh-2/publication/259869970_'Nuclear_Disaster_at_Fukushima_Daiichi_Introducing_the_Terrain'_in_Nuclear_Disaster_at_Fukushima_Daiichi_Social_Political_and_Environmental_Issues_Ch_1_Introduction/links/00b4952e47bbfbbd3a000000/Disaster-at-Fukushima-Daiichi-Introducing-the-Terrain-in-Nuclear-Disaster-at-Fukushima-Daiichi-Social-Political-and-Environmental-Issues-Ch-1-Introduction.pdf
Hoopes Halpin S (2013) The impact of Superstorm Sandy on New Jersey towns and households. Rutgers School of Public Affairs and Administration, Newark, NJ. https://doi.org/10.7282/T36H4FTS
Hunter ND (2010) The law of emergencies: public health and disaster management. Disaster Prevent Manag: Int J 19(4):516–516. https://doi.org/10.1108/dpm.2010.19.4.516.4
Kaiser Family Foundation and Episcopal Health Foundation (2017) An early assessment of Hurricane Harvey's impact on vulnerable Texans in the Gulf coast region. Kaiser Family Foundation and Episcopal Health Foundation. https://files.kff.org/attachment/Report-An-Early-Assessment-of-Hurricane-Harveys-Impact-on-Vulnerable-Texans-in-the-Gulf
Kapucu N (2006) Examining the national response plan in response to a catastrophic disaster: Hurricane Katrina in 2005. Int J Mass Emerg Disasters 24(2):271–299. https://doi.org/10.1177/028072700602400206
Kreiser M, Mullins M, Nagel JC (2018) Federal disaster assistance response and recovery programs: brief summaries. Congressional Research Service, Washington, DC. https://www.everycrsreport.com/files/20190425_RL31734_48b65fa5df693b5d2a8668b2f05aae6d59123075.pdf. Accessed 10 Aug 2018
Liu A (2006) Building a better New Orleans: a review of and plan for progress one year after Hurricane Katrina. Brookings Institution, Metropolitan Policy Program. https://www.researchgate.net/profile/Amy-Liu-29/publication/237414400_Building_a_Better_New_Orleans_A_Review_of_and_Plan_for_Progress_One_Year_after_Hurricane_Katrina/links/575957b008aec91374a3554a/Building-a-Better-New-Orleans-A-Review-of-and-Plan-for-Progress-One-Year-after-Hurricane-Katrina.pdf
Lauta KC (2014) Disaster law. Routledge. https://doi.org/10.4324/9781315867670
McCarthy FX (2011) Federal Stafford Act disaster assistance: presidential declarations, eligible activities, and funding. Congressional Research Service, Washington, DC. https://nationalaglawcenter.org/wp-content/uploads/assets/crs/RL33053.pdf
Mickelson SS, Paton N, Gordon A, Rammler D (2019) Fixing America's broken housing recovery system part one: barriers to a complete and equitable recovery. National Low Income Housing Coalition and Fair Share Housing Center. https://nlihc.org/sites/default/files/Fixing-Americas-Broken-Disaster-Housing-Recovery-System_P1.pdf. Accessed 19 March 2021

Moss D (1999) Courting disaster? The transformation of federal disaster policy since 1803. In: The financing of catastrophe risk. University of Chicago Press, pp 307–362

Muñoz CE, Tate E (2016) Unequal recovery? Federal resource distribution after a Midwest flood disaster. Int J Environ Res Public Health 13(5):507. https://doi.org/10.3390/ijerph13050507

Olshansky RB, Johnson LA (2014) The evolution of the federal role in supporting community recovery after US disasters. J Am Plann Assoc 80(4):293–304. https://doi.org/10.1080/01944363.2014.967710

Parmesan C, Morecroft MD, Trisurat Y (2022) Climate change 2022: impacts, adaptation and vulnerability. Doctoral dissertation, GIEC. https://hal.science/hal-03774939/document

Pierre JK, Stephenson GS (2007) After Katrina: a critical look at FEMA's failure to provide housing for victims of natural disasters. La Law Rev 68:443. https://heinonline.org/HOL/Page?handle=hein.journals/louilr68&div=17&g_sent=1&casa_token=66DRU5zVWxwAAAAA:w70iDjXV8Y-ol2kCqJ0vkNE8QueuJ5L0gUQ4z_DZ7wOl2zanQyW9mKR9NVFjj3yNBlXNeLGg-lM&collection=journals

Rando PG (2021) Mitigating the discretion disaster: how changes in the law can help FEMA effectuate its critical mission. Univ Cin Law Rev 90:1265. https://heinonline.org/HOL/Page?handle=hein.journals/ucinlr90&div=42&g_sent=1&casa_token=L9VQzpMt3dEAAAAA:pU2-pE7LmfhQPxvSJ3dow9EC8D2j58lgmWqRIogwQHhajqD0ZQ3LcMJ9NM_ddiho889QSIvhm0g&collection=journals

Rivera JD, Miller DS (2006) A brief history of the evolution of United States' natural disaster policy. J Public Manag Soc Policy 12(1):5–14. https://d1wqtxts1xzle7.cloudfront.net/34685535/Vol12Iss1-ABriefHistory-RiveraandMil-libre.pdf?1410331475=&response-contentdisposition=inline%3B+filename%3DA_Brief_History_of_the_Evolution_of_Unit.pdf&Expires=1726299554&Signature=P4dr4HIubhZs7XZfOZJH7SdSBpkNZL8vK9y~S5odN4vriIWHBu5GmjwSiDWgCHk1j294hCQdOAgnklvTAXUbjgUo0g7VlnXVYx2vrlVCGN4oSHjMnaSUDQX5yvmSqrDwmbmEtPbGPYmF3VKTlL2ENiFdmfyXTxgqfUOYdP~1~tDHuLe6mzJcoN1MC2DZmP7BtmkDlymHLVhsHAIEbp1S4euNl3tszRJJsl0MaEXAqxdqbENmS9e3BHF4xxi~1cjkSuMqUTEjJA9etJQyRgZ4L8ZqyCOOBrMwkVNHjXeLPvZ9~~flKD0Izn8OWNioGd63gFjjCXaujlB5y4byoYOQ__&Pair-Id=APKAJLOHF5GGSLRBV4ZA

Rose AZ, Blomberg SB (2010) Total economic consequences of terrorist attacks: insights from 9/11. Peace Econ, Peace Sci Public Policy 16(1). https://doi.org/10.2202/1554-8597.1189

Ross T (2013) A disaster in the making: Addressing the vulnerability of low-income communities to extreme weather. Center for American Progress. https://www.americanprogress.org/wp-content/uploads/sites/2/2013/08/LowIncomeResilience-3.pdf

Roth PB, Gaffney JK (1996) The federal response plan and disaster medical assistance teams in domestic disasters. Emerg Med Clin 14(2):371–382. http://pascalfrancis.inist.fr/vibad/index.php?action=getRecordDetail&idt=3120473

Schroeder SC (2018) Does america's new disaster relief law provide the relief america needs. Hous Law Rev 56:1177. https://heinonline.org/HOL/Page?handle=hein.journals/hulr56&div=42&g_sent=1&casa_token=zaSQ4t3IKGIAAAAA:SC6SllOSGd35p_u7l-xRC1Fgn65cggNrPC9Yqjc7URz_Itw3uvobNvfa-cUuAKMiBgVkxYdi_NQ&collection=journals

Sloan M, Fowler D (2015) Lessons from Texas: 10 years of disaster recovery examined. Texas Appleseed. https://www.texasappleseed.org/sites/default/files/TexasAppleseedHurricane_WhitePaper_02c_Final.pdf

Smith G, Sabbag L, Rohmer A (2018) A comparative analysis of the roles governors play in disaster recovery. Risk, Hazards Crisis Public Policy 9(2):205–243. https://doi.org/10.1002/rhc3.12133

Stafford RT, Relief D, Act EA (2013) The Stafford Act. https://www.govinfo.gov/content/pkg/COMPS-2977/pdf/COMPS-2977.pdf

Torsell CV, Jordan M (2009, January) Federal disaster recovery programs: brief summaries. Congressional Research Service, Library of Congress. https://www.everycrsreport.com/files/20110314_RL31734_3c29854ba8e9184b8634bb4c8901efd48a70e8f9.pdf

Twigg J (2004) Disaster risk reduction: mitigation and preparedness in development and emergency programming. Overseas Development Institute (ODI). https://www.preventionweb.net/files/8450_gprch14.pdf

Watts N, Adger WN, Agnolucci P, Blackstock J, Byass P, Cai W, ... Costello A (2015) Health and climate change: policy responses to protect public health. The Lancet 386(10006):1861–1914. https://doi.org/10.1016/S0140-6736(15)60854-6

Waugh WL Jr, Streib G (2006) Collaboration and leadership for effective emergency management. Public Adm Rev 66:131–140. https://doi.org/10.1111/j.1540-6210.2006.00673.x

Willison CE, Singer PM, Creary MS, Greer SL (2019) Quantifying inequities in US federal response to hurricane disaster in Texas and Florida compared with Puerto Rico. BMJ Global Health 4(1). https://doi.org/10.1136/bmjgh-2018-001191

Wilson B, Tate E, Emrich CT (2021) Flood recovery outcomes and disaster assistance barriers for vulnerable populations. Front Water 3:752307. https://doi.org/10.3389/frwa.2021.752307

Wolensky RP, Wolensky KC (1991) American local government and the disaster management problem. Local Gov Stud 17(2):15–32. https://doi.org/10.1080/03003939108433570

Chapter 6
Disaster Law in China

Yan Cui, Yafang Wen, Yinan Gao, and Rajib Shaw

Abstract China's vast territory presents diverse disaster challenges across different regions, necessitating harmonized legislation to establish a comprehensive governance and implementation framework. The country's rich cultural diversity, large population, and unique local environments further underscore the importance of a unified approach to disaster law. This chapter delves into the evolution of China's disaster legislation, examining three critical periods: the early days of the People's Republic of China, the era following the reform and opening up, and the twenty-first century. It highlights the current development characteristics of China's disaster law and contrasts its features with those of developed countries like the United States and Japan. The chapter also identifies several challenges in China's disaster law development, including the absence of a fundamental disaster law, inadequate capital investment, lack of detailed legal regulations for social organizations, and an imperfect disaster insurance system. Additionally, the chapter explores disaster law in Hong Kong and Macau, showcasing their well-structured frameworks, which emphasize interagency collaboration, public engagement, and technological integration. These regions provide valuable lessons for enhancing disaster management practices. Based on the analysis, the chapter proposes future directions for China's disaster law development. Recommendations include improving legal awareness among residents, focusing on disaster prevention amid climate change, leveraging science and technology for better disaster monitoring, and establishing comprehensive disaster laws. By addressing these areas, China can strengthen its disaster resilience and safeguard its citizens more effectively.

Keywords China · Characteristics · Climate change · Disaster law · Evolution

---

Y. Cui
School of Law, Gansu University of Political Science and Law, No. 6 Anning West Road, Lanzhou City, Gansu Province, China

Y. Wen (✉) · Y. Gao · R. Shaw
Graduate School of Media and Governance, Keio University, 5322 Endo, Fujisawa 252-0882, Japan
e-mail: wen.yafang.study@keio.jp

Y. Cui and R. Shaw (eds.), *Disaster Law*, Disaster Risk Reduction,
https://doi.org/10.1007/978-981-97-7374-9_6

6.1 Introduction

Disaster law, serving as a legal guarantee for the state to manage natural disasters, is of great significance in maintaining social stability and protecting people's lives and properties. As a country with a vast territory and diverse climate, China has traditionally faced the threat of numerous natural disasters. From ancient times to the present, effectively managing and mitigating the impact of these disasters has been a focal point for the government and all sectors of society. With the development of society and economy and the advancement of science and technology, China's legislative procedures for disaster law have undergone an evolutionary process from simple to complex and from decentralized to centralized. Especially since the reform and opening up, China has made remarkable progress in disaster law legislation, forming a relatively comprehensive legal system to adapt to the ever-changing social needs and disaster management challenges (Hu 2018).

The purpose of this chapter is to analyze the characteristics, effectiveness, and problems of China's disaster law by examining its legislative evolution and exploring future development directions. This analysis will reference official documents issued by the Chinese government, such as the National Comprehensive Disaster Prevention and Mitigation Plan for the 14th Five-Year Plan, as well as other relevant policy documents and academic literature to ensure the accuracy and authority of the content (National Commission for Disaster Reduction 2022).

Through an in-depth study of China's disaster law legislative process, we aim to gain a comprehensive understanding of the country's disaster management laws and policies. This analysis will provide valuable experiences and insights for the international community, contributing to the global discourse on disaster law. Enhancing the efficiency of disaster law legislation and implementation globally is crucial for building more resilient societies.

6.2 Evolution of the Legislative Process of Disaster Law in China

6.2.1 Early Development of the Legislative Process of Disaster Law in China

Understanding the foundation of China's early disaster legislation requires an in-depth analysis of its legislative background. In the early days of the founding of New China, the country faced the monumental task of rebuilding order. During this period, disaster management relied mainly on government administrative orders and the people's self-help efforts (Mallory 1926). As early as September 1949, the Chinese People's Political Consultative Conference (CPPCC) adopted the Common Program of the CPPCC. This document functioned as a provisional constitution and included preliminary provisions on disaster management. It mandated that the people's government should, in accordance with the national plan and the needs of the people's lives, prevent pests and diseases, provide relief from calamities, protect forests, prevent forest disasters, and prevent veterinary epidemics. This is the earliest recorded provision on disaster law in New China (Common Program of the Chinese People's Political Consultative Conference 1949).

The legislative measures of the 1950s to the 1970s marked the beginning of the institutional and systematic development of disaster prevention and control laws in New China. The enactment of the 1954 Constitution provided constitutional protection for disaster management. Additionally, the enactment of local laws and regulations began to address common natural disasters, such as floods and droughts. In January 1950, the State Council published the General Rules for the Organization of Provincial, Municipal, and County People's Governments, which allowed the people's governments of provinces, cities, and counties to formulate temporary decrees, regulations, or one-line statutes pertaining to provincial, municipal, and county governments (General Rules for the Organization of Provincial, Municipal and County People's Governments 1950). This legislation clearly defined the responsibilities and command obligations of local officials in the event of disasters and marked the beginning of local disaster prevention and management in New China.

Despite these pioneering legislative measures, early disaster legislation in New China lacked systematicity and unity. Legislative activities were scattered and mainly in the form of administrative orders. Disaster law legislation relied more on direct government intervention than on written laws. This type of legislation could respond quickly to disaster events but also limited the improvement of the legal system.

Early disaster legislation also faced several challenges. Firstly, the legislative framework was incomplete and lacked comprehensive regulation of the entire disaster management process. Secondly, there was minimal public involvement in disaster management, which limited the social mobilization and educational role of disaster law. Thirdly, disaster law did not effectively engage social organizations or communities in disaster preparedness and response. Fourthly, legislative power was decentralized, with people's governments at all levels above the county level enjoying legislative power. However, this was not local legislation in the strict sense and was more of an extension of administrative power under specific historical conditions. Five, there was no unified system or set of norms for disaster legislation. Although provinces and counties had the obligation to report major natural disasters, there were no effective laws or systems in place.

As society developed and the demand for disaster management increased, China's disaster law legislation process began to gradually move toward systematization and the rule of law. The Ministry of Emergency Management has been accelerating the legislative process for natural disaster prevention and control law, aiming to construct an all-encompassing natural disaster prevention and control system. This system covers the whole process of risk prevention and control, monitoring and early warning, rescue and relief, post-disaster relief, and recovery and reconstruction (Zhang et al. 2020).

The early development of China's disaster law legislative process has evolved from non-existence to existence, from fragmentation to unification, reflecting increased national attention to disaster management and the gradual deepening of the rule of law thinking. These specific historical cases and development trends provide an empirical basis for understanding the early development of China's disaster law legislative process. This historical perspective is crucial for appreciating the complexities and challenges that have shaped the current legislative framework and for identifying areas for future improvement.

6.2.2 Acceleration of the Legislative Process After the Reform and Opening-Up Policy

The policy of reform and opening up significantly accelerated the promotion and development of disaster law in China. In the 1980s, this policy injected new vitality into China's legislative efforts, marking the beginning of the country's modern legalization process. During this period, China began to shift from relying on administrative orders to relying on legal norms, emphasizing the role of law in disaster management.

In 1989, China responded to the United Nations International Decade for Natural Disaster Reduction (IDNDR) initiative by establishing the National Committee for Disaster Reduction (NCDR). This marked a new stage in China's disaster management legislation, reflecting a commitment to institutionalizing disaster law as part of the broader legal reforms initiated by the reform and opening-up policy (Mo 2003).

The acceleration of legislative processes during this period involved several key developments. Firstly, the formation of the NCDR and other legislative bodies was crucial in promoting the systematization of disaster management legislation. Secondly, the legislative Procedures are standardized. There was a concerted effort to standardize legislative procedures, ensuring that disaster laws and regulations were developed systematically and coherently. Thirdly, significant laws such as the Law of the People's Republic of China on Flood Control and the Regulations of the People's Republic of China on Earthquake Disaster Defense were enacted. These laws constructed a more comprehensive legal framework for disaster management, thereby improving the rule of law in this area.

One of the notable legislative efforts during this period was the introduction of the Law of the People's Republic of China on the Prevention and Control of Natural Disasters (Exposure Draft). The publication of this draft law demonstrated China's openness to incorporating international standards into its disaster law legislation (He and Zhang 2021). This period represented a positive attempt by China to build its disaster law framework by referencing and learning from the disaster legislation models of more advanced countries such as the United States and the United Kingdom, while also retaining the foundation of its own political system.

The policy of reform and opening up provided a new impetus for China's disaster law legislation. The establishment of legislative bodies and the standardization of legislative procedures promoted the improvement of the legal system. Analyzing important case studies of disaster law legislation during this period demonstrates the modernization and internationalization of China's legislative procedures in this area.

Through these developments, China has made significant strides in creating a robust and effective disaster management legal framework, aligning its laws with international practices while addressing the unique challenges posed by its vast and diverse territory.

6.2.3 Improvement of the Legislative System in the Twenty-First Century

With the advent of the twenty-first century, China's legislative procedure of disaster law has been further improved, especially during the period of "11th Five-Year Plan" and "12th Five-Year Plan", the legislative activities have been more active, and the legislative system has been gradually modernized and internationalized.

6.2.3.1 Innovation in Legislative Practice

The twenty-first century marked the modernization of China's disaster legislation, a period in which the transparency of legislation and public participation increased significantly. Compared to the disaster legislation reform after the reform and opening up, China has begun to experiment with more innovations in legislative practice, such as public participation in the legislative process and the establishment of mechanisms for legislative assessment and review. This includes soliciting public opinions through online platforms and organizing hearings and symposiums to make legislation more transparent and democratic (Emergency Response Law of the People's Republic of China 2007).

These innovations also include the application of science and technology in the legislative process, promoting the application of high-resolution satellites, Baidoo navigation and other civil space infrastructure in the field of disaster prevention, mitigation, and relief, and improving the scientific and technological content of legislation. The application of these technologies has led to more accurate disaster monitoring and early warning, which has led to better consideration of the scientific and technological needs of disaster prevention and mitigation in legislation.

Moreover, this includes the establishment of cross-sectoral and cross-regional coordination mechanisms. In order to respond more effectively to disasters, China has strengthened its cross-sectoral and cross-regional coordination mechanisms to ensure the consistency and efficiency of legislation and implementation. For example, a National Committee on Disaster Reduction has been established to coordinate disaster prevention and mitigation efforts across sectors, improving synergy in policy implementation (Li et al. 2021).

6.2.3.2 Modernization of the Legislative System

The first and foremost sign of the modernization of the legislative system is the improvement of the legal system. By revising and enacting relevant laws and regulations, such as the Flood Control Law, the Earthquake Prevention and Disaster Reduction Law, and the Emergency Response Law, in order to adapt to the new disaster management needs. The revision of these laws reflects China's growing emphasis on disaster management and its scientific understanding of disaster risk. They highlight China's pattern of adapting to and establishing a modern legislative system from the perspective of modern disaster risk management.

The modernization of the legislative system cannot be separated from the enhanced international cooperation in disaster law legislation, which has improved the internationalization of legislation by referring to international standards and best practices (Qin 2015). Through cooperation with international organizations, China has made remarkable progress in disaster management, such as participation in the "Belt and Road" international cooperation mechanism for natural disaster prevention and emergency management.

6.2.3.3 Standardization of Legislative Procedures

The standardization of the legislative process of China's disaster law is reflected in all aspects of legislative activities, including the preparation, drafting, deliberation, adoption, and implementation of legislation. The standardization of this process ensures the quality and efficiency of legislation. The legislature has started to focus on legislative assessment and review to ensure that laws are scientifically sound and effective. This approach aims to make sure that new laws can effectively address practical problems and enhance their adaptability and overall effectiveness.

The Concept and Practice of Legislative Evaluation Legislative evaluation refers to the activities of tracking, investigating, and evaluating the design, implementation effect, and problems of laws and regulations after their implementation, in accordance with prescribed procedures and standards, using scientific methods and techniques (Qiao and Cheng 2012). This process not only helps to find and solve the problems in implementation, but also puts forward suggestions to improve the laws and regulations or rules and improves law enforcement activities. Types of legislative assessment Legislative assessment can be divided into pre-legislative assessment, legislative assessment, and post-legislative assessment. Pre-legislative evaluation mainly focuses on the necessity and feasibility of legislation; intra-legislative evaluation involves the evaluation of the draft provisions, the timing of their introduction, and the institutional measures, etc.; post-legislative evaluation evaluates the effectiveness and problems of laws and regulations after they have been promulgated and implemented for a period of time. Legislative review is the process of examining the constitutionality and legality of laws and regulations. In China, legislative review usually includes record review and constitutionality review. Filing review is mainly to review local laws and regulations, autonomous ordinances and individual ordinances, and regulations to ensure that they do not conflict with the higher law (National Disaster Reduction Commission of China 2022). National Disaster Reduction Commission of China (2022) Constitutionality review, on the other hand, examines whether laws and regulations comply with the provisions and spirit of the Constitution. System of Legislative Supervision China's legislative supervision system is a mixed system that includes both abstract and concrete reviews, as well as ex ante and ex post reviews. Legislative oversight is dominated by the two modes of approval and filing, supplemented by a variety of other oversight modes, such as a combination of internal and external oversight.

6.3 Characteristics of China's Disaster Law

6.3.1 Characteristics of the Development of Chinese Disaster Law

One of the core characteristics of China's disaster law is its strong emphasis on prevention. The legal framework prioritizes preventing natural disasters by establishing basic principles and measures aimed at risk assessment and early warning systems. This prevention-focused approach has become even more pronounced after the COVID-19 pandemic, highlighting the importance of early warning and proactive measures in disaster management.

Furthermore, China's disaster law advocates for a comprehensive management approach that encompasses the entire disaster management process. This includes disaster prevention, emergency response, post-disaster recovery, and reconstruction. The goal is to integrate previously fragmented and localized disaster prevention systems and laws into a unified and comprehensive system that can be mobilized effectively. This holistic approach ensures that all stages of disaster management are addressed, providing a more resilient and coordinated response to disasters.

Moreover, China's disaster law places significant emphasis on the role of science and technology in disaster management. The application of high-resolution satellites, Beidou navigation, and other civil space infrastructure in disaster prevention, mitigation, and relief is actively promoted. These advanced technologies play a crucial role in improving the accuracy of disaster monitoring and early warning systems. The future effectiveness of these technological applications will depend on how well they are integrated and supported through legal frameworks (Chun-lan and Gang 2015).

These characteristics highlight China's proactive and comprehensive approach to disaster management, aiming to build a resilient system that leverages advanced technology and integrates all aspects of disaster response. This approach not only enhances the effectiveness of disaster management but also aligns with international best practices, reflecting China's commitment to continuous improvement and modernization of its disaster law framework.

6.3.2 Salient Features of China's Disaster Law Compared with Japan and the United States

The first and key feature of China's Disaster Law is prevention-oriented. China's disaster legal system is relatively centralized, consisting mainly of national-level laws, administrative regulations, and local regulations. In contrast, Japan's disaster countermeasures legal system is more extensive, divided into five main categories: the Basic Law, Prevention and Planning Law, Emergency Correspondence Law, Reconstruction and Rehabilitation Law, and Management Organization Law. The United States has nearly 100 related laws, such as the Stafford Act, forming a comprehensive emergency legislation system (Tierney et al. 2002).

The second salient feature of China's Disaster Law is comprehensive management and prevention-oriented. China's disaster law emphasizes comprehensive management and a prevention-oriented approach, which is evident in both the formulation and implementation of the law. While Japan and the United States also emphasize prevention and comprehensive management, China's legal system in this regard is more explicit and focused (Katada et al. 2007).

The third key feature of China's Disaster Law is its scientific and technological support. Like China, Japan has advanced earthquake early warning systems and disaster prevention technologies. However, China places particular emphasis on integrating science and technology into its legal framework and practical operations, promoting the use of high-resolution satellites and Beidou navigation for disaster management.

The fourth characteristic of China's Disaster Law is its emergency management system. China's emergency management system emphasizes unified leadership and hierarchical responsibility, differing from the standardization of emergency management in the United States and the multi-sectoral and multi-level collaborative response mechanism in Japan. China's approach focuses on central and local synergies and combines law and policy effectively.

6.4 Challenges of China's Disaster Law

The Emergency Response Law of the People's Republic of China, promulgated in 2007, outlines various legal provisions for prevention, response to sudden disasters, and post-disaster recovery. However, China's disaster law faces several challenges due to its relatively late development.

6.4.1 Lack of a Basic Disaster Law

Compared to the comprehensive legal systems of developed countries like the United States and Japan, China lacks a complete basic disaster law. While the Chinese government has issued laws and regulations for specific disasters, such as the Flood Prevention Regulations and Forest Fire Prevention Regulations, it does not have a comprehensive basic disaster law (Lixin et al. 2012). The current reliance on the 2007 Emergency Response Law means there are gaps in basic principles for disaster response and a complete disaster emergency response process. This reliance on temporary government-issued policies post-disaster highlights the political nature of China's disaster law.

Additionally, the responsibilities of various departments involved in disaster response are often unclear. Although the Ministry of Emergency Management, established in 2018, coordinates disaster response, overlapping functions and a large number of subordinate departments reduce disaster management efficiency.

6.4.2 Unclear Role of Social Organizations in Disaster Relief

Social forces, including volunteers and community organizations, play a crucial role in disaster prevention, response, and post-disaster relief. However, the participation and professionalism of these forces need improvement. The Emergency Response Law encourages social force participation in principle, but there are no clear legal provisions defining the roles and responsibilities of voluntary and non-governmental organizations in disaster prevention and relief. This ambiguity leads to slow development and weak strength of social organizations, resulting in an over-reliance on government forces, which can delay rescue efforts and exacerbate disaster losses (Zhang et al. 2020).

6.4.3 Inadequate Funding

China's vast territory and complex terrain make it one of the most disaster-prone countries in the world (Peijun et al. 2003). Despite recent investments, China's financial commitment to disaster prevention and relief remains insufficient compared to many developed countries. The gap between investment and demand is especially evident in underdeveloped rural areas (Lixin et al. 2012). Insufficient investment in basic disaster response facilities, such as shelters and emergency material storage, reduces grassroots communities' resilience to disasters, leading to significant economic losses and casualties.

6.4.4 *Lack of a Disaster Insurance System*

China's natural disaster insurance system is underdeveloped. Aside from the pilot agricultural natural disaster policy insurance, large-scale, specialized natural disaster property insurance and personal insurance have yet to be developed (Xing and Chongfu 2008). The government primarily provides post-disaster insurance for agriculture, with some efforts to promote earthquake insurance in disaster-prone areas. However, the catastrophe insurance system remains immature, requiring further development and broader implementation to provide comprehensive coverage for multiple disaster types (State Financial Supervision and Administration Ministry of Finance 2024).

6.4.5 *Imbalance in Local Legislation*

The activity of local governments in disaster law legislation is uneven, leading to regional disparities in disaster management (Cui 2004). While inter-regional legislative freedom allows for locally adapted disaster laws, it also results in an uneven level of legislative development across China. Economically underdeveloped regions in the west often lack the human and financial resources to build effective disaster laws compared to more developed eastern regions.

In summary, while China's disaster law has made significant strides, several challenges remain. Addressing these issues through comprehensive legislation, clearer roles for social organizations, increased funding, and a robust insurance system will enhance China's disaster management capabilities and resilience.

6.5 The Future Development of Disaster Law in China

6.5.1 *Improve the Awareness of Disaster Law*

Currently, China's disaster law is still evolving, and public understanding and attention to disaster law are insufficient. People lack knowledge on how to respond to disasters, protect their own interests, and quickly restore normalcy. This gap in understanding reflects the government's need to improve the disaster bill and highlights the system's current vulnerabilities. Therefore, it is essential to conduct disaster law training for relevant government personnel, encourage international cooperation, and learn from the disaster law experiences of developed countries like the United States, Japan, and European nations (Lixin et al. 2012). Additionally, using various media to popularize knowledge about disaster law can increase public awareness and emphasize the importance of adhering strictly to these laws.

6.5.2 *Focus on the Disaster Basic Law*

Establishing a National Disaster Basic Law is crucial for China. This law would outline the fundamental principles of disaster prevention and control, including the purpose, scope, guidelines, measures, organizational management, and legal responsibilities (Peijun et al. 2003). It is particularly important to implement disaster prevention organizations and early warning systems. While current Chinese laws focus on specific disasters, such as droughts, floods, and earthquakes, a comprehensive disaster basic law, akin to the Stafford Act in the United States, is necessary for unified and effective disaster management.

6.5.3 *Address Climate Change*

Climate change, accelerated by urbanization and globalization, presents significant disaster risks, including floods, heatwaves, and storms (Peduzzi 2019). Although China's current disaster laws cover early warning, response, and recovery, future revisions should address the increasing threat of climate-induced disasters. The government should focus on post-disaster prevention, response systems, and security measures to mitigate the severe impacts of climate change.

6.5.4 *Enhance Scientific and Technological Applications*

While China has made progress in disaster early warning and monitoring, the accuracy and timeliness of these systems need further improvement. Learning from advanced global techniques and technologies can help localize and enhance China's early warning systems.

Moreover, the application of information technology in disaster management is still limited. Strengthening the integration of modern technologies like big data and cloud computing with disaster management is essential. Developing advanced information technologies and integrating them to meet the professional needs of disaster prevention and mitigation will significantly improve disaster management efficiency.

6.6 Discussion

As a country highly prone to natural hazards, China has prioritized disaster management since its founding. The development of its disaster legal system has evolved from an immature and fragmented framework to adopting and adapting mature disaster laws from developed countries. This has culminated in a relatively comprehensive and unified disaster legal framework in the twenty-first century, offering valuable lessons for other developing countries in Asia.

China's disaster laws, tailored to its specific conditions, emphasize disaster prevention, comprehensive management, and the use of technological means for disaster monitoring and early warning. Compared to developed countries like the United States and Japan, China's legal system is more centralized, with the state holding significant authority to formulate and implement laws. This centralization allows for flexible responses to disaster situations. China's disaster response system emphasizes unified command from higher authorities and coordinated efforts between central and local governments, differing from the multi-level, multi-agency collaboration emphasized in the US and Japan.

However, China faces challenges in its disaster legal construction. Establishing a comprehensive national disaster basic law is crucial for providing a unified framework for disaster management. Learning from international best practices, such as the Stafford Act in the United States, could be beneficial.

Attention should also be given to the legal positioning and legitimate rights of social organizations in disaster relief. Social organizations play a vital role in disaster prevention, response, and rescue, significantly alleviating government pressure. While the government encourages their involvement, the legality, scope of activities, and other details regarding social organizations need further discussion and clarity.

Funding remains a perennial challenge. Increasing financial investments in disaster prevention, preparedness, and response infrastructure, especially in underdeveloped regions, is essential. Adequate funding ensures communities are better equipped to handle disasters and recover more quickly.

Improving the catastrophe insurance system is also critical for enhancing regional disaster resilience and protecting residents' property. Although the Chinese government is increasing the number of catastrophe insurance pilot projects, covering the entire country in the short term is challenging due to vast territorial and developmental disparities.

Continued efforts are needed to address existing challenges and enhance the legal and institutional framework for disaster management. By raising public awareness, drawing on international experience, and focusing on disaster prevention and prediction through science and technology, China can further improve disaster resilience and ensure the safety and well-being of its people.

6.7 Disaster Law in Hong Kong and Its Implementation

Hong Kong, as a Special Administrative Region (SAR) of China, has a unique legal system separate from mainland China's framework. Disaster management and legislation in Hong Kong are governed by local laws and administrative guidelines designed to handle emergencies and natural disasters effectively.

6.7.1 The Legal Framework and Authorities of Disaster Law in Hong Kong

The first key law is the Emergency Regulations Ordinance (Cap. 241) in Hong Kong. This essential legislation grants the Chief Executive in Council the authority to make regulations during emergencies or public dangers. Its broad applicability allows it to address various types of emergencies, including natural disasters.

The second key legal framework is the Fire Services Ordinance (Cap. 95) in Hong Kong. The Fire Services Department (FSD) is the main agency responsible for fire prevention, firefighting, and emergency rescue operations. This ordinance also covers the coordination of rescue services during disasters.

The third key legal framework is the Civil Aid Service Ordinance (Cap. 518) in Hong Kong. The Civil Aid Service (CAS) supports operations during natural disasters and emergencies. Their roles include search and rescue operations, emergency relief, and assisting with evacuations.

The government has established a Disaster Relief Fund to provide swift financial assistance for relief operations. This fund supports efforts for natural disasters both within and outside Hong Kong.

The key agencies and their roles of disaster law in Hong Kong is listed as follows.

1. Security Bureau: The Security Bureau coordinates disaster response and management. It oversees various emergency services and ensures appropriate measures are in place to handle disasters effectively.
2. Hong Kong Observatory: The Observatory is crucial in monitoring weather conditions and providing timely warnings about natural disasters such as typhoons, heavy rains, and landslides.
3. Hospital Authority: The Hospital Authority manages medical services during emergencies, ensuring healthcare facilities are prepared to handle a surge in patients during disasters.

6.7.2 Disaster Preparedness and Response

Hong Kong emphasizes community preparedness through public education campaigns and drills. The government regularly conducts exercises to test and improve disaster response capabilities across various departments and the public.

Furthermore, The Hong Kong Observatory provides real-time weather updates and early warning systems to the public. Systems such as the Tropical Cyclone Warning Signals and Rainstorm Warning Signals are well-known and understood by the public, ensuring timely responses to imminent threats.

Moreover, given its dense urban environment, Hong Kong invests significantly in infrastructure to withstand natural disasters. This includes flood prevention measures, slope safety initiatives, and the construction of typhoon shelters.

6.7.3 Implementation of Disaster Law in Hong Kong

The implementation of disaster law in Hong Kong involves the coordinated efforts of various government departments and agencies. The key elements are listed as follows:

(1) Legislative enforcement: Ensuring that laws and regulations related to disaster management are strictly enforced by relevant authorities.
(2) Interagency Collaboration: Promoting effective communication and cooperation among different government departments, such as the Security Bureau, Fire Services Department, and Hospital Authority.
(3) Public Engagement: Actively involving the community in disaster preparedness activities through education, training, and public awareness campaigns.
(4) Technology Utilization: Leveraging advanced technologies, such as early warning systems and disaster monitoring tools, to enhance preparedness and response capabilities.

6.7.4 Challenges and Future Directions of Disaster Law in Hong Kong

(1) Climate Change: With the increasing impacts of climate change, Hong Kong faces new challenges such as more frequent and intense storms and rising sea levels. The legal and institutional frameworks must adapt to these evolving risks.
(2) Cross-Border Coordination: As a SAR close to mainland China, cross-border coordination in disaster management is crucial. Effective communication and collaboration with mainland authorities can enhance disaster response efforts.
(3) Public Awareness and Participation: Continuous efforts are needed to maintain high levels of public awareness and participation in disaster preparedness. Engaging the community through education and involvement in drills is essential for building resilience.
(4) Technological Integration: Leveraging technology for disaster management, including the use of big data, artificial intelligence, and improved early warning systems, can enhance Hong Kong's ability to predict, prepare for, and respond to disasters.

In summary, disaster law in Hong Kong is comprehensive and involves a multi-agency approach to manage and mitigate the impacts of natural disasters. The legal framework provides the necessary authority and structure for effective disaster response, while ongoing efforts to improve preparedness and resilience are crucial in facing future challenges. Hong Kong's experience in disaster management offers valuable insights into the importance of a well-coordinated, technologically advanced, and community-engaged approach to disaster preparedness and response.

6.8 Disaster Law in Macau and Its Implementation

Macau, similar to Hong Kong, is a Special Administrative Region (SAR) of China with a legal system distinct from that of mainland China. The region is particularly susceptible to natural disasters such as typhoons and flooding, which necessitates a robust disaster management and legal framework. Macau's disaster law and implementation involve a combination of local laws, administrative guidelines, and coordinated efforts among various agencies.

6.8.1 Legal Framework and Authorities of Disaster Law in Macau

(1) **Civil Protection Law (Law No. 11/2001)**: This law is the cornerstone of Macau's disaster management legal framework. It sets out guidelines for civil protection, encompassing prevention, response, and recovery from natural disasters and other emergencies.
(2) **Legal Regime of Civil Protection (Regime Jurídico de Proteção Civil)**: This framework delineates the responsibilities of various government entities in disaster management. It provides the legal basis for coordinating civil protection activities, detailing the roles and duties of different agencies to ensure a unified response to emergencies.
(3) **Disaster Relief Fund**: Similar to Hong Kong, Macau has established a Disaster Relief Fund to provide financial assistance for relief operations both within and outside the territory. This fund supports immediate response and recovery efforts following a disaster.

6.8.2 Key Agencies and Their Roles of Implementation of Disaster Law in Hong Kong

(1) **Civil Protection Operations Center (COPC)**: The COPC is the central body coordinating disaster response in Macau. It activates during emergencies to manage and direct response efforts across the region. The center is responsible for implementing civil protection plans and ensuring effective communication among all relevant agencies.
(2) **Macau Meteorological and Geophysical Bureau (SMG)**: The SMG plays a crucial role in monitoring weather conditions and issuing timely warnings for natural disasters such as typhoons, heavy rains, and flooding. Their early warning systems are essential for disaster preparedness and response.
(3) **Fire Services Bureau (CB)**: The Fire Services Bureau is tasked with firefighting, rescue operations, and providing emergency medical services during

disasters. They play a critical role in both immediate response and longer-term recovery efforts.

(4) **Public Security Police Force (PSP)**: The PSP assists in maintaining public order during disasters, ensuring safety and security, and coordinating evacuations when necessary.

6.8.3 Disaster Preparedness and Response in Macau

Macau emphasizes the importance of community preparedness through public education campaigns, disaster drills, and simulations. These activities enhance the public's understanding of disaster risks and improve their ability to respond effectively during emergencies.

Furthermore, the SMG provides real-time weather updates and issues warnings through various channels, including television, radio, and mobile apps. Systems such as the Tropical Cyclone Signal and Rainstorm Warning System are widely recognized and understood by the public, ensuring timely responses to imminent threats.

Moreover, Macau invests significantly in infrastructure designed to withstand natural disasters. This includes flood prevention measures, reinforcement of buildings against typhoon damage, and the construction of drainage systems to manage heavy rainfall.

6.8.4 Implementation of Disaster Law in Macau

The implementation of disaster law in Macau involves coordinated efforts among multiple government departments and agencies. The key features of implementation of Disaster Law in Macau are listed as follows:

(1) **Legislative Enforcement**: This involves ensuring that all laws and regulations related to disaster management are rigorously enforced by the appropriate authorities. It is crucial that these legal frameworks are adhered to in order to maintain a high standard of disaster preparedness and response.

(2) **Interagency Collaboration**: Effective disaster management in Macau relies on seamless communication and cooperation among multiple government departments. Key players include the Civil Protection Operations Centre (COPC), the Macao Meteorological and Geophysical Bureau (SMG), the Fire Services Bureau, and the Public Security Police Force (PSP). These agencies work together to ensure a unified and efficient response to disasters.

(3) **Public Engagement**: Involving the community is a vital aspect of disaster preparedness. The government actively engages the public through education, training programs, and awareness campaigns. By doing so, they ensure that citizens are well-informed and equipped to handle potential disaster scenarios.

(4) **Technology Utilization**: Leveraging advanced technologies is essential for enhancing disaster preparedness and response capabilities. Macau employs sophisticated early warning systems and disaster monitoring tools to stay ahead of potential threats and ensure a rapid and effective response.

These elements together form the backbone of Macau's approach to disaster management, ensuring a robust and resilient system capable of handling emergencies efficiently.

6.8.5 Challenges and Future Directions in Disaster Management for Macau

The primary challenge Macau faces in disaster management is climate change. The city is increasingly encountering the impacts of this global phenomenon, with more frequent and intense storms, rising sea levels, and unpredictable weather patterns. These evolving risks necessitate continual updates and adaptations to the legal and institutional frameworks governing disaster management. It is essential that these frameworks are both robust and flexible enough to respond effectively to the changing climate. Ensuring that Macau's disaster resilience is maintained and enhanced requires a proactive approach to legislative and regulatory reform, keeping pace with the latest scientific findings and technological advancements.

The second challenge Macau faces in disaster management is cross-border coordination. Given Macau's close proximity to mainland China, effective cross-border coordination in disaster management is crucial. Enhanced communication and collaboration with mainland authorities can significantly improve disaster response efforts. By working together, both regions can share resources, information, and strategies to manage and mitigate the impacts of disasters more effectively. This cooperative approach ensures a unified and efficient response to emergencies, leveraging the strengths and capabilities of each jurisdiction to protect their communities.

The third challenge Macau faces in disaster management is public awareness and participation. Maintaining high levels of public awareness and participation in disaster preparedness is an ongoing challenge. Continuous efforts are needed to educate the community and involve them in drills and preparedness activities. Engaging the public not only builds resilience but also fosters a culture of readiness and proactive response to potential disasters. Public education campaigns, community workshops, and regular disaster drills are essential tools for keeping the population informed and prepared for emergencies. This collective effort helps to ensure that all residents, from individuals to businesses, understand their roles and responsibilities in disaster scenarios.

The fourth challenge Macau faces in disaster management is technological Integration.

The integration of advanced technologies in disaster management is essential for enhancing Macau's capabilities. Utilizing big data, artificial intelligence, and improved early warning systems can significantly improve the ability to predict, prepare for, and respond to disasters. Leveraging these technological advancements ensures that Macau remains at the forefront of disaster management practices. Technologies such as real-time data analytics, predictive modeling, and automated alert systems enhance situational awareness and enable quicker, more informed decision-making during crises.

In summary, the disaster law in Macau is comprehensive and involves a multi-agency approach to managing and mitigating the impacts of natural disasters. The legal framework provides the necessary authority and structure for effective disaster response. However, ongoing efforts to improve preparedness and resilience are crucial in facing future challenges. Macau's experience in disaster management highlights the importance of a well-coordinated, technologically advanced, and community-engaged approach to disaster preparedness and response. By continuing to address these challenges and adapting to new risks, Macau can enhance its disaster management strategies and ensure the safety and well-being of its residents. The city's proactive stance and commitment to improvement set a strong example for disaster management practices worldwide, demonstrating the power of cooperation, innovation, and public involvement in building a safer, more resilient future.

6.9 Conclusion

In the context of global climate change, disaster risks are increasing worldwide, making disaster law more crucial than ever. Disaster law provides the fundamental legal basis and institutional guarantee for all disaster management activities. It ensures that before disasters occur, government agencies can monitor risks, educate the public, and conduct evacuation drills. After a disaster, these laws facilitate an organized and efficient response, ensuring timely rescue operations and coordination among various departments. By mandating these actions, disaster laws maximize the protection of residents' lives and property, maintaining societal stability.

As a country frequently affected by natural disasters, China has been developing and improving its disaster laws. However, challenges remain due to its late start and large population. Moving forward, China must enhance its disaster laws by learning from the comprehensive systems in developed countries, tailoring improvements to its unique conditions, and raising the level of disaster legislation. Hong Kong and Macau offer valuable lessons with their well-structured frameworks, emphasizing interagency collaboration, public engagement, and technological integration. By adopting these best practices, China can strengthen its disaster resilience and better protect its citizens.

References

Chinese People's Political Consultative Conference (1949) Common program of the Chinese people's political consultative conference. CPPCC. http://www.cppcc.gov.cn/zxww/2021/04/27/ARTI1619511683099546.shtml

Chun-lan MIAO, Gang TAN (2015) Review of earthquake disaster relief management in China. North China Earthq Sci 33(2):30–35. https://doi.org/10.3969/j.issn.1003-1375.2015.02.006

Civil Aid Service Ordinance (Cap. 518): Hong Kong e-Legislation (n.d.) Civil aid service ordinance (Cap. 518). https://www.elegislation.gov.hk

Civil Aid Service, The Government of the Hong Kong Special Administrative Region (n.d.) Introduction. https://www.cas.gov.hk

Civil Protection Operations Centre (COPC) (2021) Annual report on disaster management and cross-border cooperation. COPC Reports website

Cui LX (2004) On national economy mobilization for non-military needs. J Beijing Inst Technol (Soc Sci Ed) 3:15–18

Disaster Relief Fund: The Government of the Hong Kong Special Administrative Region (n.d.) Disaster Relief Fund. https://www.gov.hk

Emergency Regulations Ordinance (Cap. 241): Hong Kong e-Legislation (n.d.) Emergency regulations ordinance (Cap. 241). https://www.elegislation.gov.hk

Emergency Response Law of the People's Republic of China (2007) Source: emergency response law of the People's Republic of China (order of the president no. 69). Retrieved from Government of China

Environment Bureau, The Government of the Hong Kong Special Administrative Region (n.d.) Hong Kong's climate action plan. https://www.climateready.gov.hk

Fire Services Bureau (FSB) (2021) Utilization of advanced technologies in disaster management. FSB Publications

Fire Services Department, The Government of the Hong Kong Special Administrative Region (n.d.) About us. https://www.hkfsd.gov.hk

Fire Services Ordinance (Cap. 95): Hong Kong e-Legislation (n.d.) Fire services ordinance (Cap. 95)

Government of Macau (2020) Disaster prevention and mitigation law. Macau SAR Government Website

He X, Zhang XY (2021) Research on climate change adaptation: international negotiation issues and domestic action strategies. Science Press, Beijing. ISBN: 9787030656469

Hong Kong Observatory (n.d.) About us. https://www.hko.gov.hk

Hong Kong Observatory (n.d.) Climate change. https://www.hko.gov.hk

Hong Kong Observatory (n.d.) Warnings and signals. https://www.hko.gov.hk

Hospital Authority, The Government of the Hong Kong Special Administrative Region (n.d.) Disaster management. https://www.ha.org.hk

Hu Z (2018) The research course, orientation and trend of Chinese history of natural disasters. J Peking Univ (Philos Soc Sci) 55(6):120–130

Information Services Department, The Government of the Hong Kong Special Administrative Region (n.d.) Public awareness campaigns. https://www.isd.gov.hk

Innovation and Technology Bureau, The Government of the Hong Kong Special Administrative Region (n.d.) Smart city blueprint for Hong Kong. https://www.smartcity.gov.hk

International Federation of Red Cross and Red Crescent Societies (IFRC) (2019) Case study: disaster law implementation in Macau. IFRC Case Studies

Kaneko Y, Matsuoka K, Toyoda T (2016) Asian law in disaster. Routledge

Katada T, Kimura H, Kodama M (2007) A study on the desirable utilization of flood hazard maps for disaster risk communication. J Jpn Soc Civ Eng, Ser D 63(4):498–508. https://doi.org/10.2208/jscejd.63.498

Li H, Wang X, Zhao X, Qi Y (2021) Understanding systemic risk induced by climate change. Adv Clim Chang Res 12(3):384–394

Lixin Y, Lingling G, Dong Z, Junxue Z, Zhanwu G (2012) An analysis on disasters management system in China. Nat Hazards 60:295–309

Macau Meteorological and Geophysical Bureau (SMG) (2021) Climate change reports and projections. SMG Website

Mallory WH (1926) China: the land of famine. American Geographical Society

Mo JH (2003) Legal governance during the SARS period: a glimpse into China's disaster law and emergency state law. Law Press. ISBN: 9787503643156

National Disaster Reduction Commission of China (2022) Opinions on strengthening the work of natural disaster prevention and control. National Emergency Management Department

Peduzzi P (2019) The disaster risk, global change, and sustainability nexus. Sustainability 11(4):957

Peijun S, Jingai W, Mingchuan Y (2003) China natural disaster system atlas

Planning Department, The Government of the Hong Kong Special Administrative Region (n.d.) Sustainable development. https://www.pland.gov.hk

Public Security Police Force (PSP) (2022) Community engagement and disaster preparedness programs. PSP Community Programs website

Qiao G, Cheng X (2012) The improvement of legal system and management mechanism for natural disaster prevention in China: lessons from the United States experience. Wuhan University Institute of Environmental Law

Qin D (2015) National assessment report on extreme weather, climate events, and disaster risk management and adaptation in China. Science Press. ISBN: 9787030461421

Security Bureau, The Government of the Hong Kong Special Administrative Region (n.d.) Emergency support unit. https://www.sb.gov.hk

Security Bureau, The Government of the Hong Kong Special Administrative Region (n.d.) Emergency preparedness. https://www.sb.gov.hk

Security Bureau, The Government of the Hong Kong Special Administrative Region (n.d.) Cooperation with mainland. https://www.sb.gov.hk

State Financial Supervision and Administration Ministry of Finance (2024) Notice on expanding the coverage of catastrophe insurance for urban and rural residential properties and further improving the catastrophe insurance system

Tierney KJ, Lindell MK, Perry RW (2002) Facing the unexpected: disaster preparedness and response in the United States. Disaster Prev Manag 11(3):222–222. https://doi.org/10.1108/dpm.2002.11.3.222.1

United Nations Office for Disaster Risk Reduction (UNDRR) (2020) Disaster risk reduction in Macau: a comprehensive approach. UNDRR Reports. https://www.undrr.org/publications

Xing S, Chongfu H (2008) Research on the insurability of natural disaster risks. J Appl Basic Eng Sci 16(3):382–392

XingQiao H (2010) Analysis of China's legal system for natural disaster prevention and control from the perspective of comparative law. Leg Syst Econ 2:36–37

Zhang L, Huang Q, Ren Q, He C, Liu J, Bai Y (2020) Evolution of earthquake disaster management policy in China: A bibliometric analysis based on laws and regulations, 1949–2018. Ziranzaihai Xuebao 29(5):11–23

Chapter 7
Disaster Law in Australia

Rong Huang and Rajib Shaw

Abstract There is no single 'Disaster Law' in Australia, as the Commonwealth Australia Constitution Act (the Constitution) devolves certain powers to State and Territory Governments. The *National Emergency Declaration Act 2020* provides for preparing for, responding to, and recovering from emergencies that cause or are likely to cause nationally significant damage. It assists the Federal Government and the State and Territory Governments in managing emergencies, and allows State and Territory Governments to implement local disaster laws simultaneously. This chapter briefly introduces the natural hazard crisis in Australia, addresses case study of Queensland floods 2010–2011 and New South Wales black summer bushfires 2019–2020, and focuses on the Australian perspectives on disaster regulation.

Keywords Disaster law · Australia · Disaster management · Federal government · State governments

7.1 Introduction

Australia is the largest country in Oceania. Although the general public does not have such an image of Australia, it is actually a disaster-prone country. Disasters have had a major impact on Australia's environment, economy, human safety, and culture. As a result, Australia has a large number of emergency management systems and disaster laws. These regulations and management procedures are in place for the purpose of disaster risk reduction and the development of disaster recovery plans.

Australia has a government department for disaster management, the National Emergency Management Agency (n.d.), which collects data from the states and territories, and provides information on disaster recovery services and various programs to reduce disaster risk and increase resilience. The department's website also records every disaster in Australia over the years and showcases innovative technologies and

R. Huang (✉) · R. Shaw
Graduate School of Media and Governance, Keio University, 5322 Endo, Fujisawa 252-0882, Japan
e-mail: rongh910@keio.jp

Y. Cui and R. Shaw (eds.), *Disaster Law*, Disaster Risk Reduction,
https://doi.org/10.1007/978-981-97-7374-9_7

designs to reduce disaster risk and improve resilience. It demonstrates the seriousness with which Australia takes disaster management and the effort it puts into preparedness and disaster response. On the other hand, Australia has three departments dedicated to responding to international crises: Emergency Management Australia, the Department of Home Affairs, and the Department of Foreign Affairs and Trade.

Australia is the sixth largest country in the world. At the same time, as Australia is a federal parliamentary constitutional monarchy, its political system is divided into three levels: Federal government, State and Territory Government, and local government. On this basis, each state entrusts some legislative, administrative, and judicial powers through the Constitution, and each state government has its own disaster management regulation. In general, this is all based on the *National Emergency Declaration Act 2020* (Australian Government 2020a), which provides a broad framework, assists each State and Territory Government to formulate specific and well-developed disaster management system based on the local situation.

The chapter is divided into two parts, the first of which provides an overview of disasters in Australia and their impacts. This part discusses some of the most common impacts and disasters, namely bushfires, floods, droughts, earthquakes, and climate change. The causes and effects of these disasters are discussed. Several case studies are demonstrated in this part to understand the actual situation of hazard crises in Australia and to provide a brief understanding of the management and subsequent impacts of different disasters and different states. The second part deals with disaster law in Australia. Specifically, this chapter discusses the disaster legislation of the Federal Government and six state governments, namely New South Wales, Queensland, South Australia, Tasmania, Victoria, and Western Australia.

7.2 Overview of Australia's Disaster and Its Impact

Australia's national report states that wildlife species are decreasing due to frequent natural hazards, climate change, and human activities (Australian Government 2021). Australia is facing an unprecedented environmental crisis and disaster management crisis. Furthermore, Australia faces rising disaster costs (Deloitte Access Economics 2016). The frequent occurrence of disasters in Australia due to climate change has also been widely discussed (Yu et al. 2020; Abram et al. 2021; Crosweller and Tschakert 2021). Therefore, it is to develop climate change mitigation and adaptation strategies to achieve the 1.5° target to improve the environmental degradation caused by climate issues in Australia. This section provides a brief introduction to the most common and most impactful disasters in Australia.

7.2.1 Climate Change

As the Australian economy relies heavily on coal for domestic power generation and as an export commodity, Australians are significant contributors to anthropogenic climate change (Head et al. 2014). Australia is suffering from severe ecological changes caused by climate change, such as hotter and drier climates, more frequent bushfires, reduced rainfall, loss of soil moisture, acidified estuaries, extinction of wild species, and a range of problems such as environmental degradation (Scanes et al. 2020; King et al. 2020; Yu et al. 2020; Abram et al. 2021; Crosweller and Tschakert 2021). According to the World Report 2022 (Human Rights Watch 2022), the Australian government's failure to take proactive climate action has exacerbated the global climate crisis. At the same time, the large-scale climate social movement is making decisive efforts. In the same year as the report was published, the Australian Senate passed the Climate Change Act (Australian Government 2022), which introduced the national target for increasing emissions reduction targets and established an independent expert review mechanism.

7.2.2 Bushfires

Australia is the country most prone to bushfires among all continents (Bradstock 2010), and therefore bushfire has become a prominent feature of the contemporary Australian environment (Sharples et al. 2016). The incidence of bushfires has been increasing in Australia, with a 40% increase between 2008 and 2013 (DRYAD 2023), with Australian fire services responding to between 45,000 and 60,000 bushfires per year (Australian Government 2008). Bushfires have also become the most serious threat to Australia's local economy and culture. The construction of infrastructure, the loss of land resources, decline of air quality, and aggravation of personal safety crisis are all serious impacts of bushfires on Australia.

The summer of 2019 has been the darkest for Australia, and for the world. The bushfires that began in July 2019 and lasted until March 2020 were the worst on record in New South Wales. Twenty-six people died, 2,448 homes were destroyed and 5.5 million hectares burned, resulting in unprecedented impacts for NSW (Australian Institute for Disaster Resilience n.d.). Normally, NSW's statutory Bushfire Danger Period starts from October to March, but the early start to the 2019 bushfire season, coupled with continued high temperatures and drought across NSW, led many local governments to announce the bushfire danger period in advance, so that warnings and preparations could be made. Although the NSW Rural Fire Service has issued Standards for Asset Protection Zones and made many suggestions to prevent and manage bushfires (n.d.), the disasters continue to escalate due to the poor temperature and environment. Moreover, this disaster has also sparked a debate in Australia about the federal government's inaction.

7.2.3 Floods

The second most significant disaster in Australia is flooding, and the second most dangerous disaster threat to human safety. Between 1900 and 2022, floods accounted for about 20% of deaths from natural hazards in Australia (Australian Government n.d.). The causes of floods are complex and interrelated, usually including extreme climate, drainage system problems, poor terrain, etc. (Halgamuge and Nirmalathas 2017), which also means that the occurrence of floods is not only caused by human activities, but also by geographical environmental factors. The Australian government has six levels of flood alert in place, with state governments having corresponding alerts and emergency contacts.

Queensland experienced severe floods in November 2010, affecting 70% of the state's area until January 2011. In total, thirty-three people lost their lives, three were missing, nearly 6000 people were evacuated, and some 28,000 houses were damaged and needed to be rebuilt. The floods took an economic and human toll on Queensland. A year later, the Final report of the Queensland Floods Commission (Queensland Floods Commission of Inquiry 2012) was submitted to the Queensland Government, claiming to suggest more constructive ways of preparing for and responding to floods, based on the experience of the 2010–2011 floods. In particular, the report recommends that the state government should assess the extent of the flood crisis, implement regional management, and develop flood planning models to facilitate local government assessment and management.

7.2.4 Drought

Drought is the third most common natural hazard in Australia and has a long history (Heathcote 1969). The impact of drought is severe for Australians and has long plagued Australian farms and rural communities. However, it is very difficult to monitor and predict it, especially the ability to know when a drought will start or end is very limited (Kiem et al. 2016). Therefore, it affects the economy of rural areas and the daily life of farmers and rural residents. As Australia has been affected by drought for a long time, Australia has established a government department called Department of Agriculture, Fisheries and Forestry, as well as developed a series of management measures and policies (Australian Government n.d.-d). The Australian government has also adopted a National Drought Agreement with state and territory governments to coordinate drought policies and implementation plans. The Australian government also working with a wide range of private sector and international organizations to help farmers and rural communities prepare for the drought.

7.2.5 *Earthquakes*

Australia has a relatively low risk of earthquakes, with an average of 100 earthquakes of magnitude 3 or greater recorded in Australia each year (Australian Government n.d.-b). As a result, state governments do not have specific emergency preparedness measures in place, other than monitoring and warning by the National Earthquake Alerts Centre at the national level (Australian Government n.d.-c).

7.3 Disaster Law in Australia

Australia's disaster crisis is far worse than people have imagined. Frequent droughts, floods, and bushfires are due to Australia's geographical location, cumulative human activities, and increasing climate change. It is obvious that the Australian government attaches great importance to disaster management, which is divided into three levels of administrative system from federal to state and territory to local. The Federal Government and the states and territories have separate administrative powers, and with the support of the local government, it is a very comprehensive disaster management system. In this section, the disaster regulation of the Australian Federal Government, central and state relationship on disaster regulation will be addressed, and state governments will be introduced, and the focuses of their disaster management will be discussed.

7.3.1 *Central and State Relationship on Disaster Legislation*

Based on The Commonwealth of Australia Constitution Act (the Australian Constitution), the states have independent legislative powers, and the states and territories have their own disaster legislation.

The central regulation is, in general, a broad policy framework that provides legislative guidance to the States and Territories. It explains Australia's disaster management system and empowers State and Territory governments to directly implement its powers and activities. Coordinating and planning the response to any emergency or disaster in any jurisdiction is the responsibility of the State or Territory Government. Also, the financial burden of disaster recovery and relief is also borne primarily by State and Territory Governments. Moreover, Federal law sets out the conditions under which a declaration of national emergency can be modified if the threat of disaster is too great: This requires consultation between the Prime Minister and the State and Territory Governments. In general, the Federal Government Act enables the Federal Government to manage disaster risks by empowering State and Territory Governments, and local governments.

7.3.2 *Disaster Law of the Australian Federal Government and State Governments*

See self-made Table 7.1.

Table 7.1 The main departments/offices that deal with disaster management and the most significant acts of each jurisdiction

Jurisdiction	Department/office	Law/plan/framework
Federal government	• National Emergency Management Agency • Australian Institute of Disaster Resilience	• Defence Act 1903 section 123AA (Australian Government 1903) • Australian Disaster Preparedness Framework (Australian Government n.d.-e) • National Emergency Declaration Act 2020 (Australian Government 2020a) • Australian Disaster Recovery Framework (Australian Government 2020b) • Australian Government Emergency Management Plans (Australian Government n.d.-f)
Queensland	• Disaster Management • Queensland Reconstruction Authority • Inspector-General Emergency Management • Queensland Fire and Emergency Services	• Disaster Management Act 2003 (Queensland Government Queensland Legislation 2003) • Standard for Disaster Management in Queensland (Queensland Government Inspector-General Emergency Management 2021) • Prevention preparedness response and recovery disaster management guideline (Queensland Government 2018)
South Australia	• Department for Environment and Water • South Australian Fire and Emergency Services Commission • Recovery • South Australian Country Fire Service	• Emergency Management Act 2004 (Government of South Australia 2004) • Fire and Emergency Services Act 2005 (Government of South Australia 2005) • State Emergency Management Plan (Government of South Australia n.d.)
Tasmania	• Tasmania State Emergency Service • Tasmania Fire Service • Tas Alert	• Emergency Management Act 2006 (Tasmanian Government 2006) • Fire Service Act 1979 (Tasmanian Government 1979) • Tasman Municipal Emergency Management Plan (Tasman Council 2020)

(continued)

Table 7.1 (continued)

Jurisdiction	Department/office	Law/plan/framework
Victoria	• Emergency Management Victoria • Vic Emergency • Forest Fire Management Victoria • Fire Rescue Victoria	• Emergency Management Legislation Amendment Act 2018 (Victoria Legislation 2018) • Emergency Management Act 2013 (Victoria Legislation 2013) • Fire Rescue Victoria Act 1958 (Victoria Legislation 1958) • Victoria's emergency management planning framework (Emergency Management Victoria n.d.)
Western Australia	• Department of Fire and Emergency Services • Western Australian Legislation • Emergency WA	• Emergency Management Act 2005 (Government of Western Australia 2005) • Fire and Emergency Services Act 1998 (Government of Western Australia 1998)
New South Wales	• Disaster Response Legal Service NSW • Department of Planning • Community Legal Centres NSW • NSW Rural Fire Service • NSW Reconstruction Authority	• NSW Submission to the Australian Senate Inquiry: Operation of the National Emergency Declaration Act 2020 (New South Wales Government 2020) • Fire Services Joint Standing Committee Act 1998 (New South Wales Government 1998) • State Emergency and Rescue Management Act 1989 (New South Wales Government 1989a) • Fire and Rescue NSW Act 1989 (New South Wales Government 1989b) • State Emergency Service Act 1989 (New South Wales Government 1989c)

7.3.3 Discussion

Disaster management by state governments follows similar principles and is planned according to the 4 phases of emergency risk reduction, emergency preparedness, emergency response, and emergency recovery. All states have a top-level department responsible for managing and responding to emergencies. However, there are subtle differences in emphasis between state's acts.

To be specific, the Queensland Act focuses on the establishment of a management group, the development of disaster management plans and guidelines to ensure that the community has access to information on disaster preparedness, relief, and post-disaster recovery, the declaration of a disaster, and the establishment of an appropriate regulatory office to record the overall timeline and process of the disaster.

The South Australian Act focuses on establishing an emergency management framework that promotes speed and efficiency in effective decision making and response in the event of an emergency, as well as promoting community resilience and reducing community vulnerability. At the same time, the South Australian Act recognizes that the key to managing emergencies is the coordinated cooperation of all sectors, including government, business, NGOs, and individuals.

New South Wales, on the other hand, focuses on departmental management, believing that an authorized government agency should be in charge once an emergency has occurred. Tasmania's Act focuses on the role of the administration and details the role of the committee in each department and process. Victoria's Act aims to provide 'all' communities with an actionable emergency management plan, recognizing the importance of advance preparation and planning and the need for information to flow between government departments and not be blocked to the public.

Besides, only the Tasmania Act and the Victoria Act do not mention insurance. The Western Australian Act focuses on disaster regionalization and local government response, and recognizes the importance of collaboration between government agencies and the public sector.

As state governments have effective authority over their territories, they control the primary functions of effective crisis prevention, preparedness, response, and recovery. Only when the crisis becomes serious enough to threaten national interests and security will cooperation and management between the Federal Government and the state and territory governments be required. Besides, the state government also establishes special department to monitor and manage the more frequent and serious hazards crisis. In fact, all state governments have dedicated bushfire-related departments to ensure their emergency management. Nevertheless, bushfires remain one of Australia's most significant natural hazards. It also shows that, to some extent, state governments need to do more to improve bushfire management.

Australia attaches great importance to disaster management. According to the actual situation of the states, it has formed targeted departments. The special disaster crisis legislation and framework try to guide the emergency management, trying to achieve the position from the preparation stage, to ensure disaster management. All three levels of government play an important role in the overall disaster management framework, which makes the system organized and practicable.

From the perspective of the federal government, its laws provide a broad framework and decentralize power. National law pays more attention to the functions and overall coordination of the federal government and does not specifically restrict the requirements and rules of the administration of the states and territories. The National Emergency Management Agency, one of the departments at the national level, is responsible for the implementation of programs, recording national disaster events, managing programs, fundings, etc. They also help develop national strategies. Central legislation is a safeguard that allows states and territories to report to the central government if their capacity is limited and allows the Prime Minister to make a national emergency declaration to take a higher level of regulation and assistance.

The State and Territory regulations are the most important regulations for the relevant region because the State and Territory governments are the administrative units that directly manage and respond to the region. They have emergency management departments in place, and they establish targeted emergency departments for the most common disasters in each state to ensure that emergency management is in place to speed up response times and reduce disaster losses. For example, NSW

Rural Fire Service in New South Wales, Forest Fire Management Victoria in the state of Victoria, Department for Environment and Water in South Australia.

Local government is the most direct and important political body in disaster management. They are the most front-line management units in accordance with the State and Territory Disaster Acts. At the same time, it is often necessary to cooperate with various sectors and non-governmental organizations and to interact directly with the public.

7.4 Conclusion

Australia's three level political system plays a role in disaster management. The Federal Government Act coordinates and provides the highest level of regulatory framework, placing actual executive power in the hands of the State and Territory Governments. The State and Territory Governments are able to establish government departments according to the specific conditions of the state, and can also focus on the frequent hazards crisis. Such administrative management and disaster management are relatively efficient.

The disaster crisis in Australia is relatively severe, and the financial expenditure due to disasters is rising. Australia has also been criticized for failing to manage disasters adequately. After constantly learning lessons and experiences from the past, Australia's disaster management is on the way to continuous improvement. Disaster management in Australia can be summed up in four steps. First, making sense of the hazards itself, its causes, and effects. Working with local intelligence to develop infrastructure or establish disaster mitigation standards. Second, make plans and coping frameworks in advance to reduce disaster risks through early assessment and calculation. The formulation of the strategy also requires the participation of the local government to develop targeted emergency management plans, so that the implementation will not be out of control due to the large gap in the actual situation of different places, resulting in worse consequences. Third, the local government responded in time to control the situation with an effective emergency response. The implementation of this step depends to a large extent on the preparation of the first and second steps, and also attaches great importance to the coordination among various sectors. Fourth, State and Territory Governments should cooperate with local governments in post-disaster recovery and reconstruction, and at the same time emphasize improving resilience for the future.

The Australian Emergency Management Act emphasizes the collaboration of multiple sectors, including government agencies, the private sector, non-governmental organizations, and individuals. The study by Crosweller and Tschakert (2021) argues that the Australian government has deliberately blurred the line of responsibility between the state and citizens, confirming that citizens have responsibilities in the planning phase. From another perspective, there may be a direct relationship between citizens and government management. The Australian Resilience Index (Parsons et al. 2021) shows that resilience and adaptation is unevenly distributed across Australia, with more densely populated areas closer to city centers being more resilient and adaptable. In areas where resources are not concentrated or are sparsely populated, the efficiency of disaster management is correspondingly low. On this basis, the role of local government is extremely important, and more emphasis is placed on the cooperation between the local government and citizens.

In conclusion, in terms of the legislation in place, Australia's disaster law is relatively complete and well-established. However, there are still gaps when we look at actual cases. This also means that a more thorough analysis of past cases and more precise disaster management planning are needed for the actual implementation.

References

Abrahams J (2001) Disaster management in Australia: the national emergency management system. Emerg Med 13(2):165–173. https://doi.org/10.1046/j.1442-2026.2001.00205.x

Abram NJ, Henley BJ, Sen Gupta A, Lippmann TJ, Clarke H, Dowdy AJ, Boer MM et al (2021) Connections of climate change and variability to large and extreme forest fires in southeast Australia. Commun Earth Environ 2(1):8. https://doi.org/10.1038/s43247-020-00065-8

Australian Government (1903) Defence act 1903. Australian Government. https://www.legislation.gov.au/C1903A00020/latest/text

Australian Government (2008) Deliberately lit vegetation fires in Australia. Australian Government. https://www.aic.gov.au/publications/tandi/tandi350

Australian Government (2020a) National emergency declaration act 2020. Australian Government. https://www.legislation.gov.au/C2020A00128/latest/text

Australian Government (2020b) Australian disaster recovery framework. Australian Government. https://www.nema.gov.au/sites/default/files/2024-08/ADR%20Framework%20October%202022.pdf

Australian Government (2021) Australia state of the environment. Australian Government. https://soe.dcceew.gov.au

Australian Government (2022) Climate change act 2022. Australian Government. https://www.legislation.gov.au/C2022A00037/latest/text

Australian Government (n.d.-a) Floods. Australian Government. https://www.acs.gov.au/pages/floods

Australian Government (n.d.-b) Earthquakes. Australian Government. https://www.acs.gov.au/pages/earthquakes

Australia Government (n.d.-c). National Earthquake Alerts Centre (NEAC). Australia Government. https://www.community-safety.ga.gov.au/data-and-products/neac

Australian Government (n.d.-d). Drought policy. Australian Government. https://www.agriculture.gov.au/agriculture-land/farm-food-drought/drought/drought-policy

Australian Government (n.d.-e) Australian disaster preparedness framework. Australian Government. https://www.homeaffairs.gov.au/emergency/files/australian-disaster-preparedness-framework.pdf

Australian Government (n.d.-f) Emergency management plans. Australian Government. https://www.homeaffairs.gov.au/about-us/ourportfolios/emergency-management/emergency-response-plans

Australian Institute for Disaster Resilience (n.d.) Bushfires—black summer. Australian Institute for Disaster Resilience. https://knowledge.aidr.org.au/resources/black-summer-bushfires-nsw-2019-20/

Bradstock RA (2010) A biogeographic model of fire regimes in Australia: current and future implications. Glob Ecol Biogeogr 19(2):145–158. https://doi.org/10.1111/j.1466-8238.2009.00512.x

Crosweller M, Tschakert P (2021) Disaster management and the need for a reinstated social contract of shared responsibility. Int J Disaster Risk Reduct 63:102440. https://doi.org/10.1016/j.ijdrr.2021.102440

Deloitte Access Economics (2016) The economic cost of the social impact of natural disasters. Australian Business Roundtable for Disaster Resilience & Safer Communities. https://australianbusinessroundtable.com.au/assets/documents/Report%20-%20Social%20costs/Report%20-%20The%20economic%20cost%20of%20the%20social%20impact%20of%20natural%20disasters.pdf

DRYAD (2023) Australia bushfire facts: challenges and resilience. DRYAD. https://www.dryad.net/post/australia-bushfire-facts-challenges-and-resilience

Emergency Management Victoria (n.d.) Victoria's emergency management planning framework. Emergency Management Victoria. https://www.emv.vic.gov.au/responsibilities/emergency-management-planning/emergency-management-planning-resource-library-0/victorias-emergency-management-planning-framework

Government of South Australia (2004) Emergency management act 2004. South Australian Legislation. https://www.legislation.sa.gov.au/lz?path=%2FC%2FA%2FEMERGENCY%20MANAGEMENT%20ACT%202004

Government of South Australia (2005) Fire and emergency services act 2005. South Australian Legislation. https://www.legislation.sa.gov.au/lz?path=%2FC%2FA%2FFIRE%20AND%20EMERGENCY%20SERVICES%20ACT%202005

Government of South Australia (n.d.) State emergency management plan. Department of the Premier and Cabinet. https://www.dpc.sa.gov.au/responsibilities/security-emergency-and-recovery-management/state-emergency-management-plan

Government of Western Australia (1998) Fire and emergency services act 1998. Government of Western Australia. https://www.legislation.wa.gov.au/legislation/statutes.nsf/main_mrtitle_337_homepage.html

Government of Western Australia (2005) Emergency management act 2005. Government of Western Australia. https://www.legislation.wa.gov.au/legislation/prod/filestore.nsf/FileURL/mrdoc_36944.pdf/$FILE/Emergency%20Management%20Act%202005%20-%20%5B01-a0-03%5D.pdf?OpenElement

Halgamuge MN, Nirmalathas A (2017) Analysis of large flood events: based on flood data during 1985–2016 in Australia and India. Int J Disaster Risk Reduct 24:1–11. https://doi.org/10.1016/j.ijdrr.2017.05.011

Head L, Adams M, McGregor HV, Toole S (2014) Climate change and Australia. Wiley Interdisc Rev: Clim Change 5(2):175–197. https://doi.org/10.1002/wcc.255

Heathcote RL (1969) Drought in Australia: a problem of perception. Geogr Rev 175–194. https://doi.org/10.2307/213453

Human Right Watch (2022) World report 2022. Human Right Watch. https://www.hrw.org/world-report/2022

Kiem AS, Johnson F, Westra S, van Dijk A, Evans JP, O'Donnell A et al (2016) Natural hazards in Australia: droughts. Clim Chang 139:37–54. https://doi.org/10.1007/s10584-016-1798-7

King AD, Pitman AJ, Henley BJ, Ukkola AM, Brown JR (2020) The role of climate variability in Australian drought. Nat Clim Chang 10(3):177–179. https://doi.org/10.1038/s41558-020-0718-z

New South Wales Government (1989a) State emergency and rescue management act 1989 no 165. NSW Legislation. https://legislation.nsw.gov.au/view/html/inforce/current/act-1989-165

New South Wales Government (1989b) Fire and rescue NSW act 1989 no 192. NSW Legislation. https://legislation.nsw.gov.au/view/html/inforce/current/act-1989-192

New South Wales Government (1989c) State emergency service act 1989 no 164. NSW Government. https://legislation.nsw.gov.au/view/whole/html/inforce/current/act-1989-164

New South Wales Government (1998) Fire services joint standing committee act 1998 no 18. NSW Legislation. https://legislation.nsw.gov.au/view/html/inforce/current/act-1998-018

New South Wales Government (2020) NSW submission to the Australian senate inquiry: operation of the National Emergency Declaration Act 2020. Australian Parliament House. https://www.aph.gov.au/DocumentStore.ashx?id=2bd9f972-fe9c-413e-a2c2-59440c474b7d&subId=706393

NSW Rural Fire Service (2006) Standards for asset protection zones. NSW Rural Fire Service. https://www.rfs.nsw.gov.au/__data/assets/pdf_file/0010/13321/Standards-for-Asset-Protection-Zones.pdf

Parliament of Australia (2020) National emergency and disaster response arrangements in Australia: a quick guide. Parliament of Australia. https://www.aph.gov.au/About_Parliament/Parliamentary_departments/Parliamentary_Library/pubs/rp/rp1920/Quick_Guides/NationalEmergencyDisasterManagement

Parsons M, Reeve I, McGregor J, Hastings P, Marshall GR, McNeill J et al (2021) Disaster resilience in Australia: a geographic assessment using an index of coping and adaptive capacity. Int J Disaster Risk Reduct 62:102422. https://doi.org/10.1016/j.ijdrr.2021.102422

Queensland Floods Commission of Inquiry (2012) Final report of the Queensland Floods Commission. Queensland Floods Commission of Inquiry. http://www.floodcommission.qld.gov.au/publications/final-report

Queensland Government (2018) Prevention preparedness response and recovery disaster management guideline. Queensland Government. https://www.disaster.qld.gov.au/__data/assets/pdf_file/0032/359465/QLD-Disaster-Management-Guideline.pdf

Queensland Government Inspector-General Emergency Management (2021) Standard for disaster management in Queensland. Queensland Government. https://www.igem.qld.gov.au/standard

Queensland Government Queensland Legislation (2003) Disaster Management Act 2003. Queensland Government. https://www.legislation.qld.gov.au/view/html/inforce/current/act-2003-091

Queensland Government Queensland Reconstruction Authority (n.d.) Queensland strategy for disaster resilience. Queensland Government. https://www.qra.qld.gov.au/qsdr

Scanes E, Scanes PR, Ross PM (2020) Climate change rapidly warms and acidifies Australian estuaries. Nat Commun 11(1):1803. https://doi.org/10.1038/s41467-020-15550-z

Sharples JJ, Cary GJ, Fox-Hughes P, Mooney S, Evans JP, Fletcher M, Fromm M, Grierson PF, McRae R, Baker P (2016) Natural hazards in Australia: extreme bushfire. Clim Chang 139:85–99. https://doi.org/10.1007/s10584-016-1811-1

Tasman Council (2020) Tasman municipal emergency management plan. Tasman Council. https://www.tasman.tas.gov.au/download/Tasman-Emergency-Management-Plan-Issued-10-December-2020.pdf

Tasmanian Government (1979) Fire service act 1979. Tasmanian Government. https://www.legislation.tas.gov.au/view/html/inforce/current/act-1979-035

Tasmanian Government (2006) Emergency management act 2006. Tasmanian Legislation. https://www.legislation.tas.gov.au/view/html/inforce/current/act-2006-012

Victorian Legislation (1958) Fire Rescue Victoria Act 1958. Victorian Legislation. https://www.legislation.vic.gov.au/in-force/acts/fire-rescue-victoria-act-1958/130

Victoria Legislation (2013) Emergency management act 2013. Victorian Legislation. https://www.legislation.vic.gov.au/in-force/acts/emergency-management-act-2013/021#rpl-main-content

Victoria Legislation (2018) Emergency management legislation amendment act 2018. Victorian Legislation. https://www.legislation.vic.gov.au/as-made/acts/emergency-management-legislation-amendment-act-2018

Victorian Legislation (n.d.) Fire Rescue Victoria Act 1958. Victorian Legislation. https://www.legislation.vic.gov.au/in-force/acts/fire-rescue-victoria-act-1958/123

Yu P, Xu R, Abramson MJ, Li S, Guo Y (2020) Bushfires in Australia: a serious health emergency under climate change. Lancet Planet Health 4(1):e7–e8. https://doi.org/10.1016/S2542-5196(19)30267-0

Chapter 8
Disaster Management Law in Türkiye

Burcak Basbug

Abstract Türkiye with its repeated experiences of earthquakes, from 1939 Erzincan earthquake, 1992 Erzincan earthquake, August 1999 Marmara earthquake to the recent 6 February 2023 Kahramanmaraş earthquakes, has evolved its legislation over time, drawing the lessons from the major disasters. There have been updates and revisions according to the needs of the community and policy makers after each event. For instance, compulsory earthquake insurance (CEI), which was introduced following the devastating 17 August 1999 Marmara earthquake (aka Kocaeli/Gölcük/Adapazarı earthquake) is one of the key developments in the insurance sector of the country. CEI is strongly supported by the legislative framework. The chapter will highlight some of the key issues in the Building Code development, Municipality Laws, and financial mechanisms in this regard.

Keywords Disaster · Development · Earthquake · Governance · Law

8.1 Introduction

Geography is not destiny! Türkiye sits in a highly seismic location. There have been series of earthquakes in the country throughout history. The decade of the 1990s was designed as the International Decade for Natural Disaster Risk Reduction. As stated in Dobrucali and Demir (2016), earthquakes and floods are the top two hazards to cause significant damage when they occur. Table 8.1 summarizes the major earthquakes in Türkiye since the 1990s, connected with the magnitude and the resulting deaths/injured. It is a scientific data, which tells us the frequency and the severity of the earthquake hazard is a serious issue to be considered in decision making process for disaster risk reduction and resilience policies of the country.

As previously stated, the country faced hundreds of earthquakes, and after each there were lessons to be learnt. It was not until 1996 that the seismicity of Türkiye has been based on a seismic hazard map and it is used as a baseline for scientists

B. Basbug (✉)
Middle East Technical University, Ankara, Turkey
e-mail: bbasbug@gmail.com

Y. Cui and R. Shaw (eds.), *Disaster Law*, Disaster Risk Reduction,
https://doi.org/10.1007/978-981-97-7374-9_8

Table 8.1 Major earthquakes in Türkiye since 1990's

Date	Location	Magnitude	Deaths/injured
13 March 1992	Erzincan	6.8	650/700
October 1995	Dinar	6.1	92/200
June 1998	Adana	6.3	144/1000
17 August 1999	Marmara region	7.4	17,480/43,953
12 November 1999	Düzce-Kaynaşlı	7.2	763/4,948
23 October and 9 November 2011	Van	7.2	604/4,152
6 February 2023	Kahramanmaraş and Eastern region	7.7 and 7.6	53,783/122,000

Source Adapted from Gulkan (2018)

as well as policy makers. In Fig. 8.1, one can observe the seismic hazard map, which was used for twenty-two years. This map has been produced as a joint work of the former General Directorate of Disaster Affairs and structural engineering departments of well-known universities such as Middle East Technical University, Bosphorus University, Istanbul Technical University, and others. Figure 8.2 is the revised version of the original map. In both maps, the North Anatolian Fault Line (NAF) starting from the east lies to the west, East Anatolian Fault Line (EAF) and the Aegean grabens are clearly observed with the color code red, indicating the locations at high risk (Table 8.2).

8.2 6 February 2023 Kahramanmaras Earthquakes

On 6 February 2023, a centennial event happened. The first earthquake hit at 04.17 am with a magnitude 7.7 at Kahramanmaras-Pazarcik district. After nine hours, around 1 pm, a second earthquake of magnitude 7.6 hit the same province but at Elbistan district. Thousands of buildings collapsed at the first one, the ones which had damaged in the morning one, collapsed in the second one in the afternoon. Even after a week, the third earthquake of magnitude 5.6 hit the same region. Scientists state that three major earthquakes in a week's time is an extreme and unique event to happen. Nobody really prepared, expected, or even simulated such a scenario. It can be named a Black Swan Event by looking at the scale of it.

The earthquake affected Hatay, Adiyaman, and Kahramanmaras directly and very severely, and additional eleven provinces such as Malatya, Sanliurfa, Osmaniye at a secondary impact. In total directly 14 provinces, a population of 15 million and at the national level all 81 provinces and a whole population of 85 million were devastated. According to AFAD report, thousands of buildings had collapsed, thousands had heavy/moderate damage, which requires to be demolished and thousands had a slight damage but local inhabitants had a fear to continue living there. The Government

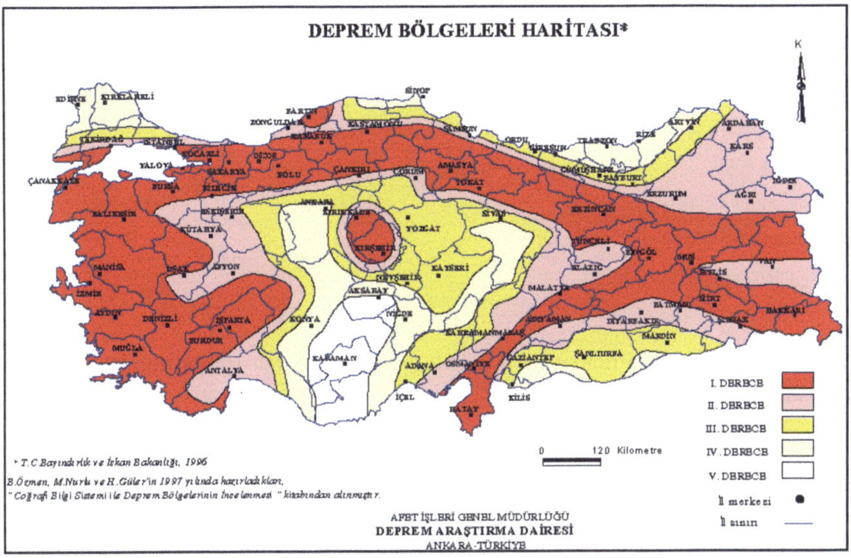

Fig. 8.1 Seismic hazard map of Türkiye in use between 1996 and 2018. *Source* https://www.afad.gov.tr/turkiye-deprem-tehlike-haritasi

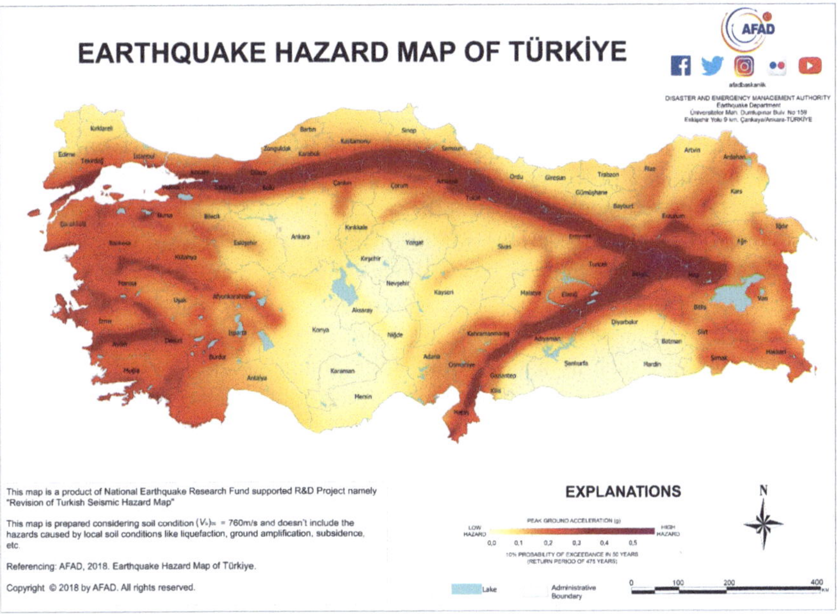

Fig. 8.2 Earthquake hazard map of Türkiye currently in use since 2018. *Source* AFAD (2024)

Table 8.2 The deadliest earthquakes in Türkiye from 1900 until August 2023

Date	Location	Magnitude	No. of deaths
6 February 2023	Kahramanmaras	7.7 and 7.5	53,783
26 December 1939	Erzincan	7.8	32,700
17 August 1999	Marmara (Kocaeli)	7.6	17,480
24 November 1976	Van	7.0	5,000
26 November 1943	Samsun	7.5	4,020

Source CRED (2023)

Report declared the estimated economic losses of more that 100 billion USD, which is gigantic.

8.3 The Implementation of Building Code

'One picture says more than a thousand words!' Figure 8.3 shows us that some buildings collapsed but the one next to it could stand. What makes the difference? In the case of Türkiye, an earthquake of magnitude more than 7.0 kills thousands of people. This should not be a routine and accustomed life. The country has the historical experience of earthquakes. The country has advanced construction technology and sectoral implementation. The country has the Building Code, which has been revised in the past following the earthquake events. What is the reason in 2023, with this experience to cause one building to collapse and kill tens of people; whereas the next building stands still and perhaps causes few injuries only.

The central government establishes the laws at the national level, but the local governments implement these laws in cities and towns. Therefore, seismic safety and design are among the main responsibilities of local municipal governments. The current Turkish Building Code is the version following the revision of the previous codes, which were legalized in 1998, 2000 and 2007. Hundreds of experts from various institutions such as national ministries, municipalities representing local government, and academia with its highly qualified civil engineers, urban planners, and architects contributed to the development of the new Code. It was published in the Official Gazette (Resmi Gazete) on 18 March 2018. As of 1 January 2019, it was activated. If the New Code is compared with the previous versions, there are new chapters on high-rise, seismically isolated, cold-formed steel, and wooden buildings. It is mainly the implementation of the Legal Code in the field by the contractors. After the Kahramanmaras earthquakes, everyone agrees and knows that the major problem is the audit and inspection process during the construction.

After the poor performance of the building stock following the 1999 earthquakes, Decree No. 595 (Building Construction Supervision) was established on 10 April 2000. Gulkan (2018) states that seismic safety and design is the main responsibility of local municipal governments. In Decree Law No. 595, there is an outline for

Fig. 8.3 Collapsed building versus standing building. *Source* Anadolu Ajansi (2023)

all buildings to be constructed in 27 seismically risky provinces, which included those affected by the 1999 Marmara and Duzce earthquakes. This Decree Law No. 595 has been replaced by Law No. 4708, which explains all details of the Building Construction Supervision at the link (https://www.mevzuat.gov.tr/mevzuatmetin/1.5.4708.pdf).

The 6 February 2023 earthquakes showed that not only the old buildings but new buildings like the Ronesans Residence in Hatay, which collapsed and killed thousands of people should be investigated. The type of construction with earthquake-resistant structure as in the regulations and on strong ground conditions are crucial components to be fairly evaluated during the inspection process of the construction.

8.4 Historical Disaster Law Developments in Türkiye

The first recorded big earthquake in the Istanbul region is called the "Little Doom's Day" dating back to 10 September 1509. It used to be believed as the Acts of God! That time, the Sultan Bayezid II declared a "ferman" the order that stated to prepare for future disasters. His orders to reconstruct the city again are considered to be the first legislative rules for earthquake resistant building construction in the country. The reconstruction process started on 23 March 1510 and ended on 1 June 1510 (Figs. 8.4 and 8.5).

Fig. 8.4 1509 Istanbul earthquake. *Source* https://www.indyturk.com/node/400141/haber/i%CC%87stanbul%E2%80%99un-alt%C3%BCst-oldu%C4%9Fu-g%C3%BCn-k%C3%BC%C3%A7%C3%BCk-k%C4%B1yamet-depremi

In 1817, Helmuth Von Moltke, a German planner and soldier, was invited to Istanbul by the Ottoman Sultan to develop new planning approaches and projects (Ozden and Erkan 2016). Von Moltke prepared plans for the reorganization and development of new measures for the fire hazard. He proposed to eliminate the dead-end streets, which were seen as the main causes of the spread of fire, and barriers for the controlling of fires. In addition, he recommended the use of masonry building materials accepted as fire-resistive, and also the development of city squares as another measure to prevent the spread of fire. Those attempts and planning decisions can be seen as the initial ideas of a mitigation approach proposed in the planning phase. In 1839, the first official development law, called "*İlmühaber*", which had some understanding of disaster risk reduction, was published (Ozden and Erkan 2016).

5 November 1882 is an important milestone in this chronological approach of legislative and administrative advancements in the Ottoman period. Then, the first time, a comprehensive law comprising of all development and building issues in a single legislative document was published and implemented (Ozden and Erkan 2016). This law, which is named as the first Development Law, was in use until the first years of the Turkish Republic. This law supported the municipal works to become widespread across the country to have development plan approaches following disasters (Ozden and Erkan 2016).

After 1923, with the declaration of the Republic of Türkiye, the Village Law (Law No. 442) was published in 1924. It is one of the first and comprehensive legislative developments of the republic. On 13 September 1924, an intensive earthquake hit the eastern part of the country with an epicenter at Erzurum province. It caused extensive damage in many settlements and left hundreds of casualties along with the loss of a great amount of livestock (Kalemli 2010). After this earthquake, a law was published in order to arrange the aid and rehabilitation works for the stricken area, that is Law

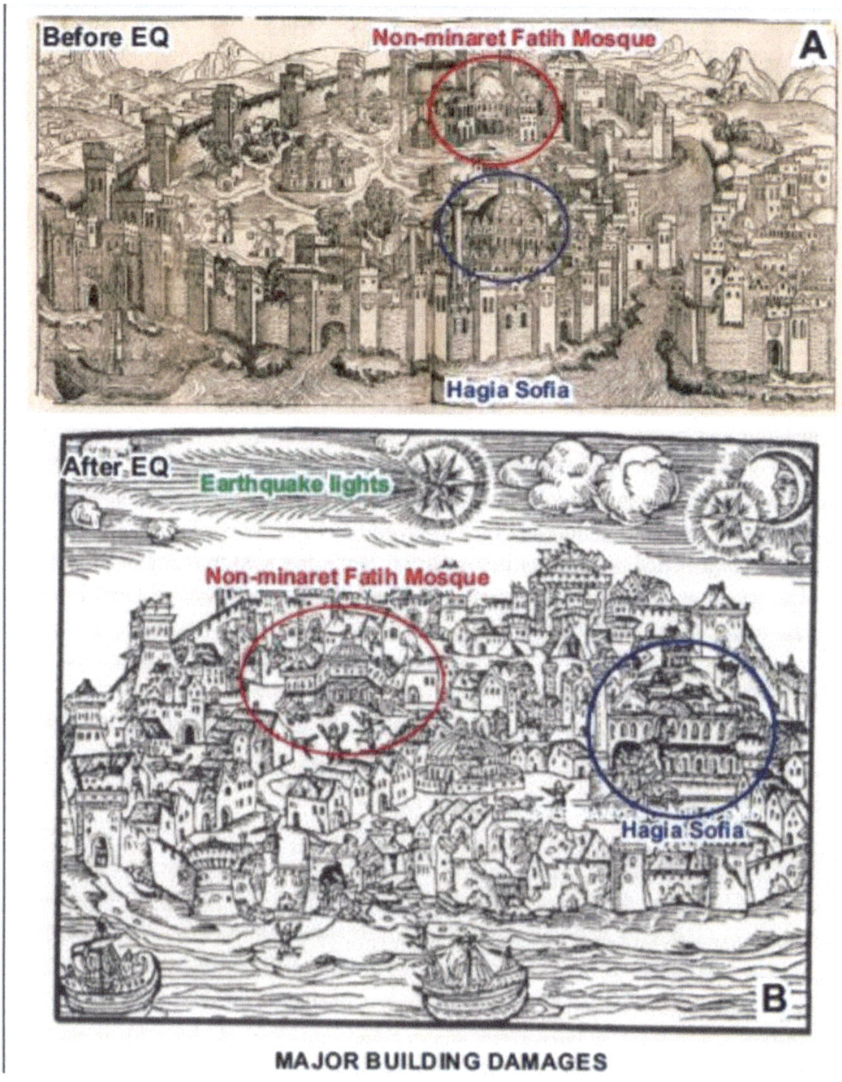

Fig. 8.5 Damage scratches in Istanbul after 1509 earthquake. *Source* https://www.indyturk.com/node/400141/haber/i%CC%87stanbul%E2%80%99un-alt%C3%BCst-oldu%C4%9Fu-g%C3%BCn-k%C3%BC%C3%A7%C3%BCk-k%C4%B1yamet-depremi

No. 516 (Ergunay 2011). The coping capacity of the new republic's institutions was too scarce to solve the adverse effects of the earthquake. Law No: 516 is the first case-specific oriented and rehabilitative arrangement of the newly founded republic (Ozden and Erkan 2016).

In 1930, the Municipality Law (Law No: 1580) came into action. It included detailed issues related to development and inspection activities, as well as disaster preparedness concepts, such as fire prevention approaches. The Law of Public Sanitation (Law No: 1593) was also developed in 1930 to organize and put into order health and sanitation issues across the country. In 1933, Law No: 2290 was legalized to have healthy and safe urban areas with coping efforts during hazardous events (Ozden and Erkan 2016).

Coming to the next decade of the 1940s, Law No: 4373 for protection against flood water and floods was introduced as the first to establish a legislative and administrative approach to flood hazard. In 1959, the well-known and used Law No: 7269 (**Disaster Law**) was published, which covered disaster coping policy. This Law 7269 has been revised several times with the type of the disasters, needs of the community, and the policy makers.

Then in 1985, a new development law was established, that is Law No: 3194. Today, it is still in use and effective all over the country although it has been criticized by building professionals in the country due to its fragmented and partial structure, which excludes the integrated approach to coping with disasters.

Following the destruction of the 17 August 1999 Marmara Earthquake, in a very short period of time in bureaucracy, on 15 November 1999, a new administrative institution was established under the title of Turkey Emergency Management Presidency by a Decree Law No: 583. The Presidency was converted to General Directorate in 2000 by another Decree Law No: 600.

Decree Law No: 587, which was activated on 27 September 2000, introduced the compulsory earthquake insurance scheme in Türkiye as the first public–private partnership in an emerging economy. The Turkish Catastrophe Insurance Pool (TCIP) is still active today. The TCIP has been tested in October 2011 Van Earthquake, October 2020 Izmir Earthquake, and the big test for this insurance model, unfortunately, occurred with the 6 February 2023 Kahramanmaras Earthquake. The pool aims to reduce the economic burden on the Government's budget but it also enforces the implementation of the earthquake-resistant construction. The TCIP became Law No: 6305 from a Decree Law, which made it stronger in implementation. Decree Laws are generally quicker to pass and be accepted at the Turkish Grand National Assembly (TBMM).

On 3 March 2000, another Decree Law: 595 in line with the reorganization of building inspections came into effect. According to this remarkable shift in building production processes, it was aimed at enhancing and developing more effective inspection activities in order to secure urban safety and health (Ozden and Erkan 2016). It transferred the building inspection responsibility from public institutions to the private sector. However, the Decree Law No: 595 was canceled by the Turkish court due to legal and administrative insufficiencies within the law. As a result, a new law, the Building Inspection Law (Law No: 4708), was published in 2001 and is still in use with revisions (Ozden and Erkan 2016).

The last legal and administrative development in this period was the establishment of then the Prime Ministry Disaster and Emergency Management Authority (AFAD) (Law No: 5902). By this law, three formerly established major institutions working in disaster coping issues were abolished and united under the umbrella agency AFAD. These institutions were: the former General Directorate of Civil Defense, the former

General Directorate of Disaster Affairs, and the Turkey Emergency Management Presidency. The aim to have AFAD was to change from top-down, centralized to bottom-up, decentralized system and give local, provincial teams more authority to prepare, to respond, and to reconstruct for any potential hazards. In 2018, since the country's jurisdictional system has changed, there is no more a Prime Minister's Office. AFAD is now connected to the Ministry of Interior, which lessens its role as the main responsible coordination agency against disaster and emergencies in the country. After the 6 February Kahramanmaras earthquakes, AFAD went into surgery and was restructured. The next disaster to happen will prove the efficiency of the new model.

Since the establishment of AFAD in 2009, there have been several publications at the national level in the context of disaster and emergency management policies and regulations of the country. These documents are listed by name below. They have been prepared with the consensus and joint efforts of the researchers, NGOs, local governments, and national governments. All are in line with the targets of the Hyogo Framework for Action 2005–2015 and the latter Sendai Framework for Disaster Risk Reduction 2015–2030.

- Turkey National Disaster Response Plan (TAMP-2012)
- Turkey National Disaster Risk Reduction Plan (TARAP) with provincial documents IRAP (2023)
- Turkey National Disaster Strategy Document (2017)
- Turkey National Disaster Risk Reduction Platform (2011)
- National Earthquake Strategy Action Plan (NESAP)/Ulusal Deprem Strateji Eylem Plani (UDSEP) in Turkish (2009)
- National Earthquake Council
- Turkey Post-Disaster Recovery Plan (TASIP-2023).

In the financial context, on 15 March 2023, Law No: 7441 has been put into effect for Disaster Reconstruction Fund. It gives the sole responsibility to the Ministry of Treasury and Finance. It organizes the fund management, donations (national and international), budget diversion, catastrophe bonds, and any action related to disaster risk finance. Line ministries such as Ministry of Agriculture, Ministry of Urbanization and Climate Change, and Ministry of Energy and Natural Resources are represented at the Board of the Disaster Reconstruction Fund.

Caglayan and Pilan (2023) discusses the international humanitarian law and regulations in the response phase of disaster risk management in link with the implementations at the national level in Türkiye. It states that disaster law is the weakest component of the international law system and structures. Therefore, this book will serve as a very important guide for international disaster community. The paper discusses how the UN and IFRC give priority and emphasis to signatories to develop a country level disaster law, where Türkiye is also committed to follow.

Ozmen (2019) summarizes the laws and regulations of the disaster and emergency management system in Türkiye. Table 8.3 lists the various related laws briefly, which have not been mentioned before.

Table 8.3 Some laws listed in relation to disaster risk reduction and resilience in Türkiye

Law No. 5302/Special Provincial Administration	Covers the provincial elements of disaster risk reduction and emergency plans
Law No. 5403 on Soil Preservation and Land Utilization	Covers the risk reduction strategies against soil losses due to landslides, wind, and flood
Law No. 5363 on Agriculture Insurance	Provides coverage for agricultural losses due to drought, earthquake, fire, hail, frost, and flood
Law No. 5366 on Usage of Timeworn Historical and Cultural Real Property with Restoration and Protection	For protection of historical and cultural heritage against disaster risk
Law No. 3234 and Law No. 6831 on Organization and Duties of the General Directorate of Forestry	For protection of forests and ecosystem against erosion, desertification, avalanche, and flood
Law No. 3234 on Organization and Duties of the General Directorate of Meteorology (MGM)	States the risk reduction policies against hydrological and meteorological hazards
Law No. 6306 on Restructuring of Areas under Risk of Disasters	Support urban transformation to build resilient structure, infrastructure, and built-in environment

Source Ozmen (2019)

8.5 Conclusion

It is important for all countries to connect development policies/regulations and disaster risk reduction and resilience strategies and actions for sustainable resilient communities and countries against surrounding hazards. Investment in strong legal capacities should contribute to the pathway for achieving Sustainable Development Goals 2030 (SDGs) and targets of the Sendai Framework for Disaster Risk Reduction 2015–2030 (SFDRR) in the local, national, and global level.

Türkiye is often exposed to natural and man-made hazards. Unfortunately, because the preparedness, prevention, and mitigation efforts are insufficient most of the time; it is hard to cope with the impact of the disaster. Therefore, there occurs economic, social, cultural, and environmental losses, when a hazard turns into a disaster. Earthquake is the main geo-hazard, which occurs less frequently but results in high severity. Then, it affects the dynamics of the whole jurisdictional system.

In recent years, hydrological and meteorological hazards such as flash floods and strong storms have also been observed with heavy consequences, which require different mitigation plans. As the number of events, type of hazards, and amount of loss varies from year to year, location to location, there is an urge to have a strong legal system, which could prevent chaotic results for disaster survivors as well as local and national governments. It is a chain reaction, if a disaster strikes and it affects multiple stakeholders. Stakeholder relations need to be managed in all three phases of disaster risk management; that is, before, during, and after. A well-established, expandible, revisable legal structure would also support the consensus and justice among the stakeholder. Solid and strong legislation should cover and respond to the needs of the communities and countries. Sustainability, equality, transparency, and accountability are crucial components of the legal wheel.

Land use regulations, building construction, agriculture investment, infrastructure, insurance, communication, education, transportation, supply and logistics, social support, and many other sectors, which are directly or indirectly affected if a disaster strikes, can only be well governed if there are strong laws and regulations to keep them strong and act together. In this aspect, Türkiye has many lessons in the past and will still continue to learn in the future.

References

AFAD (2024) www.afad.gov.tr

Anadolu Ajansi (2023) Images

Caglayan S, Pilan Z (2023) Disaster response law with national and international dimensions and February 6 earthquakes. Turk J Earthq Res 5(2):233–247

CRED (2023) Earthquakes in Türkiye: a review from 1900 to today

Dobrucali E, Demir IH (2016) Earthquake and flood disaster management regulations in Turkey. Disaster Sci Eng 2(1):1–6

Ergunay O (2011) How the 1999 earthquakes changed the disaster legislation: where we are in terms of legislation (in Turkish). In: 1st Earthquake engineering and seismology conference of Turkey, October 11–14. METU, Ankara

Gulkan HP (2018) Natural hazards governance in Turkey. In: The Oxford research encyclopedia of natural hazard science. Subject: Policy and governance. https://doi.org/10.1093/acrefore/9780199389407.013.245

Kalemli H (2010) The aid from abroad in the earthquake of Erzurum in 1924 (in Turkish). J Soc Sci Inst, Atatürk Univ 14(2):1–19

Ozden AT, Erkan B (2016) 'The shift from healer state to protector state in a 500-year period: a critical evaluation of painful development struggles in legal and administrative understanding of disaster management strategies in turkey from 1509 to 2010' in the Asian law in disasters. Routledge

Ozmen OT (2019) Turkey country report 2019. Asian Disaster Reduction Center

Chapter 9
Policies and Legislation on Disaster Risk Governance and Management in Thailand

Indrajit Pal and Nattasuda Anusonadisai Kaplin

Abstract Thailand is exposed to various natural hazards, which include coastal and fluvial flooding, drought, earthquakes, tsunamis, landslides, forest fires, heat waves, and epidemics. In the past four decades, the country's disaster management system has been built, starting with the enactment of the National Social and Development Act (1978) and the Civil Threat Prevention Act (1979) as Thailand's fundamental comprehensive disaster management laws. After the 2004 devastating Indian Ocean Tsunami struck Thailand's southern coastline communities, the Royal Thai Government further developed its disaster management system by enacting the Disaster Prevention and Mitigation Act (2007) as the primary legislative framework for disaster risk management and response (DDPM 2021). In addition, the country also developed the National Disaster Risk Management Plan (2015–2020), which highlights relatively new thinking on Disaster Risk Reduction (DRR) and disaster prevention through DRR awareness raising before, during, and after disasters, in line with the Sendai Framework for Disaster Risk Reduction (2015–2030). This chapter synthesizes the legislations and guidelines in Thailand at various levels to make the country more resilient to various natural hazards. The study will also discuss the risk governance mechanism aligned with the legislation.

Keywords Legislations · Risk governance · Thailand · Climate change · Disaster · Policy

I. Pal (✉)
Disaster Preparedness, Mitigation and Management, Asian Institute of Technology, Khlong Luang, Thailand
e-mail: indrajit-pal@ait.ac.th

N. A. Kaplin
Development Planning Management and Innovation, Asian Institute of Technology, Khlong Luang, Thailand

Y. Cui and R. Shaw (eds.), *Disaster Law*, Disaster Risk Reduction,
https://doi.org/10.1007/978-981-97-7374-9_9

9.1 Hazard Profile of Thailand

Hydrological hazards and disasters are significant concerns in many countries, with damages that can amount to up to 15% of a country's yearly GDP (UN 2015). United Nations report describes the frequency and severity of disasters are increasing, causing massive destruction to life and property, which has been exacerbated by climate change. In addition, population growth, poverty, land scarcity, urbanization, and the poor condition of flood protection and drainage infrastructure, as well as water storage facilities, have made people more vulnerable to floods and droughts. Climate change also has a major role to play in Thailand's DRR and disaster risk management systems. At the 26th United Nations Climate Change Conference of the Parties (COP26) in 2021, the country also pledged to reduce national greenhouse gas emissions by 20% by 2030. In Thailand, water-related hazards are the most common, while droughts slowly unfold calamities and induce the breakdown of social institutions and the influx of migrants, causing disturbances in the social structures of neighboring areas. Climate change is very likely to worsen this tendency, both for floods and droughts; however, different patterns in precipitation and temperatures are predicted in various regions of the world. Fluvial flooding, which constantly occurred during the past 30 years in Thailand, is caused by increasing water levels that exceed river capacity and is influenced by heavy rainfall during the monsoon season. River floods cause huge losses and damage the country's economic activities and human assets. In 2011, a hazard became a major disaster as Thailand faced colossal flooding with a widespread impact. According to a UNDRR report (2012), it took five months for the water to descend, with the loss of around 500 lives, over 12 million people affected, and disruption to huge business plants in the peri-urban area. The economic loss was more than USD 1.4 million (Figs. 9.1 and 9.2).

9.2 Historical Context

Thailand's susceptibility to natural disasters, including floods, droughts, earthquakes, tsunamis, and cyclones, has a deep historical context. Throughout its history, the country has faced periodic calamities, and traditional coping mechanisms were often community-based. The history of disaster management in Thailand is marked by a series of developments and transformations in response to the country's vulnerability to various natural and man-made disasters. The approach to disaster management has evolved, with significant milestones and lessons learned along the way (Molle et al. 2009).

1. 1970s—Early Disaster Response: Modern disaster management in Thailand can be traced back to the 1970s when the government recognized the need for a coordinated response to disasters. Early efforts focused on response and relief, with limited emphasis on preparedness and mitigation.

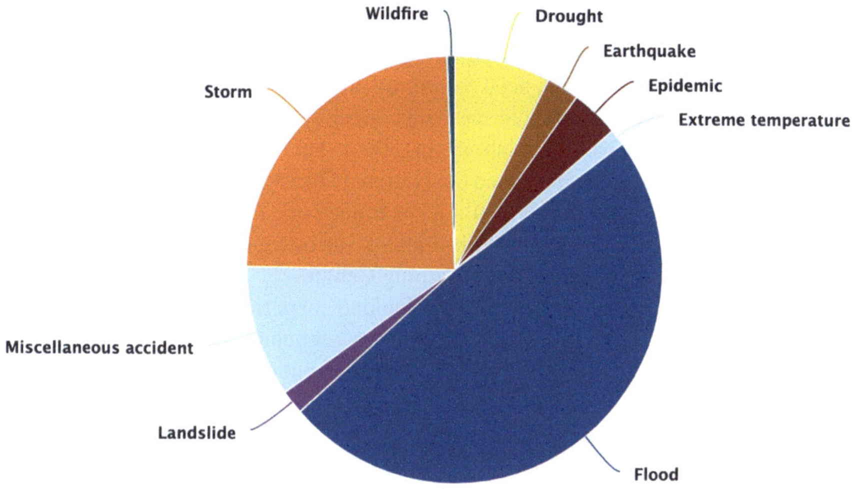

Fig. 9.1 Average annual hazard occurrence in Thailand 1980–2022. *Source* Climate change knowledge portal for development practitioners and policy makers, World Bank (2022)

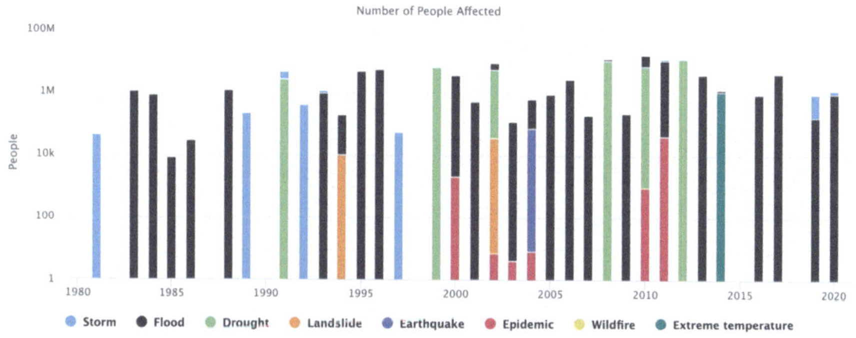

Fig. 9.2 Key natural hazard statistics 1980–2022. *Source* Climate change knowledge portal for development practitioners and policy makers, World Bank (2022)

2. 1980s—Establishment of Disaster Management Agencies: In the mid-1980s, Thailand established the Department of Disaster Prevention and Mitigation (DDPM) under the Ministry of Interior. The DDPM was tasked with overseeing disaster management activities and played a crucial role in coordinating disaster responses at the national and provincial levels.
3. 1990s—Strengthening Preparedness and Mitigation: During the 1990s, Thailand shifted its focus toward disaster preparedness and mitigation. It adopted a more proactive approach to disaster management, including the development of early warning systems and the promotion of community-based disaster risk reduction initiatives.

4. 2004—Indian Ocean Tsunami: The 2004 Indian Ocean tsunami, which struck several coastal provinces in Thailand, served as a wake-up call for the country. The disaster highlighted the need for improved tsunami warning systems, better evacuation procedures, and international cooperation in disaster response.
5. 2007—Comprehensive Legislation: In 2007, Thailand enacted the Disaster Prevention and Mitigation Act and the National Disaster Warning and Mitigation System Act. These laws provided a legal framework for disaster management, delineating the roles and responsibilities of various government agencies and establishing the National Disaster Warning Center.
6. 2011—Severe Flooding: In 2011, Thailand experienced severe flooding, affecting millions of people, and causing significant economic losses. The event prompted a reevaluation of flood management strategies and the need for improved infrastructure and water resource management.
7. 2018—Royal Decree on Water Resources Management: In response to recurrent flooding, Thailand enacted the Royal Decree on Water Resources Management, aimed at enhancing water resource management, flood control, and sustainable water use practices.
8. Recent Developments—Climate Change Adaptation: In recent years, Thailand has recognized the importance of integrating climate change adaptation into disaster management strategies. Rising sea levels, changing precipitation patterns, and increasing temperatures pose new challenges that require adaptive measures.
9. COVID-19 Pandemic: The COVID-19 pandemic, while not a natural disaster, tested Thailand's disaster management capabilities in dealing with a health crisis. The government implemented various measures to control the spread of the virus, showcasing its ability to adapt and respond to evolving threats.

9.3 Disaster Management Systems in Thailand

Thailand has a comprehensive disaster management system in place to address a wide range of natural and man-made disasters. This system includes government agencies, laws, policies, early warning systems, and coordination mechanisms to ensure effective disaster preparedness, response, recovery, and mitigation. Here is an overview of the disaster management system in Thailand (Brassard et al. 2015):

1. ***Government Agencies***: Several government agencies and departments are responsible for different aspects of disaster management in Thailand. The key agencies include:

    - Department of Disaster Prevention and Mitigation (DDPM): Under the Ministry of Interior, the DDPM is the primary agency responsible for coordinating disaster management efforts at the national level. It formulates policies, plans, and guidelines for disaster risk reduction and response.

- National Disaster Warning Center (NDWC): The NDWC is responsible for monitoring and disseminating early warnings for various hazards, including tsunamis, floods, and landslides. It plays a crucial role in ensuring timely communication and evacuation procedures.
- Royal Irrigation Department (RID): RID manages major dams and reservoirs for flood control and water resource management.
- Royal Thai Police (RTP): The RTP plays a role in disaster response, search, and rescue operations, and maintaining public order during disasters.
- Ministry of Public Health (MOPH): MOPH is responsible for healthcare services during disasters and public health emergencies.

2. ***Legal Framework***: Thailand has enacted a range of disaster governance laws, including the Disaster Prevention and Mitigation Act (2007) and the National Disaster Warning and Mitigation System Act (2007). These laws provide the legal framework for disaster management, outline the roles and responsibilities of various agencies, and establish mechanisms for disaster response and recovery.
3. ***Early Warning Systems***: Thailand has implemented a comprehensive early warning system to provide timely alerts to the public and authorities. This system includes the use of sirens, mobile phone alerts, and radio broadcasts to disseminate warnings for hazards like floods, tsunamis, and severe weather events (Aldrich et al. 2015)
4. ***Preparedness and Training***: Thailand conducts regular disaster preparedness drills and training exercises at the local and national levels. These exercises involve various agencies, emergency responders, and communities to ensure a coordinated response.
5. ***Community-Based Disaster Risk Reduction***: Thailand places a strong emphasis on involving local communities in disaster risk reduction efforts. Community-based disaster risk management (CBDRM) initiatives empower communities to identify risks, develop evacuation plans, and implement resilience-building measures.
6. ***Recovery and Rehabilitation***: After disasters, the government, with support from international partners and non-governmental organizations, engages in recovery and rehabilitation efforts. These include rebuilding infrastructure, providing financial assistance to affected individuals and businesses, and restoring essential services (Aldrich et al. 2015).
7. ***International Cooperation***: Thailand collaborates with neighboring countries and international organizations on disaster management and response. The country is part of regional initiatives, such as the ASEAN Agreement on Disaster Management and Emergency Response (AADMER), to enhance regional cooperation in disaster risk reduction and response.
8. ***Climate Change Adaptation***: Thailand recognizes the importance of climate change adaptation in disaster management. It integrates climate resilience strategies into its disaster risk reduction efforts, addressing the long-term impacts of climate change on disaster risks.

9.4 Thailand's Disaster Management Policies and Practices

The primary laws that govern disaster management in Thailand include the B.E. 2521 National Social and Development Act (1978), the B.E. 2522 Civil Threat Prevention Act (1979), and the B.E. 2550 Disaster Prevention and Mitigation Act (2007) (Sophia 2020). Other disaster management frameworks also include the National Disaster Risk Management Plan (2015–2020), Provincial and District DRM Plans; and the DRM Annual Action Plans (CEF-DM 2022). The 1978 Act inaugurated the NESDB, which advises the prime minister and the cabinet on development planning, including disaster resilience in the country, as part of the overall social and economic development framework (MOI 2021). The 2007 Act formed the DDPM, which is the principal agency that carries out disaster management planning and response in Thailand to date while setting up the National Disaster Prevention and Mitigation Committee (NDPMC) chaired by the Prime Minister and Deputy Prime Minister (MOI 2021). Both the NESDB and DDPM play a significant role in the development of disaster management and mitigation-related plans outlined below:

1. ***The Water Resource Management Master Plan (2012)***: Following the devastating flooding in 2011, the Water Resources Management Master Plan was developed by the SCWRM in Thailand, with the NESDB office serving as the SCWRM's secretariat established by the cabinet (TNC 2022). The Master plan's priorities were to clarify the tasks of government agencies responsible for water and flood management while minimizing damages and losses from future medium to large-scale floods (CEF-DM 2022).
2. ***National Disaster Prevention and Mitigation Plan (2010–2014)***: The DDPM formulated the NDPMP in 2010 to provide an outline for cross-agencies collaboration in all sectors and levels in disaster prevention, mitigation, and management. The plan identifies four strategic mechanisms: (i) impact reduction and prevention, (ii) arrangements for preparedness, (iii) disaster emergency management, and (iv) post-disaster management. Civil society organizations were also identified as supporting agencies for (ii), (iii), and (iv) components.
3. ***Strategic National Action Plan on Disaster Risk Reduction (2010–2019)***: In alignment with the Hyogo Framework for Action (HFA) and the ASEAN Agreement on Disaster Management and Emergency Response (AADMER), Thailand has prepared the Strategic National Action Plan (SNAP) to support disaster risk reduction. The plan was spearheaded by the DDPM in collaboration with other concerned government agencies, CSOs, and the private sector (TNC 2022). SNAP features four disaster risk reduction components: prevention and mitigation, preparedness, emergency response, and post-disaster management. It seeks to provide a national strategy to guide relevant government agencies in preparing their respective specific action plans. The effect of having SNAP is that DRR is mainstreamed into the planning and response of Thailand's governmental agencies (CEF-DM 2022). Additionally, SNAP also acknowledges the importance of having multi-stakeholder partnerships in disaster management, such as DDPM and other concerned governmental agencies, IFRC, ICRC, and other

Red Cross Society, UN agencies, NGOs, INGOs, foundations, Community-based Organizations (CBO), academia, and the private sector (CEF-DM 2022).

4. ***Thailand's Organizational Structure for Disaster Management***: Historically, Thailand's disaster management systems were oriented toward civil defense and emergency response. With the passing of the Disaster Prevention and Mitigation Act in 2007, the country's framework for DRM and disaster response was set up. To strengthen the government-led systems, a network of charities, Non-Government Organizations (NGO), academic institutions, and private sectors, along with community and other civil society organization (CSO) groups, have been formed to support the country's disaster risk reduction and management capabilities (ADPC 2020).

Government Agencies that lead Thailand's disaster management system are comprised of policy-level and operational-level organizations. At the policy level, the Prime Minister, or Deputy Prime Minister, is the top commander for DRM, chairing the inter-ministerial level NDPMC. The Department of Prevention and Mitigation, under the Ministry of Interior, is the secretariat for NDPMC (Fig. 9.3).

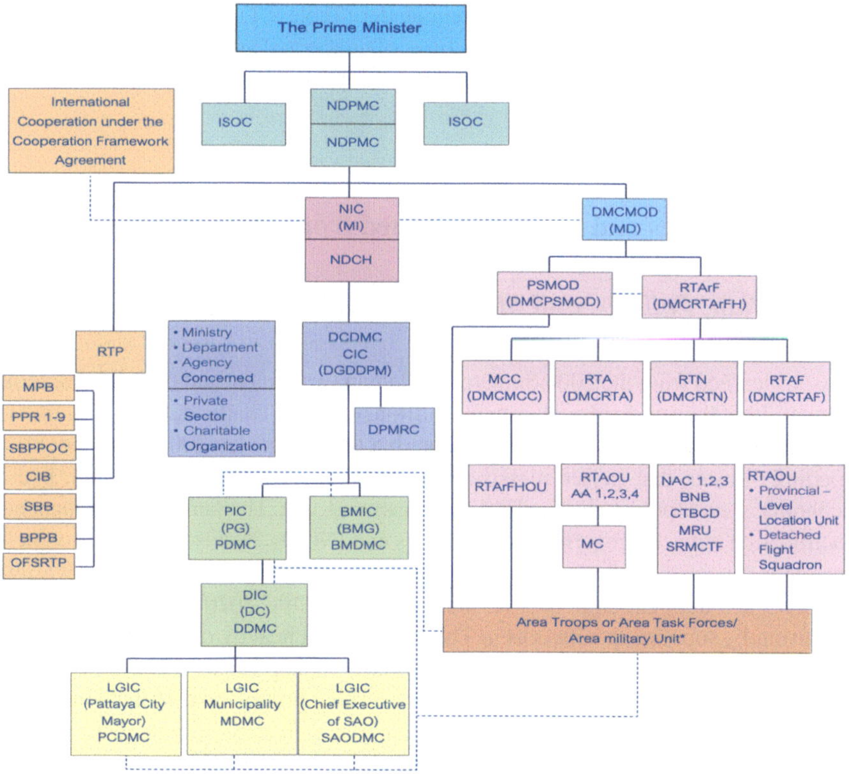

Fig. 9.3 Thailand's disaster management Chain of command, chain of communication, and key responsibilities of policy-level and operational-level agencies. *Source* NDPMC

At the operational level, agencies that are responsible for responding to a disaster are as follows:

- National Disaster Command Headquarters
- Central Disaster Management Center
- Provincial Disaster Management Centers
- Bangkok Metropolitan Disaster Management Center
- District Disaster Management Centers
- Pattaya City Disaster Management Center
- Municipal Disaster Management Center
- Sub-district Administrative Organization Disaster Management Center.

In Thailand, different authorities may declare an event as a disaster depending on the level of risk. However, for levels 1 and 2 (small-scale and medium-scale disasters), the provincial incident commander (the provincial governor) or Chief of the BMA (Bangkok Metropolitan Incident Commander) may declare an emergency if the disaster is in Bangkok (Fig. 9.4).

For level 3, the Minister of Interior is the incident commander. In a catastrophic-scale disaster level 4, the Prime Minister (PM) or Deputy Prime Minister (if assigned by the PM) is the National Incident Commander (Table 9.1). Chain of communication, chain of command, and responsibilities of concerned agencies under the DRM plan have been explained clearly following the principles of Incident Command System (Fig. 9.5).

9.5 Challenges and Lessons Learned from Major Crises

9.5.1 Plan, Policies, and Multi-stakeholder Partnerships

Lessons learned from the 2004 Sumatra-Andaman earthquake and tsunami that took almost 230,000 lives, displaced over one million people in Thailand, Indonesia, India, Sri Lanka, and nine other countries (Jayasuriya and Mccawley 2008), and the 2011 flooding disaster, that caused massive damage to the infrastructure, property, lives. Economic development in Thailand demonstrated that Thailand needs enhanced coordination between governmental agencies and INGOs, NGOs, and CBOs, which operate independently. Improved coordination and collaboration will reduce wasted resources and duplication in disaster management (ADPC 2020).

Currently, supporting networks in Thailand depend heavily on personal relationships, with no centralized platforms for disaster management, while many other ASEAN countries have set up more formal 'working groups' to distribute information, identify and collaborate on common themes as well as coordinate with relevant government agencies and other sectoral stakeholders (CEF-DM 2022). Investigators have mentioned that the Thai government's response to recent disasters did not

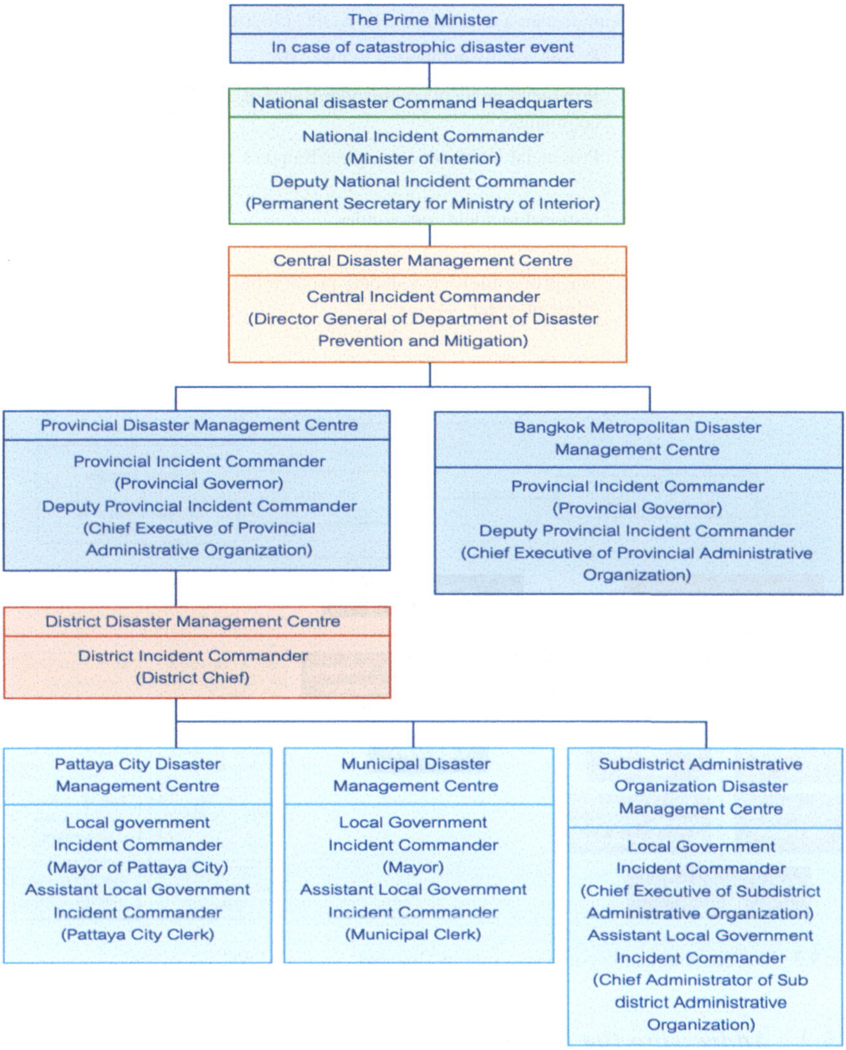

Fig. 9.4 Thailand's disaster response structure. *Source* CEF-DM

follow the adopted policies and plans, which may be because of insufficient knowledge, training, and exercises of disaster management policies and plans, on top of other political pressure (CEF-DM 2022). This resulted in ad hoc arrangements to address the unfolding incidents (ADPC 2020) (Table 9.2).

Table 9.1 Authorities that can declare a disaster. *Source* ADPC (2020)

Level	Description	Person legally authorized to make declaration of disaster areas
1	Small-scale disaster	Provincial incident commander/Bangkok metropolitan incident commander
2	Medium-scale disaster	Provincial incident commander/Bangkok metropolitan commander
3	Large-scale disaster	National incident commander
4	Catastrophic-scale disaster	The prime minister or deputy prime minister when assigned by the prime minister

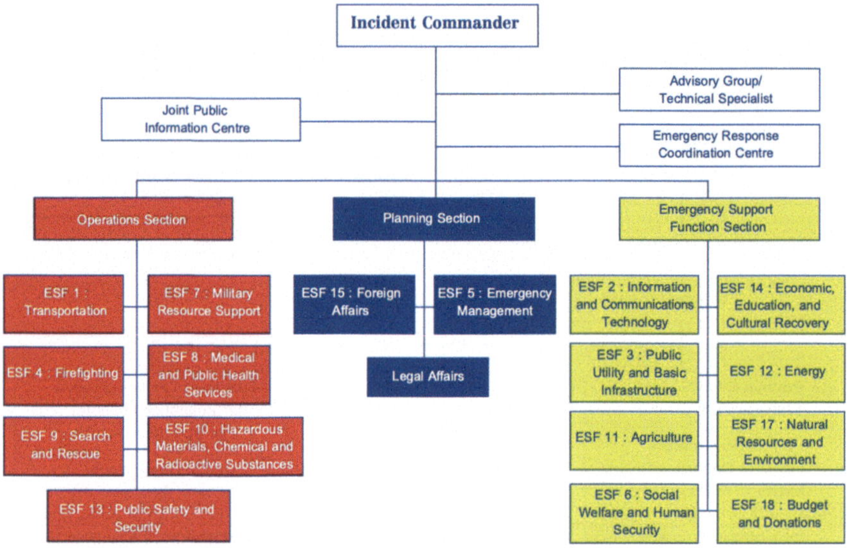

Fig. 9.5 Incident command system structure in Thailand. *Source* ADPC

9.5.2 Addressing the Needs of Vulnerable Groups

Investigators also say that there's a lack of involvement of vulnerable groups in governmental plans, policies, and partnership platforms. There is an urgent need to mainstream the inclusion of vulnerable groups in Thailand's disaster management planning and policies (CEF-DM 2022).

(a) Women—Women-headed households, older women, women with disabilities, women migrant workers, and pregnant women are not sufficiently acknowledged as vulnerable. They require appropriate services such as safety in shelters, accessible toilets, and maternal health and reproductive care (ADPC 2020).

(b) Older People—This group often has experience in handling natural hazards and disasters. However, they are usually not consulted in the process of developing

Table 9.2 Legislative policies and plans intended to enhance disaster risk reduction and climate resilience. *Source* ADPC 2020

Implementation	Plan/policy	Scope	Purpose
Department of Disaster Prevention and Mitigation	Disaster Prevention and Mitigation Act (2007)	National, provincial, district, sub-district, local community	Aims to streamline disaster management systems of Thailand by clarifying roles and coordination among stakeholders. Includes provisions for DRR
Department of Disaster Prevention and Mitigation and other agencies	National Disaster Prevention and Mitigation Plan (2015)	National, provincial, local	Outlines strategic focus areas for DRM interventions, aligned with SFDRR. Intended to cater for all levels of the government, alongside relevant stakeholders
Sub-district administration unit	DRM Action Plan (updated annually)	Local	Guides the implementation of risk management activities at the local level. Intended for the respective sub-district authorities
Provincial authorities	Provincial and District Disaster Prevention and Mitigation Plans	Provincial	Guides the implementation of DRM activities at the provincial level, implemented by province governance and supporting stakeholders

disaster risk reduction plans for their communities. Due to age-related issues such as mobility and health, some older people may need special services in times of natural disasters. The existing DRR policies and response plans do not take this into account, putting older people at greater risk (ADPC 2020).

(c) Children—Children and orphans are not sufficiently recognized as being vulnerable. They require specific services such as handling post-disaster stress via the use of child-friendly spaces, nourishing and hygienic milk and food, and safety in shelters as they face increased risk of trafficking and sexual abuse (ADPC 2020).

(d) Persons with Disabilities (PWDs)—Often, information on how to be prepared for disasters does not reach PWDs before flooding occurs. This group also lacked access to assistance and services during a disaster (ADPC 2020).

9.6 Significance of Legislation

Disaster governance laws are a crucial component of a country's legal framework designed to manage and respond to disasters effectively. These laws provide the legal foundation for disaster preparedness, response, recovery, and mitigation efforts. While specific laws and regulations can vary from one country to another, they typically cover several key aspects of disaster governance. Thailand's disaster governance laws and legislations are significant for several reasons (Hurlbert 2018):

1. Coordination and Accountability: They establish a clear hierarchy of authority and coordination among government agencies, ensuring a unified response to disasters.
2. Early Warning and Preparedness: Laws like the National Disaster Warning and Mitigation System Act prioritize early warning systems, which are crucial in minimizing casualties during sudden-onset disasters, and many disaster governance laws address the establishment and operation of early warning systems. These systems can include meteorological, seismological, and hydrological monitoring, as well as protocols for disseminating warnings to the public and relevant authorities.
3. Environmental Protection: Environmental laws contribute to disaster risk reduction by regulating activities that can exacerbate disaster impacts, such as deforestation and improper land use, and in some cases, disaster governance laws incorporate environmental protection and mitigation measures. This can include regulations to prevent deforestation, manage land use in disaster-prone areas, and promote sustainable practices that reduce vulnerability to disasters.
4. Infrastructure Resilience: Building and urban planning regulations promote resilient infrastructure, reducing the risk of damage and casualties during disasters Laws may outline procedures for post-disaster recovery and rehabilitation efforts. This includes measures to restore essential services, rebuild infrastructure, provide financial assistance to affected individuals and businesses, and address long-term recovery needs.
5. Community Engagement: These laws encourage community participation in disaster management, fostering a culture of preparedness and resilience at the local level, and disaster management laws often mandate the development of disaster preparedness plans, training programs for emergency responders, and drills or exercises to test response capabilities. These activities are crucial for ensuring a coordinated and effective response when disaster strikes and public Awareness and Education because Disaster governance laws may emphasize the importance of public awareness and education campaigns. These campaigns aim to inform the public about disaster risks, preparedness measures, and evacuation procedures to enhance community resilience.
6. Recovery and Rehabilitation: Laws may outline procedures for post-disaster recovery and rehabilitation efforts. This includes measures to restore essential services, rebuild infrastructure, provide financial assistance to affected individuals and businesses, and address long-term recovery needs.

9.7 Conclusions and Remarks

Climate change and induced hazards pose a significant challenge for Thailand, significantly impacting economic growth, livelihoods, and the achievement of the SDGs. Thailand has incorporated climate change in its national economic and social development plans (MOI 2021). Past four decades, Thailand's disaster management system has been built, implemented, and improved based on the learnings from previous disasters. While the government is leading DRR, disaster management mitigation, and preparedness, strengthening the government-led systems with a network of charities, NGOs, academic institutions, and private sectors, along with community and other civil society organization groups, have been identified as an essential step to enhance the country's disaster risk reduction and management capabilities (ADPC 2020).

In 2011, Thailand dealt with a severe flood that also prompted an impressive response at the policy and operational levels. Thailand also invested heavily in flood management, mitigation, and flood protection infrastructure, as well as integrating sectoral policies, strategies, and plans for DRR. At various levels, integrating DRR with international frameworks has been evident through the integration of policies and programs (UNDRR 2020) (Table 9.3).

Thailand's disaster governance laws and regulations form a robust and evolving framework that plays a vital role in the country's efforts to manage and mitigate disaster risks. These laws, including the Disaster Prevention and Mitigation Act (2007) and the National Disaster Warning and Mitigation System Act (2007), serve as the foundation for disaster preparedness, response, recovery, and mitigation for the country. Thailand's approach emphasizes early warning systems, community engagement, and the integration of climate change adaptation into disaster risk reduction strategies. The establishment of the National Disaster Warning Center (NDWC) and the focus on community-based disaster risk reduction initiatives highlight Thailand's proactive stance in addressing and mitigating disaster risks to climate hazards. While challenges remain, such as the need for better enforcement, increased investment in disaster resilience, and adaptation to changing climate conditions, Thailand's disaster governance laws demonstrate the commitment to mitigating climate hazards. As Thailand faces ongoing and emerging climate risks, the continued resilience of its disaster governance laws, coupled with the dedication of government and communities to their implementation, will be crucial for ensuring a safer and more secure future for the country.

Table 9.3 Integration of policies and programs to enhance Thailand's DRR plan after the 2011 floods. *Source* UNDRR (2020)

Sectoral aim	Policies/programs with potential links to Sendai framework for disaster risk reduction	Policies/programs with potential links to sustainable development goals	Policies/programs with potential links to the Paris climate agreement or environment
Disaster and climate risk reduction	National Disaster Risk Management Plan 2015 (being reviewed and updated as of 2020)	12th National Economic and Social Development Plan (NESPD 2017–2021)	Strategic Plan for Water Resource Management and Action Plan (2015–2026)
			Nationally Environmental Quality Promotion and Conservation Policy (2017–2036)
Vulnerability reduction	Thailand Healthy Lifestyle Strategic Plan (2011–2020)	National Health Strategy on Climate Change (draft) (2017–2030)	Nationally Determined Contribution Roadmap on Mitigation 2021–2030 (draft)
		Strategic Framework on Food Security (2013–2016)	National Adaptation Plan (2018)
	National Adaptation Plan (2018)	National Plan for Older Persons (2002–2021)	20 Year Energy Efficiency Development Plan (2011–2030)
		Women Development Strategy (2017–2021)	
Urban development	Bangkok Resilience Strategy 2017	20 Year Strategic Plan for Housing Development (2017–2037)	National Environmental Health Strategic Plan 2017–2021
	Bangkok Comprehensive Plan (2013)	Bangkok Comprehensive Master Plan (2014–2018)	Master Plan on Sewage and Wastewater Management 2017–2026

References

Aldrich DP, Oum S, Sawada Y (2015) Resilience and recovery in Asian disasters: community ties, market mechanisms, and governance

Asian Disaster Preparedness Center (ADPC) and UN Office for Disaster Risk Reduction (UNDRR) Disaster risk reduction in Thailand: status report 2020. https://www.undrr.org/user/login?destination=publication/disaster-risk-reduction-thailand-status-report-2020,18

Brassard C, Howitt AM, Giles DW (2015) Natural disaster management in the Asia-Pacific. Disaster Risk Reduct. https://doi.org/10.1007/978-4-431-55157-7

Hurlbert MA (2018) Adaptive Governance of Disaster, Water Governance – Concepts, Methods, and Practice. https://doi.org/10.1007/978-3-319-57801-9_1
Jayasuriya S, Mccawley P (2008) Reconstruction after a major disaster: lessons from the post-Tsunami experience in Indonesia, Sri Lanka, and Thailand. https://www.adb.org/sites/default/files/publication/155980/adbi-wp125.pdf
Molle F, Foran T, Kakonen M (2009) Contested waterscapes in the Mekong region: hydropower, livelihoods, and governance. Earthscan.
National Disaster Prevention and Mitigation Committee (2015) Thailand national disaster disaster risk management plan. http://110.78.23.212/nl/dataset/ndrmp
Sophia T (2020) Thailand country report 2020. Asian Disaster Reduction Center. https://www.adrc.asia/nationinformation.php?NationCode=764&Lang=en
Thailand Disaster Management Reference Book (2022) Center for Excellence in Disaster Management and Humanitarian Assistance. www.CFE-DMHA.ORG
Thailand's National Communication (TNC), and United Nations Framework Convention on Climate Change (UNFCCC) (2022) https://unfccc.int/sites/default/files/resource/Thailand%20TNC.pdf
UNDRR (2020) Disaster risk reduction in Thailand: status report 2020. United Nations Office for Disaster Risk Reduction (UNDRR), Regional Office for Asia and the Pacific, Bangkok, Thailand
United Nations (2015) Department of Economic and Social Affairs. https://sdgs.un.org/goals
World Bank Group (WBG) (2022) Overview: World Bank in Thailand. https://www.worldbank.org/en/country/thailand/overview

Chapter 10
Disaster Legislation in Malaysia: A Scoping Review

Nurfashareena Muhamad, Aida Soraya Shamsuddin, Lim Choun Sian, and Joy Jacqueline Pereira

Abstract The most recent Intergovernmental Panel on Climate Change (IPCC) 2023 report asserts that the effects of climate change on both humans and ecosystems are more extensive and severe than anticipated, emphasizing that the risk of future catastrophic events will escalate rapidly with each incremental degree of warming. Malaysia frequently experiences several disasters, including floods, landslides, earthquakes, and others within the country. Each year, floods stand out as the primary cause of both frequent and substantial damage, resulting in a significant loss of human life, disease outbreaks, property and crop destruction, and various other forms of loss. Between 2012 and 2019, Malaysia had the highest percentage of its population exposed to floods compared to other member states of the Association of Southeast Asian Nations (ASEAN). In December 2014, Malaysia encountered its most severe monsoon floods on record. In response to this event, the National Disaster Management Agency (NADMA) was established on 1 October 2015, following a Cabinet decision made on 26 August 2015. The Malaysian government is constantly evaluating and revising its disaster management policies and legislation to accommodate evolving risks and the challenges ahead. There are several laws related to disaster management and emergency response in the country which are designed to provide a legal framework for managing disasters, emergencies, and public protection. This chapter will offer an overview of the scope of some important legislation related to disaster management in Malaysia. It will begin with a brief overview of Malaysia's disaster governance, hazards, and risks. After that, it will delve into disaster governance, cover key institutions, and discuss key instruments and their coverage before concluding with a conclusion.

N. Muhamad (✉) · A. S. Shamsuddin · L. C. Sian · J. J. Pereira
Southeast Asia Disaster Prevention Research Initiative (SEADPRI), Institute for Environment and Development, Universiti Kebangsaan Malaysia, Bangi, Malaysia
e-mail: fasha@ukm.edu.my

Y. Cui and R. Shaw (eds.), *Disaster Law*, Disaster Risk Reduction,
https://doi.org/10.1007/978-981-97-7374-9_10

10.1 Brief Governance of Malaysia

Malaysia is a tropical nation situated in Southeast Asia. It features a unique landscape divided into two distinct regions—Peninsular Malaysia in the west and East Malaysia on the island of Borneo. It shares a northern border with Thailand. Peninsular Malaysia stretches an amazing distance of 800 km, starting from Thailand's Kra Isthmus to the southern region near Singapore and the Indonesian Islands. It showcases a varied landscape that perfectly represents its geographical diversity. Conversely, East Malaysia asserts ownership of the northern portion of Borneo, which is a mesmerizing and extensive area. Situated to the south of Indonesia and the north of Brunei, this area on Borneo Island contributes to the diverse fabric of Malaysia. This area is intriguing, with its rich landscapes and flawless integration of ethnic subtleties. Malaysia's overall land area spans 329,847 square km^2 (126,895 square miles), comprising 328,657 km^2 (126,895 square miles) of land and 1,190 km^2 (460 square miles) of water (CFE-DMHA 2022). The map of Malaysia is shown in Fig. 10.1.

The Malaysian Federation comprises 13 states and three federal territories, with 11 states and two territories situated in Peninsular Malaysia. The 13 states are Perlis, Kedah, Penang, Perak, Selangor, Pahang, Terengganu, Kelantan, Negeri Sembilan, Melaka, Johor in Peninsular Malaysia while two in Sabah and Sarawak; three federal territories are Putrajaya, Kuala Lumpur and Labuan. Among the peninsular states, nine follow a political structure rooted in historical Malay kingdoms. These states are governed by "Sultans" who inherit the throne based on the principle of agnatic primogeniture. Notably, Negeri Sembilan employs a distinct system where the ruler holds the title of "Yang di-Pertuan Besar." Concurrently, Perlis is led by a "Raja", and the throne succession is based on agnatic seniority.

Within this group of nine rulers, the selection of the federal chief of state, known as the "Yang di-Pertuan Agong," or King, follows a rotational system, with individuals serving five-year terms. Other states and former British Crown Colonies have Governors. Malaysia operates as a constitutional monarchy, signifying the presence

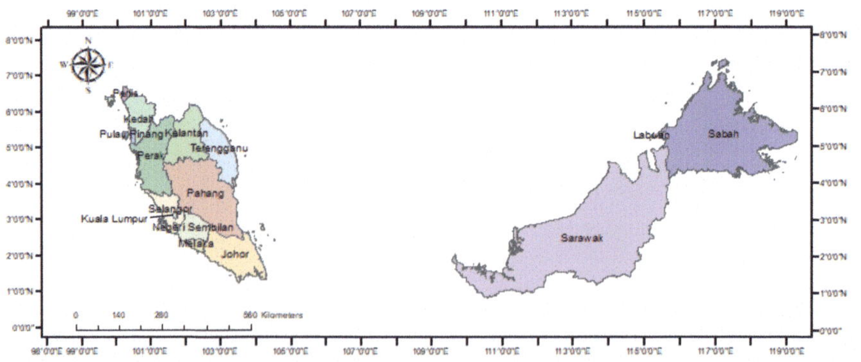

Fig. 10.1 Map of Malaysia

of a King, while a parliamentary democracy, elected by the people, governs at both the federal and state levels. The King is obligated to adhere to the rule of the government, encompassing the cabinet and parliament (MyGovernment 2021). Following the monarchy, Malaysia has an executive authority and a legislative authority. In Malaysia, the Prime Minister serves as the leader of the executive branch of the federal government, appointed by the King. The prime minister, with the King's approval, selects members of the cabinet from parliament. The federal government oversees various authorities, including the administration of justice and citizenship, formulation of foreign policies, management of internal securities, and defense.

The legislative authority structure in Malaysia is a reflection of the country's political framework, characterized by the separation of authority between the federal and state levels. Legislative affairs at the federal level are the joint prerogative of the executive branch and the two chambers of the federal parliament, constituting the foundation of democratic governance in Malaysia. The federal parliament, consisting of the House of Representatives and The Senate, embodies the nation's commitment to inclusive representation and thoughtful deliberation in decision-making. The bicameral structure guarantees thorough review and discussion of proposed legislation, thus cultivating a legislative procedure that is robust and adheres to the values of accountability and transparency.

The Senate, also known as the Dewan Negara, functions as a chamber of review and revision, wherein members appointed to represent different states and federal territories offer their perspectives during legislative deliberations. By serving as a check on the House of Representatives, this chamber enriches legislative outcomes through the provision of a forum for deliberate deliberation and constructive criticism. Meanwhile, the House of Representatives, also known as the Dewan Rakyat, serves as a tangible manifestation of the Malaysian people's direct representation as its members are elected via universal suffrage. In its capacity as the principal legislative institution, the House of Representatives deliberates on policies and legislation in a manner that reflects the varied aspirations and interests of the constituents it serves. This chamber transforms the laws and policies of the country by translating the collective will of citizenry into concrete legislative action via lively debates and consultations. In this instance, a bill's pathway to becoming law is marked by stringent assessment, which includes the need for approval from both houses and the King's assent.

Nevertheless, Malaysia's legal framework transcends the boundary of the federal realms, adopting a dual legal system. The first constituency comprises entirely of the country and is regulated by parliamentary laws that require a two-thirds majority to alter. Simultaneously, Malaysia ensures adherence to Islamic law for its Muslim populace, with the majority of the responsibility for its enforcement resting with individual states. Malaysia's justice system, in conjunction with the Sharia courts, reflects its colonial history by being influenced by the British legal tradition. The Federal Court is the highest authority in matters of constitutional interpretation and has exclusive jurisdiction in resolving disputes between states or between the federal government and the states. The Court of Appeal complements the Federal Courts by handling appeals from High Courts nationwide to ensure consistent application of the law and promote values of justice and fairness.

Currently, Malaysia still does not have a specific legislation on disasters or disaster management. In November 2023, the government of Malaysia revealed intentions to implement a special law to improve and enhance disaster management preparedness and the National Disaster Risk Reduction Policy (FMT Reporters 2023). However, there are several pieces of existing legislation related to disaster management and risk reduction. They provide a legal framework for managing disasters, emergencies, and civil protection. The key components and aspects of the disaster legislation are the National Security Act 2016 (Act 776), which provided the power for the establishment of the National Security Council that prescribes the Standard Operating Procedures under its Directive No. 20 in 1997 (revision 2012) followed by the establishment of National Disaster Management Agency (NADMA). The Civil Defence Act 1951 (Government of Malaysia 2016) tasked the Civil Defence Force to carry out partly disaster management and other roles such as humanitarian services and civil defense training. Complimentary legislation related to disaster risk reduction that prevents the creation of new risks from new development by mandatory development plans and planning control, earthworks and environment, stability of building, erosion and siltation control, and drainage design in reducing landslide and flood risks regulated by Town and Planning Act 1976 (Act 172); Uniform Building By-Law 1984; and Street, Drainage and Building Act 1974.

The following section of this chapter will elaborate on the disasters in Malaysia and will be followed by a scoping of disaster legislation of the country.

10.2 Hazards and Disaster Risks in Malaysia

Climate change presents substantial and escalating threats to our shared future. The repercussions of rising sea levels, floods, and droughts have uprooted communities, disrupted trade, and jeopardized both natural resources and the well-being of numerous individuals. Malaysia is not exempt from the physical and transitional risks associated with climate change. The heightened intensity and recurrence of climate-related incidents are amplifying the physical and liability risks to our economy. Over the past two decades, we have witnessed more than 50 disasters, impacting over three million people through displacements, injuries, and fatalities. The escalating severity and frequency of significant floods and prolonged dry periods have significantly adversely affected livelihoods, particularly in the agricultural sector.

Over the past 120 years (1900–2020), natural hazard occurrences have resulted in the highest number of fatalities, mainly when storms induce landslides and floods. Traditionally, numerous cities in the nation have developed from communities situated in low-lying areas to near rivers. However, due to swift urbanization, certain densely populated urban centers have expanded into elevated regions with steep inclines. This scenario contributes significantly to the elevated rates of floods and landslides within the country. Anticipated consequences of extreme weather events and emerging climate-related hazards include heightened vulnerability of cities and settlements to impacts such as floods, landslides, water scarcity, and coastal inundation. Floods and Landslides are the most common types of disasters in Malaysia (NADMA 2021; Affandi et al. 2023; Siti Nurkhalidah et al. 2023; Rosmadi et al. 2023). Each year, floods stand out as the predominant factor causing both regular and significant harm, leading to substantial human casualties, disease outbreaks, property and crop destruction, and various other forms of losses (Muhammad Ikhwan et al. 2023; Sharir and Roslee 2023). During the period spanning from 2012 to 2019, Malaysia bore the highest percentage of its population exposed to the devastating impact of floods among its counterparts within the Association of Southeast Asia Nations (ASEAN) (UNDRR 2020).

The latest report from the IPCC in 2023 posits that the ramifications of climate change on both human societies and ecological systems are more far-reaching and severe than previously predicted. It underscores the notion that the risk of future catastrophic events will intensify swiftly with each incremental rise in global temperature. In fact, in recent years, a number of significant disasters occurred, have shaken the country: (1) A devastating landslide disaster occurred in Batang-Kali, Genting Highland, Hulu Selangor, on December 16, 2022. The event resulted in the destruction of nearly the entire camping and agricultural site, impacting 92 individuals, with 31 reported fatalities (JMG 2023); (2) Debris flow that occurred on July 4, 2022, in the northern of Peninsular Malaysia located in Sungai Kupang, Baling, Kedah, resulted in three fatalities, 17 homes destroyed or damaged, 3,546 residents affected, and estimated losses in total of RM 25.91 million. The incident was triggered by exceptionally heavy rain in the highland area of Gunung Inas, causing numerous landslides simultaneously. This was followed by the phenomenon of debris flow in four (4) main river branches, culminating in the tragedy of debris flood and mudflow in low-lying areas, namely Kampung Iboi, and dozens of villages downstream (JMG 2023); (3) The unpredictable flood of Taman Sri Muda, Selangor in December 2021 impacting more than 300 residents and estimated losses in total of RM300 million.

Malaysia does not fall within the "Pacific Rim of Fire," making major natural hazard events like earthquakes and tsunamis uncommon. Nevertheless, the possibility of such disasters occurring in the country cannot be entirely ruled out. Instances of earthquakes with mild to moderate seismic activity have been observed, particularly in Sabah and Sarawak. In Malaysia, storms primarily manifest as localized episodes of strong winds. While infrequent, a handful of unusual incidents stemming from the trailing impact of tropical cyclones have led to heavy rainfall (Fig. 10.2). The occurrence of haze in the country is attributed to wildfires originating from peat and forest fires, originating both locally and from sources across borders.

In the upcoming years, Malaysia is projected to face a heightened occurrence of climate-related hazards. The anticipated impacts on local communities are expected to be severe due to rising sea levels, extreme temperatures, and intensified rainfall. Changes in weather patterns, characterized by more frequent and intense rainfall alongside prolonged dry spells, serve as indicators of climate change. Managing heat stress may become a challenge if global warming continues unchecked. Additionally,

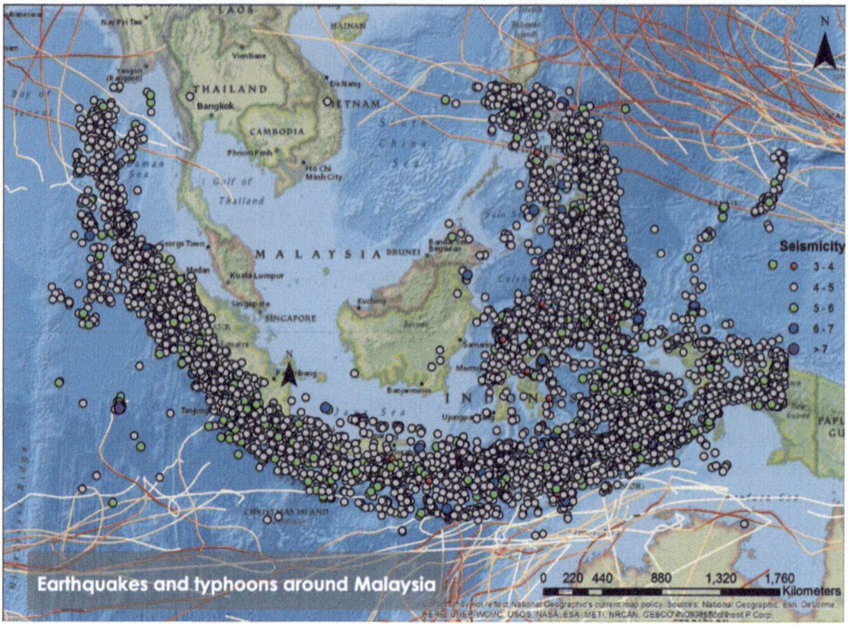

Fig. 10.2 The seismicity and typhoons around Malaysia. *Source* NADMA (2021)

potential consequences such as diminished yields in food crops, regional instability, and the associated economic and security concerns pose further challenges.

Opportunities to reduce the risk and impact of disasters in Malaysia are conveyed through a disaster management cycle. This cycle, modified to align with existing legislation, promotes consistent practices and accommodates practitioners and decision-makers from diverse backgrounds. The Disaster Management Cycle consists of five stages (Fig. 10.3): prevention, mitigation, preparedness, response, and recovery, with each phase incorporating elements of disaster risk reduction.

Disaster Prevention is an essential element of the country's risk management strategy, as it acknowledges the criticality of taking proactive actions to reduce the consequences of perils and protect communities. Malaysia implements a wide range of disaster prevention initiatives that are specifically designed to address the country's distinct socio-economic and environmental circumstances, in accordance with a comprehensive framework. At the core of these endeavors lies the seamless incorporation of disaster risk reduction into routine operations, supported by the passage of comprehensive legislation and the enforcement of rigorous land-use regulations. Through the establishment of explicit standards and guidelines, Malaysia endeavors to bolster resiliency and reduce susceptibilities with respect to emerging threats. Furthermore, Malaysia places significant emphasis on the advancement of insurance as an indispensable instrument for disaster readiness, furnishing communities with monetary protections in the event of potential losses. The prioritization

Fig. 10.3 The disaster management cycle in Malaysia

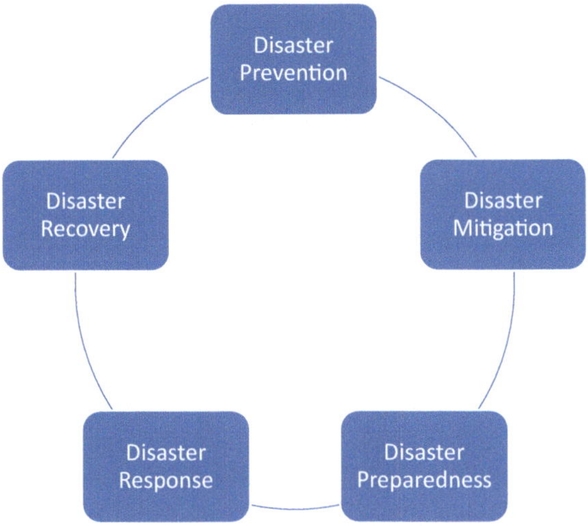

of addressing fundamental risk factors, including poverty and inequality, continues to be a central concern. Focused interventions are designed to reinforce societal resilience and promote equitable outcomes. Identification of disaster-prone areas and vulnerable populations is a critical components of Malaysia's prevention strategy, as it permits the implementation of targeted interventions and customized mitigation efforts. The establishment of efficient communication channels and early warning systems is crucial for bolstering readiness and guaranteeing prompt reactions to emergent hazards. Malaysia aims to promote safety and resilience and cultivate a culture of collaboration and engagement among various stakeholders, such as policymakers, communities, and pertinent authorities. This is achieved through the utilization of collective expertise and resources. Prevention stands out as the most economically efficient approach for mitigating the impact of hazards.

Disaster Mitigation is an essential component of the country's endeavors to enhance its resilience. Its objective is to avert the progression of perilous situations into catastrophic disasters or to reduce the extent of their consequences by implementing diverse physical interventions. In light of the wide array of hazards encountered, Malaysia implements a comprehensive strategy for risk reduction that incorporates both engineered and nature-based solution, capitalizing on technological progress and inventive approaches. Through the development of resilient infrastructure intended to endure natural hazards, engineering structures contribute significantly to Malaysia's mitigation efforts. These structures, which range from flood barriers and resilient buildings to reinforced coastal defenses, are strategically erected in order to protect vulnerable communities and reduce the impacts of natural disasters on critical infrastructure. Simultaneously, Malaysia adopts nature-based solutions as a supplementary strategy for disaster mitigation, capitalizing on the intrinsic resilience of ecosystems to provide a protective barrier against the impacts of disasters. Aside from promoting environmental sustainability and enhancing biodiversity.

Wetland restoration, mangrove rehabilitation, and afforestation initiatives provide natural defenses against inundation, erosion, and storm surges, thus mitigating the risk of disaster. In addition, Malaysia improves its mitigation capabilities through the implementation of innovative solutions and technological advances, including real-time monitoring network, predictive modeling, and data analytics, in addition to early warning systems.

Disaster Preparedness emphasizes the implementation of proactive strategies that inform the public about possible hazards and enable communities to efficiently address emergencies. Malaysia, in an effort to underscore the significance of prompt action, incorporates disaster preparedness education into its curriculum. This ensures that children commence their education with a thorough understanding of disaster risk awareness and response strategies. During this stage, emergency managers engaged in close collaboration with civil society organizations, government agencies, and community stakeholders in order to develop comprehensive action plans and bolster essential capabilities. Malaysia also additionally places a high emphasis on the upkeep of critical infrastructure and equipment, assuring that emergency response teams possess the necessary resources to execute their responsibilities efficiently. Preparing emergency responders for a wide range of scenarios through rigorous training programs fosters a culture of professionalism and preparedness within the ranks. Malaysia's preparedness efforts also include the testing and refinement of early warning methods; routine exercises and simulations are conducted to assess the effectiveness of response protocols and alert systems. In addition, Malaysia prioritizes the development of pool of competent volunteers drawn from the civilian populace, thereby leveraging on the combined capabilities of communities to enhance initiatives pertaining to emergency response.

Disaster Response in Malaysia is a well-coordinated and rapid operation that entails mobilizing essential emergency services and dispatching first responders to the impacted region swiftly. First responders, such as firefighter, police officers, and ambulance teams, are promptly deployed to offer crucial aid and help to individuals impacted by disaster. First responders receive additional backup from secondary emergency services, including specialist rescue teams trained to address specific obstacles and scenarios that may occur during the response operation. Malaysia's disaster response is highly effective due to the meticulous preparation and implementation of emergency plans developed during the preparedness phase. Emergency responders engage in regular drills, simulations, and training exercises to become acquainted with response protocols and ensure effective coordination of rescue operations. Centralized command centers are crucial for coordinating and communicating response efforts, guaranteeing efficient allocation of resources, and prompt aid to individuals in need. Malaysia focuses on community resilience and empowerment by utilizing local volunteers and grassroots organizations to enhance government-led response operations and aid in post-disaster recovery.

Disaster Recovery emphasizes the restoration of areas impacted by disaster to their pre-disaster state. This phase also involves addressing long-term challenges and making decisions once immediate needs have been addressed. Recovery activities involve various aspects, such as rebuilding destroyed property, reinstating employment possibilities, and fixing crucial infrastructure necessary for community operations. Malaysia aims to reduce risks before disasters by focusing on "building back safer", to enhance resilience against future hazards in communities and infrastructure. Malaysia proactively employs prevention and mitigation actions during the recovery phase to enhance long-term resilience, taking advantage of a "window of opportunities". By incorporating these measures into the recovery framework, Malaysia not only reconstructs what was lost but also strengthens communities and infrastructure against future disasters, demonstrating a dedication to sustainable and resilient development in challenging circumstances.

With the concern of the continuous threat of climate change, Malaysia, led by NADMA has developed a National Risk Register (NRR) that consists of a risk matrix to promote awareness about past and potential natural hazards and disasters in Malaysia. The NRR has categorized Malaysia as being exposed to seven hazards (Fig. 10.4). These include floods, tsunamis, earthquakes, landslides, storms, dry spells (droughts), and wildfires, with their ranking determined by a risk matrix. The matrix was constructed by assessing each hazard based on its likelihood and impact, utilizing a hybrid approach that incorporates information from various sources such as open data, technical departments, national reports to the United Nations of Sendai Framework Monitor, and the expert opinions of government agencies.

Various measures have been implemented to increase disaster resilience, with a primary focus on key areas outlined in the Twelfth Malaysia Plan (RMK-12). This involves carrying out evidence-based measures based on risk assessment, embracing a comprehensive strategy for climate adaptation and disaster risk reduction, enhancing early warning and disaster response systems, and enhancing disaster preparedness and recovery. The implementation of the Natural Policy on Disaster

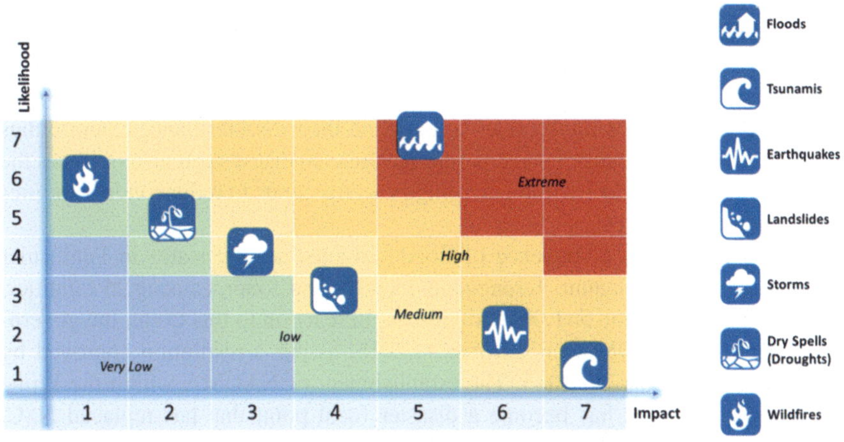

Fig. 10.4 The risk matrix was created by categorizing a hazard based on its likelihood and impact. *Source* NADMA (2021)

Risk Reduction (DRR) is a notable initiative. The strategy is designed to help the country address the impacts of climatic extremes and climate change in the future by focusing on community involvement, risk awareness, and risk finance, among other factors.

10.3 Disaster Legislation in Malaysia

Since the early 1990s, the Malaysian Government has implemented policies, infrastructure, and operational mechanisms that extend across national, state, and district levels related to disaster. These measures ensure the coordinated involvement of various government agencies and the non-government sector in addressing disaster management. The Melaka Declaration on DRR in Malaysia encapsulates the country's future directions in disaster risk reduction and its commitment to implementing the priority areas of the Hyogo Framework for Action (HFA), 2005–2015 and the Sendai Framework for DRR (SFDRR) 2015–2030. The disaster management process in Malaysia is tailored to align with prevailing legislative mandates, encourage uniform practices, and accommodate professionals from diverse disciplines.

10.3.1 Key Institutions

In Malaysia, key institutions consisting of diverse organizations, agencies, and bodies are responsible for effectively managing and responding to disasters and emergencies to protect the nation's security and well-being. The National Security Council (NSC) of Malaysia is the main organization responsible for supervising national security issues, including disaster management. The NSC released Directive No. 20 in response to the catastrophic fall of the Highland Tower condominium (Fig. 10.5). This directive aims to guide national disaster management and relief operations. Directive No. 20 requires several agencies to integrate their disaster management duties and roles, enabling organized and efficient reactions to disasters. It also oversees the handling of disaster risks by implementing proactive steps to reduce vulnerabilities and strengthen resilience.

In December 2014, a sequence of floods affected several states in Peninsular Malaysia, covering Kelantan, Terengganu, Pahang, and Johor, causing 25 fatalities, and displacing more than 541,000 individuals. In reaction to this event, the government established NADMA on October 1, 2015, as per a resolution approved by the Cabinet on August 26, 2015. The establishment of NADMA within the Prime Minister's Department has become a disaster focal point that has replaced NSC. The formation of NADMA involved the consolidation of three entities: the Disaster Management Division of the NSC, the Post-Flood Recovery Unit of the PMD, and the Special Malaysia Disaster Assistance and Rescue Agency (SMART). Functioning

Fig. 10.5 The deadliest of Highland Tower collapsed on December 11, 1993 caused the death of 48 people. *Source of photo* New Straits Time (2019)

as the primary national entity for disaster management, NADMA is tasked with developing policies and mechanisms in this field, supported by its various divisions.

The NADMA structure comprises four sectors: disaster planning and preparedness, operational implementation post-disaster, and administrative and finance (Fig. 10.6). Each sector consists of several sections. On a national scale, NADMA acts as the Secretariat for the National Disaster Management Committee, overseeing policy implementation and coordinating initiatives aligned with the disaster management cycle. The agency is also responsible for conducting public awareness programs and advocating strategic research for disaster risk reduction. In its crucial role of coordinating significant disasters in the country, NADMA manages the National Disaster Relief Trust Fund, directs the deployment of the SMART Team, and leads international humanitarian assistance efforts for disasters.

NADMA collaborates with technical agencies at the federal, state, and district levels, including disaster management secretariats and relief committees. It also engages with other organizations on regional and global platforms, focusing on disaster risk reduction. The scope and responsibilities of NADMA are based on the provisions under NSC Directive No. 20. NADMA is also responsible for ensuring that the implementation of NSC Directive No. 20 is adhered to by all relevant agencies. Generally, NADMA's scope involves coordinating all activities and collaboration before, during, and after disasters, including disaster risk prevention and mitigation activities, preparedness and disaster response activities, as well as recovery and reconstruction activities. NADMA Malaysia acts as the secretariat for the Central

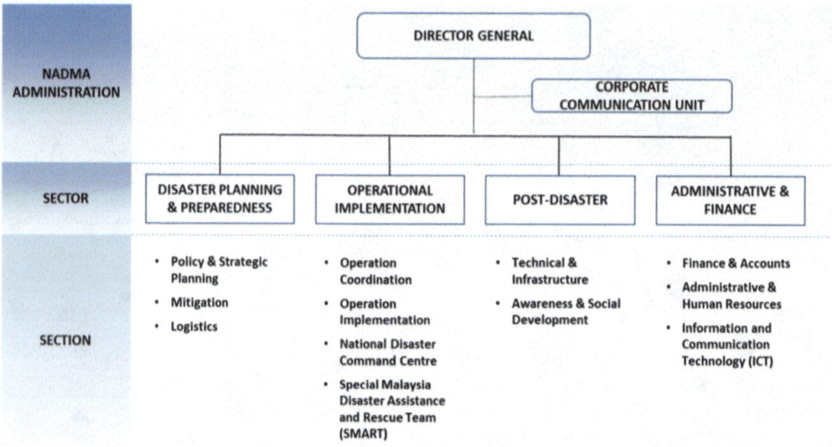

Fig. 10.6 The structure organization of NADMA consists of NADMA comprises four divisions dedicated to mobilizing its strategic and operational roles across all phases of disaster management

Disaster Management Committee (CDMC) and the National Disaster Operations Control Center (NDOCC) at the federal level.

Under NADMA, it also includes the Special Malaysia Disaster Assistance and Rescue Team, known as SMART, one of the lead disaster response agencies in Malaysia was established on August 1, 1995, following the collapse of the Highlands Towers condominium in 1993. The incident revealed the country's shortcomings in handling enormous building collapse tragedies, prompting Malaysia to seek and wait for assistance from abroad. At its establishment, the team's mandate was to carry out specialized search and rescue tasks requiring expertise, skills, and specific equipment and gear in disaster events. The headquarters of the SMART team is located on Pulau Meranti, Puchong, in the state of Selangor, Malaysia. They have received certification from the International Search and Rescue Advisory Group (INSARAG), which demonstrates their compliance with United Nations (UN) standards and their operational capability for technically challenging and complex search and rescue operations. The SMART team functions as an operational unit of the Malaysian Government, actively responding to disasters at regional and international levels. Notable examples of their assistance include search and rescue missions for tsunami victims in Aceh (2004), earthquake victims in Muzafarabad, Pakistan (2005), Leyte landslides (2006), and efforts related to the Sabah earthquake on Mount Kinabalu (2015).

In addition to NADMA and SMART, the Malaysia Civil Defence Force (APM) is also another important institution related to disaster management in the country. It is a government agency in Malaysia responsible for providing emergency response and disaster management services. Established under the Civil Defence Act 1951, the main role of the APM is to assist and support the public during emergencies, disasters, and crises. APM operates under the jurisdiction of the Prime Minister's

Department and works closely with other government agencies, local authorities, and non-governmental organizations (NGOs) to coordinate disaster response efforts. The defense function in the Malaysian Civil Defense Force includes search and rescue operations where APM personnel are trained to conduct search and rescue missions in various environments, including urban areas, forests, and bodies of water, to locate and evacuate individuals affected by disasters, such as floods, landslides, and building collapses. They also provide essential medical assistance and first aid to victims of accidents and disasters and support the deployment of medical teams and ambulances during emergencies to provide immediate medical care to those in need.

In addition, APM is involved in disaster relief and humanitarian assistance by distributing relief supplies such as food, water, shelter, and clothing to affected communities during disasters. They work with NGOs and other agencies to provide humanitarian assistance and support to displaced people and vulnerable populations. APM functions as the central coordinating agency for civil defense and disaster management activities in Malaysia. Overall, the Malaysia Civil Defence Force plays an important role in ensuring the safety and well-being of Malaysians during crises, and their efforts contribute significantly to improving the country's resilience and disaster preparedness. In addition to APM, there is also the Malaysian Fire and Rescue Department (JBPM) which is responsible for firefighting, rescue operations, and providing emergency medical services during disasters and emergencies. They also run public awareness campaigns and training programs to improve community resilience. These institutions play an important role in disaster management efforts, dealing with both natural hazards and man-made hazards such as industrial accidents or epidemics. As a result, mandates or sources of power are obtained differently.

10.3.2 Key Instruments and Its Coverage

The key instruments serve as the foundation of authority, with defining the roles and responsibilities of government agencies for disaster risk management (Sect. 3.1). This section will comprehensively cover NSC Directive No. 20: National Policy and Mechanism on Disaster Management and Relief and selected key instruments that cover Malaysia Civil Defence Force Act 1951, Emergency (Essential Powers) (No. 2) Ordinance 2021, Occupational Safety and Health Act 1994, Occupational Safety and Health Regulations (Control of Major Accident Hazards in Industry) 1996 and Environmental Quality Act, EQA 1974 (Act 127). The NSC Directive No. 20, implemented on May 11, 1997, established significant guidelines. This directive was revised in 2012 to streamline the reactive disaster response oriented guidelines into a more holistic disaster risk management that covers the cycle of disaster management. The revised version, NSC Directive No. 20: National Policy and Mechanism on Disaster Management and Relief, issued on March 30, 2012, integrated comprehensive responses, and international best practices, further empowering NADMA (MNSC 1997, 2012). The main objective of NSC Directive No. 20 is to enhance

Fig. 10.7 The NSC directive no. 20

Malaysia's disaster preparedness, response, and recovery capabilities nationwide (Fig. 10.7). It seeks to establish a coordinated and efficient approach to managing disasters and providing relief to affected communities. The key provisions of NSC Directive No. 20 are outlined in Table 10.1. This directive is complemented by a few standard operating procedures (SOP) that refine on specific hazards, e.g. flood and tropical cyclone, industry, haze petrochemical, earthquake, and tsunami; that delineate the mechanisms, duties, and responsibilities of various agencies.

To meet the requirements stated in NSC Directive No. 20, which involves the coordination of all disaster-related activities, the Disaster Management and Relief Committee (DMRC) has been established at three hierarchical levels: Federal, State, and District (Fig. 10.8). All government agencies are tasked with various aspects of DRR. The initiation of DMRC implementation depends on a number of factors, including the nature and magnitude of the incident, as well as the extent of the affected area. The Federal Disaster Management and Relief Committee (FDMRC) takes the lead for the federal government in overseeing and addressing disasters at the national level. The FDMRC is chaired by the Minister in the Prime Minister's Department. In the event of a disaster, the FDMRC gathers at the NDOCC to oversee the unfolding situation and determine disaster mitigation strategies, search and rescue operations, and emergency relief efforts. This group is responsible for managing Level 3 disasters, which involve complex events spanning a wide area across two or more states.

The State Disaster Management and Relief Committee (SDMRC) oversee disasters at the state level, operating from the State Disaster Operation Control Centre (SDOCC). Chaired by the State Secretary, the State Disaster Management Committee

Table 10.1 Key features of NSC directive no. 20 (MNSC 1997, 2012)

No.	Key features	Description
1	Establishing a National Disaster Management Committee	The directive sets up a committee that includes pertinent government agencies, non-governmental organizations (NGOs), and other stakeholders to oversee national disaster management activities. In times of disaster response and relief efforts, this committee ensures enhanced coordination and communication among multiple agencies
2	Defining roles and responsibilities	The directive delineates the roles and obligations of government agencies and organizations engaged in disaster management and relief operations. It outlines their specific responsibilities across the different stages of disaster management, spanning preparation and mitigation to response and recovery
3	Disaster risk reduction and mitigation	The directive underscores the importance of implementing measures for reducing and mitigating disaster risks. It advocates for the promotion of various strategies to minimize vulnerability to hazards. These strategies include establishing early warning systems, improving infrastructure, fostering community-based disaster preparedness, and conducting public awareness campaigns
4	Resource mobilization and coordination	The directive highlights the significance of having ample resources and funds to strengthen disaster management efforts. It underscores the need for efficient coordination and collaboration among governmental bodies, non-governmental organizations (NGOs), and private sector entities to ensure the most effective allocation of resources during emergencies
5	National Disaster Relief Fund	The directive may involve establishing or utilizing a National Disaster Relief Fund with the aim of providing financial aid and assistance to communities affected by disasters, both in the immediate aftermath and during the recovery period

addresses Level 2 events, which may not extend beyond two or more districts but have the potential to cause substantial harm to life and property. The state-level Disaster Management team coordinates assistance at the state level, particularly in terms of assets, financial aid, and human resources for disaster management, directed toward the affected districts. The District Disaster Management and Relief Committee (DDMRC) operates from the District Disaster Operation Control Center (DDOCC) and addresses disasters at the district and village levels. The DDMRC manages village-level disasters with input from the village committee, as official disaster management is not established at the village level. The DDMRC, led by the District Officer, ensures coordinated actions, adequate assets, human resources, and media management. The District Office plays a crucial role as the primary implementing agency in Level 1 disasters, which are localized and manageable incidents, ensuring coordinated responses, sufficient assets and human resources, and effective communication with the media. Additionally, Level 1 disasters are not complex

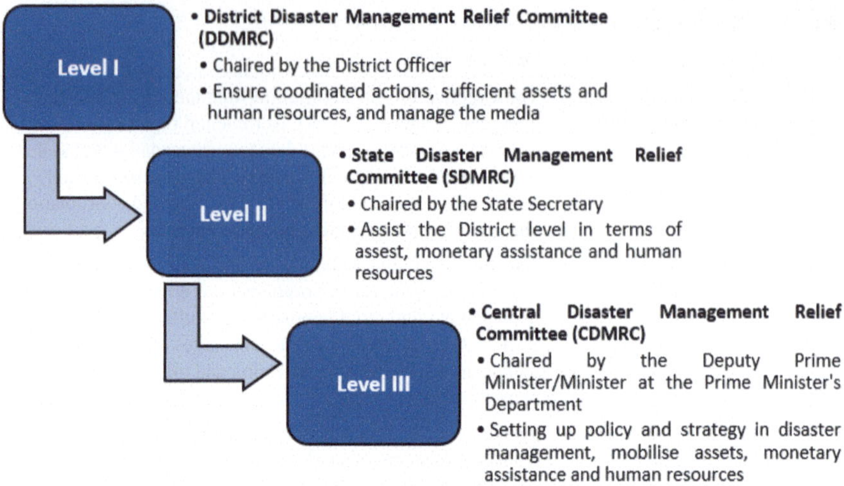

Fig. 10.8 Disaster management level in Malaysia (MNSC 1997, 2012)

and would only result in minimal damage to life and property. The District Level Authority has the capability to handle Level 1 incidents without or with limited external assistance.

The categorization of disaster severity outlined in NSC Directive No. 20 is evaluated at the district, state, and federal levels. It's crucial to emphasize that the criteria for assessing severity don't solely rely on the number of districts or states impacted by a disaster. The individual in charge at the On-Scene Command Post (OSCP), Disaster Operations Control Centre (DOCC), or the first responders present at the disaster sites may participate in collaborative discussions with other pertinent agencies to determine the appropriate activation level for a disaster. The selection of the On-Scene Commander (OSC) in the OSCP is identified based on the scale of the disaster. It may be the Officer in Charge of the Police District (OCPD), the Chief Police Officer (CPO), or the Director of Internal Security and Public Order of the Royal Malaysia Police.

In addition to NSC Directive No. 20, the Malaysia Civil Defence Force Act 1951 serves as the legislative framework for the establishment and operation of the APM. The Act outlines the functions and powers of the Civil Defence Force, which include conducting rescue operations, providing emergency medical services, distributing relief supplies, and coordinating disaster response efforts. It also stipulates provisions for the training and recruitment of personnel for the Civil Defence Force, ensuring that they are adequately prepared and equipped to respond to emergencies. Furthermore, the Act also empowers the Minister responsible for civil defense to make regulations for the better administration of the Act. It also outlines offenses and penalties for violations of the Act or its regulations. Overall, the Civil Defence Force Act 1951 provides the legal basis for the establishment and operation of the

Malaysian Civil Defence Force, outlining its functions, powers, organizational structure, and regulatory framework to ensure effective disaster management and response in Malaysia.

An example of disease control, the National Security Council Act 2016 (Act 776) enables greater jurisdiction to command and mobilize government and non-governmental entities to control the pandemic on a wider national scale. Act 776 with Prevention and Control of Infectious Diseases Act 988 (Act 342) helps Malaysia in response the global outbreak in January 2020 and the pandemic in March 2020 (Selvarajah et al. 2023). Another legislation is the Emergency (Essential Powers) (No. 2) Ordinance 2021. This ordinance is made pursuant to Article (2B) of Article 150 of the Federal Constitution in continuation of a Proclamation of Emergency issued by the King on January 11, 2021. This ordinance contains eighteen sections and one schedule that aims to provide the necessary powers required to ensure and maintain safety, economic life, and public order. This Ordinance was proclaimed for stricter movement control measures in the states that were most badly affected by the outbreak of COVID-19. Occupational Safety and Health Act 1994 on the other hand, is a comprehensive piece of legislation enacted in Malaysia to ensure the safety, health, and welfare of employees in workplaces. The OSHA 1994 applies to all sectors of employment in Malaysia, except for certain excluded categories like domestic workers and the armed forces. It covers various aspects of occupational safety and health to protect workers from workplace hazards. In Malaysian legislation, the Control of Industrial Major Accident Hazard (CIMAH) is a regulation created under the OSHA 1994. This regulation is called the Occupational Safety and Health Regulations (Control of Major Accident Hazards in Industry) 1996 or for short called CIMAH Regulation 1996.

This regulation, which is promulgated pursuant to Act 514, is applicable to all industrial activities, with the exception of nuclear installations, installations under the purview of the armed forces, vehicles or vessels engaged in the transportation of hazardous substances to or from an industrial site, as well as industrial activities that involve a quantity of hazardous substances that is equal to or less than ten percent of the threshold quantity of hazardous substances. This regulation outlines the policies and mechanisms of disaster management as a whole; the integrated roles and responsibilities of agencies involved in the stages before, during, and after a disaster occurs. This includes industrial disasters such as explosions, fires, pollution, and leakage of hazardous materials in factories or plants that process, produce, and store hazardous materials. In this regard, related agencies and local authorities can help implement early awareness and education programs related to disaster management and mobilize energy in disaster risk reduction efforts. The Environmental Quality Act, EQA 1974 (Act 127) is a significant piece of legislation in Malaysia aimed at protecting and enhancing the environment that was enacted to provide for the prevention, abatement, control of pollution, and enhancement of the environment. The primary objective of the EQA is to safeguard the environment by regulating and controlling activities that may cause pollution and degradation.

This study has reviewed the relevant elements of the selected key instruments discussed and developed a synthesis matrix coverage of disaster management instruments (refer to Table 10.2). The objective of this matrix is to assess the presence of each component within the disaster management cycle depicted in the documents. It has been observed that the NSC Directive No. 20: National Policy and Mechanism on Disaster Management and Relief, alongside the Malaysia Civil Defence Force Act 1951, are utilized to address natural hazards. On the other hand, the Emergency (Emergency Powers) (No. 2) Ordinance 2021 mainly focuses on matters related to national security, power, and emergency, as illustrated in Table 10.2, where only two sections seem appropriate for disaster response. The analysis found that, CIMAH 1996 and the Environmental Quality Act, EQA 1974 (Act 127), are employed for managing human-induced hazards (industrial disaster related) and environmental management. It is worth noting that disaster prevention and disaster mitigation received limited coverage. Nonetheless, all five documents address disaster response, with the NSC Directive No. 20 demonstrating that the majority of its Articles fall within this category. This is followed by disaster preparedness where many regulations under CIMAH 1996 are listed within this component. The NSC Directive No. 20 has been shown to cover all phases of the disaster management cycle, as does the Malaysia Civil Defence Force Act 1951 and CIMAH 1996, except for disaster mitigation.

Undoubtedly, the NSC Directive No. 20 serves as an efficient tool for disaster management and relief operations. However, its scope concerning disaster prevention instruments is somewhat constrained, hindering the achievement of a fully comprehensive disaster management approach. This limitation calls for the integration of proactive measures, including the establishment of permanent solutions aimed toward disaster risk reduction. Often, disaster management in Malaysia becomes more reactive rather than because in many situations the response or reaction is only after the disaster has occurred. This shows that Malaysia requires a comprehensive approach that covers all aspects of the disaster management cycle and includes an appropriate balance of each component of prevention, mitigation, preparedness, response, and recovery.

10.4 Conclusion

In conclusion, the review of disaster legislation in Malaysia highlights the country's dedication to proactive and adaptable governance when faced with unexpected obstacles. Malaysia has established a comprehensive legal framework that demonstrates the country's commitment to reducing the adverse effects of disasters on the environment, infrastructure, and its people. Given the dynamic nature of hazards, national resilience legislative initiatives create the basis for efficient disaster recovery and management.

Table 10.2 Synthesis matrix coverage of disaster management instruments

Disaster management/ instruments	Disaster prevention	Disaster mitigation	Disaster preparedness	Disaster response	Disaster recovery
NSC directive no. 20: National Policy and Mechanism on Disaster Management and Relief	• Article 9(18)(a) • Article 9(18)(d)	• Article 9(18)(c) • Article 10(19)(b) • Article 11(20)(a)	• Article 10(19)(d) • Article 10(19)(f) • Article 12(21) • Article 13(22) • Article 14(23)	• Article 7(15)(a) • Article 15(24)(a)(i) • Article 15(24)(a)(ii) • Article 15(24)(a)(iii) • Article 16(25)(a) • Article 16(25)(b) • Article 16(25)(c) • Article 17(32) • Article 18(33)	• Article 26(45)
Malaysia Civil Defense Force Act 1951	• Section 2B(g)		• Section 2B(d) • Section 2B(h) • Section 2B(q) • Section 2B(r)	• Section 10.2B(b) • Section 10.2B(j) • Section 10.2B(k) • Section 10.2B(s)	• Section 10.2B(l) • Section 10.2B(n) • Section 10.2B(o) • Section 8(1)
Emergency (Essential Powers) (No. 2) Ordinance 2021				• Section 7 • Section 8	
CIMAH 1996	• Regulation 21(1) • Regulation 21(2)		• Regulation 7(1)(b) • Regulation 7(2)(a) • Regulation 7(2)(b) • Regulation 10(a) • Regulation 10(b)(i) • Regulation 10(b)(ii) • Regulation 18(1) • Regulation 18(2) • Regulation 18(3) • Regulation 19 • Regulation 20	• Regulation 22(2) • Regulation 23(a) • Regulation 23(b)	• Regulation 22(4)

(continued)

Table 10.2 (continued)

Disaster management/ instruments	Disaster prevention	Disaster mitigation	Disaster preparedness	Disaster response	Disaster recovery
Environmental Quality Act, EQA 1974 (Act 127)	• The Environmental Quality Act 1974 (Act 127) in Malaysia primarily focuses on environmental protection, management, and pollution control. It provides provisions for preventing and controlling pollution, managing waste, and conserving the environment • Example, section 3 empowers the Director General to take necessary actions in case of pollution emergencies to prevent or minimize harm to the environment, public health, or property. While not explicitly focused on disaster prevention, such emergency measures can help mitigate the environmental impacts of disasters and prevent them from escalating into larger-scale crises	• The EQA 1974 aims to prevents and mitigate environmental pollution and degradation, which can help reduce the likelihood and severity of certain types of disasters, such as chemical spills, air pollution-related health crisis, or water contamination events	• Environmental impact assessment (EIA) procedures mandated by the EQA 1974 require developers to assess and mitigate potential environmental impacts of their projects. These assessments can help identify and prepare for environmental risks that may contribute to disaster, ensuring that mitigation measures are in place before disasters occur	• In the event of environmental agencies or disasters, authorities can utilize the powers granted under the EQA 1974 to respond to pollution incidents, such as chemical spills or industrial accidents, thereby minimizing environmental damage and protection public health	• While the EQA 1974 does not have specific provisions related to disaster recovery, the Act aims to protect and conserve the environment, which indirectly supports recovery efforts post-disaster. Restoration and rehabilitation of the environment following a disaster can be guided by the principles and objectives outlined in the EQA 1974

Source NSC Directive No. 20: National Policy and Mechanism on Disaster Management and Relief; Malaysia Civil Defense Force Act 1951; Emergency (Essential Powers) (No. 2) Ordinance 2021; CIMAH 1996; Environmental Quality Act, EQA 1974 (Act 127)

This scoping review has described several aspects of disaster law, which include strategies for coordination of response, preparedness, recovery, and relief and assistance. With its adaptive approach, Malaysia is well positioned to deal with emerging threats effectively and efficiently, as it is guided by insights gained from previous incidents.

Although progress has been made in disaster legislation, continued efforts to improve and revise this legislation are essential to proactively address the ever-changing nature of threats. Continuous cooperation among government entities, non-governmental organizations, and the public is essential to guarantee the effectiveness of disaster response mechanisms.

Basically, disaster legislation in Malaysia functions as more than a mere legal structure; it embodies the nation's dedication to protecting its people and fostering a resilient society equipped to deal with the complexities presented by both natural and man-made disasters. Given the dynamic environment in which Malaysia operates, its disaster legislation continues to serve as a fundamental component in creating a sustainable and protected future for all.

References

Affandi E, Ng TF, Pereira JJ, Ahmad F, Banks VJ (2023) Revalidation technique on landslide susceptibility modelling: an approach to local level disaster risk management in Kuala Lumpur, Malaysia. Appl Sci 13:768. https://doi.org/10.3390/app13020768

Centre for Excellence-Malaysia Disaster Management Reference Handbook (CFE-DMHA) (2022) https://www.cfe-dmha.org/Publications/Disaster-Management-Reference-Handbooks

Department of Mineral and Geoscience Malaysia (JMG) (2022) Laporan kajian bencana geologi banjir puing 2022 Sungai Kupang, Baling, Kedah. https://www.nrecc.gov.my/ms-my/pustakamedia/Penerbitan/Laporan%20Kajian%20Bencana%20Geologi%20Banjir%20Puing%202022%20di%20Sungai%20Kupang%20Kedah.pdf

Department of Mineral and Geoscience Malaysia (JMG) (2023) Laporan kajian bencana geologi tanah runtuh di Father's Organic Farm (Jalan Batang Kali—Genting Highlands). http://blog.jmg.gov.my/2023-01-12-01-29-07

Federal Government Gazette, Emergency (Essential Powers) (No. 2) Ordinance 202

Federal Subsidiary Legislation, Occupational Safety and Health Act 1994 [ACT 514], Occupational Safety and Health Regulations (Control of Major Accident Hazards in Industry) 1996

FMT Reporters (2023, November 30) Govt to introduce special law for disaster management. Free Malaysia Today (FMT). https://www.freemalaysiatoday.com/category/nation/2023/11/30/govt-to-introduce-special-law-for-disaster-management/

Government of Malaysia (2016) Laws of Malaysia (Act 221) Malaysia Civil Defence Force Act 1951 (Revision 2016)

Laws of Malaysia Act 127 Environmental Quality Act, EQA (1974)

Laws of Malaysia Act 221, Malaysia Civil Defence Force Act (1953)

Laws of Malaysia Act 514, Occupational Safety and Health Act (1994)

MNSC, Policy and Mechanism of Disaster Management in Malaysia (1997) Malaysia National Security Council, Prime Minister Department

MNSC, Policy and Mechanism of Disaster Management in Malaysia (2012) Malaysia National Security Council, Prime Minister Department

Muhammad Ikhwan MS, Nazmi AA, Chandramalar K, Nur Za'Imah Z, Rosliza AM, Suhainizam MS (2023) Application of Sendai Framework for disaster risk reduction in food security during flood disaster in Malaysia: a narrative review. Malays J Med Health Sci 19(4):332–341
MyGovernment (2021). https://www.malaysia.gov.my/portal/index.
National Disaster Management Agency (NADMA) (2021) National risk register. Prime Minister's Department of Malaysia, Putrajaya
Rosmadi HS, Ahmed MF, Mokhtar MB, Lim CK (2023) Reviewing challenges of flood risk management in Malaysia. Water 15:2390. https://doi.org/10.3390/w15132390
Selvarajah S, Nordin AA, Kunusagaran, MSJMNS, Saad N, Ahmad Shauki NI (2023) Country case study: Malaysia knowledge generation and exchange related to preparedness and response to the COVID-19 outbreak. https://thedocs.worldbank.org/en/doc/87b5ed4c9067a8838e783c9ad68a4829-0070012023/original/Malaysia-case-study.pdf
Sharir K, Roslee R (2023) Peta ketumpatan fizikal bagi menentukan unsur berisiko banjir di kawasan Kota Belud, Sabah, Malaysia. Sains Malaysiana 52(7):1939–1954
Siti Nurkhalidah H, Bery AA, Abir IA, Lestari W, Akingboye AS (2023) Landslides susceptibility mapping of Penang Island, Malaysia, using remote sensing and multi-geophysical methods. Earth Sci Res J 27(2):93–107
United Nations of the International Strategy for Disaster Reduction (UNISDR) (2006) Developing early warning systems: a checklist. In: Document from the third international conference on early warning (EWC III), Bonn, 27–29 March. https://www.unisdr.org/2006/ppew/info-resources/ewc3/checklist/English.pdf
United Nations Office for Disaster Risk Reduction (UNDRR) (2020) Disaster risk reduction in Malaysia: status report 2020. United Nations Office for Disaster Risk Reduction (UNDRR), Regional Office for Asia and the Pacific, Bangkok, Thailand. https://www.undrr.org/publication/disaster-risk-reduction-malaysia-status-report-2020

Chapter 11
Building a Nation of Lifesavers

How Hwa Teong and Xuan En Constance Ng

Abstract Singapore, a vibrant island city-state in Southeast Asia, may seem like a tranquil haven amid the hustle and bustle of the modern world. However, behind the scenes, the city-state is perpetually poised to address a variety of hazards through its robust disaster management framework. The Singapore Civil Defence Force (SCDF) serves as the national focal point for disaster management, coordinating with multiple stakeholders and partners to implement a comprehensive Whole-of-Society and Whole-of-Government response strategy. This multi-tiered framework includes government agencies, non-governmental organizations, and the community. The SCDF plays a pivotal role, orchestrating efforts with other agencies and the community to ensure a cohesive and effective response, aiming to realize the bold vision of "A Nation of Lifesavers."

Keywords Disaster legislation · Disaster management · Whole-of-Government · Civil defence · Disaster preparedness

11.1 Introduction

11.1.1 Disaster Landscape in Singapore

Despite being geographically situated in the world's most disaster-prone region, Singapore lies on the border of the Pacific Ring of Fire, which grants the island city-state greater immunity from major natural disasters such as earthquakes and volcanic eruptions which typically threaten the region with catastrophic impacts.

However, the country is not completely insulated from disaster risk. Singapore remains highly susceptible to climate-induced disasters such as floods and droughts. Floods in Singapore are usually a result of heavy rainfall, high tides, and drainage problems, especially in low-lying areas. During the northeast monsoon season,

H. H. Teong · X. E. C. Ng (✉)
Singapore Civil Defense, Singapore, Singapore
e-mail: constance2851@gmail.com; zohra_abdul_rahim@scdf.gov.sg

Y. Cui and R. Shaw (eds.), *Disaster Law*, Disaster Risk Reduction,
https://doi.org/10.1007/978-981-97-7374-9_11

monsoon surges bring about heavier rainstorms, in addition to the already abundant rainfall Singapore receives due to our tropical climate.[1] In recent years, Singapore has experienced more frequent and intense rainfall, with the total annual rainfall increasing at an average rate of 67mm per decade from 1980 to 2019.[2]

Coupled with the predicted sea level rise in the future, flooding and inundation are likely to pose immediate threats to our low-lying island nation. Much of our land lies only 15m above the Singapore Height Datum and approximately 30% of the island lies less than 5m above the Singapore Height Datum, rendering at least one-third of our country vulnerable to such hydrometeorological hazards.[3]

Singapore's significant industrial and petrochemical facilities pose potential hazards such as fires, chemical spills, and explosions. Despite the strict regulations in place to minimize the likelihood of these events, their potential impact on human lives, the economy, and the environment is severe and far-reaching.

In addition, epidemics and pandemics continue to remain as significant risks to our population as well, as illustrated by the SARS outbreak in 2003, the COVID-19 pandemic in 2020 and the persisting prevalence of vector-borne diseases.

These vulnerabilities are expected to increase due to increasing physical exposure and various demographic sensitivities associated with population growth, and the social and economic stratification of the populace.[4] Hence, the burgeoning threats posed by these disasters to the people, economy and infrastructure in our country demand our immediate attention to mitigate the adversities.

11.1.2 Disaster Law and Its Importance for Singapore's Disaster Management

In spite of the existing disaster risks faced, Singapore ranked 191 out of 191 countries in the 2024 Index for Risk Management (INFORM) relative ranking, marking Singapore as the lowest risk of all countries surveyed.[5] INFORM evaluates risk across 3 dimensions: (1) Hazards & Exposure, (2) Vulnerability, and (3) Lack of Coping Capacity. The second and third dimensions consider population factors that mitigate against or exacerbate the risks, such as the strength of individuals and households relative to a crisis and institutional strength respectively.

---

[1] National Library Board Singapore, "Major Floods in Singapore," n.d., https://www.nlb.gov.sg/main/article-detail?cmsuuid=51f13462-3584-4ae9-b2c6-ce72b0775c72.

[2] "Impact of Climate Change in Singapore," n.d., https://www.nccs.gov.sg/singapores-climate-action/impact-of-climate-change-in-singapore/.

[3] "Impact of Climate Change in Singapore."

[4] Chow et al. (2016).

[5] "INFORM Risk—Results and Data," n.d., https://drmkc.jrc.ec.europa.eu/inform-index/INFORM-Risk/Results-and-data/moduleId/1782/id/469/controller/Admin/action/Results.

Singapore's low-risk scores, especially in the "vulnerability" and the "lack of coping capacity" dimensions, are a testament to the comprehensive legal and operational frameworks in place that serve as a vital instrument for the necessary actions to be taken promptly, be it before, during or after a disaster. The legislative measures offer specific guidance to various stakeholders, including the government and the populace, whereas the operational frameworks assign certain duties and responsibilities to individuals and communities, compelling them to act promptly when required.

The key principle undergirding Singapore's approach toward disaster management is inter-agency coordination, as evidenced from the Whole-of Government Integrated Risk Management (WOG-IRM) framework adopted.[6] It incorporates provisions for disaster response, including medical emergencies and mass fatality management, alongside outlining an integrated approach to disaster risk reduction (DRR) across sectors and ministries.[7]

While the operational frameworks are not legally binding, existing disaster laws which tend to address a single threat of hazard, such as the Civil Defence Act and the Infectious Diseases Act, maintain the legal obligation of certain agencies and lend them the legal authority to mobilize resources and to carry out the actions required of them by the operational frameworks.

11.2 Governance Provisions Before a Disaster

11.2.1 Disaster Law

The main legislation supporting emergency preparedness and disaster management activities in Singapore are as follows.

11.2.1.1 Civil Defense Act 1986

This Act outlines the structure, establishment, and management of SCDF. It covers the establishment, upkeep, and regulation of a civil defense force, as well as the

[6] Jonathan Ng and Centre for Strategic Futures, Prime Minister's Office Singapore, "Whole-of-Government Integrated Risk Management in Singapore," *International Risk Governance Council*, https://irgc.org/wp-content/uploads/2018/09/6.-Jonathan-NG_IRGC-Beijing-2013_WOG-IRM-in-Singapore.pdf.

[7] "Singapore Disaster Management Reference Handbook 2017," *Resilience Library, IFRC* (Center for Excellence in Disaster Management & Humanitarian Assistance, May 2017), accessed January 13, 2024, https://www.google.com/search?q=cfe-dm+2017&oq=cfe-dm+2017&gs_lcrp=EgZjaHJvbWUyBggAEEUYOdIBCDI0NDZqMGo0qAIAsAIA&sourceid=chrome&ie=UTF-8.

execution of the force's duties and authority during national emergencies, and related matters.[8]

More notably, sections 102 and 103 of the Act provide for the declaration of state of civil defense emergency and grants the SCDF special powers during an emergency respectively. The Act allows for the Minister to declare a state of civil defense emergency in any part or district in Singapore when deemed appropriate. During which, the Commissioner is legally authorized, under this Act, to execute a series of actions to support operations according to his discretion.[9]

11.2.1.2 Fire Safety Act 1993

This Act establishes the legal framework for imposing fire safety standards on commercial and industrial properties and mandates the participation of the management and owners of these properties in fire emergency preparedness.

11.2.1.3 Civil Defense Shelter Act 1997

This Act provides a legal framework to mandate the provision of civil defense shelters in all new houses, flats, and appropriate buildings owned by statutory boards. It also allows for the designation of specific areas within buildings as civil defense shelters for individuals seeking refuge during a state of emergency and regulates the use of these shelters.[10]

11.2.1.4 Infectious Diseases Act 1976

This Act includes provisions for the prevention and management of infectious diseases. It covers the notification of specific diseases, grants authority to the Director-General of Health to mandate medical examinations or treatment, and to restrict public gatherings that may contribute to the spread of disease. The Act also allows the Minister of Health to declare a public health emergency and by extension, demarcate restricted areas and to prohibit or restrict movement.[11]

---

[8] "Civil Defence Act 1986—Singapore Statutes Online," October 28, 2022, https://sso.agc.gov.sg/Act/CDA1986.

[9] "Civil Defence Act 1986—Singapore Statutes Online."

[10] "Civil Defence Shelter Act 1997—Singapore Statutes Online," December 31, 2021, https://sso.agc.gov.sg/Act/CDSA1997?ValidDate=20211231&ProvIds=P11-#P11.

[11] "Infectious Diseases Act 1976—Singapore Statutes Online," May 2, 2023, https://sso.agc.gov.sg/Act/IDA1976?ProvIds=P13-#pr17A.

11.2.2 Operational Disaster Management Frameworks

11.2.2.1 Whole-of-Government Integrated Risk Management (WOG-IRM)

In the wake of the 2003 SARS outbreak, the WOG-IRM policy framework was developed in 2004 to identify risks and to implement a process to analyze and manage said risks.[12] The WOG-IRM approach seeks to improve risk awareness within the government and among the public. It integrates medical response systems during emergencies, mass fatality management, legislation for reducing risks related to fire safety and hazardous materials, coordination of police operations, management of information and media during crises, and the involvement of public–private partnerships in emergency preparedness.[13]

The framework operates both in peacetime and during national emergencies. Four key agencies constitute the core disaster management structure: (1) Strategic Planning Office (SPO), (2) Homefront Crisis Ministerial Committee (HCMC), (3) National Security Coordination Secretariat (NSCS), and (4) Ministry of Finance (MOF).[14]

The HCMC is headed by the Ministry of Home Affairs (MHA). In peacetime, MHA is the primary policy-making governmental body for safety and security. During national emergencies, MHA typically assumes the role of supervisory authority, although there are instances in which the Ministry of Health (MOH) gains authority such as a public health emergency.[15]

11.2.2.2 Operation Civil Emergency Plan (Ops CE Plan)

The Operation Civil Emergency Plan (Ops CE Plan) is under the purview of the SCDF, which is the agency responsible for managing and activating this plan in the event of large-scale civil and natural disasters.[16] The Ops CE Plan is the national plan developed to address emergencies that require multi-agency response such as structural collapse, aircraft incidents, hazardous materials (HazMat) incidents, terrorism,

---

[12] "Singapore Disaster Management Reference Handbook 2017."

[13] "Singapore Disaster Management Reference Handbook 2021," *Center for Excellence in Disaster Management and Humanitarian Assistance* (Center for Excellence in Disaster Management and Humanitarian Assistance, September 2021), accessed January 11, 2024, https://www.cfe-dmha.org/LinkClick.aspx?fileticket=DW0AlEU959M%3d&portalid=0.

[14] National Security Coordination Secretariat (1826) *Days: A Diary of Resolve: Securing Singapore Since 9/11* (National Security Coordination Secretariat, Singapore 2006).

[15] "Singapore Disaster Management Reference Handbook 2021."

[16] "Singapore Disaster Management Reference Handbook 2021."

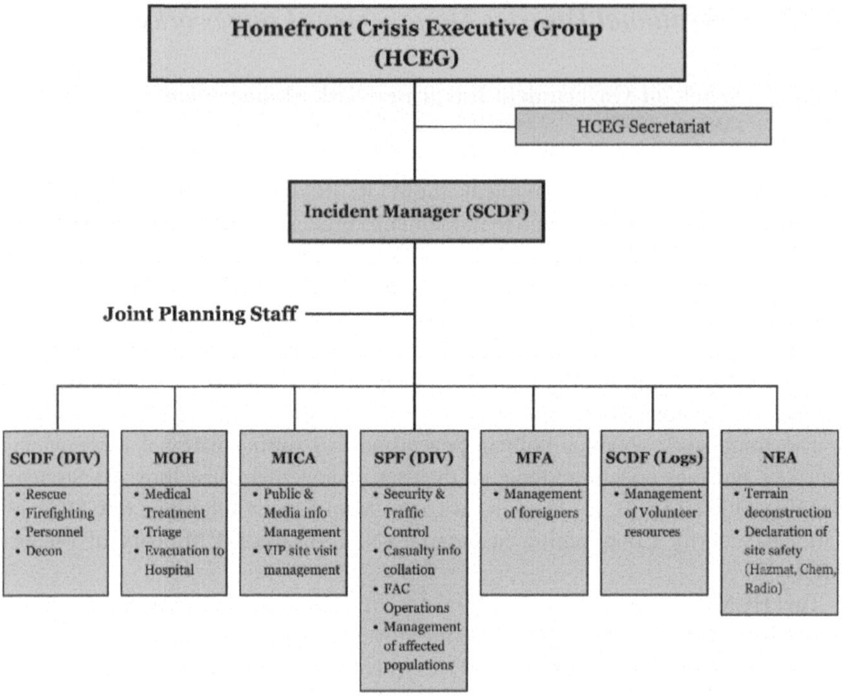

Fig. 11.1 Singapore Whole-of-Government Framework for Incident Management (*Source* Constance Ng, modified from Singapore Civil Defence Force[19])

major fires, and acts of terrorism involving chemical, biological, radiological, and/or explosive (CBRE) agents.[17]

As the Incident Manager (IM), the SCDF will command, control and coordinate the entire operations by directing all response forces, with the support of a group of specialists from various government agencies organized into the Joint Planning Staff (JPS).[18] The SCDF will be guided by the Homefront Crisis Executive Group (HCEG) (Fig. 11.1).

The Ops CE Plan has proven to be more than a sound theoretical framework, through its successful execution and management of real-life disasters on multiple occasions. On 20 April 2004, part of the Nicoll Highway, a major road in Singapore,

[17] Singapore Civil Defence Force, "Emergency Response in Singapore," Slide show, International Federation of Red Cross and Red Crescent Societies, October 2012, https://www.rcrc-resilience-southeastasia.org/wp-content/uploads/2018/01/2012-SCDF-Emergency-Response-in-Singapore-powerpoint-presentation.pdf.

[18] Singapore Civil Defence Force, "Singapore's National Civil Emergency Management Structure," Slide show, Asian Disaster Reduction Center, 2006, https://www.adrc.asia/acdr/2006seoul/documents/006b_country_presen/Singapore.pdf.

[19] Singapore Civil Defence Force, "Singapore's National Civil Emergency Management Structure."

Fig. 11.2 SCDF Command Post set up to manage the Nicoll Highway rescue operations in 2004[23]

collapsed and caved into a subway line tunnel that was under construction.[20] As outlined in the Ops CE Plan, SCDF functioned as the IM, and the JPS, such as the Land Transport Authority (LTA) and the Building and Construction Authority (BCA), were activated to support the operations.[21] The four-day rescue operation saved three lives and uncovered three bodies (Fig. 11.2).[22]

On 28 September 2011, the Ops CE Plan was implemented to manage a fire that broke out at an oil refinery on the offshore island of Pulau Bukom. The situation, described as "complex and multi-dimensional", was unprecedented and required joint efforts to tackle.[24] The JPS, such as the Public Utilities Board (PUB), the National Environmental Agency (NEA) and the Maritime and Port Authority of Singapore (MPA), were activated to assist SCDF by providing specialist advice and ensuring proper execution of the orders by their respective ground forces (Fig. 11.3).[25]

---

[20] Singapore Civil Defence Force, "Day-to-Day Operations: Nicoll Highway and Other Incidents," *Rescue 995* (Singapore Civil Defence Force, 2015), accessed February 14, 2024, https://www.scdf.gov.sg/docs/default-source/scdf-library/r995/volume_1_issue_2(1).pdf.

[21] Singapore Civil Defence Force, "Emergency Response in Singapore."

[22] Singapore Civil Defence Force, "Day-to-Day Operations: Nicoll Highway and Other Incidents."

[23] Singapore Civil Defence Force, "Emergency Response in Singapore."

[24] National Library Board Singapore, "Pulau Bukom Fire (2011)," n.d., https://www.nlb.gov.sg/main/article-detail?cmsuuid=e33470da-288f-4487-b54f-4c89fd0bd2d4.

[25] Singapore Civil Defence Force, "Emergency Response in Singapore."

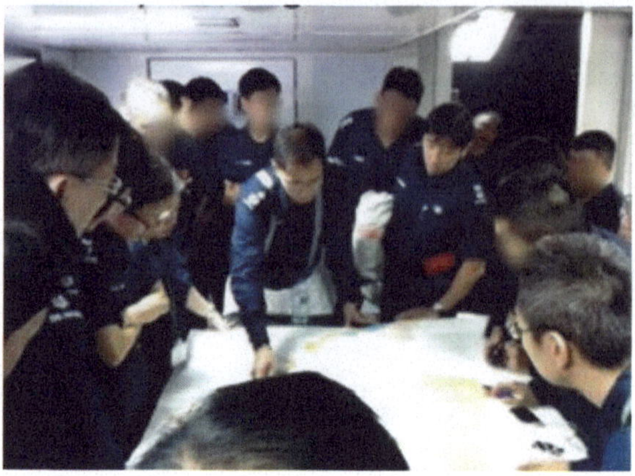

Fig. 11.3 SCDF command post set up to manage the Pulau Bukom fire operations in 2011[26]

11.3 Implementation During a Disaster

11.3.1 Activation of Emergency Powers

11.3.1.1 Coordination of Government Agencies

Singapore's disaster response strategy is built upon a multi-tiered framework that involves government agencies, non-governmental organizations, and the community. The existing frameworks are supported by our disaster laws, which provide the legal framework for relevant agencies to take necessary action.

During times of crises, MHA leads at the strategic level of incident management via the Homefront Crisis Management System (HCMS). The HCMS provides a ministerial committee accountable for all crisis situations in Singapore (Fig. 11.4).[27]

11.3.2 SCDF's Role in Disaster Response

The SCDF has a pivotal role within Singapore's inter-agency framework, coordinating response efforts with other agencies to ensure a cohesive and well-organized approach. In both peacetime and in times of disasters. With the legal framework outlined in the Civil Defence Act which allows for the mobilization and deployment of the SCDF, the Force remains ready to handle crises at national, regional, and international levels.

---

[26] Singapore Civil Defence Force, "Emergency Response in Singapore."

[27] "Singapore Disaster Management Reference Handbook 2021."

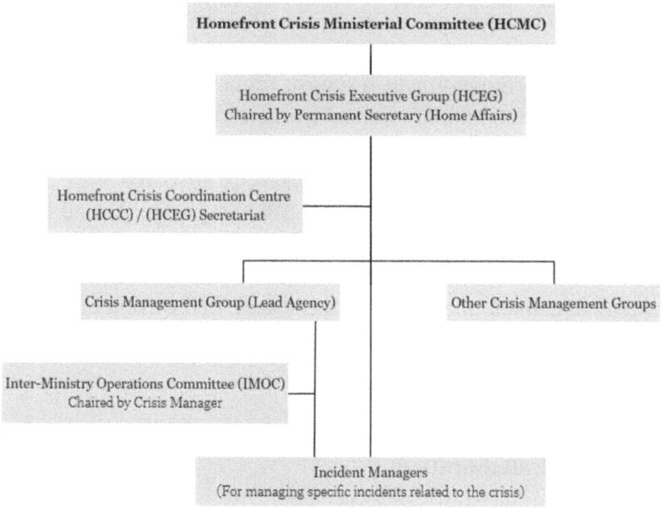

Fig. 11.4 Structure of the homefront crisis management system (*Source* Constance Ng, modified from National Security Coordination Secretariat[28])

11.3.2.1 Internal Roles and Responsibilities

The SCDF has specialized teams dedicated to different types of emergencies, such as the Disaster Assistance and Rescue Team (DART) for Urban Search and Rescue (USAR) operations and the CBRE teams for HazMat incidents. With well-trained personnel, the SCDF can respond to most emergencies and hazards, including firefighting and rescue operations, emergency medical services, and HazMat management.

To facilitate timely warnings, the SCDF maintains and operates the Public Warning System (PWS), consisting of sirens distributed across the island to alert the public of imminent threats to lives and property. Additionally, other broadcast systems like the SMS Public Alert System and the SGSecure mobile application are accessible during emergencies. These warning systems complement the upcoming nationwide sensor network, which monitors atmospheric anomalies that could impact public health and safety.

11.3.2.2 Promoting Inter-Agency Collaboration

During peacetime, the SCDF collaborates with other agencies such as the MOH, the Ministry of Defence (MINDEF), and the Singapore Police Force (SPF) to ensure a unified and effective response to complex emergencies. National-level

[28] National Security Coordination Secretariat, 1826 *Days: A Diary of Resolve: Securing Singapore Since 9/11* (National Security Coordination Secretariat, Singapore 2006).

emergency exercises are carried out to assess the readiness of relevant agencies in addressing different scenarios. First initiated in 1997, Exercise Northstar aims to validate the whole-of-government response framework and enhance emergency response and coordination among national agencies in Singapore. The most recent Exercise Northstar, held in March 2023, simulated a terrorist attack on various oil tanks and petrochemical pipelines. The exercise involved over 300 personnel from different agencies, including the SCDF, SPF, Singapore Armed Forces, MOH, Maritime and Port Authority of Singapore (MPA), and private companies. These exercises promoting effective interagency communication and coordination are vital for successful management of actual complex crises. In the event of a major disaster, the SCDF will activate the Ops CE Plan, and take on the role of IM, delegating roles and responsibilities to the involved agencies.

11.3.2.3 Regional Collaborations

At the regional level, the SCDF is Singapore's national focal point for disaster management. As a member of the ASEAN Committee on Disaster Management (ACDM), Singapore, often represented by SCDF, works with fellow ASEAN Member States to establish an effective and efficient approach to disaster management, covering prevention, mitigation, preparedness, response, recovery, and global leadership. This involves sharing resources, exchanging knowledge, and conducting joint exercises to improve disaster management capabilities. This collaboration enables the sharing of expertise and resources with ASEAN partners, enhances capacities, and fosters regional stability and resilience. It also reinforces the region's collective capacity to address large-scale disasters that transcend national borders.

11.3.2.4 Community Involvement

SCDF recognizes that the public plays a fundamental role in Singapore's preparedness as well. Since 2016, the SCDF has been working toward a Transformation 2025 vision of cultivating *A Nation of Lifesavers*. To realize this objective, the SCDF has been actively involving the community in various public education programs aimed at strengthening the nation's overall resilience and emergency preparedness.

As the decade of transformation is nearing its close, SCDF is already looking forward to launching its next phase of Transformation 2030 with initiatives that will capitalize on the strong foundation of community partnership SCDF has built.

11.4 Conclusion

In sum, Singapore has established a robust framework of disaster law and regulations to effectively address and respond to various disaster threats. Multiple national-level stakeholders play an important part in the management of emergencies and disasters in Singapore and are elemental in supporting disaster response and preparedness. Of which, the SCDF is the main agency in Singapore overseeing disaster response and management. The nation's multi-agency approach, supported by comprehensive legal and operational frameworks, has allowed for effective and efficient responses in times of need. Singapore's success in disaster response has also allowed the country to take a leading role in regional and international collaborations to further enhance its preparedness and response capabilities.

References

"Civil Defence Act 1986—Singapore Statutes Online,". Accessed 28 Oct 2022. https://sso.agc.gov.sg/Act/CDA1986

"Civil Defence Shelter Act 1997—Singapore Statutes Online,". Accessed 31 Dec 2021. https://sso.agc.gov.sg/Act/CDSA1997?ValidDate=20211231&ProvIds=P11-#P11-.

"Impact of Climate Change in Singapore," n.d. https://www.nccs.gov.sg/singapores-climate-action/impact-of-climate-change-in-singapore/

"Infectious Diseases Act 1976—Singapore Statutes Online," May 2, 2023. https://sso.agc.gov.sg/Act/IDA1976?ProvIds=P13-#pr17A

"INFORM Risk—Results and Data," (n.d.) https://drmkc.jrc.ec.europa.eu/inform-index/INFORM-Risk/Results-and-data/moduleId/1782/id/469/controller/Admin/action/Results.

National Library Board Singapore. "Major Floods in Singapore," (n.d.) https://www.nlb.gov.sg/main/article-detail?cmsuuid=51f13462-3584-4ae9-b2c6-ce72b0775c72

National Library Board Singapore. "Pulau Bukom Fire (2011)," (n.d.) https://www.nlb.gov.sg/main/article-detail?cmsuuid=e33470da-288f-4487-b54f-4c89fd0bd2d4

National Security Coordination Secretariat (2006) 1826 days: a diary of resolve: securing Singapore Since 9/11. National Security Coordination Secretariat, Singapore, 2006

Ng, Jonathan and Centre for Strategic Futures, Prime Minister's Office Singapore. "Whole-of-government integrated risk management in Singapore." International risk governance council. 2013. https://irgc.org/wp-content/uploads/2018/09/6.-Jonathan-NG_IRGC-Beijing-2013_WOG-IRM-in-Singapore.pdf

Singapore Civil Defence Force (2024) "Day-to-Day Operations: Nicoll Highway and Other Incidents." Rescue 995. Singapore Civil Defence Force, 2015. Accessed 14 Feb 2024. https://www.scdf.gov.sg/docs/default-source/scdf-library/r995/volume_1_issue_2(1).pdf

Singapore Civil Defence Force (2012) "Emergency Response in Singapore." Slide show. International federation of red cross and red crescent societies, October 2012. https://www.rcrc-resilience-southeastasia.org/wp-content/uploads/2018/01/2012-SCDF-Emergency-Response-in-Singapore-powerpoint-presentation.pdf

Singapore Civil Defence Force (2006) "Singapore's National Civil Emergency Management Structure." Slide show. Asian Disaster Reduction Center, 2006. https://www.adrc.asia/acdr/2006seoul/documents/006b_country_presen/Singapore.pdf

"Singapore Disaster Management Reference Handbook." (2024) Resilience Library, IFRC. Center for excellence in disaster management & humanitarian assistance, May 2017. Accessed 13

Jan 2024. https://www.google.com/search?q=cfe-dm+2017&oq=cfe-dm+2017&gs_lcrp=EgZjaHJvbWUyBggAEEUYOdIBCDI0NDZqMGo0qAIAsAIA&sourceid=chrome&ie=UTF-8
"Singapore Disaster Management Reference Handbook 2021." (2024) Center for excellence in disaster management and humanitarian assistance. Center for excellence in disaster management and humanitarian assistance, September 2021. Accessed 11 Jan 2024. https://www.cfe-dmha.org/LinkClick.aspx?fileticket=DW0AlEU959M%3d&portalid=0

Chapter 12
Disaster Law in Indonesia

Ariyaningsih, Riyan Benny Sukmara, Rizqi Bachtiar, Arsyad A. Iriansyah, and Rajib Shaw

Abstract In response to the 2004 Aceh tsunami, the Indonesian government issued Presidential Regulation No. 83/2005 establishing the National Coordinating Agency for Disaster Management. Following that, Indonesia has focused on disaster risk reduction. Furthermore, the government implemented Disaster Management Law No. 24/2007, followed by Presidential Regulation No. 8 on the National Disaster Management Agency (BNPB) in 2008. The legislation provides scope for establishment of disaster departments in local governments and identifies focal person for DRR (Disaster Risk Reduction) in the local level. Given the importance of understanding disaster legislation, the chapter will elaborate on some of the key aspects of disaster legislation in Indonesia.

Keywords BNPB · Disaster law · Disaster legislation · Indonesia · National disaster management agency

Ariyaningsih (✉) · R. Shaw
Graduate School of Media and Governance, Keio University, Tokyo, Japan
e-mail: ariyaningsih@lecturer.itk.ac.id

Ariyaningsih
Department of Urban Planning, Institut Teknologi Kalimantan, Kalimantan, Indonesia

R. B. Sukmara
Department of Civil Engineering, National Central University, Taoyuan City, Taiwan

Department of Civil Engineering at Institut Teknologi Kalimantan, Kalimantan, Indonesia

R. Bachtiar
School of Politics and International Studies, University of Leeds, Leeds, UK

Department of Governmental Science, Brawijaya University, Jawa Timur, Indonesia

A. A. Iriansyah
Indonesian National Agency for Disaster Management (BNPB), Jakarta Timur, Indonesia

Y. Cui and R. Shaw (eds.), *Disaster Law*, Disaster Risk Reduction,
https://doi.org/10.1007/978-981-97-7374-9_12

12.1 Introduction

The climate is undergoing significant changes and has emerged as an important issue in recent decades (Kjellstrom et al. 2007). The global impact of climate change was extensively researched by various researchers worldwide. Multiple studies showed over twelve pieces of evidence indicating climate change, including rising temperatures on land and in oceans, increased ocean temperatures, glaciers melting, and changes in the environments of species and timing of life events (Higgins 2014). Furthermore, climate change repercussions present a substantial threat to various sectors, including biodiversity and human well-being (Pörtner et al. 2022). Both communities and companies are vulnerable to climate-related hazards encompassing both the tangible risks presented by changing weather patterns and fewer tangible risks arising from societal and economic changes (Arribas et al. 2022). However, it is the fact that globalization has led to the widespread impact of climate change in various regions that lack direct connections (Linnenluecke 2017). In the context of a globalization scheme, dependence on the worldwide supply chain will have an impact on the global economy if climate change threatens one or many countries (Woods 2007).

Indonesia is highly vulnerable to climate-related hazards, making it one of the most disaster-prone countries globally (Widiachristy and Rachmanto 2021). The characteristics mentioned above of Indonesia pose a threat to the surrounding nations as well (Ariyaningsih et al. 2022). In addition, more than sixty percent of the districts in Indonesia are highly vulnerable to flooding. Also, Indonesia has seen numerous natural hazards like earthquakes, tsunamis, volcanic eruptions, cyclones, and landslides in the past (Trias and Cook 2021). Tsunamis had the most significant impact in terms of fatalities. The 2004 Indian Ocean Tsunami inflicted the most extensive destruction (Fig. 12.1).

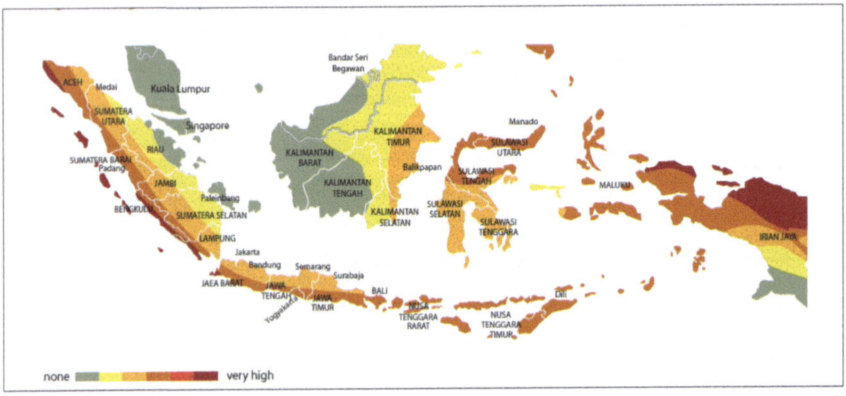

Fig. 12.1 Degree of exposure to natural hazards (*Source* authors with adapted from UNOCHA, 2006)

Moreover, the safety, livability, and prosperity of communities throughout Indonesia are being affected by the country's increasing exposure and vulnerability to the risks of disasters due to rapid development and climate change. Integrating disaster risk reduction into spatial designs is also crucial (Ariyaningsih et al. 2022). This signifies a critical milestone for Indonesia's disaster risk management (DRM) endeavors and underscores the significance of using risk-informed planning to strengthen the resilience of urban areas against disasters. Furthermore, it is crucial to consider the primary implications for policymakers, the correlation between urbanization and disaster resilience, and the necessity of establishing an optimal balance between risk reduction, preparedness, and post-disaster recovery (Joerin et al. 2014).

Disaster risk is a crucial aspect of public policy, and Indonesia has made significant efforts to enhance its resilience (Sukhwani et al. 2021). After the catastrophic 2004 Indian Ocean Earthquake and Tsunami, it became apparent that there was an urgent requirement to enhance disaster awareness and understanding (Oktari et al. 2018). After that, there has been a notable improvement in the legislative and institutional frameworks related to disaster risk management (DRM), with the approval of the Law on Disaster Management (UU 24–2007) and the Spatial Planning Law (UU 26–2007) in 2007 (Law No. 26 Year 2007 On Spatial Management 2007). The National Disaster Management Authority or Indonesia National Agency for Disaster Management (BNPB) was established in 2008 to enhance the coordination of disaster risk management (DRM) responsibilities among governmental bodies, non-governmental organizations (NGOs), international collaborators, and other appropriate stakeholders. The nation has established globally acknowledged protocols for emergency response and community-driven post-disaster recovery. Nevertheless, there are still obstacles to overcome, such as the need for better coordination, adequate human resources and technical capabilities, systematic integration of risk into development processes, resilience of infrastructure, and the establishment of sustainable and efficient financing mechanisms for both risk reduction and preparedness and recovery efforts (Drosou et al. 2019).

Typically, the advancement of disaster governance in Indonesia involves modifications to organizations and shifts in values. Past research on disaster management law includes the reinstatement procedure to guarantee that the government's attention is directed toward both natural and man-made disasters, including those caused by COVID-19 (Hapsari and Zenurianto 2016). Understanding the disaster law in Indonesia is crucial as it prevents individuals from making improper choices. This chapter aims to comprehend the laws and regulations regarding disasters in Indonesia. It includes an introductory section highlighting the significance of disaster legislation and resilience in the country.

Furthermore, the second sub-section focuses on the review of disasters occurring in Indonesia. Following that, the focus shifts to the third sub-chapter, which explores into a topic of disaster law. In the fourth sub-chapter, a review of stakeholders is conducted. The fifth sub-section contains some discussion on disaster law in Indonesia. In the end, this chapter concludes with a conclusion.

12.2 Overview of Disaster Type in Indonesia

Indonesia stands as one of the world's most disaster-prone countries (Amri et al. 2020) and is known as the "supermarket of disasters" (Butt 2014). Among the various hazards it faces, hydro-meteorological hazard, including flood, typhoons, drought and others, emerge as the most recurrent, significantly impacting a substantial populace. Hydro-meteorological hazards present a major threat to human civilization. This is primarily caused by the escalating intensity of these hazards, a consequence of climate change, global warming, and decreasing environmental carrying capacities. Indonesia's vast and varied geography, consisting of more than 17.000 islands, exposes it to a wide range of topographical conditions, making it susceptible to climate change and hydro-meteorological hazards. Majority of regions in Indonesia are susceptible to the risk of flood, landslides, soil erosion, and intense rainfall over rainy season, which span from October to March. Concurrently, several areas of Indonesia, particularly in in the eastern regions, are undergoing a period of drought (Basuki et al. 2022). Small islands, particularly, are at higher risk due to climate change-induced hazards such as rising sea levels and drought.

Furthermore, certain coastal areas on major islands have issues associated with increased sea level, coastal flooding, and land subsidence. Regarding the drought issues, small Islands have difficulty maintaining a sufficient supply of clean water due to limited freshwater sources and limited capacity for water storage on land such as rivers and ponds/lakes. Another challenge associated with the drought is the occurrence of El Nino phenomenon.

Several areas in Indonesia have experienced water scarcity since June or the beginning of August 2023. According to the forecasted data from Indonesian Meteorological, Climatological, and Geophysical Agency (*Badan Meteorologi, Klimatologi, dan Geofisika, BMKG*) points to several areas were estimated indicated a high likelihood of experiencing decreased rainfall intensity of about 0–20 mm below normal condition in August to September 2023. In response, BKMG launched an early warning related to water scarcity in certain areas such as Java, Bali, and Southern Sumatera (Reliefweb 2023). In contrast to drought events, several regions in Indonesia grapple with flooding, particularly in low-lying areas. Floods in Indonesia create practically weekly headlines in print and electronic media (Sulaeman et al. 2019). Flood occurs when the amount of water flowing through drainage channel or rivers exceeds the flow rate at which the surrounding land can absorb and handle it (Setiadi et al. 2023). Regarding water balance, flooding is a form of surface runoff because the water cannot be infiltrated, flowed, and evaporated in river basins (Guo et al. 2014). Flood hazard can arise due to high rainfall intensity without adequate drainage systems. Unregulated land use and massive land cover change also contribute to flood occurrence as they reduce infiltration areas. Rainfall that transforms into runoff cannot be effectively infiltrated, leading to increasing flood discharge.

Flooding can also result from the reduced capacity of rivers, either due to sedimentation, hydro-dynamic phenomena or anthropogenic activities such as illegal settlement on the riverbank. Regarding flood hazards, Jakarta is one of Indonesia's regions that are highly exposed to floods. Due to its geographical location in delta area, Jakarta is inherently susceptible to flooding (Dudal 2005). Flood hits Jakarta almost every year and become worse. A major flood hit Jakarta in 1996, 2002, 2007, 2013, 2014, and 2020. One of the major flood events in Jakarta occurred in 2007 and was regarded as a national disaster, resulting in losses nearly 680 million USD, inundation over 60% of the land area, 79 casualties and the displacement of over 500.000 people (Octavianti and Charles 2019). In January 2013, intensive rainfall also led to the flooding of 98.000 houses in 124 villages. As a result, 40.000 people were evacuated and 20 people lost their lives. The estimated total damage caused by this major flood amounts to approximately 775 million USD (Wijayanti et al. 2017). In 2020, another major flood event occurred in this Capital City of Indonesia, resulting in catastrophe losses. The rainfall during this flood event set a new record since 1866, with a cumulative amount of around 366 mm per day. 173.000 inhabitants were evacuated, with 60% of the residential area being inundated. The death toll stood at 66, and the estimated losses amounted to approximately 700 million USD (Lubis et al. 2022).

Another famous natural hazard frequently occurring in Indonesia is a Landslide (Muntohar et al. 2021). Landslides are destructive natural hazards that mainly impact localized areas, unlike other natural hazards like earthquakes, floods, droughts, and hurricanes. Landslides are primarily the result of a complex interaction of various factors, including dynamic triggers like earthquakes and rainfall, ground conditions such as slopes, geological conditions, and soil types, as well as anthropogenic disturbance such as deforested slopes and road cuts (Hidayat et al. 2019). According to data published by the National Disaster Management Agency (Badan Penanggulangan Bencana Nasional, BNPB), 9569 recorded landslide occurrences have occurred from 1815 to 2023. These disaster events have had significant consequences, resulting in 3.193 casualties, 374 missing persons, 3.322 injuries. Additionally, approximately 149.729 people were evacuated (BNPB 2023). Due to these numbers, Indonesia ranks among the top three countries with the highest percentage of landslide fatalities (Kirschbaum et al. 2010) (Fig. 12.2).

Located amidst the intersecting tectonic plates of Asia and Australia, Indonesia occupies a high-risk zone for tectonic activity, which frequently results in earthquakes and tsunamis (Hsu et al. 2006) and have caused the most deaths in Indonesia (Desinventar 2024). One of the severe and deadliest disasters in Indonesia was the Aceh Tsunami in 2004, which was triggered by an 8.9 magnitude earthquake in the Indian Ocean, claiming the lives of 167.000 people in Aceh Province and Nias Islands (North Sumatra Province) (Rahiem et al. 2021). Apart from the Aceh Earthquake and Tsunami, Indonesia has experienced several major earthquakes in the past decades that resulted in numerous casualties. These include the Yogyakarta earthquake in 2006, which claimed 5782 lives and left over 36.000 injured (Nichols 2007); the Padang earthquake in 2009, resulting in 1117 fatalities (Chian et al. 2019); and the Palu earthquake in 2018, causing 2113 deaths, 1309 missing and 4612 injuries (Widiyanto et al. 2019).

Indonesia, home to over a hundred active volcanoes, has faced substantial volcanic eruptions throughout its history. Among these cataclysmic events, the Mount

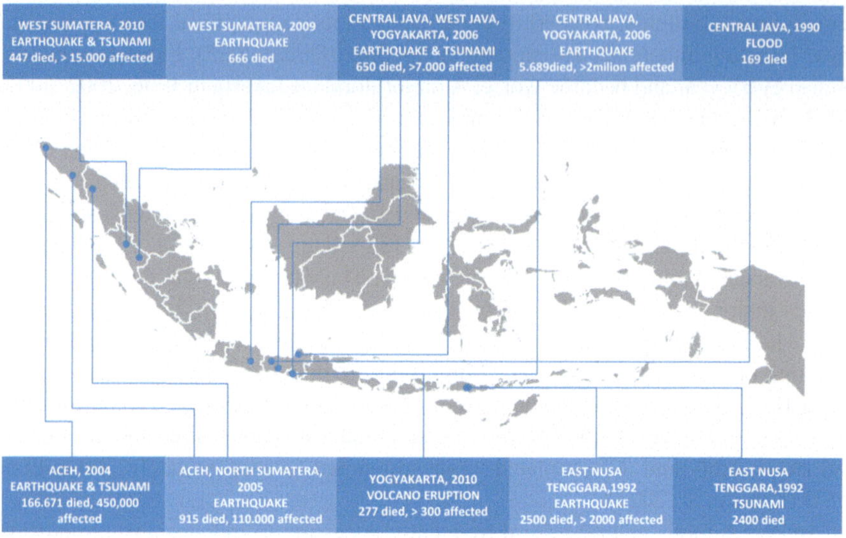

Fig. 12.2 Disaster in Indonesia (*Source* adapted from Dibi—http://dibi.bnpb.go.id)

Tambora eruption in 1815 stands as the largest recorded volcanic eruption, killing over 12.000 people through direct hazard and an estimated 49.000 more due to subsequent famine, disease, and crop failure (Brown et al. 2017), Additionally, the famous Krakatoa eruption in 1883 resulted in thousands of fatalities. More recently, the significant Merapi volcanic eruption in 2010 claimed the lives of 367 people, injured 277 and forcibly over 400.000 people residing within a 20-km radius of the summit (Bakkour et al. 2015).

Indonesia also encounters Man-made disasters such as forest and land fires which predominantly occur during summer when the land becomes dry. These occurrences are not classified as natural hazards, as 99% of them stem from human actions due to sheer negligence or unintended actions (Sitanggang et al. 2018). Forest and land fires encompass burning incidents in forest and/or land, triggered by either natural factors or human activities, resulting in adverse environmental effects and leading to ecological, economic, socio-cultural, and political losses (MoEF 2016). The areas at risk of these fires span the islands of Sumatera, Java, and Kalimantan, encompassing a total area exceeding 14 million hectares (Kusumasari 2019). Based on the documentation data on forest fires in Indonesia, 2015 witnessed the most severe forest fire event between 2013 and 2022. The total impacted area was approximately 2.611.411,44 hectares (MoEF 2023), with an estimated cost of around 16 billion USD (World Bank 2016). A significant proportion of this territory exhibits abundant biodiversity and is a refuge for endangered animals such as orangutans, tigers, rhinos, and elephants (World Bank 2016). Fire emits substantial amounts of carbon into the atmosphere, significantly contributing to air pollution and climate change (Edwards et al. 2020). Moreover, these fires have caused more than half a million respiratory diseases in Indonesia and Singapore, and around a hundred thousand premature deaths have been linked to them (Koplitz et al. 2016). The primary contributors to Indonesia's Forest fires, particularly in Kalimantan (Borneo Island), include large palm oil companies, small local plantation companies, and local landowners (Saharjo 2022).

Another "significant controversy" in the history of Man-made disasters in Indonesia occurred in 2006, referred to as Lumpur Sidoarjo or LUSI (Sidoarjo Mudflow). The mud eruption was caused by a drilling procedure that applied excessive pressure to the porous and permeable limestone around 2830 m below the land surface. As a result of unprotected steel casing, pressure induces hydraulic fracturing and leads the propagation of the fracture to the surface. This resulted in the eruption of pore fluid and some sediment. The mudflow rates, ranging from 7000 to 150.000 m^3 per day, have remained consistently high for 173 days since the eruption began (Davies et al. 2007). By the middle of 2007, over 30 million m^3 of mud, with temperatures ranging from 70 to 100 °C, had erupted (Geoffrey S. Plumlee et al. 2008) and continued to do so until the time of writing this article in January 2024. The mud has inundated more than 749 hectares encompassing industrial estates, agriculture areas, the Surabaya-Gempol Toll road, and densely populated settlements (Humaida et al. 2010), with over 40.000 people forced to be displaced (Andreas et al. 2011). This catastrophe had far-reaching effects in various sectors, encompassing the economy, society, community culture, physical infrastructure, ecology (such as land deformation and earth movement), flammable gas bursts, and degradation of groundwater and air quality (Novenanto 2015).

12.3 Disaster Management Legislation in Indonesia

Disaster management in Indonesia is an essential part of the national development process through various actions carried out before, during, and after the occurrence of a disaster. The primary purpose of Law Number 24/2007 on Disaster Management is to address each disaster phase, which encompasses the pre-disaster, response, and post-disaster phases. The establishment of the National Disaster Management Agency was authorized by Presidential Regulation No. 8/2008 (Benny Sukmara and Shyan Wu 2021). The agency was formerly known as the National Coordinating Agency for Disaster Management. It was established under Presidential Regulation No. 83/2005, replacing the previous agency known as the National Coordinating Agency for Disaster Management and Refugee Management, which was established under Presidential Decree No. 3/2001. The National Disaster Management Agency (BNPB) serves as the principal coordinating body for government agencies. The Regional Disaster Management Agency (BPBD) is the central hub for disaster management at the provincial and district/city levels.

Nonetheless, to enhance the execution of disaster management in Indonesia, forums were established at both the national and local levels on an informal basis. A National Platform (Planas) was established nationally, with representatives from civil society, the business sector, universities, the media, and international organizations. Indonesia has a hierarchical structure of disaster management agencies, which are categorized into different tiers.

A. **National Level**

The Indonesian government established several encouraging national disaster management legislation in anticipation of the increasing risk in the future. National disaster management policies and frameworks should be used as references, guidelines, directives, and contextual factors while developing local government disaster management plans. Nowadays, Indonesia has constructed a disaster management roadmap with long-term objectives, as detailed in the National Disaster Management Master Plan (RIPB) for 2020–2044, referring to Presidential Regulation Number 87 of 2020. The article regulates the vision, goal, objectives, and targets for disaster management, including policies and strategies, as well as the path for executing RIPB from 2020 to 2044.

The Disaster Management Vision for 2020–2044 is "Understanding a Resilient Indonesia for Sustainable Development," including the disaster resilience concept. According to this concept, Indonesia is capable of withstanding, absorbing, adapting, and recovering from the effects of disasters and climate change in a timely, effective, and efficient manner. Achieving this objective is critical to achieving and maintaining high levels of economic growth, poverty reduction, and long-term welfare enhancement. This vision is then converted into three missions for the Disaster Management Plan from 2020 to 2044, which are as follows:

(1) Creating robust and sustainable catastrophe management.
(2) Developing professional, inclusive disaster management governance.
(3) Providing high-quality emergency disaster response and recovery services.

The Disaster Management Master Plan (Rencana Induk Penanggulangan Bencana-RIPB) is established for the period from 2020–2044, referring to the phases of the first National Long-Term Development Plan (RPJPN) that ends in 2025, as well as the second RPJPN stage, which runs from 2025 to 2045. Furthermore, RIPB for the years 2020–2044 is consistent with the Paris Agreement in the framework of the United Nations Framework Convention on Climate Change, the United Nations Sustainable Development Goals (SDGs) 2015–2030, and the Sendai Framework for Disaster Risk Reduction (SFDRR) 2015–2030. Within based on The RIPB roadmap's aims for 2025–2029 serve as an example of translation (Table 12.1).

In addition, the RIPB is transformed into The National Disaster Management Plan (RENAS PB), which is a comprehensive framework encompassing policies, strategies, and targeted measures designed to accomplish national disaster management (DM) goals within a 5-year timeframe (2020–2024). RENAS PB serves as an essential framework for developing program and activity plans for all disaster management parties, including national and local stakeholders. Periodic evaluations and expert assessments, conducted at intervals of no more than 5 years, constitute a systematic process to examine the effectiveness of RENAS PB. This guarantees the plan's flexibility in response to the evolving circumstances, enabling essential

Table 12.1 Roadmap for the Implementation of RIPB (National Disaster Management Master Plan) Phase 2025–2029

Policy	Strategy	Ripb focus 2025–2029
Enhancing Effective and Efficient Disaster Management Legislation	a. Improving adaptability and sustainable legal regulations and disaster management implementation b. Improving disaster management norms, standards, procedures, and criteria	Harmonization of Legal Regulations in Disaster Management
Improving Collaboration in Disaster Management between Ministries/Agencies and Stakeholders	a. Improving coordination and collaboration between ministries/agencies, local governments, the Indonesian National Armed Forces, the Indonesian National Police, academics, businesses, communities, the media, and other disaster management stakeholders b. Developing and improving an integrated and sustainable early warning system, data, and disaster information services based on one map, one data policy principles	a. Developing technical self-sufficiency and disaster industrialization b. Providing easy access to integrated early warning systems for multiple-threat disasters
Strengthening investment in disaster risk management in accordance with the projection of increased disaster risks, taking into account spatial planning and area arrangement	a. Developing and implementing preparedness programmes and disaster risk management while taking into account spatial planning and area arrangement b. Increased investment and use of various innovative financing mechanisms, including risk transfer, for catastrophe mitigation c. Optimising integrated disaster mitigation funds	a. Implementing sufficient investments in catastrophe risk reduction to promote resilience b. Implementing collaborative disaster risk governance at the central and regional levels

(continued)

Table 12.1 (continued)

Policy	Strategy	Ripb focus 2025–2029
Strengthening Disaster Management Governance to Increase Professionalism, Transparency, and Accountability	a. Strengthening the skills and professionalism of disaster management organisers and practitioners b. Strengthening the execution of minimal service standards in disaster management c. Strengthening information transparency and communication, planning system quality, and monitoring and evaluation in disaster management d. Encouraging stakeholder involvement in disaster management governance to increase accountability e. Establishing disaster-resilient districts/ cities, villages, and communities f. Creating disaster-resilient infrastructure g. Strengthening disaster education and knowledge management among communities and stakeholders	1. Increasing insight into catastrophe risk, topography, climate change adaptation, social resilience, and public health resilience 2. Providing a timely, effective, and coordinated emergency disaster response 3. Implementing integrated spatial planning in cities and settlements to improve disaster resilience, climate change adaption, and social and health resilience 4. Providing protection for vulnerable marine and coastal habitats
Strengthening capacity and capability for rapid and dependable disaster emergency response	a. Increasing the amount and quality of human resources in emergency catastrophe response b. Increasing the readiness and dependability of logistics and equipment for disaster response c. Improving the management of community help during emergency disaster response d. Improving institutional quality and leveraging science and technology e. Accelerating the recovery of critical facilities and infrastructure	Availability of human resources who have expertise and professionals in the field of disaster management

(continued)

Table 12.1 (continued)

Policy	Strategy	Ripb focus 2025–2029
Accelerating Post-Disaster Recovery in Affected Regions and Communities to Build Back Better	a. Improving post-disaster rehabilitation and reconstruction planning by spatial considerations responsive to disaster risks b. Improving the quality of life in disaster-affected communities c. Developing disaster-resistant infrastructure, housing, and settlements d. Improving the quality of socioeconomic recovery, natural resource management, and environmental restoration	a. Enhancing the efficiency, security, and long-term viability of the restoration process in areas affected by disasters, with a particular emphasis on mitigating the likelihood and impact of future disasters b. Achieving infrastructure that is of superior quality, dependable, enduring, and capable of withstanding disasters

Source Presidential regulation 87/2020 on Disaster Management Master Plan

modifications to synchronize with the present condition of disaster management affairs.

B. **Provincial Level**

The national disaster management policies' objective is to provide guidance to relevant sectors or organizations in their endeavors to mitigate the risk of disasters, effectively respond to emergencies, and facilitate recovery following a disaster. These guidelines aim to encompass all Disaster Management (DM) areas at the municipal and provincial levels. Disaster management plans are a collection of initiatives designed to accomplish goals related to reducing the risk of catastrophes, responding to emergencies, and facilitating the process of recovery and reconstruction. These programs can be implemented by the relevant fields or sectors, based on their characteristics, tasks, and obligations. In Indonesia, the planning framework is described as follows:

(a) *Rencana Pembangunan Jangan Menengah Nasional* (RPJMN), or National Medium-Term Development Plan, is a national development planning framework that aims to achieve medium-term development goals at the national level.
(b) *Rencana Pembangungan Jangka Menengah Daerah* (RPJMD) Provinsi is a provincial Medium-Term Regional Development Plan. It is a planning document that specifies provincial development priorities and plans over a specific time.
(c) *Rencana Pembangunan Jangkan Menengah Daerah* (RPJMD) Kabupaten/ Kota refers to the district or city's Medium-Term Regional Development

Plan. This planning document establishes the direction for local development and initiatives while considering each district or city's unique needs and characteristics.

As required by Law Number 24 of 2007 and Government Regulation Number 21 of 2008, local government's Disaster Management Plan (RPB) must be included as an integral part of the development plan. The development plan mentioned here is the Medium-Term Regional Development Plan (RPJMD), corresponding to the RPB document's 5-year term. Support, contribution, and cooperation procedures must be coordinated to avoid overlaps. The National Medium-Term Development Plan (RPJMN), Provincial Medium-Term Development Plan (RPJMD Provinsi), and District/City Medium-Term Development Plan (RPJMD Kabupaten/Kota) all help to identify targets and frameworks for actions at the district/city level.

According to Minister of Home Affairs Regulation Number 86 of 2017, to formulate RPJMD, development issues must be identified, and other planning documents must be reviewed before strategic regional problems may be developed. In this perspective, RPB is viewed as one of several planning documents that must be analyzed as input into the process of developing regional strategic concerns. In Addition, the regulation is translated into the Minimum Service Standards (SPM) for Disaster Sub-Divisions, which are under the control of public order and community protection. At the provincial level, SPM is responsible for supervising the implementation of SPM for Disaster Sub-Divisions in districts and cities.

(a) Assisting with the implementation of SPM for Disaster Sub-Divisions in district/city regions using data collecting results and basic service requirements estimations.
(b) Compiling Disaster Risk Assessment and Disaster Management Plan papers to assist district/city regional governments in meeting the SPM for Disaster Sub-Divisions.
(c) Encourage district/city regional governments to form SPM Implementation Teams by issuing a Regional Head Decree (SK Kepala Daerah).
(d) Assisting in the establishment of programmes, actions, and sub-activities to meet the SPM, while ensuring compliance with Minister of Home Affairs Regulation No. 90/2019 and Minister of Home Affairs Decree No. 050–5889 Year 2021.
(e) Overseeing and guaranteeing the integration of programmes, activities, sub-activities, and budgets for the implementation of SPM in regional planning documents, as well as the review of the Regional Medium-Term Development Plan (RKPD) and Regional Budget (APBD).
(f) Encouraging district/city regional governments to develop actions by issuing local regulations from the regional head.

C. **Local Level**

Indonesia is experiencing a significant and transformative change in how disasters are seen and managed, occurring on both local and national levels. The initial change is transitioning from focusing on responding to emergencies to prioritizing preparedness and mitigating risks. The enactment of the Disaster Management Law in 2007, in response to the 2004 Aceh Tsunami, played a crucial role in forming both National and Regional Disaster Management Agencies. Indonesia's adoption of the HFA, the decentralization process, and the second shift have prompted a greater emphasis on implementing disaster risk reduction (DRR) measures at the local level. According to a study conducted by Djalante et al. (2012), implementing the DRR strategy in Indonesia primarily emphasizes local efforts. However, the study found that while DRR institutions have been successfully established at the national level, this success has not been extensively replicated at the local level. Each of the 33 provinces in Indonesia has implemented Regional Disaster Management Agencies (BPBDs), however, only 144 out of the total 497 local governments now possess BPBDs (BNPB, 2011). Therefore, the current 30% establishment of BPBDs is below BNPB's intended goal.

At the regional level, the Indonesian Government guarantees the allocation of funds for disaster management services in sub-district areas of districts and cities. This is done by implementing the Minimum Service Standards (SPM) as outlined in the Minister of Home Affairs Regulation No. 101 of 2018 on Technical Standards for Basic Services. The Minimum Service Standards (SPM) for Sub-Division of Disasters impose a duty on regions to deliver services to their populations. This standard has three fundamental services, which are subsequently elaborated into 12 sub-activities (Table 12.2).

Table 12.2 Matrix of the minimum service standards (SPM) for sub-division of disasters

No	Disaster management program	Sub disaster management
1	Disaster-prone services for information	a. Preparing catastrophe risk assessments b. Providing socialisation, communication, information, and education on disaster vulnerability (specific to each type of disaster)
2	The Disaster Prevention and Preparedness Service	a. Disaster Management Planning b. Continuity Plan Development c. Disaster Prevention and Mitigation Training d. Preparedness Drill e. Operational Control and Infrastructure. Disaster Response Planning f. Provide safety and disaster preparedness equipment
3	Search and Rescue Operations for Disaster Victims	a. Activation of the Emergency Disaster Command System b. Rapid response to disasters c. Search, rescue, and evacuation of victims d. Prompt response to KLB and priority zoonotic diseases

12.4 Stakeholders for Disaster Management in Indonesia

The main objectives of disaster management are to encourage engagement and collaboration between the public and private sectors during the pre-disaster phase, emergency response, and recovery. The government and local governments encourage all parties to participate in disaster management. This comprises financial assistance, execution of disaster risk mitigation efforts, emergency response, rehabilitation, reconstruction, and disaster management decision-making. Indonesia uses the term "pentahelix" to describe disaster management stakeholders at the local level, which include Regional Government Agencies (OPD), Regional People's Representative Council (DPRD), TNI/Polri, non-governmental organizations, mass media, business entities, universities, community organizations, religious organizations, and others.

These parties are viewed as resources and capacities able to assist the region in disaster management activities, and they can engage and play roles alone and with others. Non-governmental organizations, universities, community organizations, and religious organizations offer village-level empowerment and community resilience-building programmes. Businesses operating in disaster-prone locations are vested in safeguarding their assets. Furthermore, the DPRD takes a strategic approach to allocating disaster management budgets. Mapping these parties' resources and capacities is critical because they have the ability to help create resilience at the regional and neighborhood levels. As a result, disaster management planning is envisaged to serve as a tool for integrating stakeholder frameworks and action plans into disaster management implementation.

Every stakeholder involved in disaster preparedness, response, and recovery has roles to play, as laid out in the 2007 Law on Disaster Management. The regional disaster management agencies (BPBD) at the provincial and district levels collaborate with BNPB to coordinate various aspects of disaster risk management (DRM), even though numerous national and local agencies are responsible for implementing the institutional arrangements and legal framework. In addition, regarding funding allocation for DRM activities, the Ministry of Finance distributes national budget resources to BNPB and line ministries. A contingency budget is also set aside to address unforeseen crises, such as disaster disasters. Municipal governments adopt a comparable budgeting method for expenses linked to DRM.

Several measures have been implemented to create a legal structure for the advancement of DRM, which includes Law Number 24/2007. In addition, articles 33–35 of Law Number 24/2007 describe the three disaster management phases: pre-disaster, emergency response, and post-disaster. Moreover, according to Government Regulation Number 21/2008 on the Implementation of Disaster Management, an action plan for Disaster Risk Reduction (DRR) must be created, including a national and regional plan. The National Action Plan on Disaster Risk Reduction (DRR) will be developed thoroughly and unified, with participation from government, non-governmental, and business-related groups. BNPB is coordinating this effort.

Table 12.3 Stakeholders related to disaster management in Indonesia

Ministry	National agency	Private sector/NGO	Academia
Ministry of National Education	Monetary and Development Control Agency	Indonesia Red Cross	Most of the university in Indonesia
Ministry of National Development Planning	Geospatial Information Agency	Caritas Germany	Korea Institute of Science and Technology
Ministry of Defence	National Agency of Auditing	Swiss Confederation	
Ministry of Public Works	National Research and Innovation Agency	Japan International Cooperation Agency	
Ministry of Agriculture	National Search and Rescue Agency	Asia Development Bank	
Ministry Coordination of People's Welfare	National Agency of Meteorology, Climatology and Geophysics	Islamic Development Bank	
		The International Organization for Migration	
		UNICEF	
		Indonesian National Nurses Association	
		United Nations Population Fund	
		United Nations Development Programme	

Source BNPB (2024)

The President of the Republic of Indonesia leads a steering group comprised of experts and professionals in Disaster Risk Reduction (DRR), along with the support of 13 government ministries and organizations/agencies for the National Disaster Management Agency (BNBP). The disaster management agencies are established nationally and in 33 provinces and 497 local governments (cities and regencies) (BNPB, 2011). Here is the list of stakeholders that make cooperation with BNBP (Table 12.3).

12.5 Discussions: *Indonesia's Disaster Law: Problem or Panacea?*

As mentioned in the previous section. (2), due to its large archipelago and varied topography, Indonesia is vulnerable to various natural calamities, such as floods, earthquakes, tsunamis, and volcanic eruptions. The danger increases annually because of significant human interventions in the natural system, a lack of preparedness for mitigation, and the region's propensity for disasters. Hence, as Ayuningtyas et al. (2021) and Putra and Matsuyuki (2020) mentioned, improving disaster management should be the government's primary focus. That transformation to understand disaster in the contemporary era as a "social turn" (Da Costa 2016) is crucial to handling any disaster. Disasters can no longer be a divine act. Instead, it is part of human activities and reactions. In other words, disasters are now recognized to be caused by a combination of factors, including inadequate response systems and misunderstanding or human errors, rather than being driven by hazards per se.

The paradigm shift in disasters is applied toward a more proactive, comprehensive, and risk-informed strategy to mitigate disasters. From the upstream, disaster regulation to disaster management generally delineates the legal structure for mitigating, preventing, responding to, and recovering from disasters. The regulation should specify the rights and obligations of people and communities, set forth the roles and responsibilities of government institutions, and offer procedures for organizing actions linked to disasters. The rule also makes it easier for government agencies, non-governmental organizations, and foreign entities to coordinate and collaborate because it offers a legal framework outlining different parties' roles in disaster management. In Indonesia, the government has implemented several disaster management laws and regulations in response to risks and vulnerabilities. Nevertheless, significant obstacles still stand in the way of the nation's catastrophe legislation being implemented successfully.

Law Number 24 of 2007 concerning Disaster Management provides the legal basis for managing disasters in Indonesia. Despite being outdated, this legislation remains Indonesia's primary legal framework for catastrophes. For disaster management planning, the law is translated into Presidential Decree Number 87 Year 2020 on Master Plan for Disaster Management 2020–2044. In the medium term, the plan is interpreted in a five-year medium-term document, which is National Plan Countermeasures Disasters 2020–2024. Furthermore, the law is supported by another law specifically regulating health quarantine, Law Number 6 Year 2018 on Health Quarantine. However, there is a tendency for the disaster laws in Indonesia to emphasize natural hazards rather than non-natural hazards (Wati and Bantam 2023).

As located on the Pacific Ring of Fire, Indonesia is known to have a variety of potential disasters, such as erupting volcanoes, earthquakes, and tsunamis. The situation is logical for paying more attention to natural hazards. However, the COVID-19 outbreak, a non-natural hazards that has recently affected most countries, including Indonesia, exposes the loophole in the laws. Indonesia seems unprepared, at least from the legislation, to prevent the outbreak. Although Indonesia has made progress in creating disaster legislation, the structure of laws and regulations may still have certain holes or discrepancies. Overlapping authorities and a lack of clarity in duties and responsibilities may hamper the seamless execution of disaster management strategies. For example, Lele (2021) exposes a disagreement on handling COVID-19 between the governor of DKI Jakarta and the central government. In 2020, the central government opted to centralize addressing the pandemic by adopting the large-scale social restrictions (PSBB) policy. Still, the local government had other choices for stopping the spread of COVID-19. As a result, for the COVID-19 handling, the centralized approach was implemented. At least nine new legal products were issued by the central in the name of emergency: two Presidential Regulations, four Presidential Decrees, one Government Regulation, one Presidential Instruction, and one Government Regulation in place of Law (Roziqin et al. 2021).

The legal framework should be reviewed and updated regularly to maintain coherence and handle new issues. This entails clarifying the functions of different agencies, expediting the regulatory procedures, and encouraging responsibility in applying disaster legislation. The master plan and the medium-term disaster management plan have made it one of the main priorities (Table 12.4).

The plans above seem to overcome institutional and contextual problems that may hinder the implementation of disaster management at all levels of government in Indonesia. Institutionally, Indonesia is a big country with a decentralized structure that employs a range of institutions and local rules. There are 81,626 villages, 70,244 sub-districts, 514 regencies and cities, and 24 provinces total. Different regions may have different policies in reaction to any disasters. Furthermore, the Indonesian government's development of an institutional framework and political commitment to disaster management also paved the way for forming the National Disaster Management Agency (BNPB) and its local agency, the Regional Disaster Management Agency (BPBD). However, there are concerns about collaborations and engagement with regional agencies, BPBD. Inconsistencies in decision-making, task execution, and resource allocation might result from BNPB and BPBD's lack of clarity and poor collaboration. This may make regional catastrophe management less effective. In addition, the government and, in some cases, NGOs were criticized for their interactions with local communities, which were perceived as being authoritative and male-dominated. The stakeholders were condemned for imposing predetermined disaster risk reduction (DRR) plans on communities without adequately involving them in the process of developing and designing activities.

Through legal mechanisms, such as the rights given under village and local government law, as well as community-driven committees and forums, local stakeholders

Table 12.4 Differences between master plan and medium term plan

Master plan 2020–2044 (BNPB(a), 2020)	Medium-term plan 2020–2024 (BNPB(b), 2020)
Strengthening effective and efficient disaster management laws and regulations:	Strengthening and harmonization of disaster management systems, regulations, and governance that are effective and efficient, with strategies:
1. Improving the quality of legislative regulations and implementation in adaptive and sustainable disaster management	1. Strengthening and harmonization of laws and regulations in disaster management
2. Improve the quality of norms, standards, procedures, and criteria for disaster management	2. Increasingly strengthening disaster management governance professional, transparent, and accountable

have the ability to influence and control decision-making and actions related to disaster risk reduction (DRR). Modifying the disaster management law is essential to express the state's efforts to safeguard its citizens. This is since several policy instruments currently require adjustments, ranging from defining the scope and timing of disasters to redefining the authority of regional heads in disaster management (Arif 2022). In order to manage those issues, the disaster management law was included in the 2020 National Legislative Program (*Prolegnas*) (Nugroho 2020), which was relevant to the plans. It made the 2021 revision of the law necessary. The need to revise the disaster law is urgent because it is essential to handle the complex issues arising from natural and man-made disasters. Disaster laws are crucial for safeguarding people and property first and foremost. In order to ensure a cohesive and successful response, the comprehensive law makes it easier for government agencies, non-governmental organizations, and foreign entities to coordinate and collaborate.

However, political disagreement between elites in Parliament and the central government has failed the plan to amend. With multiple political parties and a history of forming and breaking alliances, Indonesia's political landscape is characterized by a high degree of fragmentation. A democratic system naturally produces a diversified political environment, but too much fragmentation might make it difficult to build strong coalitions. Although the Indonesian Democratic Party of Struggle (PDIP) is currently the ruling and majority party in the Parliament, it failed to accommodate the need to revise the law. From the Parliament's perspective, the amendment of the law should strengthen the role of the BNPB, while they criticized the central government's refusal to include the BNPB nomenclature in the proposed legislation and their choice to leave out sections regarding the state funding allotment.

There are numerous arguments and complaints to conclude that BNPB needs to be strengthened. One topic that comes up often is the uncertainty surrounding the functions and duties of BNPB, which can occasionally cause problems with executing policies and specific actions. The BNPB's policies have been criticized for their limits. Some contend that because the BNPB has substantial executive authority, its role is typically more strategic and coordinated. As Article 13 of the Disaster Management Law mentions, BPNB has two main functions: formulating and coordinating disaster management policies. Consequently, in some circumstances, BNPB can have trouble carrying out the essential operational procedures. However, there is no political consensus in the central government or parliament to strengthen the agency. This means that the institutional problems that hindered disaster management in the past will remain in place in the future.

In addition, the political commitment of the government can be linked to the execution and distribution of required funds as well as the creation of suitable institutional and legal frameworks that support disaster management initiatives. In fact, there is a huge gap between the funding for disaster management and the total economic loss caused by disasters in Indonesia. Frimawan (2021) mentions that there is a significant annual financial imbalance because of the limited funds and bureaucracy to allocate the funds. Rigid laws and regulations restrict how disaster contingency funds can be used, and parliamentary permission is frequently needed. Whether a disaster event is deemed a national disaster or seen as nationally extremely significant determines the source of funds for the emergency response phase following the disaster. Limited contingency budgets, on the other hand, call for reallocating and modifying central or regional government budgets. This takes time and approval from parliament, and the process of preparing and approving the budget will impact the availability of additional funding sources for a given period. For that reason, the parliament preferred a minimum allocation from the national budget to have flexibility in using the budget when a disaster occurs. The scheme is also regulated in the education sector, where at least 20% of the APBN (National Budget) is allocated to education. However, it failed to accommodate because the central government refused to regulate it. The situation makes the procedural and contingency funds for disaster management still experienced by the country.

The DM Law seeks to guarantee the engagement of the community in decision-making about disaster management activities. It grants the right to any individual to participate and oversee these actions, following a controlled process for disaster management. The latest progress report from BNPB highlights the primary obstacle to decentralized disaster risk governance as the insufficient allocation of resources to the local level and the scarcity of human resources in the regions. There is a need to prioritize the provision of technical and financial capacity-building to local communities. This can only be achieved by coordinated government efforts with the assistance of several partners. Several initiatives have been implemented to tackle this disaster law issue; however, due to the vastness and intricacy of Indonesia, it has proven to be a challenging endeavor. The 'Disaster Resilient Village' program, led by BNPB, aims to encourage community involvement in Disaster Risk Reduction (DRR) at the village level.

12.6 Conclusion

As the outdated law is still valid, it takes a multifaceted approach to overcome these obstacles because of the failure to amend it. This should involve deliberate human resources and technology infrastructure investments, coordination with local leaders to incorporate disaster law into cultural contexts, and focused public awareness efforts aimed at varied communities. Furthermore, cultivating regional and global alliances can facilitate the exchange of knowledge and capacity development, augmenting Indonesia's capability to navigate and alleviate the aftermath of catastrophes via efficacious derivative legal frameworks. The capacity of governmental entities engaged in disaster management must be strengthened via strategic investments in technology infrastructure and human resources. During times of crisis, response speeds, coordination, and overall efficacy can be significantly enhanced by providing workers with adequate training and deploying cutting-edge technologies. Constructing a resilient and adaptable disaster management system requires this investment. In addition, cultivating regional and global alliances can furnish Indonesia with invaluable assets, avenues for exchanging information, and cooperative structures. Interaction with other nations and international organizations facilitates the sharing of best practices, lessons discovered, and creative ways to manage disasters. These collaborations aid in creating a networked, resilient system that can lessen the effects of disasters on a larger scale. It can also attract another source of disaster funds that still hinder disaster management in Indonesia.

References

Amri A, Hanifa NR, Tebe Y, Lassa J, Pradipta GC, Furqon MR, Nangkiawa L (2020) National evaluation of the disaster-safe school programme. In: National secretariat of disaster-safe school. Resilience Development Initiative

Andreas H, Abidin HZ, Kusuma MA, Gumilar I (2011) After four years of ground displacements following LUSI mud volcano eruption; sign of its ending eruption. In: FIG working week 2011, May, 18–22

Ariyaningsih, Sukhwani V, Shaw R (2022) Vulnerability assessment of Balikpapan (Indonesia) for climate change-induced urban flooding. Int J Disaster Resil Built Environ. https://doi.org/10.1108/IJDRBE-08-2021-0111

Arribas A, Fairgrieve R, Dhu T, Bell J, Cornforth R, Gooley G, Hilson CJ, Luers A, Shepherd TG, Street R, Wood N (2022) Climate risk assessment needs urgent improvement. Nat Commun 13(4326). https://doi.org/10.1038/s41467-022-31979-w

Ayuningtyas D, Windiarti S, Sapoan Hadi M, Fasrini UU, Barinda S (2021) Disaster preparedness and mitigation in indonesia: a narrative review. Iran J Public Health 50(8):1536–1546. https://doi.org/10.18502/ijph.v50i8.6799

Bakkour D, Enjolras G, Thouret JC, Kast R, Mei ETW, Prihatminingtyas B (2015) The adaptive governance of natural disaster systems: Insights from the 2010 mount Merapi eruption in Indonesia. Int J Disaster Risk Reduct 13:167–188. https://doi.org/10.1016/j.ijdrr.2015.05.006

Basuki TM, Nugroho HYSH, Indrajaya Y, Pramono IB, Nugroho NP, Supangat AB, Indrawati DR, Savitri E, Wahyuningrum N, Purwanto Cahyono SA, Putra PB, Adi RN, Nugroho AW, Auliyani D, Wuryanta A, Riyanto HD, Harjadi B, Yudilastyantoro C, Simarmata DP (2022) Improvement of integrated watershed management in indonesia for mitigation and adaptation to climate change: a review. Sustainability (Switzerland) 14(16):1–41. https://doi.org/10.3390/su14169997

Benny Sukmara R, Shyan Wu R (2021) The 20 th cross-strait symposium on environment, resources and ecological conservation 印度尼西亞三馬林達的洪水管理:最新進展 flood management in Samarinda, Indonesia: recent progress. https://doi.org/10.20944/preprints202102.0524.v1

BNPB (2023) Data Informasi Bencana Indonesia. Badan Nasional Penanggulangan Bencana (BNPB)

Brown SK, Jenkins SF, Sparks RSJ, Odbert H, Auker MR (2017) Volcanic fatalities database: analysis of volcanic threat with distance and victim classification. J Appl Volcanol 6(1). https://doi.org/10.1186/s13617-017-0067-4

Butt S (2014) Disaster management law in Indonesia: from response to preparedness? In: Butt S, Nasu H, Nottage L (eds) Asia-pacific disaster management: comparative and socio-legal perspectives. Springer, pp 1–303. https://doi.org/10.1007/978-3-642-39768-4_9

Chian SC, Wilkinson SM, Whittle JK, Mulyani R, Alarcon JE, Pomonis A, Saito K, Fraser S, Goda K, Macabuag J, Offord M, Hunt-Raby AC, Sammonds P, Franco G, Stone H, Ahmed B, Hughes FE, Jirouskova NK, Kaminski S, Lopez J (2019) Lessons learnt from the 2009 padang indonesia, 2011 Tōhoku Japan and 2016 muisne Ecuador earthquakes. Front Built Environ 5(June):1–20. https://doi.org/10.3389/fbuil.2019.00073

Da Costa K (2016). Disaster Law by Kristian Cedervall Lauta New York: Routledge, 2015, 157 pp. £ 90.00; Hardcover. Eur J Risk Regul 7(3):642–644. https://doi.org/10.1017/S1867299X00006176

Davies RJ, Swarbrick RE, Evans RJ, Huuse M (2007) Birth of a mud volcano: east Java. GSA Today 17(2). https://doi.org/10.1130/GSAT01702A.1

Desinventar (2024) Disaster profile: Indonesia. Desinventar.org

Drosou N, Soetanto R, Hermawan F, Chmutina K, Bosher L, Hatmoko J (2019) Key factors influencing wider adoption of. Water 11(6):1–20. https://www.mdpi.com/2073-4441/11/6/1234

Dudal R (2005) Soil of Southeast Asia. In A Gupta (ed) The physical geography of Southeast Asia. Oxford University Press

Edwards RB, Naylor RL, Higgins MM, Falcon WP (2020) Causes of Indonesia's forest fires. World Dev 127. https://doi.org/10.1016/j.worlddev.2019.104717

Plumlee GS, Casadevall TJ, Wibowo HT, Rosenbauer RJ, Johnson CA, Breit GN, Lowers HA, Wolf RE, Hageman PL, Goldstein H, Anthony MW, Berry CJ, Fey DL, Meeker GP, Morman SA (2008) Preliminary analytical results for a mud sample collected from the LUSI Mud Volcano, Sidoarjo, East Java, Indonesia: U.S. Geological Survey Open-File Report 2008–1019. U.S. Geological Survey (USGS)

Guo J, Li H-Y, Leung LR, Guo S, Liu P, Sivapalan M (2014) Links between flood frequency and annual water balance behaviors: a basis for similarity and regionalization. Water Resour Res 50(2). https://doi.org/10.1002/2013WR014374

Hapsari RI, Zenurianto M (2016) View of flood disaster management in Indonesia and the key solutions. Am J Eng Res (AJER) 5(3):140–151

Hidayat R, Sutanto SJ, Hidayah A, Ridwan B, Mulyana A (2019) Development of a landslide early warning system in Indonesia. Geosciences 9(10):1–17. https://doi.org/10.3390/geosciences9100451

Higgins PAT (2014) Climate change risk management. The American Meteorological Society, An AMS Policy Program Study

Hsu Y-J, Simons M, Avouac J-P, Galetzka J, Sieh K, Chlieh M, Natawidjaja D, Prawirodirdjo L, Bock Y (2006) Frictional afterslip following the 2005 nias-simeulue earthquake, sumatra. Science 312:1921–1926. https://doi.org/10.1126/science.1126960

Humaida H, Zaennudin A, Sutaningsih NE, Sulistiyo Y (2010) Semburan gas dan dampaknya terhadap lingkungan di sekitar Lumpur Sidoarjo. J Lingkung Dan Bencana Geol 1(1). https://doi.org/10.34126/jlbg.v1i1.5

Joerin J, Shaw R, Takeuchi Y, Krishnamurthy R (2014) The adoption of a climate disaster resilience index in Chennai, India. Disasters 38(3):540–561. https://doi.org/10.1111/disa.12058

Kirschbaum DB, Adler R, Hong Y, Hill S, Lerner-Lam A (2010) A global landslide catalog for hazard applications: method, results, and limitations. Nat Hazards 52(3):561–575. https://doi.org/10.1007/s11069-009-9401-4

Kjellstrom T, Friel S, Dixon J, Corvalan C, Rehfuess E, Campbell-Lendrum D, Gore F, Bartram J (2007) Urban environmental health hazards and health equity. J Urban Health 84(SUPPL. 1):86–97. https://doi.org/10.1007/s11524-007-9171-9

Koplitz SN, Mickley LJ, Marlier ME, Buonocore JJ, Kim PS, Liu T, Sulprizio MP, DeFries RS, Jacob DJ, Schwartz J, Pongsiri M, Myers SS (2016) Public health impacts of the severe haze in Equatorial Asia in September-October 2015: demonstration of a new framework for informing fire management strategies to reduce downwind smoke exposure. Environ Res Lett 11(9). https://doi.org/10.1088/1748-9326/11/9/094023

Kusumasari B (2019) Natural Hazards Governance in Indonesia. Nat Hazard Sci. https://doi.org/10.1093/acrefore/9780199389407.013.234

Law No. 26 Year 2007 On Spatial Management (2007)

Linnenluecke MK (2017) Resilience in business and management research: a review of influential publications and a research agenda. Int J Manag Rev 19(1):4–30. https://doi.org/10.1111/ijmr.12076

Lubis SW, Hagos S, Hermawan E, Respati MR, Ridho A, Risyanto, Paski JAI, Muhammad FR, Siswanto, Ratri DN, Setiawan S, Permana DS (2022) Record-breaking precipitation in Indonesia's capital of Jakarta in early January 2020 Linked to the Northerly Surge, Equatorial Waves, and MJO. Geophys Res Lett 49(22). https://doi.org/10.1029/2022GL101513

MoEF (2016). Regulation of the minister of environment and forestry number p.32 year 2016 concerning on forest and land fire management. Ministry of Environment and Forestry (MoEF)

MoEF (2023) Indication forest fires area. Ministry of Environment and Forestry (MoEF)

Muntohar AS, Mavrouli O, Jetten VG, Van CJ, Hidayat R (2021) Development of landslide early warning system based on the satellite-derived rainfall threshold in Indonesia. In: Casagli N, Tofani V, Sassa K, Bobrowsky PT, Takara K (eds) Understanding and reducing landslide disaster risk. Volume 3: monitoring and early warning. Springer. https://doi.org/10.1007/978-3-030-60311-3_26

Nichols JM (2007) The 2006 Yogyakarta earthquake—a preliminary study of deaths. WIT Trans Built Environ 93:207–213. https://doi.org/10.2495/ERES070201

Novenanto A (2015) Membangun Bencana: Tinjauan Kritis atas Peran Negara dalam Kasus LapindoKasus Lapind. Masy: J Sosiol 20(2).

Octavianti T, Charles K (2019) The evolution of Jakarta's flood policy over the past 400 years: the lock-in of infrastructural solutions. Environ Plan C: Polit Space 37(6):1102–1125. https://doi.org/10.1177/2399654418813578

Oktari RS, Shiwaku K, Munadi K, Syamsidik, Shaw R (2018) Enhancing community resilience towards disaster: the contributing factors of school-community collaborative network in the tsunami affected area in Aceh. Int J Disaster Risk Reduct 29:3–12. https://doi.org/10.1016/j.ijdrr.2017.07.009

Pörtner H-O, Roberts DC, Tignor MMB, Poloczanska E, Mintenbeck K, Alegría A, Craig M, Langsdorf S, Löschke S, Möller V, Okem A, Rama B (eds) (2022) IPCC, 2022: climate change 2022: impacts, adaptation, and vulnerability. contribution of working group II to the sixth assessment report of the intergovernmental panel on climate change. Cambridge University Press. https://doi.org/10.1017/9781009325844

Putra DI, Matsuyuki M (2020) The disaster-management capabilities of local governments: a case study in Indonesia. J Disaster Res 15(4):471–480. https://doi.org/10.20965/jdr.2020.p0471

Rahiem MDH, Rahim H, Ersing R (2021) Why did so many women die in the 2004 Aceh Tsunami? Child survivor accounts of the disaster. Int J Disaster Risk Reduct 55:102069. https://doi.org/10.1016/j.ijdrr.2021.102069

Reliefweb (2023) Indonesia: drought—2023–2024. Reliefweb

Roziqin and Mas'udi, S. Y. F., & Sihidi, I. T. , 2021 Roziqin A, Mas'udi SYF, Sihidi IT (2021) An analysis of Indonesian government policies against COVID-19. Public Adm Policy 24(1):92–107. https://doi.org/10.1108/PAP-08-2020-0039

Saharjo BH (2022) Research for fire prevention management in Indonesia (Smoke, Haze, Ghg Emission Reduction, and Deforestation). J Trop Silviculture 13(1):1–13. https://doi.org/10.29244/j-siltrop.13.01.1-13

Setiadi S, Sumaryana A, Bekti H, Sukarno D (2023) The flood management policy in Bandung city: challenges and potential strategies. Cogent Soc Sci 9(2). https://doi.org/10.1080/23311886.2023.2282434

Sitanggang IS, Istiqomah N, Syaufina L (2018) Fire spot identification based on hotsport sequential pattern and burned area classification. Biotropia 25(3). https://doi.org/10.11598/btb.2018.25.3.676

Sukhwani V, Napitupulu H, Jingnan D, Yamaji M, Shaw R (2021) Enhancing cultural adequacy in post-disaster temporary housing. Prog Disaster Sci 11:100186. https://doi.org/10.1016/j.pdisas.2021.100186

Sulaeman D, Pradana A, Hamzah H (2019) 3 main causes of floods in Indonesia and how to prevent them. World Resources Institute (WRI) Indonesia

Trias APL, Cook ADB (2021) Future directions in disaster governance: insights from the 2018 Central Sulawesi Earthquake and Tsunami response. Int J Disaster Risk Reduct 58:102180. https://doi.org/10.1016/j.ijdrr.2021.102180

Wati KM, Bantam DJ (2023) Identify mitigation levels disaster FES Unjaya students based survey knowledge disaster and extension non-structural mitigation management field. Jurnal Mantik 7(2):868–877. https://doi.org/10.35335/mantik.v7i2.3893

Widiachristy L, Rachmanto AS (2021) the effectiveness of Jakarta smart city application in enhancing community resilience in facing flood risk. J Arch Environ 20(1):45. https://doi.org/10.12962/j2355262x.v20i1.a9034

Widiyanto W, Santoso PB, Hsiao SC, Imananta RT (2019) Post-event field survey of 28 September 2018 Sulawesi earthquake and tsunami. Nat Hazard 19(12):2781–2794. https://doi.org/10.5194/nhess-19-2781-2019

Wijayanti et al., 2017 Wijayanti P, Zhu X, Hellegers P, Budiyono Y, van Ierland EC (2017) Estimation of river flood damages in Jakarta, Indonesia. Nat Hazards 86(3):1059–1079. https://doi.org/10.1007/s11069-016-2730-1

Woods M (2007) Engaging the global countryside: Globalization, hybridity and the reconstitution of rural place. Prog Hum Geogr 31(4):485–507. https://doi.org/10.1177/0309132507079503

World Bank (2016) The cost of fire Indonesia—an economic analysis of Indonesia's 2015 fire crisis. World Bank

Chapter 13
Disaster Legislation in the Philippines

Ma. Theresa P. Pamaong and Rajib Shaw

Abstract The Republic Act 10121 or the Philippine Disaster Risk Reduction and Management Act of 2010 aims to strengthen the Disaster Risk Reduction (DRR) programs of the local government in dealing with disasters. A salient feature of the law is the creation of the Local Disaster Risk Reduction and Management Fund (LDRRMF) which allocates 5% of government funds to support disaster risk management activities. This study highlights the status, challenges, and gaps in the governance of the local government in implementing this unique system of resource allocation as an innovative tool to mainstream disaster risk reduction into development planning.

Keywords Disaster risk reduction · Disaster governance · Local government

13.1 Introduction

The World Risk Report (2023) ranks the Philippines as the No. 1 country among 193 countries most vulnerable to disasters. The country achieved a World Risk Index (WRI) of 46.86 in its latest report. Around 19–20 tropical cyclones enter the Philippine Area of Responsibility (PAR) every year (PAG-ASA 2022) and 12, 628 earthquakes were recorded in 2021 (DOST-PHIVOLCS 2021). Its geographic location near the Pacific Ocean and the Pacific Ring of Fire is one of the factors that make the country prone to typhoons and earthquakes.

The Philippines has over 7,100 islands and is home to 109,035,343 Filipinos (Philippine Statistics Authority 2021). The Filipino people are known to be resilient, particularly in handling disasters. Victoria (2003) provides the concept of resilience firmly rooted despite the strong winds. This is shown during the time of the COVID-19 pandemic. COVID-19 exacerbated institutional, social, and political issues to grapple with its impacts. The economy is one of the sectors that was highly affected by

Ma. T. P. Pamaong (✉) · R. Shaw
Graduate School of Media and Governance, Keio University, 5322 Endo, Fujisawa 252-0882, Japan
e-mail: matesapam@keio.jp

Y. Cui and R. Shaw (eds.), *Disaster Law*, Disaster Risk Reduction,
https://doi.org/10.1007/978-981-97-7374-9_13

the pandemic. Economic activities were limited due to the social distancing protocols that were implemented. The pandemic provides a paradigm shift in how people live. It presents an opportunity for people and the government to work together in formulating measures to address it. These measures and resilience have worked together to pave for the economic recovery of the country. The economic recovery growth of the country has increased to 7.6% in 2022 from 5.7% in 2021 (World Bank 2023). This achievement underscores the importance of continuous efforts and initiatives and the dynamic partnership of the people and the government to improve one's society.

Similarly, the Philippine government is continuously gearing up its capabilities to ensure the safety and security of the people in addressing environmental issues such as climate change. The Philippines is the first country in Asia to enact a specific piece of legislation on climate change (IFRC 2020). The Republic Act No. 9729 or the Climate Change Act of 2009 aims to mainstream climate change into government policy, to plan frameworks, and to implement programs to address the impacts of climate change. Furthermore, the country has put forward and become more proactive in disaster legislation with the Republic Act No. 10121 or the Philippine Disaster Risk Reduction and Management Act of 2010 in the aftermath of Typhoon Ketsana in 2009 (Caspellan 2022). Its salient feature is its multi-hazard approach in dealing with disasters specifically, highlighting the importance of disaster risk reduction and empowering communities and local governments with their roles to develop resilience. The passage of the law is a crucial step as it serves as the blueprint and sets the direction to attain its goal. This goal will be achieved by building an effective governance to utilize the available resources. Local Government Units (LGUs) in the country play an important role in the implementation of the law. Section 21 of RA 10121 stipulates the creation of a local calamity fund to be known as the Local Disaster Risk Reduction and Management Fund (LDRRMF). A fund not less than 5% of the estimated revenue is allotted for disaster risk management activities in the areas of pre-disaster preparedness, procurement of life-saving rescue equipment and supplies, and post-disaster activities. Further, 30% is appropriated and will be allocated as a Quick Response Fund (QRF) or stand-by fund for relief and recovery programs of communities affected by disasters. The 5% fund allotment is aligned with the Local Government Code of 1991, which also requires 5% of annual lump-sum appropriations for relief, rehabilitation, reconstruction, and other works or services in connection with calamities that may occur during the budget year. The unused local appropriations for the current year will be transferred to a special trust fund of the LGU under the LDRRMF for future use and will be reverted to the LGU's general budget if unutilized after five years (Qian et al. 2020).

This chapter highlights the status, challenges, and gaps in the governance of the local government in implementing this unique system of resource allocation as an innovative tool to mainstream disaster risk reduction into development planning. This study utilizes a desk review of online secondary resources from journal articles, humanitarian agency reports, and public documents such as policy documents, annual reports, and training manuals as well as studies related to local governance were examined to understand disaster governance in the context of the Philippines to capture the phenomenon. The keywords of disaster law, Philippine disaster, and LGU in the Philippines were used in the online search of the documents.

13.2 Status of the Disaster Legislation in the Philippines

The disaster legislation of the Philippines traces back to Presidential Decree No. 1566 by former President Ferdinand Marcos Sr. on June 11, 1978. The decree aims to strengthen the national programs and measures in handling disasters at national, regional, and local levels. It provides the legal basis for the establishment of the National Disaster Coordinating Council (NDCC) which consists of nineteen (19) government officials from different government agencies that will work in times of disaster. Its provision allows for the creation of an organizational structure for the regional and local levels to respond during disasters. In addition, it entails a two percent (2%) fund allocation to be solely used for disaster preparedness programs such as the construction of physical facilities and training of disaster action teams to equip them in conducting their operations.

Figure 13.1 shows the summary of the disaster legislation in the Philippines. Currently, RA 10121 represents an advanced model for a law related to climate and disaster resilience (IFRC 2020). Before RA 10121 was passed into law, the passage of Republic Act No. 9729, or the Climate Change Act of 2009 was enacted. The law aims to incorporate disaster risk reduction measures into climate change plans and to establish the Climate Change Commission (CCC). CCC is an independent and autonomous institution equivalent to a national government agency. It is mandated to formulate government policies relating to climate change. Proactive disaster legislation in the country enables a dynamic synergy in the interaction of governance, climate, disaster, and community participation. These interactions were improved by the existing laws enacted in the country particularly the Republic Act No. 7160 and Republic Act No. 8425 on October 10, 1991, and June 30, 1998, respectively.

The Republic Act No. 7160 or the Local Government Code of 1991 aims to ensure fiscal sustainability, strengthen local autonomy, and avoid duplication of responsibilities between the National Government and the LGUs (DBM 2022). The law provides a clear division of roles and responsibilities between the national and local governments. It represents one of Southeast Asia's most comprehensive legislation on sub-national authority on the political, administrative, and fiscal aspects of governance (Shair- Rosenfield 2016). The law empowers LGUs to exercise their political powers which is aligned with section 13, Article X of the 1987 Constitution where local government units may group themselves, consolidate, or coordinate their efforts, services, and resources for purposes commonly beneficial to them by the law (Official Gazette n.d.). Its passage provided a policy and legal framework for multiple entry points to an inclusive and participatory approach in creating platforms for citizen and civil society organizations to improve local governance (Brillantes & Cabo 2006).

Legislation	Title	Description
RA 9003	Ecological Solid Waste Management Act of 2000	a national policy on managing solid waste in the country
RA 10821	The Children's Emergency Relief and Protection Act of 2016	emergency relief and protection of children before, during and after disasters and other emergency situations.
RA No. 7077	Citizen Armed Force or Armed Forces of the Philippines Reservist Act.	Section 7: Reservist's mission to assist in relief and rescue during disasters or calamities
RA No. 10174	The People's Survival Fund Act	Amendment of RA 9729 (Climate Change Act) in establishing The People's Survival Fund, a long stream finance for adaptation projects of local government units and local/community organizations aimed at increasing resilience of communities and ecosystems to climate change
Executive Order No. 137, s 2021	Accelerating And Harmonizing Aid And Humanitarian Operations Of The National Government During Disasters And Emergencies	Institutionalize "Aid and Humanitarian Operations Nationwide" *AHON* Convergence Program to enhance and unify delivery of social amelioration services
Executive Order No. 137, s 1999	Declaring The Month Of July Of Every Year As National Disaster Consciousness Month And Institutionalizing The Civil Defense Deputization Program	Increase in the disaster awareness of every Filipino and appreciate government's disaster preparedness programs
Executive Order 29	Renaming The National Disaster Consciousness Month To National Disaster Resilience Month And Shifting Its Focus From Disaster Awareness Building To Disaster Resilience	Promotion of the significance of disaster resilience
Executive Order 24	Constituting The Disaster Response And Crisis Management Task Force	A task force that focuses only on disaster preparedness and response

Fig. 13.1 Summary of the disaster legislation in the Philippines. *Source* Accessed through Government online databases and compiled by the authors

Similarly, the Social Reform Agenda (SRA) was created during the administration of former president Fidel V. Ramos. The Social Reform Agenda will be defined in equal partnership with different sectors where meaningful consultation and participation in governance will be promoted (PSSC 1995). The SRA is the administration's response to address poverty and act as a mechanism to spur economic development in the country. The passage of Republic Act No. 8425 or the Social Reform and Poverty Alleviation Act institutionalizes and enhances SRA. The law became the cornerstone in institutionalizing democratic practices and participation of marginalized groups and sectors in local and national governance (PSSC 1995). It empowers different various local communities to amplify their voices to improve local governance.

RA 7160 and Republic Act No. 8425 build a landscape for the national government to decentralize political powers to the local government. The decentralization is initiated to increase the productivity of LGUs in catering the needs of their constituents (Porio 2017). This decentralization allows LGUs to formulate policies and solutions that are crucial and necessary in their decision-making process, particularly during disasters. It provides a tool to examine how the politics of disasters may be utilized to formulate better, equitable, and inclusive policy choices (Delos Santos 2023). This is the main goal that the RA 10,121 wants to achieve.

13.3 Overview of the Republic Act. No. 10121 or the Philippine Disaster Risk Reduction Act of 2010

RA No. 10121 was enacted into law by former President Gloria Macapagal-Arroyo on May 27, 2010. This legislation seeks to provide holistic, participatory, institutionalized, proactive, and collaborative roles for LGUs and Non-Government Organizations (NGOs) to build resilient communities (Pellini et al. 2013). The law is a substantial development from PD No. 1566 where it focuses on the preparedness aspects yet frames DRRM from the standpoint of emergency response (Caspellan 2022).

The law institutionalized the National Disaster Risk Reduction Management Council (NDRRMC) which consists of thirty-eight (38) member agencies and serves as the policymaking body to plan, coordinate, supervise, and formulate the National Disaster Risk Reduction and Management Plan or the NDRRMP. The NDRRMP sets the goals and specific objectives to reduce disaster risks, particularly in the aspects of disaster prevention and mitigation, disaster preparedness, disaster response, and disaster rehabilitation and recovery. The plan ensures the incorporation of disaster risk reduction and climate change adaptation into local development plans and programs as a mechanism for sustainable development. Figure 13.2 illustrates the hierarchical structure of the councils.

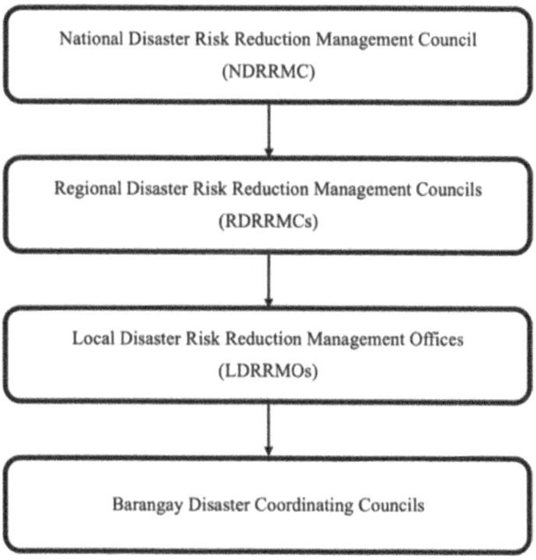

Fig. 13.2 The hierarchical structure. *Source* Author's illustration

13.4 National Government Initiatives for Local Governance

13.4.1 Performance Challenge Fund

The Performance Challenge Fund (PCF) is a financial grant program of the Department of the Interior and Local Government (DILG) that recognizes LGUs' excellence in governance in the areas of transparency, accountability, participation, and service delivery. It incentivizes qualified LGUs who have implemented development projects included in their Annual Investment Program (AIP). The Seal of Good Local Governance (SGLG) defines the eligibility requirement of the LGU to be qualified for the grant. The LGU should meet the core components that are assessed namely (a) peace and order, (b) environmental protection, and (c) Business-friendliness and competitiveness (ULAP n.d.). The financial grant received can be utilized as an additional budget for their local development projects.

13.4.2 KAlamidad at Sakuna LAbanan, SAriling Galing ang Kaligtasan **Gawad Kalasag (GK Seal and Special Awards for Excellence)**

The *Gawad Kalasag* (GK) is an award program that was established in 1998 by the National Disaster Risk Reduction Management Council (DRRMC) through the Office of Civil Defense (OCD). The OCD is the implementing arm of NDRRMC and an organization within the Department of National Defense (DND). It was then transformed into the Gawad KALASAG Seal and Special Awards for Excellence in Disaster Risk Reduction and Management and Humanitarian Assistance. Figure 13.3 shows the category and incentives for GK awardees. The award created a performance and compliance assessment mechanism to recognize the community efforts of the LGUs in localizing the initiatives of NDRRMC such as the institution of DRRM councils and offices (Pineda 2023). It aspires to strengthen disaster resilience through a "whole-of-society" approach to promote inclusivity and participation in DRR-CCA practices.

13.4.3 Operation **L!sto**

The Department of the Interior and Local Government—Local Government Academy (DILG—LGA) created Operation L!STO in 2014. It is a national advocacy program about disaster preparedness. It serves as a guide for government officials and personnels on the actions on handling disasters. Also, it aims to train the L!STO

CATEGORIES		INCENTIVES
GK Seal for Local DRRM Councils and Offices	1. Local DRRM Councils and Offices	Plaque of Recognition: GK Seal of Excellence Beyond Compliant: Gold Plaque Fully Compliant: Silver Plaque
GK Special Awards for Civil Society Organizations	2. Volunteer Organizations (Emergency Response)	Top Awardee: Plaque plus Php 300,000.00 1 Finalists: Plaque plus Php 100,000.00
	3. Peoples Organizations	
	4. Local Civil Society Organizations	
GK Special Awards for GEMs	5. Basic Local Government Emergency Management and Response Team (GEMs) for 4th to 6th Class Municipalities	Top Awardee: Plaque plus Php 300,000.00 1 Finalists: Plaque plus Php 100,000.00
	6. Advance Local Government Emergency Management and Response Team (GEMs) for Provinces, Cities, and 1 st to 3 rd Class Municipalities	
GK Special Awards for Hospitals	7. National Government Hospitals	Top Awardee: Plaque plus Php 300,000.00 2 Finalists: Plaque plus Php 100,000.00
	8. Local Government Hospitals	
	9. Private Hospitals	Top Awardee: Plaque plus Php 100,000.00 2 Finalists: Plaque plus Php 50,000.00
GK Special Awards for Schools	10. Higher Education Institution	Top Awardee: Plaque plus Php 300,000.00 2 Finalists: Plaque plus Php 100,000.00
	11. Public Elementary Schools	
	12. Public High Schools	
GK Special Awards for Private Organizations	13. Private Organizations (Business/Corporate)	Top Awardee: Plaque plus Php 100,000.00 2 Finalists: Plaque plus Php 50,000.00
GK Special Recognitions	14. Heroic Act (Individual/Group Living)	Plaque of Recognition Plus Php 50,000
	15. Heroic Act (Individual/Group Posthumous)	
	16. Special Recognition for Individuals 17. Special Recognition for Organizations	Plaque of Recognition

Fig. 13.3 The Gawad Kalasag Award Category and its corresponding Incentives. *Source* National Disaster Risk Reduction and Management Council (NDRRMC), Memorandum Circular No 001, 2023

teams in national and local governments. Its main goal is to institutionalize and standardize local protocols and platforms for disaster management in the country. The Local Government Academy (LGA) under the DILG conducts the training for LGU personnel.

Noteworthy is DILG's creation of a Quality Assurance System (QAS) specifically for the use of barangay level. Figure 13.4 shows the landing home page of the website and the training manuals being used. QAS has two components namely the Quality Assessment Tool (QAT) and BDRRM Plan Template. QAS is used to assess the quality and status of the BDRRM Plan BDRRM Committee. The BDRRM plan provides a checklist of essential items that should be included in the quality and

Fig. 13.4 Homepage website of quality assurance system (top) and training manuals for local government unit personnel (bottom). *Source* Department of the interior and local government—local government academy

comprehensive plan. The BDRRM Plan Template is used to formulate plans for the Barangay Disaster Risk Reduction and Management Committee (BDRRMC). Different people from the community are represented to promote inclusivity in the planning process. Figure 13.5 shows the hazard-specific manuals tailored for city and municipal government units in training local government officials.

13.5 Local Government in the Philippines

Figure 13.6 illustrates the Local Government Structure of the Philippines. The Philippines has 17 regions, 81 provinces, 33 highly urbanized cities, 108 component cities, 1,488 municipalities, and 42,046 barangays (Philippines Statistics Authority 2021). The *barangay* is the smallest political unit in the local government of the country. Noteworthy is that more than half of the *barangays* are at risk of disasters. Developing capabilities is essential to resilience. Disaster Preparedness is one of the key components. Disaster Preparedness is defined as the "knowledge and capacities developed by the governments to assist professionals in the response and recovery of organizations, communities, and individuals to effectively anticipate, respond to, and recover from the impacts of likely, imminent, or current hazards." (NDRRMC 2015).

Fig. 13.5 Hazard-specific manuals for city and municipal government. *Source* Department of the Ir and Local Government—Local Government Academy

The achievement of disaster resilience in the local government requires an enabling environment where the exercise of political powers spurs a great dynamic of partnership that fosters active community participation that lies in the delivery of local governance.

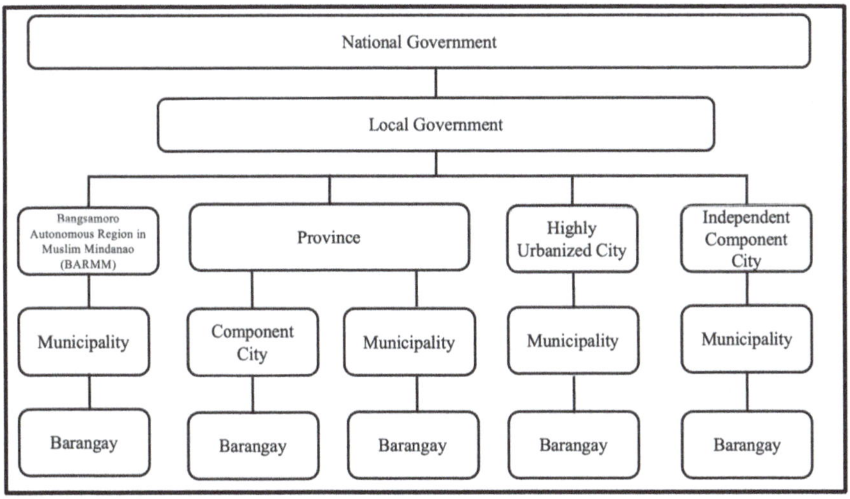

Fig. 13.6 The local government structure of the Philippines. *Source* Authors' illustration

13.5.1 Local Governance

The capability of a government to govern efficiently and effectively is the core of public service. It produces an enabling environment for both public officials and citizens to create harmonious synergy for the benefit of society. This is exemplified in the governance of disasters which is an essential component to achieve it. The DILG through the Bureau of Local Government Supervision (BLGS) organized a disaster preparedness assessment of the LGUs in 2014. The assessment has shown a preparedness rate of the country at 73.9% for 1,676 Local Government Units (LGUs) included in the assessment (NDRRMC 2015).

The result of the preparedness rate reveals that a lot of work should be done particularly in the aspect of disaster preparedness in the country. During the onset of the implementation of DRRM, a delay in the local level implementation of DRRM exists because there are no incentives to institutionalize DRRM offices and the 5% calamity fund can be tapped without building it (Pellini et al. 2013). There is no repercussion if they comply or not. Similarly, financial resources management is crucial to develop better plans and strategies. This requires an effective leader to realize it. This exceptional leadership is recognized by the DILG through the PCF. However, 20 percent of municipalities are not eligible to receive PCF grants because they do not meet the requirements (Sicat et al. 2022). The PCF put forward excellent governance and compliance with the creation of disaster plans. On the other hand, in the context of human capital, there is a notion that community engagement is synonymous with more expenses (transportation, food, honorarium), and investment returns are not guaranteed in the long run (Domingo & Manejar 2021). Likewise, local government units' interaction with community partnerships shows that a total of 555 (43.4%) LGUs had a mechanism for partnership or networking with the private sector; 198 (15.5%) LGUs received commendations from their partners; 423 (33.1%) LGUs have minimal or limited interoperability in mobilizing them. Lastly, 301 (23.5%) LGUs had no partnership at all (COA 2022). In addition, public officials are more likely to spend on projects that can show results during their term in office (Delos Santos 2023). Their views about community engagement, and political motivations affect their priority in making decisions pertaining to disasters. Local political tensions present in the area hinder as well in the process such as in the case of Cotabato. Cotabato is located on the island of Mindanao. Its borders traverse across the Bangsamoro Autonomous Region in Muslim Mindanao where a high risk of not only natural hazards exists but the notion of human-induced incidents (Domingo & Manejar 2021). Moreover, these factors influence not only on how they interact with their jurisdiction but also with the national government. Noteworthy is that this perspective makes them allocate fewer resources to pre-disaster activities and expect the national government to rescue them when a disaster occurs in their jurisdiction (Delos Santos 2023). This can lead to coordination practices that can exacerbate the improvement in developing disaster resilience in the country. The Super Typhoon Yolanda in 2013 and the Marawi Siege in 2017 offer significant perspectives on the coordination of the government during disasters.

Bangon Marawi projects amounting to P 56.803 million were not fully distributed to beneficiaries due to erring suppliers/contractors and unsupported LGUs (Qian et al. 2020). Trust with authorities is a pinnacle of good governance that can foster good community partnerships. However, excessive reliance on partnerships can be a recipe for destruction as witnessed in Tacloban for the super typhoon Yolanda. The local government is highly dependent on outside sources for recovery and rehabilitation (Paragas et al. 2016). They were overwhelmed with the outside sources that the establishment of a unified system should be created for an equal distribution of resources. Delos Santos (2023) argues that when the national government controls financial resources, human losses during disasters are fewer. This brings forth a greater challenge in the essence and implementation of the DRRM law in the country.

13.5.2 Expenditure

The Philippine government has increased its fund allotment for climate change adaptation and mitigation from PHP 195 billion in 2017 to PHP 289 billion in 2022 but its total budget declined from 6.99 to 5.77 percent in the same period (NEDA, 2022). The 2022 Annual report released by the Commission on Audit (COA) shows that a total of 1,517 LGUs allocated a total amount of P 43.790 billion for its LDRRMF for CY 2022. It flagged 218 LGUs that were not able to optimally utilize their LDRRMF and funds of 204 LGUs, amounting to at least d1.346 billion, were utilized for purposes other than the activities that were prescribed in the law (COA 2022). Similarly, the study of Qian et al. (2020) is a pioneer panoramic review of post-disaster spending in the country to serve as a guide in studying total disaster expenditures and related processes. It reveals that an average of six percent (6%) of LGUs have used LDRRMF allocation for other activities and 20% do not properly report the use of funds. This budget allocation stems from the local government's priorities in terms of disasters. Brucal et al. (2020) argue that the allocations of national funds are not proportionate to storm impacts where certain areas received significantly higher amounts of national aid compared with areas that experienced worse impacts. This disparity in budget allocation makes the situation worsen. Likewise, the NDRRMC was mainly used for post-disaster activities and quick response funds for agencies (NEDA 2022). A misalignment of fund allocation exists in the local government and efforts for disaster risk reduction are put on a halt. Figure 13.7 shows the spending patterns of the local and municipal governments in the context of disasters. It reveals that the local governments put the highest priority on the procurement of equipment while the least priority is on the conduct of seminars and training. The proper fund allocation of disaster funds poses a grave challenge and the monitoring of actual expenditures in the agency and LGUs is insufficient which led for the government to track and assess the progress in the climate agenda (NEDA 2022).

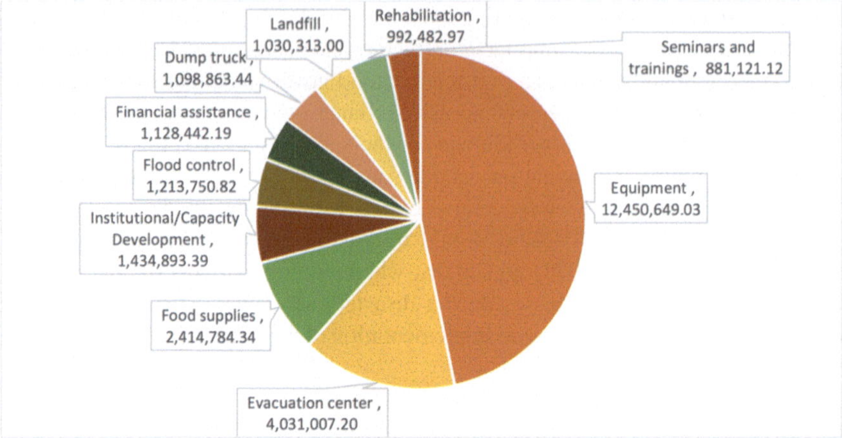

Fig. 13.7 Spending patterns of municipal and city local governments. *Source* Domingo and Manejar (2021)

13.6 The Role of the National Government

The disaster legislation in the Philippines has established different avenues for the local and national government to work together to achieve a resilient country. Its core is on mainstreaming disaster risk reduction into development planning particularly in the local government. This creates opportunities to put disaster management as a crucial step in providing better solutions and services for the interest of the people. The national government has created various measures to empower the LGUs to develop their capabilities in handling disasters. It attempts to build an open and dynamic partnership between the national government and LGUs by providing different avenues of participation. Noteworthy are the fund allocation, award system programs, and capacity-building projects for the LGUs. The allocation of funds solely for disaster risk management efforts enhances the capability of the local government to empower its political leaders and the community to leverage their capabilities in disaster management. The allocation of funds allows the LGUs to shape the direction of how disaster management will work in the best interest of their locality.

Next, the award system programs particularly the Performance Challenge Fund and Gawad Kalasag Award by DILG and NDRRMC respectively serve to acknowledge the efforts not only of the LGUs initiatives but also the participation of the people in promoting disaster risk reduction. This award system encourages cooperation and collaboration between the local government units and the community to mainstream disaster risk reduction in their locality. It sets the standard and commitment of the LGUs to sustain and innovate their disaster management programs. However, creating standards for these awards should be created with caution. Understanding the different existing capabilities of the LGUs such as their current human resource, logistical support, and economic situation to organize initiatives should be considered. These standards can mislead the main motivation and intention of the main cause of creating these awards.

Lastly, the capacity-building projects for the LGUs particularly with the launch of DILG-LGA's advocacy program Operation *L!sto*. These programs institutionalize disaster risk reduction efforts as a crucial activity for the local government officials in the country. It empowers them to be adept in various roles and responsibilities to ensure the safety and security of their constituents. It enables them to create various ways of community engagement in different sectors such as the youth, professionals, and community workers, among others to participate in strengthening their disaster risk reduction capabilities in their area.

The existing efforts of the national government to promote and strengthen disaster resilience in the country highlight the importance of active participation and partnership of the local government. Its effectiveness lies at the core of dynamic and proactive systems in the local government implementation.

13.7 The Role of Local Government

The local government units (LGUs) are a front liner in providing services during disasters and their role in disaster management has been put into the spotlight with the existing disaster legislation in the country. The local public official's leadership is important to achieving the goals of disaster risk reduction. The political motivation and priority of public officials influence the decision-making and fund allocation of the local government. The law emphasizes the promotion of disaster risk through disaster preparedness. The current expenditure of the LGUs situates their current priority toward disaster management. It reveals that the LGUs center their funds on infrastructures and logistical support more than human resources. There has been a focus on the recovery more than the preparedness programs. Next, the coordination of the public and private sectors in delivering goods and services during disasters is crucial. Thus, establishing a dynamic network and fostering good relationships should be put into highlight in the planning activities. The core of this network and relationship is with people. The people in the community are the valuable assets that the local government units should put into its core. Their skills and knowledge can contribute to the programs being implemented by their local government to strengthen efforts in dealing efficiently and effectively with disasters.

13.8 Conclusion

Disasters are inevitable events in our existence on earth. Disaster risks are evolving and the level of uncertainty for the future is certain. The future is grappling as we live in our present thriving to address environmental issues such as the impacts of climate change. We cannot do it alone. Institutions and communities should work together to engage in a conversation to create sustainable solutions. The government plays a role in mitigating it and in reducing the risks. The engagement and commitment of the government set a clear direction for a country.

This study demonstrates a multidisciplinary perspective in understanding the local and national disaster governance that exists in the Philippines. The Philippine government is ramping up its capability to enhance its disaster resilience. The study presented an overview of the historical development, status, and challenges in the implementation of the RA 10121 or the DRRM Act of 2010. The establishment of LDRRMF serves as an important tool not only for the allocation of disaster funds but the integration of disaster risk reduction in development planning particularly at the grassroots level. The study has demonstrated how synergy can be created between the local and national governments for disaster risk reduction highlighting the experience of the Philippines. Developing disaster resilience is not an overnight process nor a one-size-fits-it-all solution. Rather, creating platforms for collaborative participation and bringing them on a deck requires the establishment of trust, transparency, and truth between shareholders and local government.

The Philippine experience demonstrates the interplay of top-down and bottom-up approaches where both have a proactive engagement to address disaster risks. Many disaster laws are enacted in the country tackling various disaster issues and their relation to development issues. It emphasizes the integration of disaster risk reduction in development planning. This put forward the conversation of disaster into societal issues that call for the humanities and social science discipline participation to formulate long-term solutions. RA 10121 highlights the important function of the local government in achieving disaster resilience. This is also translated into how local officials govern their jurisdiction. The political motivation and priority of public officials influence the decision-making and fund allocation of the local government. The emphasis of the law is the promotion of disaster risk through disaster preparedness. However, local government efforts are more aligned in achieving short-term goals than long-term goals. This is attributed to the idea of the prestige and achievements that are tied to the public officials which they can accomplish during their terms. Thus, public interest sits in the corner. Similarly, the value of human capital development is necessary because it serves as an important tool for progress, and this is true as well with disaster education. However, there is a scarce fund allocation to enhance the skills and knowledge of DRRM practitioners. Noteworthy is that no matter how sophisticated the procured equipment is, if they do not have a knowledgeable staff to handle them, all efforts will be in vain, and it will only worsen the situation. This scarcity of funds for training is also the main reason why despite the large number of disasters the country has experienced, the country is still not resilient. Education plays an important role in disaster resilience. It empowers a community to engage in conversations through this platform. Many lives are lost, and infrastructures are destroyed. Public officials are pointing their fingers at others and the cycle of blaming games persists. The implementation of the law in the local government should put forward its goals and not be put to a halt. Despite its limitations, the national government is striving to encourage participation by granting qualified local governments to receive a financial grant. This adds to their fund budget and fortifies their commitment to attain DRRM goals.

Nevertheless, disaster governance in the Philippines offers the interaction of disaster resilience and development planning which is promulgated by crafting proactive disaster legislation to address disaster risk. The allotment of government funds solely for the promotion of disaster risk reduction demonstrates the government's commitment to contribute to disaster resilience. The active participation of the local government in mobilizing partnerships in the community is the core of this engagement.

References

Brucal A et al (2020) Disaster impacts and financing: local insights from the Philippines (Policy Report).Center for climate change economics and policy. https://www.lse.ac.uk/granthaminstitute/wp-content/uploads/2020/06/GRI_policy_report_Disaster-impacts-and-financing_Local-insights-from-the-Philippines.pdf

Brillantes A, Cabo W (2006) Towards greater local democratic governance: a view from the Philippines. In: Nakamura A (ed) Comparative studies of public administration IX civil society and local governance, pp 125–145. https://www.soumu.go.jp/main_content/000336608.pdf

Caspellan PA (2022) International disaster law at the domestic level: the Philippines. Yearb Int Disaster Law Online 3(1):502–511. https://doi.org/10.1163/26662531_00301_026

Commission on Audit (2022) Consolidated report on the audit of disaster risk reduction management (DRRM) funds for the year ended December 31, 2022. https://www.coa.gov.ph/reports/disaster-risk-reduction-and-management-reports/. Accessed 5 Jan 2024

Delos Santos R (2023) Fiscal decentralization and disaster mitigation: evidence from the Philippines [Master's Degree, The University of Tokyo]. https://www.pp.u-tokyo.ac.jp/wp-content/uploads/2016/02/02_51218206Thesis2023S_revised-v2.pdf

Department of Budget and Management (2022) 2022 DBM annual report produced by the advocacy, communications, and training service (ACTS) of the department of budget and management. https://www.dbm.gov.ph/wp-content/uploads/Reports/2022-DBM-Annual-Report-0616232.pdf. Accessed 4 Jan 2024

Diokno C, Castillo A, Maddawin R (2021) Philippine local government public expenditure review: a survey of national government local government support programs. Philippine Institute for Development Studies.

Diokno–Sicat et al (2022) Local government conditional grants: the seal of good local governance and the performance challenge fund. Philipp J Dev 46(1). https://pidswebs.pids.gov.ph/CDN/document/1684374222_646582ce4e466.pdf. Accessed 05 Jan 2024

Domingo S, Manejar A (2021) Policy, institutional, and expenditure review of bottom-up approach disaster risk reduction and management. Discussion Paper no. 2021–03. Philippine Institute for Development Studies. https://www.pids.gov.ph/publication/discussion-papers/policy-institutional-and-expenditure-review-of-bottom-up-approach-disaster-risk-reduction-and-management.

International Federation of Red Cross and Red Crescent Societies (2020) Addressing specific vulnerabilities through integrated climate and disaster risk governance lessons from the Philippines. https://disasterlaw.ifrc.org/sites/default/files/media/disaster_law/2021-05/IFRC-Philippines-Full-Report-Natoli_2020.pdf. Accessed 30 Dec 2023

Local Government Academy (2024) Technical guide notes barangay disaster risk reduction management plan and committee (English). https://alertandready.ph/qatportal/sites/default/files/B.%20Technical%20Guide%20Notes_English.pdf. Accessed 10 Jan 2024

Local Government Academy (2021) Annual report 2021. https://cdn.lga.gov.ph/publication/attachments/1657697981.pdf. Accessed 15 Dec 2023

Local Government Academy (2018) Homepage of quality assurance system [screenshot image]. https://www.alertandready.ph. Accessed 06 Jan 2024

National Disaster Risk Reduction and Management Council (2023) Memorandum circular No 0001, 2023 guidelines for 23rd Gawad KALASAG seal and special awards for excellence in disaster risk reduction and management and humanitarian assistance

National Disaster Risk Reduction and Management Council (2015) National disaster preparedness plan 2015–2028. vol 1. https://www.rcrc-resilience-southeastasia.org/wp-content/uploads/2018/01/2015-National-Disaster-Preparedness-Plan-2015-2018-Vol-1.pdf. Accessed 10 Oct 2023

National Economic and Development Authority (2022) Philippine Development Plan 2023–2028. https://pdp.neda.gov.ph/philippine-development-plan-2023-2028/. Accessed 15 Dec 2023

Official Gazette (n.d) The constitution of the republic of the Philippines. https://www.officialgazette.gov.ph/constitutions/1987-constitution/

Paragas G, Rodil A, Pelingon L (2016) Tacloban after Haiyan: working together towards recovery. International Institute for Environment and Development. http://www.jstor.org/stable/resrep02718

Philippine Atmospheric, Geophysical and Astronomical Services Administration (2022) Pagasa 2022 annual report. https://pubfiles.pagasa.dost.gov.ph/pagasaweb/files/transparency/PAGASA_2022%20AR(preview).pdf Accessed 14 Dec 2023

Philippine Institute of Volcanology and Seismology (2021) Annual report. https://www.phivolcs.dost.gov.ph/index.php/publications/annual-report. Accessed 10 Dec 2023

Pineda J (2023) Gawad KALASAG entries for national evaluation increase by 22.3% in 2023 - OCD. Philippine information agency. https://pia.gov.ph/news/2023/08/04/gawad-kalasag-entries-for-national-evaluation-increase-by-223-in-2023-ocd

Porio E (2017) Citizen participation and decentralization in the Philippines. In Berenschot W, Nordholt HS, Bakker L (eds) Citizenship and democratization in Southeast Asia, pp 31–50. Brill. http://www.jstor.org/stable/https://doi.org/10.1163/j.ctt1w76ws5.6

Pellini A et al (2013) Natural disasters and urban resilience in the Philippines: key definitions and policies. In: Towards policy-relevant science and scientifically informed policy: political economy of the use of knowledge and research evidence in urban resilience interventions in the Philippines, pp 9–23. http://www.jstor.org/stable/resrep50491.7

Philippine Social Science Council (1995) The social reform agenda. Philipp J Public Adm 39(2):218–229. https://www.pssc.org.ph/wp-content/pssc-archives/Philippine%20Journal%20of%20Public%20Administration/1995/Num%202/11_The%20Social%20Reform%20Agenda.pdf. Accessed 15 Dec 2023

Philippine Statistics Authority (2021) Facts and figures Philippine standard geographic code – as of 30 June 2021 (Infographics). https://psa.gov.ph/sites/default/files/infographics/PSGC%20Infographics.pdf?width=950&height=700&iframe=true. Accessed 10 Dec 2023

Qian R, Signer B, Tatiana Skalon T, Zidni Marohombsar Z (2020) Public expenditure review disaster response and rehabilitation in the Philippines. https://doi.org/10.1596/35064. Accessed 15 Dec 2023

Shair-Rosenfield S (2016) The causes and effects of the local government code in the Philippines: locked in a Status Quo of weakly decentralized authority? J Southeast Asian Econ 33(2):157–171. http://www.jstor.org/stable/44132299

Union of Local Authorities of the Philippines (n.d). DILG-BLGD and ULAP conduct performance challenge fund breakthrough summit. News. https://ulap.net.ph/ulap-news/news/110-dilg-blgd-and-ulap-conduct-performance-challenge-fund-breakthrough-summit.html

Victoria LP (2003) Community-based disaster management in the Philippines: making a difference in people's lives. Philipp Sociol Rev 51:65–80. http://www.jstor.org/stable/44243073

World Bank (2023) Philippines. https://www.worldbank.org/en/country/philippines/overview

Chapter 14
Disaster Law in Bangladesh: Current Scenario, Management Strategies and Challenges

Md. Hosenuzzaman, Ummoy Sumaia Shammy, Mohammad Golam Kibria, and Md. Anwarul Abedin

Abstract Bangladesh is a highly disaster-prone country suffering from natural and anthropogenic disasters. Therefore, the government has developed a comprehensive legal framework and laws to address disaster management and mitigation. These disaster management laws and frameworks have been a major focus, with investments in disaster management significantly decreasing. The government of Bangladesh has already implemented different laws regarding disaster management in coordination with the stakeholders, and Bangladesh has made significant strides in improving its disaster resilience. The laws were put into practice to make coordination among different institutions for building up infrastructure to effectively manage all types of disasters. This chapter will discuss the history of disaster in Bangladesh, different disaster risk management processes, institutional management strategies and coordination with different stakeholders, disaster management plans in Bangladesh, and the overall challenges for effective disaster management in Bangladesh.

Keywords Disaster laws · Challenges in disaster management and disaster resilience

14.1 Introduction

Legislation is crucial to implement disaster risk management (DRM) in society by executing risk reduction and mitigation activities (Shreve and Kelman 2014; Josephson et al. 2017). In the rapidly changing global climate and an increasing frequency of natural disasters, the importance of robust legal frameworks for disaster

Md. Hosenuzzaman · M. G. Kibria · Md. A. Abedin (✉)
Laboratory of Environment and Sustainable Development, Department of Soil Science, Bangladesh Agricultural University, Mymensingh, Bangladesh
e-mail: m.a.abedin@bau.edu.bd

U. S. Shammy
Department of Agro-Meteorology, Agricultural University, Mymensingh, Bangladesh

Y. Cui and R. Shaw (eds.), *Disaster Law*, Disaster Risk Reduction,
https://doi.org/10.1007/978-981-97-7374-9_14

risk management cannot be overstated. The use of policies and techniques for disaster risk reduction to prevent new disaster risk, lessen current disaster risk, and manage residual risk that helps to increase resilience and lower disaster losses is known as disaster risk management (Nirupama 2013). Community-based disaster risk management encourages the participation of potentially affected local communities in disaster risk management (Räsänen et al. 2020). This involves hazard, vulnerability, and capacity assessments conducted by the community as well as their participation in the design, execution, monitoring, and assessment of local disaster risk reduction initiatives. The disaster risk management cycle is a continuous process by which governments, private sector, development partners, communities and civil society plan to reduce the impact of disasters, respond during and immediately after a disaster, and take actions to recover after a disaster has occurred. In other words, disaster risk reduction (prevention and mitigation) and disaster management (the conventional preparedness, response, and recovery operations) are included in DRM. In the context of Bangladesh, a country prone to various natural calamities, the intersection of law and disaster management takes on a critical role in safeguarding lives, property, and the overall resilience of the nation.

This chapter delves into the intricate web of disaster law in Bangladesh, providing an insightful exploration of the current scenario, existing legal frameworks, and the challenges that emerge in the pursuit of effective disaster management. Bangladesh, nestled in the delta of major rivers and characterized by its vulnerability to cyclones, floods, and earthquakes, has forged a dynamic legal landscape to address the multifaceted challenges posed by natural disasters.

14.2 History of Disaster in Bangladesh

Natural disasters have a long history in Bangladesh. Following its independence on December 16, 1971, the newly formed nation experienced storms and floods in 1972. The disaster is still in rising trend. Bangladesh encountered a total of 297 natural disasters (Fig. 14.4) from 1972 to 2017, during these 46 years, (Baten et al. 2018). According to reports of EM-DAT (CRED), it was found that natural disaster happened every year in Bangladesh since 1972. It was found that same types of natural disasters occurred frequently in Bangladesh. Storm (tropical & convective), flood, and epidemics are frequent among the natural disasters in Bangladesh.

It has been observed that throughout the specified timeframe, storms happened 141 times, accounting for approximately 47% of all disasters. Floods are the next most common natural disaster, accounting for 29% of all natural disasters. Of all the natural calamities, droughts and landslides occur less frequently. There have been nine geophysical disaster earthquakes and twenty-two climatological disasters with extremely high temperatures (Sapir 2017).

14.3 The Disaster Risk Management Process

This covers an in-depth knowledge of the three primary phases of disaster risk management, as illustrated in Fig. 14.1.

14.3.1 Stages of disaster management

All aspects of preparing for and responding to disasters are included in disaster management, including pre-, during-, and post-disaster planning. The goals are to reduce human suffering, prevent fatalities, warn the public and authorities of potential risks, minimize property damage and economic loss, and expedite the recovery process. The following are the three main phases of the actions that are conducted in disaster risk management (Fig. 14.2).

14.3.1.1 Pre-disaster (Before a Disaster)

Pre-disaster measures are those undertaken to lessen losses to people and property that could result from a possible hazard. For instance, risk assessment, preparedness and early warning, launching awareness campaigns, fortifying the weak structures already in place, creating plans for home and community disaster management, etc. Activities associated with preparedness and mitigation are those risk-reduction strategies implemented at this stage.

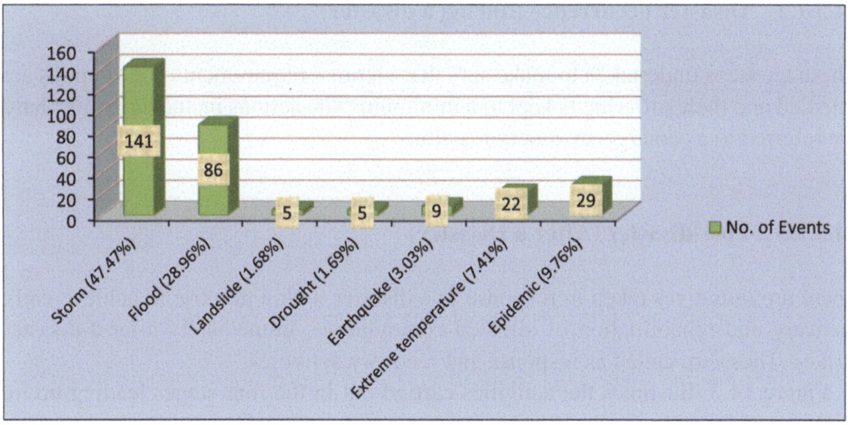

Fig. 14.1 Frequency of Natural Disaster in Bangladesh since 1972. (EM-DAT/CRED)

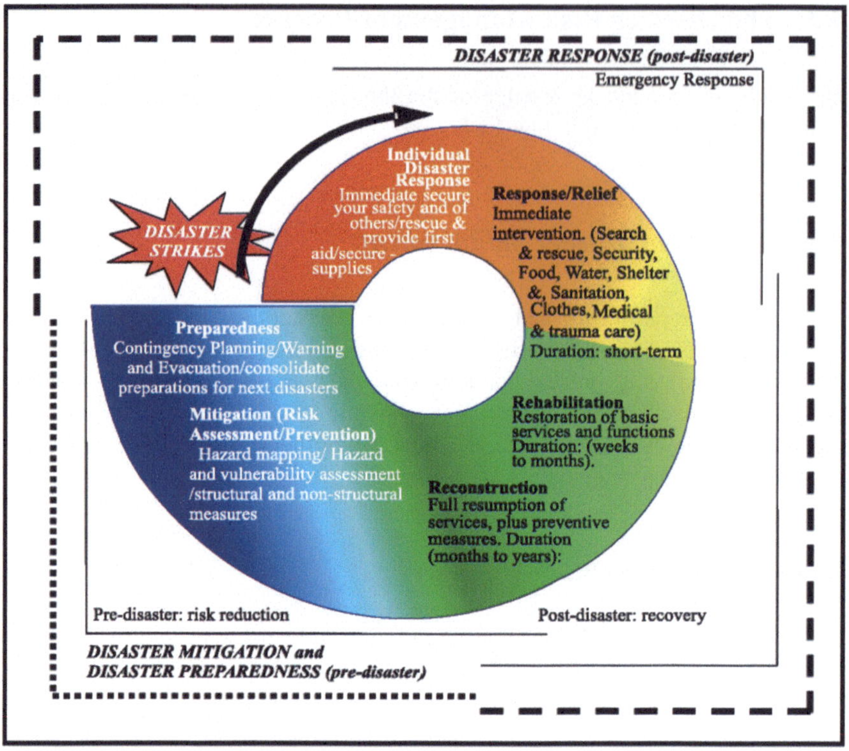

Fig. 14.2 Stages of disaster management. *Source* Khan et al. (2008)

14.3.1.2 Disaster occurrence (during a disaster)

These are steps undertaken to make sure that victims' requirements and supplies are satisfied and their suffering is kept to a minimum. The actions included in this phase are referred to as emergency reaction actions.

14.3.1.3 Post-disaster (After a Disaster)

There are initiatives taken in response to a disaster with a purpose to achieve early recovery and rehabilitation of affected communities, immediately after a disaster strikes. These are called as response and recovery activities.

Figure 14.3 illustrates the activities carried out in the four stages leading up to, during, and following a disaster.

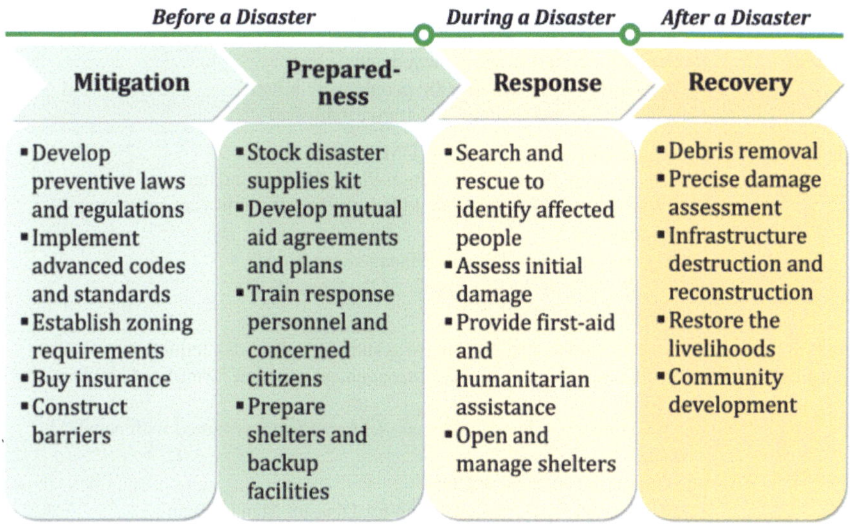

Fig. 14.3 Activities in various phases of disaster management. *Source* Sun et al. (2020)

14.4 Evolution of Disaster Management in Bangladesh

Traditional disaster management has primarily focused on disaster relief and recovery over the course of the last 50 years. However, after the devastating floods in 1988 and the 1991 cyclone, the Bangladesh government adopted a holistic approach that included hazard identification and mitigation, community preparedness, and integrated response efforts (Haque 2023). In order to improve risk management capacity of communities and reduce their vulnerability, relief and recovery efforts are now organized within every risk management framework. The Ministry of Relief and Rehabilitation reorganized as the Ministry of Disaster Management and Relief, in keeping with the paradigm shift from relief and response to comprehensive disaster management in 1973. The Ministry of Food and Disaster Management (MoFDM) was the new name given to it. All agencies involved in national disaster management are coordinated by MoFDM. Under MoFDM, the Disaster Management Bureau (DMB) is in charge of raising the public awareness about the potential risks of both natural and man-made hazards, as well as developing initiatives and programmes that will better equip vulnerable populations and government officials to lessen the effects of disasters. The MoFDM's technical arm, the DMB, oversees and plans all disaster management-related initiatives at all levels, from the national to local. The trajectory of disaster management in Bangladesh is presented in Table 14.1.

1993 saw the renaming of the Ministry of Relief and Rehabilitation as the Ministry of catastrophe Management and Relief, in keeping with the paradigm shift from relief and response to comprehensive catastrophe management. Once more, the Ministry of Food and Disaster Management (MoFDM) was the new moniker. National efforts to handle disasters are coordinated by MoFDM.

Table 14.1 Disaster management evolution in Bangladesh

1970's	Response focused disaster management: • 1970 Gorkey cyclone, 300,000 people were killed • 1972 cyclone preparedness program established
1980's-1990's	Emerging disaster management (DM) approaches • 1987–88 huge flood, Flood Action Plan (FAP) formulated • 1991 cyclone, 138,000 people killed, shifting from disaster response to preparedness • 1993 constitution of Disaster Management Bureau • 1997 Drafting of Standing order of Disasters (SoD) • 1998 prolonged flood
2000 to onwards	Forward towards a comprehensive system including risk reduction • 2000 Comprehensive disaster management program formulated and launched in 2004 • 2005 Ministry of Food and Disaster Management renamed with new DM vision • 2006 revised AoB for MODM • 2010Revised SOD, National Plan for Disaster Management • Disaster Management Act in place • Disaster management (DM) Policy drafted

14.5 Legal Context of Disaster Management in Bangladesh

The appropriate legislation, policies, and best practices framework are provided by Bangladesh's regulatory framework for disaster management, which governs how disaster risk reduction and emergency management are handled and carried out in the country (Fig. 14.4). The following are included in the framework (NPDM 2010).

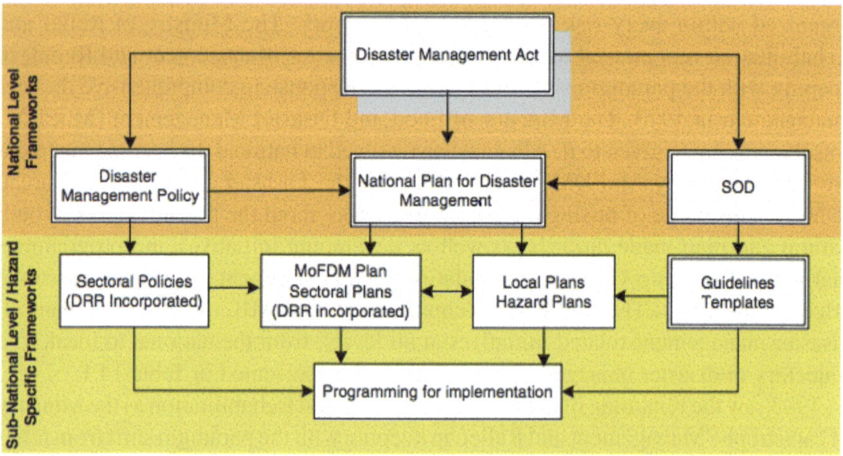

Fig. 14.4 Disaster management regulatory framework. *Source* Shaw et al. (2013)

However, Disaster Management (DM) in Bangladesh is guided by a number of national, regional and global drivers, which, among others includes

a. The Disaster Management Act 2012
b. The Disaster Management Policy 2015
c. The Standing Orders on Disasters (SOD) 2019
d. The National Plan for Disaster Management (NPDM) 2020
e. The SAARC Framework for Action (SFA) and
f. The Sendai Framework for Disaster Risk Reduction (SFDRR) 2016–2030.

14.5.1 Disaster Management Plans at Various Levels

Bangladesh has various disaster management plans (Fig. 14.5), aimed to work at different administrative strata (Shammin et al. 2022). The plans includes:

i. National Disaster Management Plan
ii. District Disaster Management Plan (DDMP)

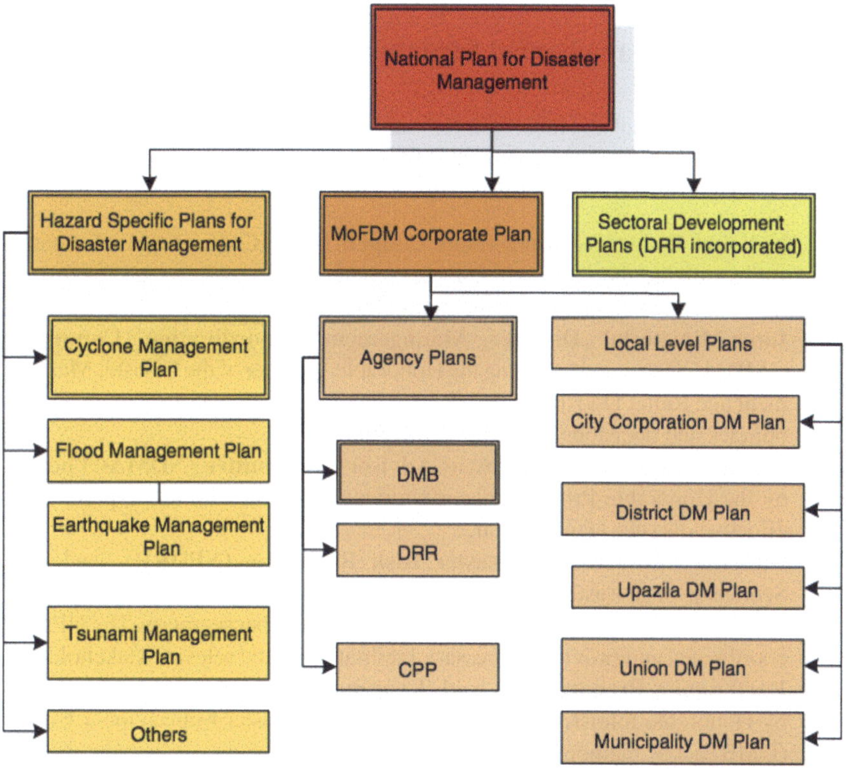

Fig. 14.5 Different levels of disaster management plans in Bangladesh. *Source* Shaw et al. (2013)

iii. Upazila disaster Management Plan (UzDMP)
iv. Union Disaster Management Plan (UDMP)
v. Pourashava/City Corporation Disaster Management Plan
vi. Sectoral development plans incorporating risk reduction
vii. Hazard Specific Disaster Management Plan

   (a) Earthquake management plan
   (b) Cyclone Shelter Plan
   (c) Disaster Resilient Cluster Housing
   (d) Tsunami response plan etc.

The Bangladesh National Plan for Disaster Management, on the other hand, is a tactical document that will be in force for a specific amount of time. This overarching plan offers the general guidelines required by pertinent sectors and all levels of disaster management committees to design and carry out their role-specific plans. Planning for disaster risk reduction and emergency management will be led by the Disaster Management and Relief Division (DM&RD), which serves as the focal ministry for these areas.

14.6 Disaster Management Structures in Bangladesh

Bangladesh has national and local disaster management mechanisms in place. Below is a figure that depicts the role, responsibility, and authority (Fig. 14.6). The national disaster management structure of Bangladesh is as follows:

(i) **National Disaster Management Council (NDMC)** in charge of creating and reviewing the policies for disaster management and giving orders to all relevant stakeholders, under the honourable prime minister.
(ii) **Inter-Ministerial Disaster Management Co-ordination Committee (IMDMCC)** headed by acting the Honorable Minister of the Disaster Management and Relief Division (DM&RD) to put into practice disaster management policies and decisions of NDMC/Government.
(iii) **National Disaster Management Advisory Committee (NDMAC)** headed by the Honorable Prime Minister nominated person who has experience in effective disaster management.
(iv) **National Platform for Disaster Risk Reduction (NPDRR)** headed by Secretary of Disaster Management and Relief Division (DM&RD) and Director General (DG), DMB functions as the member secretary. The NPDRR coordinates and provides necessary facilitation to the relevant stakeholders.
(v) **Earthquake Preparedness and Awareness Committee (EPAC)** headed by Honorable minister for MoFDM and DG, Disaster Management Bureau (DMB) act as member secretary.

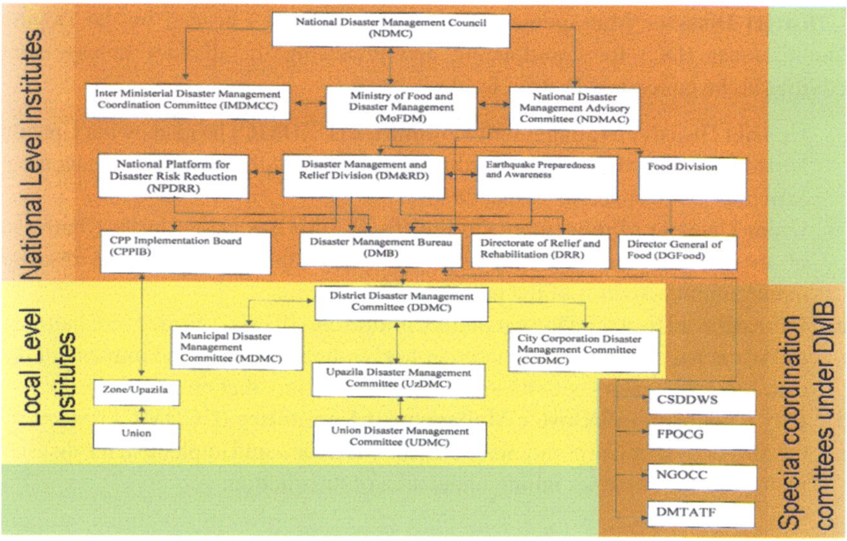

Fig. 14.6 Institutions of disaster management in Bangladesh. *Source* Shaw et al. (2013)

(vi) **Cyclone Preparedness Program Implementation Board (CPPIB)** headed by the Secretary, DM&RD to review the preparedness activities in the face of the initial stage of an impending cyclone.

(vii) **Cyclone Preparedness Program (CPP)** Policy Committee headed by Honorable Minister, MoFDM and Secretary, DM&RD act as member secretary. Disaster Management Training and Public Awareness Building Task Force (DMTATF) headed by DG, DMB to coordinate the disaster related training and public awareness activities of the Government, NGOs and relevant other organizations.

(viii) **Focal Point Operation Coordination Group of Disaster Management (FPOCG)** headed by the DG of DMB to coordinate and review the activities of various departments/agencies related to disaster management and also to review the Contingency Plan prepared by concerned departments.

(ix) **NGO Coordination Committee on Disaster Management (NGOCC)** headed by the Director General of DMB to coordinate and review the activities of concerned NGOs in the country.

(x) **Committee for Speedy Dissemination of Disaster Related Warning/ Signals (CSDDWS)** headed by the Director General of DMB in order to examine, ensure and find out the strategies and approaches for the speedy dissemination of warning/signals among the people.

Disaster Management Structure of Bangladesh (at sub-national levels) is as follows:

District Disaster Management Committee (DDMC) headed by the Deputy Commissioner (DC) for coordinating and reviewing the disaster management activities at the concerned District level.

(a) **Upazila Disaster Management Committee (UZDMC)** headed by the Upazila Nirbahi Officer (UNO) to coordinate and review the disaster management activities at the concerned Upazila level.
(b) **Union Disaster Management Committee (UDMC)** governed by the Chairman of the Union Parishad to coordinate, review and implement the disaster management activities of the particular Union.
(c) **Pourashava Disaster Management Committee (PDMC)** headed by Chairman of Pourashava (municipality) in order to coordinate, review, and implement the disaster management activities within its area of jurisdiction.
(d) **City Corporation Disaster Management Committee (CCDMC)** headed by the Mayor of City Corporations to coordinate, review and implement the disaster management initiatives falling under area of jurisdiction.

14.7 Stakeholder Involvement in Disaster Risk Management

Following the destructive flood in 1988 and the cyclone in 1991, the idea of creating a national disaster plan began to take shape (Haque and Uddin 2013). It was clear at the time that disaster preparedness could be included into the process of socioeconomic development at the local, regional, national, and household levels, providing the community with the long-term capacity to reduce disaster risk and vulnerability. The Government of Bangladesh (GoB) was also assisted in taking action against disaster preparedness by this concept. Figure 14.7 illustrates how different stakeholders at different levels play their roles in helping communities and their inhabitants reduce the risk of disaster by implementing both structural and non-structural solutions.

14.8 Overall Challenges for Effective Disaster Management in Bangladesh

Bangladesh faces several challenges in effective disaster management due to its geographical location, topography, and socio-economic conditions. Some of the overarching challenges include:

1. **Geographical Vulnerability**

   - **Cyclones and Storm Surges:** Bangladesh is prone to tropical cyclones and storm surges, especially during the monsoon season. The low-lying coastal areas are highly vulnerable to these natural disasters.

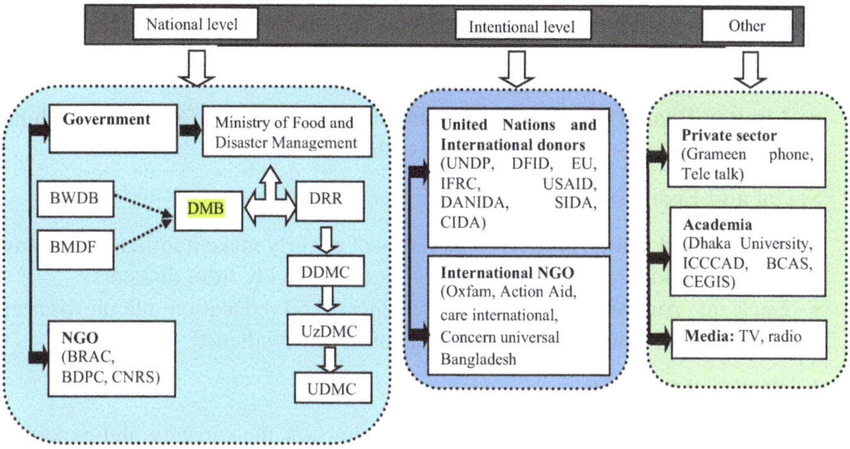

Fig. 14.7 A flow diagram shows various stakeholders involved in disaster management in Bangladesh

- **Flooding:** The country experiences regular riverine flooding due to heavy monsoon rains and the overflowing of major rivers like the Ganges and Brahmaputra.

2. **Population Density and Urbanization**

- **High Population Density:** Bangladesh is one of the most densely populated countries in the world (Streatfield and Karar 2008). This makes it challenging to evacuate and manage large numbers of people during disasters.
- **Rapid Urbanization:** Unplanned urbanization increases vulnerability, as many settlements are located in high-risk areas.

3. **Limited Resources and Infrastructure**

- **Resource Constraints:** Bangladesh faces limitations in financial and technological resources for disaster preparedness, response, and recovery.
- **Inadequate Infrastructure:** Insufficient infrastructure, especially in rural areas, hinders effective disaster response and recovery efforts.

4. **Climate Change Impact**

- **Sea Level Rise:** Bangladesh has potential risk of to sea level rise due to climate change, exacerbating the risk of storm surges and flooding.
- **Changing Weather Patterns:** Climate change contributes to unpredictable weather patterns, making it challenging to anticipate and prepare for disasters.

5. **Poor Early Warning Systems**

- **Communication Challenges:** Inadequate communication infrastructure in remote areas hampers the dissemination of early warnings and evacuation instructions.
- **Limited Reach:** Despite efforts to improve early warning systems, reaching all vulnerable communities remains a challenge.

6. **Social and Economic Factors**

   - **Poverty and Vulnerability:** High levels of poverty make it difficult for many people to adopt resilient measures or recover quickly from disasters.
   - **Lack of Awareness:** Limited awareness and education about disaster preparedness contribute to a lack of community resilience.

7. **Institutional Capacity**

   - **Capacity Building:** Some institutions may lack the capacity and expertise needed for effective disaster management.
   - **Coordination Challenges:** Coordination among various agencies and levels of government can be challenging, leading to gaps in the overall disaster response.

8. **Rural Agriculture Dependence**

   - **Agricultural Impact:** A significant portion of the population relies on agriculture. Disasters can have a severe impact on crops, leading to food insecurity and economic losses.

9. **Health and Sanitation Concerns**

   - **Disease Outbreaks:** Post-disaster, there is an increased risk of disease outbreaks due to compromised sanitation and health facilities.

The lack of integration in many sectors, programs, policies, and related project implementation at local levels reduces effective disaster management. The main obstacles are a lack of capacity among actors and institutions, poor governance, inadequate mechanisms for allocating resources and funding, inadequate coordination and collaboration, a lack of information, knowledge, and communication sharing, gaps in policy, political, social, and cultural struggles, and difficulties in implementing and mainstreaming (Islam et al. 2020). Addressing these challenges requires a comprehensive and coordinated approach involving government agencies, non-governmental organizations, communities, and international partners. Investments in infrastructure, early warning systems, community education, and sustainable development practices can contribute to building resilience in the face of disasters.

14.9 Conclusion

In the intricate tapestry of disaster law in Bangladesh, our exploration has unveiled a complex yet resilient framework designed to address the ever-present threat of natural calamities. As we conclude this chapter, we reflect on the dynamic landscape of disaster management, recognizing both the progress made and the hurdles that persist. The current scenario in Bangladesh reveals a nation that has learned from the painful lessons of the past. Legislative measures, such as the Disaster Management Act, have laid the foundation for a comprehensive approach to disaster response and recovery. The establishment of dedicated institutions, the refinement of early warning systems, and the integration of community-based initiatives exemplify the proactive strategies in place to minimize the impact of disasters on lives and livelihoods. However, the journey toward effective disaster management is fraught with challenges. Limited resources, the complexities of managing urban vulnerabilities, and the ongoing battle against climate change pose formidable obstacles. It is imperative for stakeholders, both within and beyond the legal sphere, to collaborate and innovate, ensuring that the legal frameworks in place evolve to meet the evolving nature of disasters. Yet, the true measure of success lies in the sustained implementation of these strategies, empowering communities to face the uncertainties of the future. As we confront the challenges woven into the fabric of disaster law in Bangladesh, we are reminded that the pursuit of resilience is an ongoing endeavor. This chapter serves not only as a snapshot of the current state of affairs but as a call to action. It beckons policymakers, practitioners, and communities alike to continue the dialogue, to innovate, and to forge a path toward a more resilient Bangladesh.

References

Baten A, González PA, Delgado RC (2018) Natural disasters and management systems of Bangladesh from 1972 to 2017: Special focus on flood. OmniSci: Multi-Discipl J 8(3):35–47

Haque CE, Uddin MS (2013) Disaster management discourse in Bangladesh: a shift from post-event response to the preparedness and mitigation approach through institutional partnerships. In: Approaches to disaster management-examining the implications of hazards, emergencies and disasters. IntechOpen.

Haque M (2023) Paradigm shift in disaster management: Bangladesh experience. In: International handbook of disaster research, pp 1773–1780. Springer Nature Singapore, Singapore

Islam S, Chu C, Smart JC (2020) Challenges in integrating disaster risk reduction and climate change adaptation: exploring the Bangladesh case. Int J Disaster Risk Reduct 47:101540

Josephson A, Schrank H, Marshall M (2017) Assessing preparedness of small businesses for hurricane disasters: Analysis of pre-disaster owner, business and location characteristics. Int J Disaster Risk Reduct 23:25–35

Khan H, Vasilescu LG, Khan A (2008) Disaster management cycle-a theoretical approach. J Manag Mark 6(1):43–50

Nirupama N (2013) Disaster risk management. In: Bobrowsky PT (ed) Encyclopedia of natural hazards. Encyclopedia of earth sciences series. Springer, Dordrecht. https://doi.org/10.1007/978-1-4020-4399-4_300

Räsänen A, Lein H, Bird D, Setten G (2020) Conceptualizing community in disaster risk management. Int J Disaster Risk Reduct 45:101485

Sapir GD (2017) EM-DAT [Internet]. The emergency events database—Universite catholique de Louvain UCL)-CRED, Brussels, Belgium; 2017. www.emdat.be

Shammin MR, Firoz R, Hasan R (2022) Frameworks, stories and learnings from disaster management in Bangladesh. Clim Chang Community Resil 239

Shaw R, Islam A, Mallick F (2013) National perspectives of disaster risk reduction in Bangladesh. In: Disaster risk reduction approaches in Bangladesh, pp 45–62

Shreve CM, Kelman I (2014) Does mitigation save? Reviewing cost-benefit analyses of disaster risk reduction. Int J Disaster Risk Reduct 10:213–235

Streatfield PK, Karar ZA (2008) Population challenges for Bangladesh in the coming decades. J Health Popul Nutr 26(3):261

Sun W, Bocchini P, Davison BD (2020) Applications of artificial intelligence for disaster management. Nat Hazards 103(3):2631–2689

Chapter 15
Disaster Management Act of India

Sujata Saunik, Anuska Ray, and Rajib Shaw

Abstract India faces natural disaster risks like earthquakes (affecting 59% of land), floods (impacting 12%), cyclones, and droughts (threatening 68% of cultivable land), along with man-made crises like accidents, fires, CBRN emergencies, etc. To address this need, the Disaster Management Act was passed in 2005 in the aftermath of the 2004 tsunami, establishing a system under the leadership of the Prime Minister, encompassing the National Disaster Management Authority (NDMA), National Disaster Response Force (NDRF) and state-level offices. This legislation prioritizes disaster prevention, mitigation, and introduces the NDMF to fund prevention efforts, ensuring comprehensive disaster management and risk reduction in the country. The Disaster Management Act of 2005 is a cornerstone of disaster management in India and serves as a model for state-level legislation. While it has made significant contributions to disaster management, there are opportunities for improvement, particularly in empowering local communities and integrating disaster management with development efforts which are explored in this chapter.

Keywords Disaster management act · National disaster management authority · State disaster management authority · National disaster response force · All hazards approach

15.1 Introduction

The Indian subcontinent stands as one of the world's most disaster-prone regions, owing to its expansive landmass, dense population, and distinctive geo-climatic conditions. According to a recent study conducted by the United Nations Office for Disaster Risk Reduction (UNISDR), India ranked third globally among the top five countries most affected by disasters. Approximately, 55% of the nation's total area is vulnerable to seismic activities ranging from scale III-V. Additionally, 68% of

S. Saunik (✉) · A. Ray · R. Shaw
Graduate School of Media and Governance, Keio University, 5322 Endo, Fujisawa 252-0882, Japan
e-mail: ssaunik@gmail.com

Y. Cui and R. Shaw (eds.), *Disaster Law*, Disaster Risk Reduction,
https://doi.org/10.1007/978-981-97-7374-9_15

the cultivated land is prone to drought while a substantial 4 crore area is susceptible to flooding. Landslides are the main concern in the sub-Himalayan and Western Ghats region and India's coastal states are prone to strong cyclonic activity. In the year 2015, India experienced approximately 19 natural disasters of varying magnitudes, resulting in substantial losses and damages exceeding $3.30 billion.

An analysis by the Council on Energy, Environment and Water (CEEW) reveals that out of 35 states and union territories, a substantial 27 face significant vulnerability to extreme hydro-meteorological disasters and their interconnected repercussions. The northern and north-eastern areas face a higher vulnerability to severe flooding events and their corresponding consequences. Meanwhile, the eastern and southern regions are marked as highly vulnerable to extreme cyclonic events, with an increasing propensity for cyclones, floods, and droughts occurring simultaneously. Moreover, the southern and western regions are the most exposed to extreme droughts, experiencing recurring impacts year after year, with a predominant influence on agricultural droughts. Since the 2000s, the northern, eastern, and central zones have exhibited moderate vulnerability, primarily due to meteorological and agricultural droughts. In contrast, the north-eastern region displays the least vulnerability to extreme drought event. The composite indexing indicates that over 59 percent of districts in the eastern zone are highly vulnerable to extreme cyclone events, while more than 41 percent of districts in the western zone are considered cyclone hotspots. Additionally, the analysis reveals an increasing vulnerability to cyclones along the western coast during the last decade (2010–2019). The surge in drought-like conditions across India triggers a cyclogenesis process, leading depressions to escalate into deep depressions and ultimately into cyclonic storms over the warming Indian Ocean. These cyclones, coupled with floods, render several districts along the eastern and western coasts vulnerable to all three extremes, presenting substantial challenges for mitigation and adaptation in these regions.

Furthermore, a notable surge in extreme events has been observed across India since 2005, primarily attributed to landscape disruptions. Studies have underscored the impact of alterations in the landscape on the occurrence of extreme events, while factors like the urban heat island effect, land subsidence, and microclimate changes further intensify extreme events within India.

15.2 Introduction to the Disaster Management Act 2005 Disaster Management Before the Act

Before the enactment of the Disaster Management Act in 2005, India's approach to disaster management was largely disorganized and fragmented. There was no centralized agency responsible for coordinating disaster management efforts, resulting in a reactive and uncoordinated response to disasters. Responsibilities for disaster management were spread across various ministries and departments, leading to role ambiguity, duplication of efforts, and confusion.

Furthermore, the absence of a centralized authority hindered effective coordination of disaster response efforts at the state and district levels, often causing delays and inefficiencies. Additionally, most resources were allocated to disaster response and relief, with little emphasis on disaster preparedness and mitigation, making India more susceptible to disasters.

This fragmented approach resulted in several issues, including delayed and ineffective disaster responses, resource wastage due to duplicate efforts, and a lack of focus on preventing and mitigating disasters. In the light of this, The Disaster Management Act of 2005 was introduced with an aim to address these challenges by establishing the National Disaster Management Authority (NDMA), State Disaster Management Authorities (SDMAs), and District Disaster Management Authorities (DDMAs) to oversee disaster management at the national, state, and district levels, respectively.

Disaster management act focuses on efficient disaster management and related aspects. It establishes institutional frameworks to develop and oversee disaster management strategies. Additionally, it ensures government departments take proactive measures for disaster prevention, mitigation, and swift response.

Important aspects of this legislation involve establishing the National Disaster Management Authority (NDMA) headed by the Prime Minister, State Disaster Management Authorities (SDMAs) overseen by Chief Ministers, and District Disaster Management Authorities (DDMAs) led by Collectors/District Magistrates/ Deputy Commissioners. Additionally, it requires the formation of distinct Executive Committees at both national and state levels. Furthermore, it institutes the National Institute of Disaster Management (NIDM) to improve capabilities and the National Disaster Response Force (NDRF) for swift responses (The Disaster Management Act, 2005 Government of India, Ministry of Home Affairs (Fig. 15.1).

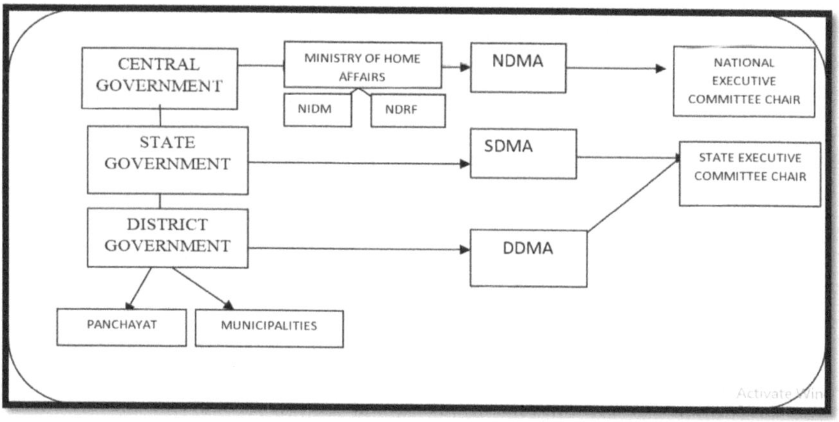

Fig. 15.1 Legal institutional framework- disaster management act 2005. *Source* The Disaster Management Act, 2005 Government of India, Ministry of Home Affairs, National Disaster Management Authority

Furthermore, the Act directs concerned Ministries and Departments to develop their own plans aligned with the National Plan. Financial mechanisms such as response funds, the National Disaster Mitigation Fund, and similar funds at state and district levels are created for disaster management purposes. Moreover, the Act delineates specific roles for local bodies in managing disasters.

15.3 Objectives and Scope

The Disaster Management Act of 2005 is designed to facilitate the efficient handling of disasters. It represents a significant change in India's approach to disaster management, emphasizing the importance of mitigation, prevention, and preparedness. Regarded as the principal legislation governing both natural and man-made disasters, this Act sets up the National Disaster Management Authority at the Central Level and replicates a similar structure at the state and district levels.

15.4 Context and Necessity of the Act

The Constitution of India does not have any explicit provision about disaster management. Despite being one of the world's lengthiest constitutions, the non-inclusion of disaster management in the constitution may probably be explained by three interrelated reasons. Firstly, a constitution typically outlines the fundamental structure of a nation, emphasizing fundamental rights and delineating legislative, administrative, and financial competencies among different levels of government. In this context, disaster management was considered a subject that should be left to the discretion of the government of the day to formulate appropriate policies and administrative frameworks (The Disaster Management Act, 2005 Government of India, Ministry of Home Affairs, National Disaster Management Authority, 2005). Secondly, during the drafting of the constitution, disaster management was not deemed as significant as to warrant inclusion within its provisions (The Disaster Management Act, 2005 Government of India, Ministry of Home Affairs, National Disaster Management Authority, 2005). Lastly, the existence of colonial-era tools like the Famine Code and a well-established administrative machinery for disaster response may have led the constitution makers to believe that the existing mechanisms were adequate to manage disasters in the future. Consequently, disaster management did not find a place in the elaborate division of legislative subjects between the central and state governments (The Disaster Management Act, 2005 Government of India, Ministry of Home Affairs, National Disaster Management Authority, 2005).

Traditionally, disaster management fell under the jurisdiction of the states due to the geographical distribution of disaster-prone areas within their boundaries. The states were considered the first responders to crises caused by natural disasters. However, as the subject gained importance in governance, questions arose regarding its appropriate legislative jurisdiction. The conventional responsibility of states for disaster management became burdensome, given the increasing frequency and severity of disasters. It was argued that states lacked both the financial resources and technical expertise to manage larger-scale disasters effectively. Consequently, states welcomed the central government's involvement, allowing it to enact laws, initiate administrative measures, and provide financial support in the realm of disaster management, despite this being a traditionally state-centric domain.

Despite the Constitution's relative silence on disaster management, clues about the intent of the constitution makers regarding its legislative locus can be gleaned from the placement of core subjects related to natural and man-made disasters. For example, flood and drought, two significant natural disasters in India, are closely linked to water excess and deficiency in rivers and other water sources within specific regions. By implication, managing these issues was considered within the purview of the relevant government level in the federal system. Additionally, the doctrine of residuary powers in the Indian constitution suggests that subjects not allocated to any level of government would automatically fall under the Central Government's domain. As disaster management is not explicitly listed in the constitution's schedules, it can be implied that the Central Government has legislative competence over it, falling under the provisions of Article 248, which deals with residuary legislative powers. Furthermore, constitutional provisions in the Union List and State List underscore the legislative competence of the Central Government over inter-state rivers and river valleys, while states retain authority over water-related subjects. This constitutional arrangement primarily pertains to water and its impact on specific natural disasters like floods and droughts, leaving other disasters unaddressed. Ultimately, the enactment of the Disaster Management Act, 2005, drew on constitutional provisions related to 'Social Security and Social Insurance; Employment and Unemployment' in the concurrent list to establish legislative competence for the Central Government in disaster management.

15.5 Evolution of the Disaster Management Act 2005

The Disaster Management Act 2005 was enacted in response to the pressing need for a comprehensive legal framework to address the increasing frequency and severity of disasters in India. This legislation was prompted by the 2004 Indian Ocean tsunami, which exposed the inadequacies of the existing disaster management infrastructure

Table 15.1 Chronological events of evolution of disaster management act in India

Year	Activity
1990s	The UN General Assembly designated the 1990s as "International decade for natural disaster reduction". The disaster management cell was established under Ministry of Agriculture"
1999	In response to the disaster as a national priority, the government of India took decisive actions by forming the High-Power Committee and subsequently the National committee by Mr J.C Pant, secretary of the Ministry of Agriculture following the Gujarat Earthquake
2002	There is a shift in policy of providing relief in the form of financial aid to adopting a more comprehensive and integrated approach in effectively addressing disaster so the disaster management division has undergone a shift to the Ministry of Home Affairs
2005	The disaster management act enacted by the government of India envisaged the establishment of national disaster management authority headed by the prime minister and state disaster management authority headed by the chief minister aimed to institute a comprehensive approach to disaster management implementation

Source The Disaster Management Act, 2005 Government of India, Ministry of Home Affairs, National Disaster Management Authority (2005)

and response mechanisms. This act was formulated following extensive deliberations and recommendations by the High-Power Committee on Disaster Management. It serves as the foundational legal framework for disaster management in the country, outlining the roles and responsibilities of national agencies and creating a comprehensive structure for disaster management at various levels (Table 15.1).

15.6 Implemetation of the Disaster Management Act

The National Disaster Management Authority (NDMA) originated on May 30, 2005, under the Prime Minister's leadership via an executive order. Later, upon the implementation of the Disaster Management Act in 2005, the NDMA was formally established on September 27, 2006. Its leadership included the Prime Minister as Chairperson and nine other members, with one designated as Vice-Chairperson.

The NDMA's responsibilities encompass developing policies and guidelines for disaster management, to be followed by various Government of India Ministries, Departments, and State Governments. It also entails providing instructions to State Authorities in crafting State Plans and executing necessary actions for disaster management.

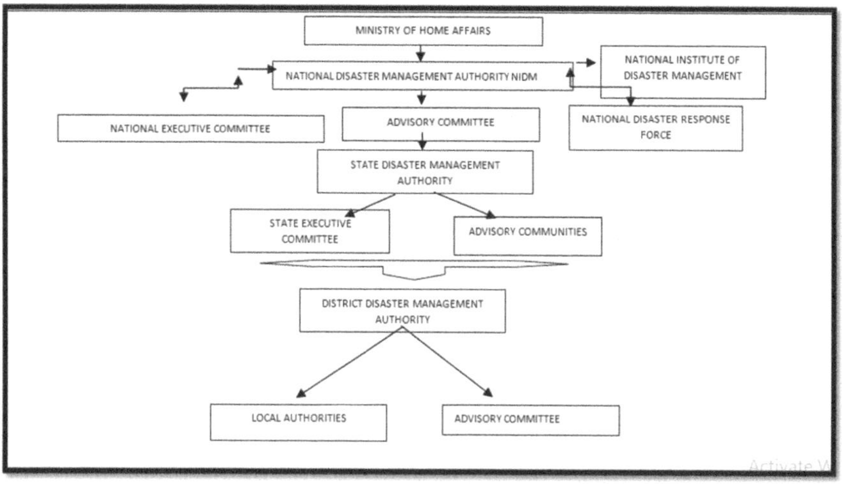

Fig. 15.2 Disaster management structure in India. *Source* The Disaster Management Act, 2005 Government of India, Ministry of Home Affairs, National Disaster Management Authority (2005)

15.7 Interpretations of Key Provisions

The Act empowers the National Disaster Management Authority (NDMA) to formulate national policies, plans, and guidelines for disaster management. It also emphasizes the role of State Disaster Management Authorities (SDMAs) and District Disaster Management Authorities (DDMAs) in implementing these policies at the state and district levels, respectively. Furthermore, it outlines the responsibilities of various stakeholders, including government agencies, local authorities, and non-governmental organizations, in disaster management efforts. The Act encourages a proactive approach, emphasizing the importance of risk assessment, mitigation measures, and capacity-building to reduce vulnerabilities and enhance resilience (Fig. 15.2 and Table 15.2).

15.8 Characteristics of the Act

A. Roles and Responsibilities of Central and State Governments

The Ministry of Home Affairs takes charge of managing most natural disasters for the Government of India, except for drought, hailstorm, and pest attacks handled by the Ministry of Agriculture. The Disaster Management Division within the Ministry oversees these responsibilities.

During disasters, the primary responsibility for relief, rehabilitation, and response lies with the respective State Governments. The Central Government supports these

Table 15.2 Roles and responsibilities of institutions

Institutions	Roles	Responsibilities
National disaster management authority	Its role is laying down policies and guidelines on disaster management that would be followed by different ministers in departments of government of India and state government in taking measures for disaster risk reduction. It also laid down guidelines to be followed by the state authorities in drawing state plants and suitable measures for disaster risk reduction	• State policies for handling disasters • Approve plans prepared by Indian government ministers • Give instructions to government departments for including disaster prevention in their project • Make sure disaster policies are followed • Suggest money allocation for disaster prevention • Help other countries hit by disasters • Provide guidelines to national institute of disaster management • Take extra steps to handle disasters
State disaster management authority	State outlines its plans for managing disasters Agrees with plan based on national guidelines Gives the nod to specific departments disaster plans Coordinate plans and implementation Suggests financial support for disaster readiness Review and check departmental plans include disaster prevention In a crisis chairperson of state authority control full actions but the state authority powers must later agree	• Create awareness campaigns about disaster risks and safety measures • Developing training materials and modules for campaign • Identify vulnerabilities and report them annually • Provide guidelines to include disaster prevention in development plans • Design projects in various sector for disaster risk reduction • Assess departmental development plans • Create plans for post disaster recovery • Set minimum standards of providing relief • Coordinating national and state level plans • Review and update state level response plans and guidelines • Establishing emergency operation centres • Offer expertise and advice to the district authorities • Design and implement projects in line with national schemes • Organize regular practice drills to test response readiness- it helps people to be prepared in advance at the time of real emergency
District disaster management authority	The state government must create disaster management in every district of the state with a chairperson and co-chairperson	• In charge of planning, organizing, and carrying out disaster management efforts • Follow the recommended steps outlined in the guidelines for disaster management • Reviewing any building projects in the district to ensure safety standards • Organizing and carrying out assistance efforts and responding to disaster at district level

Source The Disaster Management Act, 2005 Government of India, Ministry of Home Affairs, National Disaster Management Authority (2005)

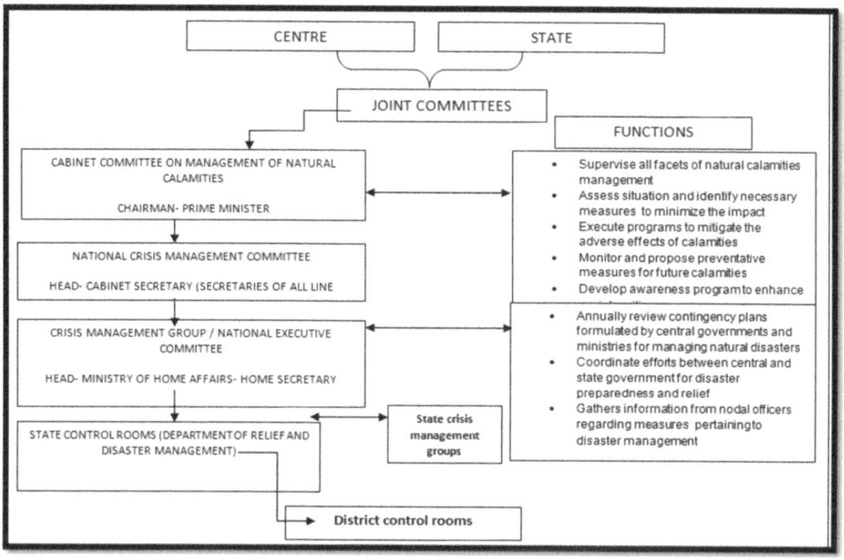

Fig. 15.3 Hierarchy level frameworks of roles and responsibilities. *Source* The Disaster Management Act, 2005 Government of India, Ministry of Home Affairs, National Disaster Management Authority (2005)

efforts by providing logistical and financial aid, deploying specialized teams, and arranging essential supplies like medical aid, communication restoration, and other necessary resources.

The Disaster Management Division closely monitors disasters and similar situations, collaborating with affected states and various Central Ministries like Health, Defence, Civil Aviation, and Food Supplies to facilitate strategic support. Coordination among departments happens through several committees at both Central and State levels (Fig. 15.3).

2 Role of State Government

In India's federal structure, the primary responsibility for responding to natural calamities lies with the State Government. However, the Central Government extends support, both in terms of resources and finances, especially during significant disasters. The level of assistance provided by the national government is determined based on the severity of the calamity, the required relief scale, and the State's financial resources.

In most states, Relief Commissioners oversee relief measures in natural disaster situations. In their absence, the responsibility falls on the Chief Secretary or a designated officer nominated by them. The Relief Commissioners or Chief Secretaries manage relief operations at the state level, coordinating with Collectors or Deputy

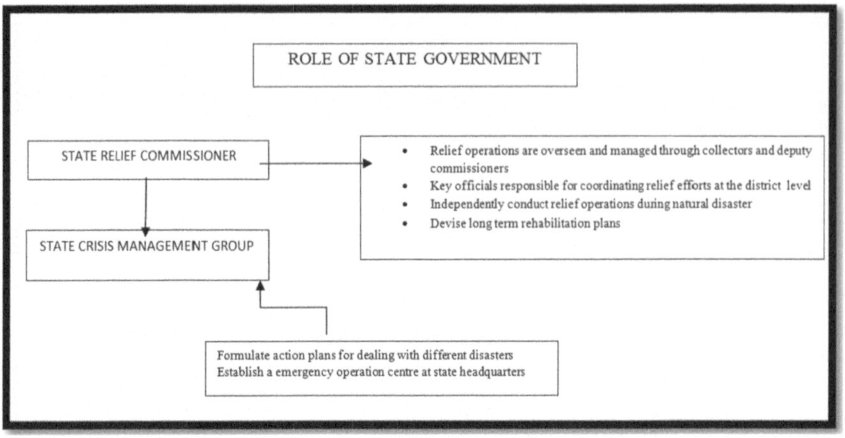

Fig. 15.4 Role of State Government. *Source* The Disaster Management Act, 2005 Government of India, Ministry of Home Affairs, National Disaster Management Authority (2005)

Commissioners at the district level. States have autonomy in organizing relief operations and planning long-term rehabilitation measures, often receiving support from the Central Government based on Finance Commission recommendations (Fig. 15.4).

3 **Role of Districts**

District Administrations are mandated to prepare Contingency Plans tailored to potential disasters in their area. These plans follow a national framework, detailing preparedness, required relief materials, involved departments, and an effective monitoring system.

During emergencies, the District Magistrate oversees and coordinates various departments' actions. The Collector often gains heightened powers for disaster mitigation and relief, sometimes informally, ratified later by higher authorities.

At the district level, a Relief Committee comprising officials, non-official members, local legislators, and Members of Parliament reviews relief measures (Table 15.3).

15.9 Response System NDRF—National Disaster Response Force Under Disaster Management Act 2005

According to section 44 (1) of the DM Act, 2005, the National Disaster Response Force (NDRF) was established to provide specialist response to threatening disaster situations or disasters. The National Authority (NDMA) exercises general superintendence, direction, and control of the Force, while the Director General of NDRF appointed by the Central Government has command and supervision.

Table 15.3 Functions of the districts administrations

Administrations	Functions/activities
The district administration	• Tasked with government contingency plans • Create specific plans based on potentials disasters adhere to national guidelines • Cover preparedness, relief materials and involved departments • Robust feedback and monitoring system is established
District magistrate	• In emergencies, collector oversees all district level department • During operations collectors' authority increases with specific orders • State administrative culture allows informal use of high powers by the collector in emergencies • Decisions made by the collector are later officially approved
District relief committee	• It includes both official and non-official members including local legislator and members of parliament • Purpose is to assess the relief measures
Sub-district administration	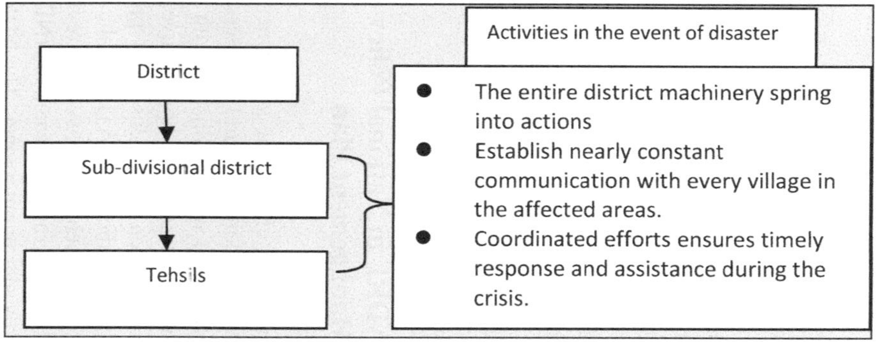

Source The Disaster Management Act, 2005 Government of India, Ministry of Home Affairs, National Disaster Management Authority (2005)

The Task Force established to review the DM Act, 2005, revealed that the NDRF is intended to provide specialized skills and capabilities for rescue operations or a 'specialist response'[1]. When a disaster occurs, the community and various security forces including the police, central armed police forces, and armed forces all participate in response functions. However, recent disaster experiences have revealed that search and rescue activities require specific equipment, training, and expertise that may not always be available within the existing forces. Therefore, the aim of the NDRF is to develop specialized skills and capabilities for rescue operations at various levels.

The NDRF was originally formed by converting eight battalions from various central armed police forces including the (BSF), (ITBP), (CISF), (CRPF) with the intention of developing them as a specialized force. As demand for specialized response in vulnerable areas and disaster sites grew, the NDRF expanded from the initial eight battalions to sixteen battalions of central armed police forces stationed in different vulnerable locations throughout the country. Despite various challenges such as limited infrastructure, training, and equipment, the NDRF has managed to improve its efficiency and has become the largest and most dedicated disaster response force in the world. The NDRF is now trained and equipped according to international standards, allowing it to handle any type of natural or manmade disaster, including those involving chemical, biological, radiological, and nuclear hazards.[2]

15.10 NDRF in National Policy and National Disaster Management Plan

Through sustained efforts, the government has made significant improvements in its readiness to address natural disasters. In compliance with the (DM) Act of 2005, the (NPDM) was established with the goal of creating a safe and resilient India by implementing a comprehensive, proactive, multi-disaster approach that is technology-driven and focused on prevention, mitigation, preparedness, and response. In 2016, the (NDMA) issued the first National Disaster Management Plan, which was subsequently reviewed and revised in 2019.

The Indian government created the (NDRF) to offer specialized assistance in the event of a disaster or emergency. The NDRF currently consists of 16 battalions that will be strategically located as necessary. These battalions will work closely with designated state governments and will be accessible to them in the event of any serious disaster situation. While all NDRF battalions are responsible for managing natural disasters, four battalions will receive specialized training and equipment to handle emergencies related to Chemical, Biological, Radiological, and nuclear events. National Disaster Management Authority (NDMA) issued the first National Disaster Management Plan, which was subsequently reviewed and revised in 2019.

The Indian government created the (NDRF) to offer specialized assistance in the event of a disaster or emergency. The NDRF currently consists of 16 battalions that will be strategically located as necessary. These battalions will work closely with designated state governments and will be accessible to them in the event of any serious disaster situation. While all NDRF battalions are responsible for managing natural disasters, four battalions will receive specialized training and equipment to handle emergencies related to chemical, biological, radiological, and nuclear events.

15.11 Other Agencies Initiated by Government of India

Government of India has initiated different nodal agencies for early warning for different disaster (Table 15.4).

15.12 Example 1-Nepal Earthquake

In April 2015, Nepal experienced a powerful earthquake measuring 7.8 on the Richter scale. This caused extensive damage to both life and infrastructure, and there was a concern that a humanitarian crisis was imminent. The earthquake was felt across Northern India as well. To assist with the aftermath, the National Disaster Response Force sent 16 Urban Search and Rescue teams to Nepal, which included over 700 rescuers and 18 trained dogs equipped with the latest technology. The government of India directed this effort.

The NDRF teams were able to rescue 11 injured individuals and retrieve 133 bodies from the rubble. Additionally, they set up six medical camps and aided 1,219 people. The NDRF also played a crucial role in distributing relief materials to those affected by the earthquake in Nepal, with a total of 1,176.571 tonnes of supplies delivered via rail, road, and air routes. The MHA and NDMA also helped with this distribution effort (Fig. 15.5).[3]

15.13 Example 2-Fukushima Nuclear Disaster, Japan 2011-Stellar Response Amidst Nuclear Leakage

In one of the most devastating disasters of the decade, Japan Triple Disaster (2011), earthquake and thereafter tsunami and successive nuclear leakage at Fukushima nuclear power plant, a 46-member team of NDRF, led by the then Comdt. Shri Alok Avasthy, was deployed at Ongawa from 27 March to 07 April 2011 for the first ever overseas operation of NDRF since its inception (Fig. 15.6).

While most of the international search and rescue teams started returning from the affected area fearing their safety in wake of the nuclear leakage, CBRN trained and equipped team of NDRF braving adverse weather conditions continued with their

Table 15.4 Different nodal agencies initiated by government of India

Disaster	Agencies	Definitions	Activities
Cyclone	Indian meteorological department	It plays a crucial role in predicting and monitoring the cyclone disturbances also disseminating timely warnings and advisory bulletins. IMD, Delhi acts as a regional specialized meteorological centre that provides the tropical cyclone advisories to the world meteorological organization	Pre cyclone watch (72 h before) Cyclone alerts (48 h before) Cyclone warning (28 h before) Post landfall outlook (12 h before)
Floods	Central water commission	It plays a crucial role in delivering timely forecast and alerts regarding incoming floods to the village communities located in close proximity to the river	Observing and collecting the hydrological and hydro meteorological data Sending the data to forecasting centres Analysing data and making forecasts Sharing forecast through social networks
Tsunami	Indian national centre for ocean information service	It was established after the Indian ocean tsunami in 2004 by the ministry of earth science. This system designed for tsunami watch, warning and alert. It offers crucial details regarding seismic events including time, epicentre location and depth of an earthquake in the ocean and promptly issues bulletin to ensure safe and preparedness to the coastal communities	The system detects earthquake of magnitude of over 6 within less than 20 min of occurrence The report of occurrence is sent to ministry of home affairs (MHA) within 25 to 30 min mentioning the location and magnitude The information is sent to various communication channels and agencies

(continued)

Table 15.4 (continued)

Disaster	Agencies	Definitions	Activities
Landslides	Geological survey of India	Established in 1851 as a government organization under the ministry of mines headquartered in Delhi. It plays a crucial role in coordinating geological studies, landslides, hazard zonation, monitoring landslides. It helps the concerned ministries departments, central and state government in landslide prevention, mitigation measures in landslide reduction and also responding in the Himalayan and sub-Himalayan regions	They study the shape of the land, materials and then generate data on area, shape, slope, infiltration and permeability of soil of the basin. Also, drainage patterns, landform and longitudinal profiles Based on the acquired data and information they prepare flood hazard map indicating prohibited area, restricted cautionary and flood free zones The studies and information are also used by the central water commission, water resource development authorities, urban planning authorities, ministry of agriculture and environment authorities
Avalanches	Snow and avalanche study establishment	This is a branch of DRDO situated in Chandigarh, with a main objective is to conduct research in the realm of snow and avalanches	It offers avalanche control strategies and predictive assistance to the armed forces It serves as the central authority responsible for disseminating advisories and alerts regarding avalanches throughout the nation

Source The Disaster Management Act, 2005 Government of India, Ministry of Home Affairs, National Disaster Management Authority (2005)

Fig. 15.5 Nepal Earthquake. *Source* NDRF 2015 https://www.ndrf.gov.in/operations/nepal-earthquake-apr-2015

Fig. 15.6 Fukushima, Japan Nuclear Disaster. *Source* NDRF 2011 https://www.ndrf.gov.in/operations/japan-tsunami-mar-2011

search and rescue operations and managed to retrieve seven bodies from under the debris, more than two weeks after the disaster occurred in the area. In addition to this, they found and turned in cash worth fifty million yen and other valuable items they came across. The NDRF team received high praise from the local authorities, media, and the public for their commendable efforts.[4]

15.14 Conclusion

This chapter delves into the significance of the Disaster Management Act in India and examines the pivotal role played by the National Disaster Response Force (NDRF) in disaster management, illustrated through examples. The current framework of disaster management in India comprises the National Disaster Management Authority (NDMA), State Disaster Management Authority (SDMA), and District Disaster Management Authority (DDMA), each operating at different hierarchical levels.

Furthermore, the chapter delves into the roles of these entities in ensuring the effective implementation of the Disaster Management Act at various levels, emphasizing the importance of coordination and collaboration between national, state, and local authorities to save lives during calamities.

With the establishment of the NDRF under the Disaster Management Act, disaster response capabilities have seen rapid augmentation and refinement, resulting in more efficient rescue operations and increased protection of lives. The NDRF's contributions to disaster management extend beyond national borders, with the force actively participating in international disaster mitigation efforts, underscoring its importance on a global scale.

Despite the significant strides made in disaster management, there exist avenues for further enhancement, particularly in empowering local communities and integrating disaster management efforts with broader developmental initiatives. The chapter explores these opportunities for improvement, aiming to foster a more comprehensive and inclusive approach to disaster management that prioritizes community resilience and sustainable development.

References

Amri A, Hanifa NR, Tebe Y, Lassa J, Pradipta GC, Furqon MR, Nangkiawa L (2020) National evaluation of the disaster-safe school programme. In: National secretariat of disaster-safe school. Resilience Development Initiative

BIMSTEC (2020) The Bay of Bengal initiative for multi-sectoral technical and economic cooperation. https://bimstecdmex2020.in/

Das P (2012) Disaster management in India: policy review and institutional structure. Asia Pac J Soc Sci. https://www.gcoedu.in/pdf/evs1.pdf

NDRF (2011) National disaster response force. https://www.ndrf.gov.in/operations/japan-tsunami-mar-2011

NDRF (2015) https://www.ndrf.gov.in/operations/nepal-earthquake-apr-2015

NIDM (2022) National institute of disaster management. https://nidm.gov.in/pdf/trgreports/2022/September/Report_26-30September2022sg.pdf

Nomani MZM, Parveen R (2020) Covid-19 pandemic and application of disaster management act, 2005: promises and pitfalls. Int J Pharm Res. https://search.bvsalud.org/global-literature-on-novel-coronavirus-2019-ncov/resource/en/covidwho-995161

Pandey RK (2016) Legal framework of disaster management in India. ILI Law Rev Winter. https://ili.ac.in/pdf/p13_rajendra.pdf

SAADMEX (2015) South Asian annual disaster management exercise. https://www.preventionweb.net/event/south-asian-annual-disaster-management-exercise-saadmex-2015

Shah AJ (2011) An overview of disaster management in India. Disaster Management 2011. https://www.researchgate.net/publication/271440240

Sharma RK, Chawla R, Kumar S (2010) Chlorine Leak on Mumbai port trust's Sewri Yard: a case study. J Pharm Bio Allied Sci

Verma A, Dimri S (2023) Legal developments for disaster management in India. Forthcoming, Environ Unsustainable Life. https://www.researchgate.net/publication/365991648

Chapter 16
Disaster Management Law in Nepal

Namita Poudel, Avani Dixit, Naomi Kato, and Rajib Shaw

Abstract The Gorkha Earthquake 2015 was the latest in a series of major disasters that Nepal has faced, and it prompted the government to pass the Disaster Risk Reduction and Management Act 2017 to improve the country's ability to cope with disasters. In December 2019, the National Disaster Risk Reduction and Management Authority was created. Furthermore, the Constitution of Nepal 2015 defines the powers and jurisdiction on disaster risk management of the three tiers of the government: federal, provincial, and local levels. The Disaster Risk Management Act's provisions, their state of execution, and their relationship to the nation's decentralized government structure will all be covered in this chapter.

Keywords Nepal · Disaster law · DRM authority · Decentralization

16.1 Introduction

Nepal is highly vulnerable to multiple hazards throughout the country due to its fragile mountain terrain, tectonic movement, diverse climatic conditions, and inappropriate land use, which create and exacerbate the risk of meteorological, hydrological, geological, biological, and man-made hazards (GoN 2018). Changes in the global and regional climate system are also exacerbating extreme weather events. Extreme rainfall damages crops and other livelihood assets and causes landslides and floods. Furthermore, the country is landlocked and one of the least developed countries in the world. As a result, several disasters occur every year and these disasters have caused many casualties in Nepal throughout its history (Adhikari and Gautam 2022).

Systematic efforts on disaster risk management in Nepal began after 1982 when the Natural Disasters (Relief) Act was promulgated (MoHA 2019).In particular,

N. Poudel (✉) · A. Dixit · N. Kato · R. Shaw
Graduate School of Media and Governance, Keio University, 5322 Endo, Fujisawa 252-0882, Japan
e-mail: namitapoudel@keio.jp

Y. Cui and R. Shaw (eds.), *Disaster Law*, Disaster Risk Reduction,
https://doi.org/10.1007/978-981-97-7374-9_16

Table 16.1 Disaster incidents and impact (2015–2021)

Year	No. of incidents	Dead	Injured	Affected family	Private house destroyed		Estimated loss (USD 1 = NRP 120)
					Partial	Complete	
2015	978	9,304	22,661	828	299,378	773,936	7,871,579
2016	2,370	486	764	13,241	1222	3,428	23,436,490
2017	2,460	490	737	19,073	14,427	1,927	20,806,545
2018	3,919	478	2,902	8,180	1880	2,505	36,182,433
2019	4,538	489	2,452	25,264	6873	4,939	39,245,919
2020	3,770	559	1,175	11,314	3330	1,959	14,676,841
2021	4,215	509	1,773	6,583	1580	2,044	21,190,103
Total	22,250	12,315	32,464	84,483	328,690	790,738	163,409,909

Source DRR Portal (2023)

the Deurali (Pokhara) landslide of 1974 and the Bajhang earthquake of 1980 triggered the enactment of the Natural Disasters Act. It must be noted that Nepal is one of the first countries in South Asia to introduce an act on disaster risk management—although the act focused mainly on relief and response with a little emphasis on preparedness, it is still considered a cornerstone by DRM practitioners. Nepal has been changing its approach to disaster management since then, influenced by international developments and global pe (Vij et al. 2020).

In recent years, the Government of Nepal (GoN) has recognized the imperative for ex-ante and ex-post approaches for disaster risk management (DRM) due to the escalating human casualties and the loss or damage of assets. On average, Nepal faces more than 500 disasters per year, ranging from small to large scale. In terms of recent disasters, Nepal faced the Gorkha earthquake in 2015, the Terai floods in 2017, landslides in 2020 and 2021, and post-monsoon rains in 2021 highlighting the diverse emergencies that the Nepalese Government has to confront.

In this Table 16.1, Families affected by the 2015 Nepal earthquake are not included. The government of Nepal (GoN) estimated that the 2015 earthquake directly affected 866,635 private houses and indirectly eight million people. The economic impact excludes the loss incurred during the 2015 earthquake estimated at USD 14.3 billion.

16.2 Review of Nepal Disaster Law

The necessity for a disaster management system became evident during the Bajhang Earthquake of 1980, which led to more than 200 deaths, 5600 injuries, and significant economic losses (Earthquake Hazard Program 2024). The disaster prompted the creation of the National Calamity Relief Act 2039 (1982), which primarily addressed relief and response efforts by defining the roles and responsibilities of security agencies (police and army) and assigning the responsibility for disaster relief and response to the Ministry of Home Affairs (MOHA). During that period, the majority of countries' disaster-related efforts were mostly focused on relief and response. The Table 16.2 provides a summary of the progress in disaster-related laws in Nepal.

The Constitution of Nepal 2015[1] as well as the DRRM Act gives responsibilities for DRM to all three levels of government—Federal, Provincial, and Municipal. The potential for overlapping mandates due to the division of roles and responsibilities among different government levels is evident, and such fragmentation can hinder timely ex-ante and ex-post activities. Schedule 7 of the Constitution states that both federal and provincial governments are responsible for disaster readiness, rescue, relief, and recovery. Schedule 8 assigns local-level disaster management to local governments only. Schedule 9 says that disaster management is the joint responsibility of federal, provincial, and local governments. Therefore, the Constitution stipulates that all three levels of government must share the responsibility of reducing and managing disaster risks.

Reducing disaster risk is critical for sustainable development in Nepal as it is highly prone to multiple hazards like earthquakes, floods, landslides, and glacial lake outburst floods. Nepal was among the first countries to align its national disaster risk reduction strategy with the Sendai Framework for Disaster Risk Reduction (SFDRR) after it was adopted in 2015. The SFDRR provides overarching priorities and guiding principles.

Key priorities for Nepal aligned with the SFDRR include: (i) Understanding disaster risk—Nepal needs more detailed risk assessments, risk mapping, vulnerability data, and research on local hazards and vulnerabilities, (ii) Strengthening disaster risk governance—Efforts are ongoing to decentralize disaster management and empower local authorities to lead community action. But more resources and capacity building are needed, (iii) Investing in resilience—Nepal requires major investments to upgrade vulnerable infrastructure, retrofit unsafe buildings, and promote climate and disaster resilient agriculture, water resources, and urban development, (iv) Enhancing disaster preparedness—Early warning systems, emergency response capacities, resource stockpiling, evacuation planning and drills, and community preparedness all need strengthening and (v) Ensuring inclusive and multi-sectoral action—Disaster management must involve all sections of society including women, poor, disabled, aged, and marginalized groups.

The SFDRR principles of primary responsibility by states, shared responsibility across stakeholders, and partnership with regional and global actors also hold relevance as Nepal cannot tackle disaster risk alone. SFDRR provides Nepal with a relevant framework to guide policies, planning, and programs to reduce existing risks and prevent future risks. However major investments, capacity building, and coordinated efforts across government, private sector, and communities are essential to realize this in practice.

[1] https://lawcommission.gov.np/en/wp-content/uploads/2021/01/Constitution-of-Nepal.pdf.

Table 16.2 Progress of disaster-related laws in Nepal

Disaster-related decisions by the government	Year	Remarks
National Calamity Relief Act 2039 (1982) (First Amendment 1989, Second Amendment 1992) (MoHA 1982)	1982, 1989, 1992	The National Disaster Risk Reduction and Management Act of 2017 has superseded this act
Soil and Watershed Conservation Act, 2038 (GoN 1982)	1982	Focuses on controlling natural hazards such as floods, landslides, and soil erosion
National Building Code (NBC) (First revision 2020) (Mahal and Kathmandu 1994)	1994, 2020	It was drafted in 1994, however, it was endorsed by the Government only in 2004 and gazette in 2006. The NBC was not made mandatory throughout the country; municipalities could choose not to endorse the NBC depending upon the resources available to them. In the aftermath of the 2015 earthquakes, the Government made it mandatory to implement the NBC throughout the country
Building Act, 2055 (1998) (First Amendment 2007) and Building Regulations 2066 (Bir Bikram Shah Dev 1998)	1998, 2009	Legalize the NBC and provide technical guidance to municipalities to enforce NBC for engineered and non-engineered houses
Construction Business Act, 2055 (GoN 1999)	1999	Focused on licensing schemes for construction companies. This essentially classified companies based on their resources, expertise, and experience into Class A, B, C, and D)
Local Self Governance Act, 2056 GoN 1999	1999	Gave authority to sub-national governments, including the mandate to work on different aspects of disaster risk management
Local Government Operation Act, 2074 (Local Government Operation Act 2017)	2017	outlines the obligations, rights, and responsibilities of both urban and rural municipalities for the various stages of disaster risk management
National Urban Policy, 2064 (GoN 2007)	2007	The guiding document for urban development in Nepal
National Strategy for Disaster Risk Management in Nepal, 2066 (NSDRM 2009)	2009	First milestone document which looked at risks from multiple hazards and recommended actions based on the Hyogo Framework for Action
The National Disaster Response Framework (First Amendment in 2019) (NDRF 2013)	2013	Focuses on the efficient coordination and execution of disaster preparedness and response endeavors

(continued)

Table 16.2 (continued)

Disaster-related decisions by the government	Year	Remarks
Act Related to the Reconstruction of Earthquake Affected Structures, 2072 (GoN 2015)	2015	The Act established the National Reconstruction Authority (NRA), which focused on the reconstruction of the damages caused by the 2015 Gorkha earthquake. NRA has completed its mandate and ceased to examine 2021
National Climate Change Policy, 2068 (First Amendment 2019) (GoN 2019)	2011, 2019	Covers adaptation strategies, mitigation measures, technology transfer, capacity building, financial mechanisms, and international cooperation
Disaster Risk Reduction and Management Act 2017 (amended in 2018) and corresponding Disaster Risk Reduction and Management Regulation 2019 (MoHA 2019)	2017, 2018, 2019	Replaced the National Calamity Relief Act 2039. Covers ex-ante and ex-post DRM activities. Devolves roles and responsibilities for DRM to federal, provincial, district, and local-level governments. Does not cover climate change-related activities
The Environment Protection Act, 2053 (First Amendment 2019) (Environment Protection Act, 1997, 1997)	1997, 2019	Focuses on environmental pollution, degradation, impacts on the environment and biodiversity, and climate change. Please note that climate change is solely covered by this act
National Policy for Disaster Risk Reduction (National Policy 2018)	2018	Focuses on fulfillment of Nepal's commitment to the Sendai framework for disaster risk reduction
Disaster Risk Reduction National Strategic Plan of Action (GoN 2018)	2018	

The National Policy for Disaster Risk Reduction 2018 provides an overarching framework aligned with the Sendai Framework to guide Nepal's efforts to minimize disaster risks and impacts. It aims to protect development gains through whole-of-society engagement. The Policy calls for integrating disaster risk reduction into all development policies, planning, and programs as a national priority. It emphasizes understanding and addressing local-level risks and vulnerabilities. The Policy focuses on enhancing preparedness, response, recovery, and building back better capabilities. It promotes the utilization of science, technology, innovation, and indigenous knowledge to inform risk reduction. The Policy stresses inclusive DRR through social mobilization and protection of vulnerable groups. It highlights the need for partnerships between the government, private sector, communities, and media for effective DRR implementation. The Policy guides strengthening legal, policy, and institutional systems for disaster risk governance. It outlines approaches for adequate resource allocation and mainstreaming DRR into budgets. It calls for evidence-based monitoring, periodic review, and updating of DRR strategies, plans, and programs across all tiers of government and society. The policy creates an enabling environment and strategic direction to achieve risk-informed, resilient development in Nepal through whole-of-society action.

Nepal's Disaster Risk Reduction National Strategic Plan of Action 2018–2030 was formulated as the means for implementing the National Policy for Disaster Risk Reduction. The strategic plan of action provides a comprehensive roadmap rooted in local realities to guide advancement across all aspects of disaster risk reduction. It reflects Nepal's strong policy commitment to reducing disaster vulnerabilities and building long-term resilience. The Strategic Plan provides a 12-year roadmap to guide Nepal's disaster risk reduction efforts aligned with the Sendai Framework. The aim is to build a disaster-resilient Nepal by reducing existing risks, preventing future risks, and enhancing response capacity.

The seven strategic priorities identified are understanding disaster risk, strengthening disaster risk governance, investing in resilience through structural and non-structural measures, enhancing disaster preparedness for effective response, promoting disaster risk reduction for sustainable development, improving social protection mechanisms against the impact of disasters, promoting participatory approach involving communities, private sector, media, and others. Cross-cutting issues highlighted include climate change adaptation, community involvement, and inclusive DRR for vulnerable groups. The implementation roles are defined for federal, provincial, and local governments. Responsibilities include policy and regulation, technical assistance, capacity building, planning, budget allocation, monitoring, and evaluation. Detailed costing of priority programs is provided to support budget advocacy and resource mobilization from the government, donors, and other partners. Monitoring frameworks and indicators are outlined to track progress over the 12-year timeline.

The institutional framework for DRRM spans disaster risk reduction, preparedness, response, and recovery. The National Council, Executive Committee, NDRRMA, and Disaster Management Committees at the Province, District, and Local levels are the institutional arrangements according to the Disaster Risk Reduction and Management Act of Nepal 2017 (Fig. 16.1).

The Ministry of Home Affairs oversees disaster management while local authorities facilitate community-based disaster risk management. In 2019, Nepal established the NDRRMA to coordinate, facilitate, operate, and manage DRRM activities nationwide. The prime minister chairs the apex body for disaster management called the DRRM National Council, which provides strategic direction, approves DRRM policies, and formulates related strategies. The Disaster Executive Committee (EC) handles operational matters including DRRM guidelines, plans, executive decisions, and implementation. It is chaired by the Home Minister. In order to create DRRM policies and plans, the EC also collaborates with government ministries. The National Council and the EC both have the NDRRMA as their secretariat. Local and provincial governments are in charge of disaster preparedness and management under their own DRRM agencies. In order to enhance cooperation amongst DRRM stakeholders,

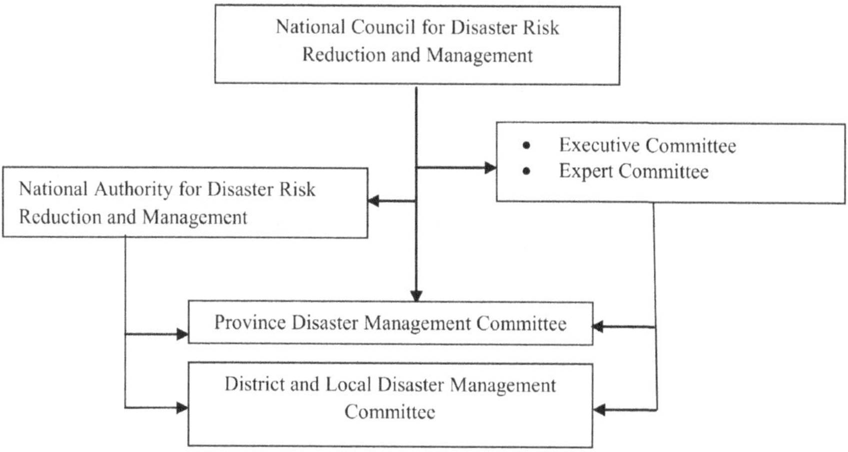

Fig. 16.1 DRRM institutions according to the DRRM Act, 2017 (MoHA 2019)

including the government, UN, bilateral partners, NGOs, media, academia, business sector, and affected communities, the National Platform for Disaster Risk Reduction (NPDRR) was established along with operating guidelines. This platform, which contains nine thematic groups, is chaired by the chief executive of the NDRRMA. To coordinate disaster preparedness and response, the Government of Nepal (GoN) and agencies have established a network of Emergency Operations Centers (EOCs). The Ministry of Home Affairs operates a National EOC alongside district EOCs in all 77 districts. Provincial EOCs coordinate with the national and district EOCs. Some municipalities have also set up EOCs, but many lack adequate staffing and equipment. Additionally, the Health Ministry runs Health EOCs nationwide which were crucial in responding to the COVID-19 pandemic. The GoN has established eight Humanitarian Staging Areas at major ports and four support base stations in strategic geographic locations. There are plans to expand these facilities further across Nepal. There are DRRM institutions in place. However, more training, resources, and decentralized capacity are needed for effective early warning and post-disaster response, especially in remote areas.

16.3 Progress and Challenges Status of Disaster Law

In this section, the progress and challenges of the Disaster Act established in 2017 and the National Policy for Disaster Risk Reduction 2018 of Nepal has been closely observed. The latest act, policy, and strategies comparatively cover strategies for multiple hazards. Even though there have been considerable advancements with current policy guidelines, a myriad of challenges persists, as evidenced in diverse policy documents. Based on existing documents available on NDRMA, DPnet, and research articles positive advancements arising from the Act and policy directives have been listed out followed by complexities and challenges that have been addressed to inherent in policy implementation.

Formulated three tiers of the disaster management committee: As mentioned in the review Sect. 16.2, policy amendment, formulating guidelines and new challenges take the lead in the implementation part too. Following the National Disaster Risk Reduction Policy of 2018, objectives number 5.2. is to strengthen disaster risk governance for disaster risk reduction and management, disaster management committees have been established at three administrative levels: provincial, district, and local. These committees are functioning in all 7 provinces, 77 districts, and 753 local wards. In addition, each province has appointed a designated disaster focal person. This initiation from the government helped to understand the concept of disaster preparedness and about global agenda at the local level (GoN 2023). Several districts have already developed pre-disaster and pre-monsoon plans, which delineate and allocate specific responsibilities. The responsibility of the district disaster committee is to identify and collect the samples of rocks, soil, and water from the designated areas in the river, rivulets, and ponds within the community in pre-monsoon plans of districts. Considering policy to achieve the target objective's organizational structure of the government agencies involved in disaster risk reduction at all levels. Additionally, NDRMA is actively working for effective operation and management of disaster risk reduction and management by taking a coordinated approach with local, provincial, and federal body.

Information Dissemination through web the portal: Second, the next step has been taken in disaster information dissemination aligning with objectives 5.1 of NDRRP 2018 to increase understanding of disaster risk and ensure access to information related to disaster risk at all levels. Since the establishment of NDRMA (National Disaster Risk Management Authority) based on the Disaster Risks Reduction and Management Act, 2074 (2017), this authority actively diffuses the information through "Bipadportal" integrated and comprehensive Disaster Information Management System (DIMS) in the national language. The word "Bipad" means disaster in Nepali language, so people understand the meaning and disaster-related news, however, very limited people who work in the disaster sector and researchers only use these websites. Bipadportal has been updating real-time data encompassing various aspects, including details on disaster incidents, risk assessments, and information on damage and loss to enhance the information dissemination process. Its core concept is a bottom-up approach to disaster data collaboration, with a nationwide gateway coupled with distinct platforms for federal, state, and local authorities. The system's integrated data can facilitate post-disaster event coordination and disaster communication, as well as enhance each DM cycle step. People working in this field can utilize this portal as a source of information because it covers disaster news, training, capacity-building programs, disaster meetings, and pertinent work in its daily and monthly bipod bulletin. However, many local people from villages with limited internet access or not familiar with IoT (Internet of Things) are unaware of this website and information even though they are living in disaster-prone areas.

Third, based on NDRPP 2018 policy objective number 5.4 is to enhance disaster resilience by increasing public and private investment in disaster risk reduction, non-government organizations, and international non-government organizations are also working for preparedness, capacity building, and mitigation. NGOs and INGOs have been working in the disaster sector for a long time and after the 2015 earthquake, the involvement of these sectors has increased dramatically. Involvement NGOs and INGOs were active in the disaster field even before ore 2015 Gorkha earthquake. However, awareness regarding disasters was very limited to a handful of people. Recent work by UKAID in partnership with Rajapur municipality has implemented a new approach for risk communication during flood time in the presence of the local disaster management authority. It aims to show that disaster education through Mugal art is an effective way to educate local people about flood education. Murals are an effective means of disseminating important information about what people can do before, during, and after a flood to lessen its effects. A mural, for instance, may show how early warning systems are put into place, alert the public about flood threats, and provide details on safe havens and evacuation routes (Fig. 16.2).

Acknowledgement of disaster management in sectoral guidelines: In 2023, Human consumer rights include consumer rights disaster time in its guidelines. There is a lot of focus on incorporating disaster management ideas into the process of creating guidelines and rules, which includes giving consumer rights during disasters recognition and priority. Human rights commissioners have made major efforts to identify fundamental rights that ought to be protected since they recognize how vulnerable consumers are in times of distress. This recognition includes preventing artificial scarcity, price increases, and the sale of inferior products or services that violate human rights. It also includes supporting initiatives like counteraction, livelihood restoration, and recovery that are grounded in humanistic ideals and congruent norms.

Fig. 16.2 Mugal art in the wall for flood risk communication. *Source* THT (2023)

Furthermore, a crucial component of putting consumer rights first is making sure that people are safely relocated from places in danger of calamities.

Disaster Management Act and National Disaster Management Policy 2018 concepts of disaster preparedness are well spread. Formulation of a committee at the local level helps to share information at a local level and the involvement of international and national non-government organizations and coordination between these sectors help to understand vulnerability to some extent. However, there are several challenges to implementing this policy.

Lack of Identification of Local Knowledge and Skill: Although policy concept number 6.5 highlights the use of science and technology based on local characteristics and optimum utilization of local skills, labor shortages for post-construction are a major problem in building back better after every disaster. The absence or inadequacy of local knowledge and skills creates challenges in successfully putting policies into practice. This could impede the desired outcomes and successful execution of planned initiatives or regulations. For instance, recent earthquake in Nepal, the Jajarkot Earthquake of 2023, skilled labor shortages were observed, and it also impacted the quality and pace of construction, potentially leading to delays or compromises in the technical aspects of building earthquake shelters. Furthermore, several problems, such as bureaucratic hold-ups in the disbursement of funding for the construction of temporary housing, have left many individuals affected by earthquakes living in hazardous conditions, which are made worse by extremely cold weather (DPNet 2023). Even though the NDRRMA released monies to the DDMC, which subsequently transferred them to local governments, the procedure for allocating grants to individuals has been considerably.

Lack of awareness: Although raising awareness of disaster risk reduction is important and falls under the purview of the NDRMA's work obligations and rights, examples from recent earthquakes indicate that the implementation aspect is still lacking. The construction method, earthquake-retarding homes, and susceptibility are unknown to the people living in the disaster-prone area. People are unaware of this changing construction process, despite the urgent need for safer housing and the advocacy of experts and concerned parties for a shift from traditional mud and stone construction to more earthquake-resistant techniques using materials like bamboo, wood, concrete, and steel. Considering the region's history of seismic activity and the likelihood of more significant earthquakes in the future, this change in building methods is essential. Individuals who are still building flimsy mud and stone homes, an activity (DPNet 2023).

Decentralization and coordination mechanism: The National Disaster Risk Reduction and Management Authority lacks control over security mobilization during humanitarian crises, recruiting and mobilizing human resources is challenging, rules governing decision-making authority in foreign aid mobilizations, limitations on financial decision-making, and reliance on the Ministry of Home Affairs for cabinet decisions are just a few of the challenges the Authority faces despite the passage of the

Disaster Risk Reduction and Management Act of 2017. Effective disaster management is further complicated by the agencies' ambiguous response requirements and frequent leadership changes. Regarding whom oversees responding to disasters of different sizes, there is a lack of clarity in the cooperation between the three branches of government. There are overlaps in the roles and responsibilities between district and national policies.

Dilemma in Budget allocation: National Disaster Risk Reduction and Management Authority (NDRRMA) has allocated budget as per requirements, but people nevertheless facing difficulties because of bureaucratic obstacles and delays in distributing funds. The fund complies with the Disaster and Natural Relief Fund Regulations of 2063 as well as the Natural Disaster Relief Act of 2039. The Prime Minister Disaster Relief Fund does not recognize the NDRRMA, which was established under the Disaster Risk Reduction and Management Act of 2074. According to officials, the funds were transferred to the NDRRMA after the government approved their provision of Rs 1 billion last year; however, this took almost five months. According to NDRRMA authorities, relief and rescue efforts must fall within the purview of the Central Fund Authority in order to reach the target group on time (DPNet 2024; My Republica 2024). Houses were damaged by monsoon-related disasters in 2023; according to NDRRMA statistics, 5,918 households were impacted, and only Rs 10 million was supplied to the affected regions for relief and rescue efforts. It has not been received or documented in detail if the district has given the relief cash to the victims of the disaster.

Building code implementation: More than 90% of the housing units have been constructed by families people as per their own requirements and financial status. So, most of the houses including engineered buildings in Nepal are highly susceptible to earthquake of event moderate intensities, due to very less knowledge of earthquake safety measures (UNCRD 2009). Consequently, the result in the figure has been shown in Table 16.3 from the 2015 earthquake. Due to non-earthquake resistance, more than 498,852 were fully and 256,697 horsepower lds damaged. The requirements for reconstruction underline the significance of rebuilding houses and settlements according to disaster-resistant standards such as BBB as per PDNA, After the 2015 earthquake, the Government of Nepal established the National Reconstruction Authority (NRA) is dedicated to the reconstruction of buildings and infrastructures in the earthquake. The NRA also developed a policy to provide three-stage grants to these owners to reconstruct their damaged houses in an owner-driven principle. Additionally, to receive the grant, a building should be seismic resistant complying with building code NBC 105. Various prototype model buildings, minimum requirements, and guidelines were formed under the NBC. However, implemention part has been lacking due to the lack of availability of expert engineers to design the buildings and as a result, the owners built the houses according to their style and requirements (Shrestha et al. 2021).

Lack of capacity building: The venture faces a significant shortfall due to the lack of capacity-building initiatives at the local level. Disaster response capacity-building efforts are heavily dependent on NGOs and INGOs, which experts argue is counterproductive for the state. This dependency undermines national capacity and

Table 16.3 No of damage houses in the 2015 earthquake

	Low strength masonry	Cement mortared masonry	Reinforced concrete	Total
Fully damaged	474,025	18,214	6,613	498,852
Partially damaged	173,867	65,859	16,971	256,697

Source PDNA Nepal (2015)

fosters a parasitic relationship. Additionally, there is a noticeable inconsistency in the allocation of resources for capacity building. Over-reliance on security forces for response operations is another issue. While the Nepal Army and police forces are crucial for search and rescue, responsibilities such as health protection, relief material management, temporary shelter management, and food and drinking water management should be handled by the respective departments. Due to insufficient orientation, district and municipality-level officials exhibit a reluctance to engage in disaster response efforts, influenced by the preconceived notion that disaster response is not their responsibility. This lack of training and capacity building, coupled with conflicting responsibilities, hampers effective disaster management (Malla et al. 2020).

Inadequate investment on safety net, innovation, and technology: Policy has focused on an appropriate technology for disaster risk reduction conducting the study and research on geology, seismology, geographical information system, remote sensing system, satellite technology, radar technology and early warning system including modern and traditional technologies. However, each investment plan has been limited on paper only. There are few consultation on multi-hazard early warning systems going on under the NDRMA leadership and few have been installed in river basin, policy yet to do a lot for effective early warning system and protect human causalities and infrastructure. The NDRRMA provisioned determination and implementation of instruments; procedures of disaster risk transfer, insurance and social security, which includes disaster management fund, agriculture and livestock insurance, soft loan, farmer's welfare fund, disaster response fund, and promotion of agriculture insurance. However, there are significantly fewer or no financial instruments as such reduced tax and impact fees in landslide-affected regions (Adhikari and Gautam 2022).

Resettlement challenges internally displaced people at low risk: Research carried out in several villages of Nepal shows that there are multiple challenges to resettle the internally displaced people at low risk (Rieger 2021).

(a) Emotional attachment: numerous elderly people seemed to experience emotional and psychological stress while living in temporary settlements. Due to emotional attachment towards original place, people prefer to back despite of disaster vulnerability.
(b) Finical problem: Integrated settlement in villages seemed to delay because of government housing grant.

(c) Lack of income generator: In new low risk place become prominent challenge. Providing opportunity in new place is not enough for people, they want income generator work so that they can feed their family.
(d) Not enough space for everybody.
(e) Lack of farmland.

16.4 Discussion

This section discusses how the institutional, legislative, and implementation of plans and policies could be improved for both ex-ante and ex-post contexts.

Structure and coordination: The structure and staffing of NDRRMA should be meticulously designed to reflect a steadfast commitment to DRR, and this commitment should be ingrained in every aspect of the organization's framework, ranging from its hierarchical structure, coordination with government and non-government agencies including private sector, to the competencies, dedication, and capacity of its staff. Beyond MOHA, the ambit of the NDRRMA's structure and coordination functions should be expanded to encompass various government offices, provincial entities, local governments, I/NGOs, and private sector. To facilitate this collaboration and enhance both horizontal and vertical linkages, the creation of an inter-ministerial working group for government agencies and revitalizing National Platform for DRR may prove to be effective. In these forums, the NDRRMA may create different work streams, such as multi-hazard disaster risk assessment, preparedness, response, disaster risk transfer (insurance) and recovery and reconstruction.

Professional human resources: NDRRMA should attract and retain a cadre of highly qualified professionals with diverse expertise in fields such as geology, meteorology, engineering, community development, and emergency management. These professionals should not only possess technical proficiency but also a profound understanding of the socio-economic and cultural dynamics of the communities they serve. In addition to technical experts, the staff should include individuals skilled in risk communication, community engagement, and capacity-building to ensure a holistic and inclusive approach to disaster risk reduction. Furthermore, continuous training and capacity-building programs for the NDRRMA staff are also crucial. This ensures that they remain abreast of the latest advancements in disaster management, technology, and methodologies. Additionally, fostering a culture of innovation within the organization can promote the development and implementation of cutting-edge strategies for disaster risk reduction.

Disaster Response: So far, the disaster response mandate has been given to Nepal Police, Armed Police Force and Nepal Army; but there are also confusion and coordination issues between these agencies. Therefore, NDRRMA may benefit to create a specialized and dedicated National Disaster Response Force (NDRF) sourcing human resources from the three agencies. This team or a division may be given responsible for developing and implementing comprehensive preparedness plans, conducting regular drills and simulations, and be ready for quick deployment.

NDRRMA needs to ensure availability of necessary resources and equipment to the NDRF. The establishment of an NDRF will stand out as a proactive measure to bolster the country's capabilities in managing the immediate aftermath of disasters. This force should be strategically positioned across the country, ready for rapid deployment to disaster-stricken areas. Moreover, the NDRF should collaborate closely with other relevant agencies, both within the country and internationally, to ensure a coordinated and efficient response to emergencies.

16.5 Conclusion

In conclusion, Nepal has implemented standardized disaster regulations in response to its own circumstances. The 2015 Gorkha earthquake opened the door throughout the country to develop national and local level policy. The execution of the plan at the highest level has been inadequate, leading to a failure to make advancements in compliance with regulations. Unclear and undedicated responsibilities under Nepal's disaster law are a significant shortcoming, causing challenges in disaster response. Immediate action is needed to implement policies at all three levels and clarify organizational roles for disaster management.

Acknowledgements The first author acknowledges the living support provided by Japan Science and Technology (JST) of Japan.

References

Adhikari BR, Gautam S (2022) A review of policies and institutions for landslide risk management in Nepal. Nepal Public Policy Rev 93–112. https://doi.org/10.3126/nppr.v2i1.48397

Bir Bikram Shah Dev B (1998) The building act 2055-Nepal law commission (Issue 2). https://lawcommission.gov.np/en/?cat=511

DPNet (2024) Quad-Day_Jajarkot_EQ_Report_(6–9 Jan 2024) 2024–01–11 03–11–57 (1). ORC. https://www.dpnet.org.np/resource-detail/1699

DRR Portal (2023) Government of Nepal Nepal disaster risk reduction portal Kathmandu, Nepal. http://www.drrportal.gov.np/

Earthquake Hazard Program (2024) Earthquake hazards program. https://earthquake.usgs.gov/earthquakes/eventpage/usp0001959/executive

Environment Protection Act, 1997 (1997)

GoN (1982) Land and Watershed Conservation Act, 2039. www.lawcommission.gov.np1www.lawcommission.gov.np

GoN (1999) Construction Business Act 1999

GoN (2007) Nepal urban policy

GoN (2015) Government of Nepal, Ministry of Law and Parliamentary Affairs

GoN (2018) National_policy_strategic_Plan_Disaster_Managment_2018–2030

GoN (2019) National climate change policy

Government of Nepal (2023) BIPAD portal. Ministry of Home Affairs. https://bipadportal.gov.np

Local Government Operation after structural change of the country: implications in RERP For Knowledge and Information Prepared by: RERP, PMO, Itahari (nd)

Local SelfGovernance Act 2055 1999 (1999)

Mahal B, Kathmandu N (1994) Nepal national building code requirements for state-of-the art design an introduction government of Nepal ministry of physical planning and works department of urban development and building construction

Malla SB, Dahal RK, Hasegawa S (2020) Local level disaster response in Nepal: investigating the government agencies. Bull Depart Geol 22:17–23. https://doi.org/10.3126/bdg.v22i0.33410

MoHA (1982) National calamity act

MoHA (2019) DRRM act

My Republica (2024) Despite enough funds in Prime Minister Disaster Relief Fund, victims struggle to access aid—myRepublica—The New York Times Partner, Latest news of Nepal in English, Latest News Articles. Newspaper. https://myrepublica.nagariknetwork.com/news/delays-in-disaster-relief-funds-cause-suffering-for-victims/

National Policy (2018) National policy for disaster risk reduction

NDRF (2013) National disaster response framework (NDRF) Government of Nepal Ministry of Home Affairs

NSDRM (2009) National strategy for disaster risk management (NSDRM): draft i national strategy for disaster risk management in Nepal final draft

PDNA Nepal (2015) Nepal earthquake 2015 post disaster needs assessment national planning commission Kathmandu 2015

Rieger K (2021) Multi-hazards, displaced people's vulnerability and resettlement: post-earthquake experiences from Rasuwa district in Nepal and their connections to policy loopholes and reconstruction practices. Progr Disaster Sci 11. https://doi.org/10.1016/j.pdisas.2021.100187

Shrestha RK, Parajuli HR, Poudel B (2021) Building typologies and code compliance issues of reconstructed houses after 2015 Mw 7.8 Gorkha, Nepal earthquake: experience from Dhading District earthquake. Progr Disaster Sci 10. https://doi.org/10.1016/j.pdisas.2021.100155

UNCRD (2009) From code to practice challenges for building code implementation and the further direction of housing earthquake safety UNCRD United Nations centre for regional development disaster management planning hyogo office

Vij S, Russell C, Clark J, Parajuli BP, Shakya P, Dewulf A (2020) Evolving disaster governance paradigms in Nepal. Int J Disaster Risk Reduct 50. https://doi.org/10.1016/j.ijdrr.2020.101911

Chapter 17
Legal and Policy Developments for Effective Disaster Management: A Review of Disaster Laws and Policies in Sri Lanka

Deepthi Wickramasinghe, Vihanga Amarakoon, Yasaswi Madawala, and Dilisha Gunawardena

Abstract Sri Lanka is a tropical island prone to multi-hazards due to its diversity in eco-geological and socio-economic settings. The application of legal and policy instruments for disaster management has emerged as a noteworthy development in the recent legal history of the country. Good practices and guidelines existed that principally focused on community preparedness and relief in disasters. Conversely, the Indian Ocean Tsunami disaster in 2004 which caused massive suffering and losses in Sri Lanka was a landmark event that led to the enactment of the Sri Lanka Disaster Management Act of 2005, which gave rise to the formal establishment of disaster management institutions, disaster management plans, and policies. With the development of understanding of disaster risk and vulnerability, the paradigm shifted to develop frameworks to cover all aspects of disaster management, from preparedness to mitigation, response, and recovery. This chapter describes the legal and policy framework for disaster management and mandates to key institutions for policy and capacity development at different levels. It reviews the resources, plans, and strategies used to manage different risk, factors including climate change and unsustainable development. The chapter concludes with suggestions for further development of policy and law that aim to strengthen disaster risk reduction and build community resilience.

Keywords Disaster laws and policies · Sri Lanka · Natural hazards · National disaster management practices

---

D. Wickramasinghe (✉) · V. Amarakoon · Y. Madawala · D. Gunawardena
Department of Zoology and Environment Sciences, Faculty of Science, University of Colombo, Colombo, Sri Lanka
e-mail: deepthi@zoology.cmb.ac.lk

Y. Cui and R. Shaw (eds.), *Disaster Law*, Disaster Risk Reduction,
https://doi.org/10.1007/978-981-97-7374-9_17

17.1 Introduction

Disaster Management encompasses activities aimed at controlling disasters and emergencies, providing a structured framework to assist communities in high-risk situations, and facilitating prevention or recovery from disasters. Its primary objective is to safeguard communities by diminishing the likelihood of catastrophic events and addressing vulnerabilities. Disaster Management is a dynamic process that involves functions such as planning, organizing, actuating, and controlling. This operational process includes preventive measures, mitigation strategies, and preparedness for emergency response and recovery (Math et al. 2015).

The core purpose of Disaster Management is to ensure the timely and appropriate provision of assistance to disaster victims, ultimately leading to a swift and effective recovery. The framework is designed with the goal of normalizing people's lives in a short timeframe while minimizing casualties and property losses. An essential aspect of Disaster Management is the implementation of well-defined steps to control disasters, enabling immediate and timely rescue of victims, along with expeditious post-disaster recovery efforts. Mitra and Shaw (2022) suggest fundamental design principles and a conceptual framework for Integrated Disaster Resilience (IDR) through the application of a Whole Systems Approach.

Covering an expanse of 65,000 square kilometers with a population of 22.156 million (Department of Census and Statistics 2021), Sri Lanka is characterized by a primary topographic feature—a mountain massif shaped like an anchor, situated in the south-central part of the island. The island's topography, combined with variations in regional climate (see Fig. 17.1 Map of Sri Lanka indicating three major climatic zones and topographic zonation), serves as a fundamental factor contributing to the diverse contrasts observed in various aspects across the region.

The escalation of disaster risk, hazards, and impacts in Sri Lanka can be attributed to various factors. Population dynamics, growing demands for natural resources like water and land, swift and uncontrolled urbanization, and development planning lacking consideration for disaster risk and exposure are among the primary contributors to this trend. According to a recent study, approximately 87% of Sri Lanka's population resides in areas identified as moderate or severe hotspots for disasters (Disaster Management Centre 2024).

Against this backdrop, this chapter describes the legal and policy framework for disaster management and mandates to key institutions for policy and capacity development at different levels. It reviews the resources, plans, and strategies used to manage different risk, factors including climate change and unsustainable development.

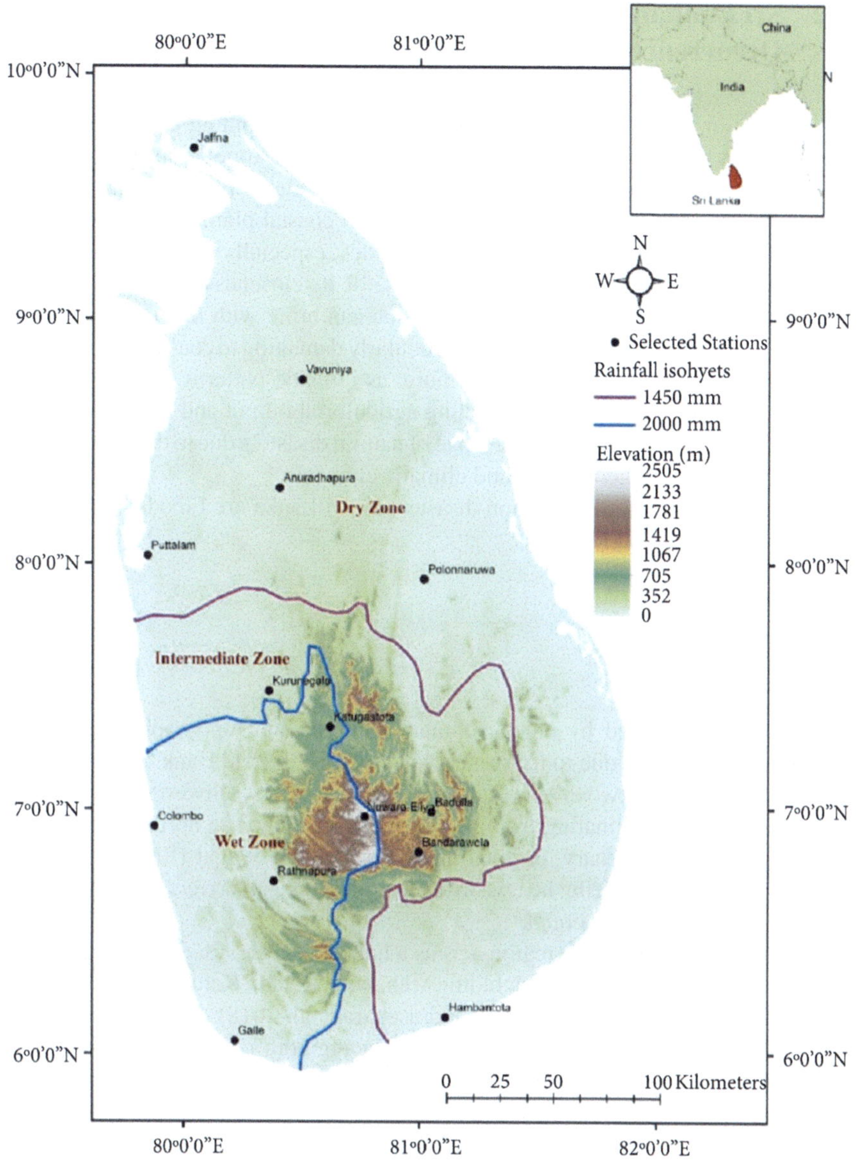

Fig. 17.1 Map of Sri Lanka indicating three major climatic zones and topographic zonation (Senatilleke et al. 2022)

17.2 Sri Lankan Context of Common Disasters and their Occurrence from 2004 to Today

Sri Lanka, a country known for its lush landscapes and stunning coastline, suffers from a variety of natural disasters. Sri Lanka's location, topography, and climate all contribute to the country's vulnerability to natural catastrophes (Alahacoon et al. 2018). The varied terrain—which consists of both coastal plains and hilly areas—increases the likelihood of flooding and landslides, especially during the monsoon season (Ratnayake and Herath 2005). Because of its closeness to the equator, Sri Lanka is vulnerable to tropical cyclones, which can bring with them severe winds, torrential rain, and storm surges that are particularly damaging to coastal communities (Srisangeerthanan et al. 2015). Furthermore, as climatic patterns change, drought frequency and intensity increase, affecting agricultural output and water resources. Sri Lanka is naturally vulnerable to a range of natural disasters due to the convergence of these geographical, geological, and climatic elements.

Accordingly, among the common disasters in Sri Lanka are Floods, Landslides, Cyclones, Wildfires and Droughts.

17.2.1 Floods

Sri Lanka, characterized by unique climatic patterns and topography, frequently faces destructive floods due to its tropical location (The World Bank Group 2021a). The island experiences two distinct monsoon seasons—the southwest monsoon from May to September, originating from the Indian Ocean, and the northeast monsoon from November to February, originating in the Bay of Bengal (Ranatunge et al. 2003). These monsoons bring heavy, prolonged rains, causing rivers to overflow and low-lying areas to be submerged.

The country's aerographic region acts as a hub for a river system with 103 rivers and associated basins, where 10, including Mahaweli, Kelani, Kalu, Nilwala, and Gin, are significantly prone to flooding (Chandrasekara et al. 2018). Sri Lanka is ranked 56th out of 191 countries for flood exposure, facing both riverine and flash floods (Patankar 2017). Predictions indicate an increased risk of flooding due to climate change-driven extreme weather events. Historical records from 1974 to 2004 reveal a rising trend in floods (Nisansala et al. 2019).

Floods in Sri Lanka have diverse and severe impacts, displacing communities, causing immediate loss of life, and damaging ecosystems, agriculture, and infrastructure (The World Bank Group 2021b). Waterborne illnesses often surge post-floods, posing additional public health challenges. Notable flood events include the 2017 disaster during the southwestern monsoon, claiming 219 lives, affecting 879,778 people, and incurring a total expenditure of 995.7 million LKR (Ministry of National Policies and Economic Affairs 2017). Similarly, heavy monsoon rains in June 2008 led to flash floods, causing 16 fatalities and impacting 173,778 people in multiple

Fig. 17.2 Floods in Kalutara district of Sri Lanka (2022). Photo credit—Vihanga Amarakoon

Fig. 17.3 Floods in Ratnapura district of Sri Lanka (2022). Photo credit—Vihanga Amarakoon

districts (WHO 2008). These incidents underscore the urgent need for effective flood management strategies in Sri Lanka. Figures 17.2 and 17.3 were taken during the floods in Kalutara and Ratnapura districts in Sri Lanka in 2022.

17.2.2 Landslides

Sri Lanka faces a persistent and severe threat of landslides due to its diverse geography. The primary cause of landslides is heavy and sustained rainfall, especially during the monsoon seasons, impacting the central highlands characterized by lush flora and steep slopes (Abeysinghe et al. 2004). Deforestation and inappropriate land use practices exacerbate this risk, as forest cover, a stabilizing element, is reduced, leading to increased slope instability (Perera et al. 2018). Anthropogenic activities such as land clearing for farming or infrastructure development further elevate the risk of landslides. Geological factors, including rock types and soil forms, also contribute to the varying susceptibility of different areas in Sri Lanka (Jayathissa et al. 2019).

Specific regions, such as the central highlands encompassing Kandy, Nuwara Eliya, and Badulla, and the Knuckles Mountain Range, are particularly vulnerable due to their steep slopes and heavy monsoon-season rainfall (Hemasinghe et al. 2018). The Ratnapura District, known for gem mining, faces heightened vulnerability due to extensive soil disturbance from mining operations (Kumara and Premasiri 2016).

Tragic events in Sri Lanka highlight the severe consequences of landslides. On October 29, 2014, monsoon rains triggered a landslide near Haldummulla, resulting in over a hundred fatalities and submerging approximately 150 dwellings in mud and debris (Ranasinghe et al. 2019). On May 17, 2016, another significant landslide occurred near the Aranayaka Divisional Secretariat, claiming more than 150 lives and destroying numerous houses due to continuous rainfall from May 14 to May 17, 2016 (International Organization of Migration 2016). This landslide occurred on the northeast facing slope of the Samasariya Hill in Dippitiya (Dang et al. 2018). These incidents underscore the urgent need for effective landslide risk management strategies in Sri Lanka.

17.2.3 Cyclones

Located in the Indian Ocean, Sri Lanka is no stranger to the destructive power of cyclones, which frequently rage over the country, leaving a path of devastation in their wake. The island nation is vulnerable to the whims of these violent storms, which bring with them torrential rainfall, strong winds, and storm surges due to its placement along main cyclone routes.

The Arabian Sea and the Bay of Bengal are the primary birthplaces of cyclones that affect Sri Lanka; they intensify over the warm waters before moving toward the island (Bhardwaj and Singh 2019). The island's intricate shoreline creates many weak spots where storm surges can breach and submerge coastal areas, increasing the island's vulnerability to cyclones.

Beyond the immediate destruction, cyclones have an influence on Sri Lanka's agriculture, fisheries, and coastal populations' means of subsistence (Weerasekara et al. 2021). A vital part of the country's economy, agriculture frequently takes the brunt of violent storms, destroying crops and leaving fertile area flooded. In addition, cyclones cause havoc to marine life's regular routines and jeopardize fishermen's safety, which disrupts the fishing sector.

Several cyclones have made their landfall in Sri Lanka leading to heavy rainfall and floods. Some of such are Cyclone Mala (2006), Cyclone Nisha (2008), Cyclone Jal (2010), Cyclone Roanu (2016) and Cyclone Ocki (2017) (Mohanty et al. 2022).

17.2.4 Wildfires

Known for its beautiful landscapes and abundant biodiversity, wildfires pose an unexpected but growing threat to Sri Lanka. The island's ecosystems, wildlife, and human communities are seriously under risk from wildfires, even though they are less frequent than in some other areas.

In Sri Lanka, a mix of man-made and natural elements frequently starts wildfires. The presence of flammable vegetation combined with windy and dry conditions makes it easier for wildfires to spread (Heenatigala 2021). Unauthorized land clearing, carelessness, and agricultural practices are among the human activities that contribute to the start and quick spread of wildfires.

Wildfires have effects that go beyond just destroying plants right away. Numerous plant and animal species can be found in Sri Lanka's different habitats, which range from dry-zone forests to tropical rainforests. In addition to causing habitat degradation, wildfires pose a threat to the survival of endangered and endemic species (Shibayama et al. 2006).

Sri Lanka experienced disastrous wildfires in 2023 in the areas of Ella which is a popular tourist destination, Puttlam, Vavuniya, and Hambanthota districts (Makumbura et al. 2024).

17.2.5 Droughts

Sri Lankan droughts are mostly caused by variations in rainfall patterns that are impacted by the monsoon season. The southwest monsoon, which runs from May to September, and the northeast monsoon, which runs from November to February, are the two main monsoon seasons on the island. Periods of water scarcity are caused by variations in precipitation, which are influenced by variations in the strength and length of these monsoons (Gunda et al. 2015).

Sri Lanka experiences more frequent and severe droughts as a result of climate change. Prolonged dry spells are caused by altering meteorological events, elevated temperatures, and altered precipitation patterns (Shelton et al. 2021). During droughts, groundwater depletion is a major worry. Water tables are strained by the excessive extraction of groundwater for domestic, industrial, and agricultural purposes, which exacerbates the effects of dry spells (De Silva and Kawasaki 2018).

Drought-like conditions impacted Sri Lanka in August 2023 with the lack of rainfall and water shortages in reservoirs (Sri Lanka: Drought – Aug 2023, 2023).

17.2.6 *Tsunami*

While Tsunami is not a common disaster in Sri Lanka, the one that stuck in 2004 managed to leave some devastating memories in the minds of the locals due to the massive destruction that happened.

A massive underwater earthquake off the Indonesian coast of Sumatra caused the tsunami waves that followed to hit Sri Lanka's shoreline on December 26 with never-before-seen strength (Rossetto et al. 2006). More than 30,000 people lost their lives as a result of the devastating effect, which also left extensive damage along the coastal districts (Kaplan et al. 2009). The waves struck the island's eastern and southern beaches hardest, leaving a path of destruction that called for a significant international humanitarian response. In addition to physically altering Sri Lanka's terrain, the 2004 tsunami brought disaster preparedness, law, and early warning systems back into the public eye in an effort to lessen the effects of subsequent tsunamis (Mulligan and Nadarajah 2011).

17.3 The Disaster Management Centre of Sri Lanka

In order to protect the country against a variety of natural and man-made disasters, the Disaster Management Centre (DMC) of Sri Lanka is essential. The DMC was founded in 2005 in the wake of the terrible tsunami (Hettiarachchi and Weeresinghe 2014). It is housed under the Ministry of Public Security and has grown into a strong organization that specializes in disaster response, preparedness, and recovery (Siriwardana et al. 2018). The DMC collaborates and coordinates with a range of stakeholders, including foreign partners, governmental organizations, and non-governmental organizations, from its headquarters in Colombo.

17.3.1 *Sections of the DMC of Sri Lanka*

To effectively fulfill its obligations in terms of disaster preparedness, response, and recovery, the DMC of Sri Lanka is divided into a number of sections and divisions (Wanninayake 2018).

17.3.2 *Roles of the DMC in Sri Lanka (Karunarathne and Gress 2022)*

Disaster preparedness is one of the DMC's main responsibilities. The center works on early warning system development, hazard mapping, and risk assessment. The

DMC makes sure that communities are aware of approaching disasters so that appropriate evacuations and preparedness measures may be implemented. It does this by employing meteorological data and innovative technologies.

The DMC has a pivotal role in organizing disaster response during times of crisis. The Operations Division oversees the logistics of relief operations and dispatches emergency response teams and resources. To guarantee a cohesive and successful response, this coordination entails working with numerous government departments, non-governmental groups, and foreign partners.

Additionally, the DMC is actively involved in reconstruction and recovery after disasters. The center works to evaluate the harm that natural catastrophes create, arranges for the relief goods to be distributed, and helps the impacted areas start over. In order to address both immediate and long-term requirements, cooperation with local authorities, humanitarian groups, and other stakeholders is required.

The Planning and Mitigation Division develops policies and plans to reduce vulnerabilities and increase community resilience in the context of catastrophe risk reduction. The DMC conducts educational campaigns, capacity-building exercises, and community awareness activities to equip people and organizations to endure and successfully respond to catastrophes.

The institution acts as a focal point for disaster management research and development. To keep ahead of new difficulties, the Research and Development Division conducts research, gathers statistics on disaster trends, and investigates cutting-edge technologies. Strategies and policies are continuously improved with the help of this information.

Additionally, the DMC actively participates in capacity building and training. Workshops, exercises, and instructional programs are arranged by the Training and Capacity Building Division to improve the abilities of individuals and groups engaged in disaster management. By taking a proactive stance, stakeholders may be sure they are equipped to address a variety of crisis situations.

17.4 Sri Lanka Disaster Management Act No. 13 of 2005

The Sri Lanka Disaster Management Act No. 13 of 2005 (hereafter referred to as the Act), is the primary national legislation related to disaster risk management (Abdeen et al. 2021). The primary objective of Act is to safeguard the lives of individuals and the environment in Sri Lanka from the impacts of natural disasters. This is achieved through the development of national policies and plans, as well as the establishment of centrally coordinated committees and institutions tasked with implementing these policies and plans (Siriwardana et al. 2018).

As stipulated in Section 2 the Act of the provisions have been made to ensure that the disaster management framework of Sri Lanka is spearheaded by a National Council for Disaster Management (NCDM) carried out through the Disaster Management Centre (DMC) (Sri Lanka Disaster Management Act 2005). When considering the constitution of the NCDM, the Act (Section 3) ensures that the President, prime minister, opposition leader, opposition representatives, ministers of a wide range of subject matters and even provincial representatives are included as members of the council (Sri Lanka Disaster Management Act 2005). Thus, the Act is able to ensure compliance of the "all of government representation" principle of the Sendai Framework for Disaster Risk Reduction (United Nations Office for Disaster Risk Reduction 2015) and establish a strong and able apex body for disaster management in Sri Lanka (Abeysinghe and De Mel 2019; Ministry of Disaster Management 2018). A comprehensive and clear account of the role and responsibilities of the NCDM is provided for in Section 4 of the Act (Sri Lanka Disaster Management Act 2005). Inter alia, the NCDM is responsible for responding to disaster emergency situations, formulating the national disaster management policy, formulating and implementing the National disaster management plan and the National Emergency Operation plan and the implementation of disaster management programmes. The Act also provides that the foremost role of the NCDM is to "take all steps necessary to counter any disaster or impending disaster" and it can be achieved by implementing, coordinating and being accountable for the disaster management initiatives of a variety of institutions that belong to the disaster management framework (named in the Act) (Sri Lanka Disaster Management Act 2005). The Act provides the NCDM with the unique and overarching responsibility and ability to approve plans and make decisions in relation to disaster management (Abeysinghe and De Mel 2019). Therefore, it is evident that establishment of the NCDM and its roles is a major contribution drawn from the Act toward a better disaster management framework in Sri Lanka.

The National Council for Disaster Management (NCDM) in Sri Lanka, established by the Act, faces practical shortcomings attributed to loopholes in the legislation. Despite the Act's theoretical soundness, the NCDM has not fully met its responsibilities. Notably, the council's infrequent meetings, falling below the mandated quarterly requirement, and the misuse of quorum provisions have been identified.

For instance, only 13 meetings occurred from 2005 to December 2018, with an average attendance of six members instead of the required 14. Additionally, ministers' absence, substituted by representatives, has hindered timely decision-making at the cabinet level. These loopholes have led to prolonged delays in approving crucial disaster preparation, reduction, and mitigation strategies. Administrative failures, such as the delayed completion of the 'Road Map for disaster management 2005–2015' and the non-issuance of gazette notifications on government department disaster management plans, underscore the urgent need for improvements in Sri Lanka's national legislation on disaster risk management. This analysis is based on studies by Abeysinghe and De Mel (2019) and Siriwardana et al. (2018).

17.5 Divisions and Responsibilities of the DMC

The Disaster Management Centre of Sri Lanka is composed of different divisions with various tasks and responsibilities (see Table 17.1 Divisions and Responsibilities of the DMC).

Table 17.1 Divisions and responsibilities of the DMC

Division	Responsibilities
Operations division	Coordinate and oversee operational aspects of disaster response, manage resources, deploy emergency teams, ensure timely and effective response during emergencies
Planning and mitigation division	Develop disaster risk reduction strategies, mitigation plans, and community awareness programs; formulate policies to enhance the country's resilience against various hazards
Information and communication technology (ICT) division	Manage technology for early warning systems, data management, and communication during disasters
Training and capacity building division	Organize training programs, workshops, and drills to enhance the skills and preparedness of individuals and organizations involved in disaster management
Research and development division	Conduct research on disaster trends, vulnerability assessments, and innovative technologies to inform DMC's strategies
Coordination division	Coordinate efforts among government agencies, NGOs, and international partners; foster collaboration for a unified response
Public awareness and education division	Manage public awareness campaigns, educational programs, and outreach initiatives to educate the public about disaster risks and response procedures
Finance and administration division	Manage financial resources, budgeting, financial planning, and general administrative tasks for the smooth functioning of the DMC

17.6 National Disaster Management Policy

The Sri Lanka Disaster Management Act No. 13 of 2005 provides guidelines for the formulation of the National Disaster Management Policy (SLNDMP) (Section 4(a)) and the National Disaster Management Plan (NDMP) to ensure an effective disaster management framework in Sri Lanka (Sri Lanka Disaster Management Act 2005). The SLNDMP serves as the main policy for disaster management and in disaster risk reduction (DRR) and is built on global standards and the Sendai principles. The National Policy on Disaster Management outlines strategies to safeguard the people, property, and environment of Sri Lanka from disasters (Siriwardana et al. 2018). This policy encompasses provisions to ensure the resilience of infrastructure and economic development in disaster-prone regions, optimization of resources for activities related to preparedness, prevention, response, relief, reconstruction, and rehabilitation, promotion of public awareness and training initiatives to empower individuals in safeguarding themselves from disaster fostering capacity building among residents in vulnerable areas and to emphasize pre-disaster planning, preparedness, and mitigation, while maintaining and enhancing capabilities for post-disaster relief, recovery, and rehabilitation (National Policy on Disaster Management 2014).

However, several shortcomings in the guidelines for the formulation of the policy and its content can be identified (Siriwardana et al. 2018). It has been identified that the guidelines in the Act provide no direction that requires the SLNDMP to be formulated in a manner that encompasses the sustainable development goals and its disaster risk reduction strategies (Siriwardana et al. 2018). As a result, if Sustainable Development Goals (SDG) such as SDG 12 relating to food waste generation were considered in the policy, it is arguable that risks of disasters such as the Meethotamulla disaster could have been reduced (Ravishan 2017). Secondly, while the Act provides that the policy be formulated to ensure risk management and increase preparedness, the manner in which these requirements must be met is left vague to the viewer (Siriwardana et al. 2018). However, if the "best fit for best practice" principle was included within the formulation guidelines, legal provisions can be made to ensure that the traditional methods that have been effective long before disaster management frameworks, are incorporated with modern twists to reduce risks (Siriwardana et al. 2018). Finally, the guidelines in the Act lack provisions to encompass the "Build back better" principle in the SLNDMP. Therefore, it is argued that the policy fails to provide authority for a Post Disaster Assessment which is an essential tool in disaster risk reduction and can be used as a measure of the effectiveness of the disaster management strategies in place (Abeysinghe and De Mel 2019; Siriwardana et al. 2018).

17.7 National Disaster Management Plan

Since 2005, two main disaster management plans have been formulated and implemented: The Road Map for Disaster Risk Management—Towards a Safer Sri Lanka (2006–2016) and the National Disaster Management Plan (2013–2017) (Disaster Management Centre 2022).

The National Disaster Management Plan (NDMP) for 2022–2030 outlines a strategic, multi-disciplinary approach to establish a disaster risk management framework in the country. It emphasizes collaboration across sectors, ministries, and agencies, the plan spans the entire disaster management cycle (Disaster Management Centre 2022). Some key aspects include pre-disaster measures, advocating for a comprehensive understanding of risk and coherent national frameworks, with investments in both structural and non-structural risk reduction. Strengthening disaster preparedness is highlighted for effective response and recovery. During disasters, the plan focuses on emergency response measures, and in the post-disaster phase, it covers relief, recovery, assessment, rehabilitation, relocation, and reconstruction. The long-term perspective includes sustained community resilience development through a "build back better" approach, emphasizing collaboration and participation from multiple stakeholders for effective implementation (Disaster Management Centre 2022).

17.8 Other Strategies for Disaster Risk Management

Institutional Arrangements

Sri Lanka has adopted a wide array of disaster risk management strategies to facilitate and bring to life the actions stipulated on the plans and policies related to disaster risk management (Disaster Management Centre 2014). A key strategy amongst them are the institutional arrangements that the government has made with the Provincial Council, District, Divisional, Grama Niladhari, and Village levels. To implement this at the ground level, technical committees have been appointed as specified in the Act, which will include specialists and members representing different stakeholder agencies handling different natural and human-induced hazards covered in the Act. These committees have been tasked with providing advice in specific disaster risk management activities to the institutions. This form of decentralization has permitted even the village-level institutions to be involved in disaster risk reduction (Caruson and MacManus 2012). The longevity of this strategy has been ensured by linking these institutions to the DMC (Disaster Management Centre 2014). This Sri Lankan framework embraces both the horizontal and the vertical collaboration concepts as suggested by Caruson and MacManus (2012) and Bae et al. (2016). Despite this, the need for effective and efficient multi-agency collaboration has been highlighted with respect to the handling of disasters in the past in Sri Lanka. For instance, a study conducted by Abdeen et al. (2021) draws on examples from the October 2014 landslide in Badulla and the 2017 floods to highlight the concerns over the degree of collaboration that exists between the agencies involved in disaster management.

Risk Assessment, Data Collection, Research and Analysis

The DMC aims to promote research as a tool to recognize, analyze, and assess disaster risk, deterioration of such risk, predict future scenarios, and to determine strategic measures to manage disaster risk. In the ongoing efforts, multi-hazard mapping, vulnerability, and risk assessments have been continuously conducted to consolidate all disaster-related information and hazard maps in a centralized repository. This ensures accessibility and facilitates technology transfer, particularly in collaborative projects with international agencies. Priority areas for mapping have been determined based on the severity of vulnerability, sector importance (e.g., education, health, housing, agriculture), and ongoing development projects. Integrating disaster risk reduction at the initial stages of development has also been emphasized by the DMC. This initiative also promotes research studies conducted by agencies and universities to enhance the disaster information database, focusing on prone areas, social issues, and specific hazards such as technological and human-induced risks resulting from unsustainable development. The Sendai Framework expands upon the Hyogo Framework for Action (HFA) by incorporating both natural and human-made hazards, broadening the range of activities related to recovery, rehabilitation, and reconstruction (Disaster Management Centre 2014). Emphasizing various hazard types necessitates a comprehensive understanding of their essential features, such as magnitude, duration, and frequency. To achieve this, there may be a need to enhance the National Hazard Profile developed by the DMC.

Early Warning (EW) Centres

Another key strategy initiated by the Sri Lankan government are the Early Warning (EW) centres to ensure effective early warning communication in events of hazards (Abdeen et al. 2021). These EW Centres collaborate closely with the special police emergency section, focusing on community and police awareness regarding early warning and immediate actions. The centers establish reliable communication systems, incorporate alternatives, and coordinate with public media for timely information dissemination DMC (Disaster Management Centre 2014). As part of their role they must consistently inform relevant administrative bodies and local committees. Additionally, communities and sea-dependent individuals likely to be affected receive prompt notifications from the EW Centres, contributing to effective disaster preparedness and response (Disaster Management Centre 2014).

Disaster Preparedness and Response Plans

The requirement to develop Disaster Preparedness and Response Plans (based on guidelines circulated by the DMC) by all government units, private sector, and educational units can be viewed as another strategy implemented by the government to manage risks posed due to human and natural disasters (Disaster Management Centre 2014). A notifying feature is the consideration of disaster resilience amongst communities and the steps taken by the DMC to promote micro-financing schemes to reduce the vulnerability of hazard-prone populations. This can be viewed as a positive step to overcome the vicious cycle of poverty and disaster (Abdeen et al. 2021).

Training, Public Awareness, and Education

The Disaster Management Centre (DMC) employs key strategies such as Training, Public Awareness, and Education to ensure sustainable management of disaster risks (DMC 2014). Training initiatives, tailored to the capacities of different authorities, involve identifying target groups, including government, private sector, NGOs, informal sector, and Community Based Disaster Risk Management. Plans cover all phases of the Disaster Management Cycle, addressing specific district needs and coordinating with existing efforts. Public awareness programs, with a focus on livelihood development and poverty reduction, are implemented by the Ministry of Disaster Management (2018). Collaboration with relevant agencies integrates disaster management into educational curricula at school and tertiary levels.

A project initiated in 2017 integrates global environmental and disaster risk management agreements into Sri Lanka's sustainable development, with completion in December 2018. Awareness programs under this project target diverse groups, including people, public officers, political authorities, small and medium-scale businesspersons, and journalists, emphasizing the importance of using metadata in decision-making processes. This comprehensive strategy successfully addresses training and awareness needs across various sectors and community levels.

Promoting Different Stakeholders Toward DRM

Promoting different stakeholders outside the government structure for "Achieving Maximum Effect" in disaster risk response is a decentralized strategy implemented by the DMC (Disaster Management Centre 2014). This has been done to enhance disaster response and recovery through the private sector which has been encouraged to form associations and develop individual plans aligned with the National Plan and guidelines of the National Disaster Management Policy (Ministry of Disaster Management 2018). The DMC aims to assist in organizing and building the capacity of these groups, coordinating with them to access resources for post-disaster response and integrating them into the National Resource database. The DMC also promotes a culture of volunteerism at various levels, encouraging registration and training of volunteer groups, as well as recognizing and rewarding volunteers and employers who support volunteerism (Disaster Management Centre 2014). Additionally, the DMC acknowledges the vital role of the media, emphasizing their responsibility to provide accurate and timely information to the public. Collaborating with NGOs and INGOs is another strategy implemented by the DMC to garner support for disaster management activities, including the inclusion of their resources in the National Resource database. A framework for the operations of the NGOs and INGOs in Sri Lanka during disasters has also been established to facilitate the role of these organizations and adopting a Code of Conduct for NGOs (Disaster Management Centre 2014).

17.9 Disaster Management Policies and Laws: A Way Forward

Strengthening disaster management policies and laws is essential for enhancing a nation's resilience and response capabilities. Some important aspects that need further strengthening and upscale present legal regime and policies could include the following.

Inclusive Stakeholder Engagement: Involve a diverse range of stakeholders in the development, review, and updating of disaster management policies. This includes government agencies, local communities, non-governmental organizations, academia, and private sector entities. Inclusive decision-making processes ensure that policies reflect the needs and perspectives of all relevant parties. There is a growing emphasis on community-based strategies within national disaster risk reduction (DRR) plans, acknowledging the essential contribution of communities in both pre-disaster preparedness and post-disaster recovery (Shaw et al. 2012).

Research on Disaster-related Issues: The country exhibits a noticeable gap in investigations, data analysis, and interpretation, particularly in areas that are crucial but have been relatively neglected. These neglected aspects encompass disaster finance, insurance, economic impacts, and the psychology of victims, as highlighted by Amarakoon et al. (2024b). Additionally, there is a need to explore the connections between climate change and disasters. Addressing these aspects is imperative for comprehensive development and a more thorough understanding of the multifaceted dimensions of disaster management.

Integration of Technology: Leverage technological advancements, such as remote sensing, artificial intelligence (AI), and geographic information systems (GIS), for more accurate and timely data collection, risk assessment, and early warning systems. Incorporating cutting-edge technology enhances the effectiveness of disaster management policies.

Legislation Review and Update: Regularly review existing disaster management legislation to identify gaps and areas for improvement. Laws should be updated to incorporate lessons learned from past incidents, emerging risks, and international best practices. This ensures that legal frameworks remain robust and adaptable to new challenges.

International Cooperation: Foster collaboration and information-sharing with international partners. Learning from global experiences and best practices can enrich a country's disaster management policies. Participating in regional and international networks facilitates mutual assistance during large-scale disasters.

By adopting these strategies, governments can strengthen their disaster management policies and laws, ultimately enhancing their ability to protect lives, property, and the environment in the face of disasters.

17.10 Discussion

This chapter discussed the disaster laws, frameworks, and other related legislation in Sri Lanka and their strengths and weaknesses. It also provides some important insights on how the disaster management can be strengthened further within the local and national levels of the country.

With climate change and due to many other factors, the natural hazards have been rapidly increasing around the world (Berz et al. 2001) and the situation in Sri Lanka is of no difference. Due to high frequency in rainfall throughout the past few years, floods and landslides have increased in intensity vastly (Ratnayake and Herath 2005). The change in rainfall patterns has attributed toward the prolonged droughts in some regions of the country (Lyon et al. 2009). The El-Nino conditions have impacted on the severe cyclones generated at the Bay of Bengal bringing intensified influences on Sri Lanka (Bhardwaj et al. 2019). Apart from the natural causes, human influences have also been affecting the increase of natural hazards in the country. For instance, the unsustainable land use practices have attributed to the wildfires occurring within the country in the recent history (Rathnayake et al. 2020). Against this backdrop, it has become clear that Sri Lanka needs stronger policies to face the upcoming natural hazards, which may bring more severe impacts than expected.

The DMC is currently playing a remarkable role within all the phases of disaster management cycle. However, more workloads can be anticipated along with the increase of disaster risk within the country and therefore, DMC needs to be strengthened further with policies and practices both.

As discussed in this chapter, Sri Lanka has well-written and properly formulated policies and other legislation related to disaster management. However, loopholes can be seen in the implementation of those policies, as explained. Such weaknesses can be overcome by proper communication with relevant stakeholders and refining the policies to match the timely needs (Ngqwala et al. 2017). Also, as discussed, it is of prime importance to align the disaster policies with the SDGs to minimize the disaster impacts as well as to be coordinated with the disaster frameworks of other countries in order to receive their support in crisis time (Vadivelu 2021).

Further, as mentioned in the chapter, collaborating with the local level stakeholders is essential for better disaster management practices and it needs to be improved more within the country. The local level officers and other stakeholders perform an important role during disasters, by directly interacting with the affected communities, especially by maintaining the temporary shelters (Malalgoda et al. 2016). Their role should be recognized further within the disaster management context and more provisions are needed through policies and frameworks to increase their working capacity.

This chapter provides some guidance for further research needed in the future regarding the disaster law in Sri Lanka. It is important to understand the discourses for the gap between policymaking and implementation and provide practically feasible solutions to fill the gap. Also, using a bottom-up approach in disaster policymaking can be beneficial too when considering the immense disaster knowledge processed by the local communities. According to Amarakoon et al. (2024a), the indigenous knowledge owned by the disaster-affected communities can be potentially used in disaster policymaking process so that the years of disaster experience of the locals can be put into a better use.

Finally, while Sri Lanka's disaster policies and laws are well-structured, there is room for further enhancement to offer clearer guidance to stakeholders in addressing future heightened disaster risks.

17.11 Conclusion

Disaster management policies and laws play a crucial role in safeguarding communities, ensuring a coordinated response, and mitigating the impact of natural or man-made disasters. In Sri Lankan disaster management context, the legal framework and policies provide a structured approach to preparedness, response, recovery, and mitigation efforts. This chapter sheds light to some common and recurrent disasters in Sri Lanka and comprehensive disaster management policies which help in defining the roles and responsibilities of the Disaster Management Center, which is the key authority in managing disasters in the island. Elaborations on strategies in disaster management that include institutional arrangement, Research that encompasses data gathering, and analysis, Disaster preparedness plans as well as training and public awareness are presented. Moreover, disaster management policies that contribute to the establishment of early warning systems and efficient communication channels, facilitating timely and effective responses to emerging threats are explained in this chapter. Finally, some important aspects that need further strengthening and upscale present legal regime and policies are discussed as a way forward.

In essence, robust disaster management policies and laws are instrumental in fostering a culture of preparedness, guiding resource allocation, and ultimately enhancing the overall resilience of societies in the face of unforeseen challenges.

Acknowledgements The authors are grateful for the support extended by the Department of Zoology and Environment Sciences, University of Colombo, Sri Lanka.

References

Abdeen FN, Fernando T, Kulatunga U, Hettige S, Ranasinghe KDA (2021) Challenges in multi-agency collaboration in disaster management: a Sri Lankan perspective. Int J Disaster Risk Reduct

Abeysinghe B, Iwao Y, Bandara S (2004) Development of a risk assessment methodologyfor landslides in Sri Lanka. Nihon Jisuberi Gakkaishi 41(2):131–141. https://doi.org/10.3313/jls.41.131

Abeysinghe S, De Mel N (2019) Disaster management in Sri Lanka: a case study of administrative failures (briefing note), Verite Research

Alahacoon N, Matheswaran K, Pani P, Amarnath G (2018) A decadal historical satellite data and rainfall trend analysis (2001–2016) for flood hazard mapping in Sri Lanka. Remote Sens 10(3):448. https://doi.org/10.3390/rs10030448

Amarakoon V, Dharmarathne G, Premasiri R, Mukherjee M, Shaw R, Wickramasinghe D (2024a) Potential for the complementary and integrative use of citizen science and modern science in flood risk reduction: a case study from Sri Lanka. Int J Disaster Risk Reduct 104331

Amarakoon V, Trafford J, Udeshika T, Amarasekara DS, Wickramasinghe D (2024b) Towards happy relief campers: surfacing psycho-social issues, conflicts and other problems for flood-affected residents and officials in Kuruwita, Sri Lanka. Int J Disaster Risk Reduct 101. https://doi.org/10.1016/j.ijdrr.2024.104259

Bae Y, Joo YM, Won SY (2016) Decentralization and collaborative disaster governance: evidence from South Korea. Habitat Int 52:50–56

Berz G, Kron W, Loster T, Rauch E, Schimetschek J, Schmieder J, Siebert A, Smolka A, Wirtz A (2001) World map of natural hazards–a global view of the distribution and intensity of significant exposures. Nat Hazards 23:443–465

Bhardwaj P, Singh O (2019) Climatological characteristics of Bay of Bengal tropical cyclones: 1972–2017. Theoret Appl Climatol 139(1–2):615–629. https://doi.org/10.1007/s00704-019-02989-4

Bhardwaj P, Pattanaik DR, Singh O (2019) Tropical cyclone activity over Bay of Bengal in relation to El Niño-Southern Oscillation. Int J Climatol 39(14):5452–5469

Caruson K, MacManus SA (2012) Interlocal emergency management collaboration: vertical and horizontal roadblocks. Publius 42(1):162–187

Chandrasekara SSK, Uranchimeg S, Kwon H, Lee SO (2018) Coastal flood disaster in Sri Lanka-May 2017: exploring distributional changes in rainfall and their impacts on flood risk. J Coastal Res 85:1476–1480. https://doi.org/10.2112/si85-296.1

Dang K, Sassa K, Konagai K, Karunawardena A, Bandara RMS, Hirota K, Tan Q, Ha ND (2018) Recent rainfall-induced rapid and long-traveling landslide on 17 May 2016 in Aranayaka, Kagelle District. Sri Lanka. Landslides 16(1):155–164. https://doi.org/10.1007/s10346-018-1089-7

De Silva M, Kawasaki A (2018) Socioeconomic vulnerability to disaster risk: a case study of flood and drought impact in a rural Sri Lankan community. Ecol Econ 152:131–140. https://doi.org/10.1016/j.ecolecon.2018.05.010

Department of Census and Statistics (2021) http://www.statistics.gov.lk/

Disaster Management Centre (2014) National Disaster Management Plan 2013–2017

Disaster Management Centre (2022) National Disaster Management Plan 2022–2030

Disaster Management Centre (2017) Situation report

Disaster Management Centre (2024) http://www.dmc.gov.lk/index.php?option=com_content&view=featured&Itemid=101&lang=en

Government of Sri Lanka (2005) Report of Sri Lankan parliament select committee on natural disasters. https://www.parliament.lk/uploads/comreports/1476092317082517.pdf

Gunda T, Hornberger GM, Gilligan JM (2015) Spatiotemporal patterns of agricultural drought in Sri Lanka: 1881–2010. Int J Climatol 36(2):563–575. https://doi.org/10.1002/joc.4365

Heenatigala M (2021) Influence of climate change on forest fire occurrence and distribution of Sri Lanka and modeling of forest fire. https://doi.org/10.15760/mem.71

Hemasinghe H, Rangali R, Deshapriya NL, Samarakoon L (2018) Landslide susceptibility mapping using logistic regression model (a case study in Badulla District, Sri Lanka). Procedia Eng 212:1046–1053. https://doi.org/10.1016/j.proeng.2018.01.135

Hettiarachchi S, Weeresinghe S (2014) Achieving disaster resilience through the Sri Lankan early warning system: good practises of disaster risk reduction and management. Procedia Econ Finance 18:789–794. https://doi.org/10.1016/s2212-5671(14)01003-x

International Organization for Migration (2016) Sri Lanka floods and landslides—Situation report 25 may 2016

Jayathissa G, Schröder D, Balke K, Fecker E (2019) Landslide hazard zonation in Sri Lanka: an assessment of manual and GIS based automated procedure in preparation of Geology weight map. Int J Eros Control Eng 11(4):116–123. https://doi.org/10.13101/ijece.11.116

Kaplan M, Renaud FG, Lüchters G (2009) Vulnerability assessment and protective effects of coastal vegetation during the 2004 Tsunami in Sri Lanka. Nat Hazard 9(4):1479–1494. https://doi.org/10.5194/nhess-9-1479-2009

Karunarathne AY, Gress DR (2022) The role of organizational networks in ameliorating flood disaster impacts: a case study of flood inundated rural and urban areas in Sri Lanka. Int J Disaster Risk Reduct 71:102819. https://doi.org/10.1016/j.ijdrr.2022.102819

Kumara SBA, Premasiri RHM (eds) (2016) Analysis of spatial distribution of landslides in Ratnapura district Sri Lanka. In: Proceedings of the international conference on multidisciplinary approaches - 2016. http://dr.lib.sjp.ac.lk/handle/123456789/5919
Lyon B, Zubair L, Ralapanawe V, Yahiya Z (2009) Finescale evaluation of drought in a tropical setting: case study in Sri Lanka. J Appl Meteorol Climatol 48(1):77–88
Makumbura RK, Dissanayake P, Gunathilake MB, Rathnayake N, Kantamaneni K, Rathnayake U (2024) Spatial mapping and analysis of forest fire risk areas in Sri Lanka – Understanding environmental significance. Case Stud Chem Environ Eng 9:100680. https://doi.org/10.1016/j.cscee.2024.100680
Malalgoda C, Amaratunga D, Haigh R (2016) Overcoming challenges faced by local governments in creating a resilient built environment in cities. Disaster Prevent Manag Int J 25(5):628–648
Math SB, Nirmala MC, Moirangthem S, Kumar N (2015) Disaster management: mental health perspective. Indian J Psychol Med 37(3):261–271. https://doi.org/10.4103/0253-7176.162915
Ministry of Disaster Management (2018) Annual performance report
Ministry of National Policies and Economic Affairs (2017) Sri Lanka rapid post disaster needs assessment. Ministry of Disaster Management. https://lk.one.un.org/wp-content/uploads/2017/11/PDNA-Sri-lanka-2017.pdf
Mitra A, Shaw R (2022) Systemic risk from a disaster management perspective: a review of current research. Soc Sci Res Netw. https://doi.org/10.2139/ssrn.4140988
Mohanty A, Dubey A, Singh RB (2022) The major cyclonic disasters in Sri Lanka. In: Cyclonic disasters and resilience, pp 129–153. https://doi.org/10.1007/978-981-19-1215-3_5
Mulligan M, Nadarajah Y (2011) Rebuilding community in the wake of disaster: lessons from the recovery from the 2004 Tsunami in Sri Lanka and India. Commun Dev J 47(3):353–368. https://doi.org/10.1093/cdj/bsr025
National Council for Disaster Management (2014) National policy on disaster management
Nisansala WDS, Abeysingha NS, Islam A, Bandara AMKR (2019) Recent rainfall trend over Sri Lanka (1987–2017). Int J Climatol 40(7):3417–3435. https://doi.org/10.1002/joc.6405
Ngqwala NP, Srinivas CS, Tandlich R, Pyle DM, Oosthuizen R (2017) Participatory multi-stakeholder platforms in disaster management in South Africa. J Disaster Res 12(6):1192–1202
Patankar A (2017) Colombo: exposure, vulnerability, and ability to respond to floods. In: Exposure, vulnerability, and ability to respond to floods, Colombo. https://doi.org/10.1596/1813-9450-8084
Perera ENC, Jayawardana D, Jayasinghe P, Bandara RMS, Alahakoon N (2018) Direct impacts of landslides on socio-economic systems: a case study from Aranayake, Sri Lanka. Geoenviron Disasters 5(1). https://doi.org/10.1186/s40677-018-0104-6
Ranasinghe AKRN, Bandara RMS, Puswewala UGA, Dammalage TL (2019) Efficacy of using radar induced factors in landslide susceptibility analysis: case study of Koslanda, Sri Lanka. Nat Hazards Earth Syst Sci. https://doi.org/10.5194/nhess-2018-335
Ranatunge E, Malmgren BA, Hayashi Y, Mikami T, Morishima W, Yokozawa M, Nishimori M (2003) Changes in the Southwest Monsoon mean daily rainfall intensity in Sri Lanka: relationship to the El Niño-Southern oscillation. Palaeogeogr Palaeoclimatol Palaeoecol 197(1–2):1–14. https://doi.org/10.1016/s0031-0182(03)00383-3
Ratnayake U, Herath S (2005) Changing rainfall and its impact on landslides in Sri Lanka. J Mt Sci 2(3):218–224. https://doi.org/10.1007/bf02973195
Rathnayake CW, Jones S, Soto-Berelov M (2020) Mapping land cover change over a 25-year period (1993–2018) in Sri Lanka using Landsat time-series. Land 9(1):27
Ravishan (2017) A brief history of the Meethotamulla Garbage dump. Roar Reports, 23 April 2017. https://roar.media/english/reports/reports/a-brief-history-of-the-meethotamulla-garbage-dump
Rossetto T, Peiris N, Pomonis A, Wilkinson S, Del Re D, Koo R, Gallocher S (2006) The Indian Ocean tsunami of December 26, 2004: observations in Sri Lanka and Thailand. Nat Hazards 42(1):105–124. https://doi.org/10.1007/s11069-006-9064-3
Section 10, Sri Lanka Disaster Management Act, No. 13 of 2005
Section 2, Sri Lanka Disaster Management Act, No. 13 of 2005

Section 3, Sri Lanka Disaster Management Act, No. 13 of 2005
Section 4, Sri Lanka Disaster Management Act, No. 13 of 2005
Section 6, Sri Lanka Disaster Management Act, No. 13 of 2005
Senatilleke U, Abeysiriwardana HD, Makumbura RK, Anwar F, Rathnayake U (2022) Estimation of potential evapotranspiration across Sri Lanka using a distributed dual source evapotranspiration model under data scarcity. Adv Meteorol 2022:1–14. https://doi.org/10.1155/2022/6819539
Shaw R, Takeuchi Y, Krishnamurthy RR, Pereira JJ, Mallick F (2012) Universities and community-based disaster risk reduction. In: Community, environment and disaster risk management, pp 55–66. https://doi.org/10.1108/s2040-7262(2012)0000010010
Shelton S, Ogou FK, Pushpawela BG (2021) Spatial-temporal variability of droughts during two cropping seasons in Sri Lanka and its possible mechanisms. Asia-Pac J Atmos Sci 58(1):127–144. https://doi.org/10.1007/s13143-021-00239-0
Shibayama T, Ashton MS, Singhakumara B, Griscom HP, Ediriweera S, Griscom BW (2006) Effects of fire on the recruitment of rain forest vegetation beneath Pinus caribaea plantations, Sri Lanka. Forest Ecol Manag 226(1–3):357–363. https://doi.org/10.1016/j.foreco.2006.01.016
Siriwardana CSA, Jayasiri G, Hettiarachchi S (2018) Investigation of efficiency and effectiveness of the existing disaster management frameworks in Sri Lanka. Procedia Eng 212:1091–1098. https://doi.org/10.1016/j.proeng.2018.01.141
Sri Lanka: Drought - Aug 2023 (2023, October 16) ReliefWeb. https://reliefweb.int/disaster/dr-2023-000151-lka
Srisangeerthanan S, Lewangamage C, Wickramasuriya SS (2015) Tropical cyclone damages in Sri Lanka. Wind Eng JAWE 40(3):294–302. https://doi.org/10.5359/jawe.40.294
The World Bank Group (2021a) Sri Lanka - vulnerability. Climate change knowledge portal. Accessed 13 June 2022 https://climateknowledgeportal.worldbank.org/country/sri-lanka/vulnerability
The World Bank (2021b) FROM crisis to green, resilient, and inclusive recovery. J Econ 114
United Nations Office for Disaster Risk Reduction (2015) Sendai framework for disaster risk reduction 2015–2030. https://www.unisdr.org/files/43291_sendaiframeworkfordrren.pdf
Vadivelu V (2021) Disaster risk management in the SDG era. Eval Environ Int Dev 278
Wanninayake WMSB (2018) Roles and responsibilities of government stakeholder agencies in managing disasters–reviewing Sri Lankan experience. J Trop Environ 1(1)
Weerasekara SH, Wilson C, Lee BL, Hoang V, Managi S, Rajapaksa D (2021) The impacts of climate induced disasters on the economy: winners and losers in Sri Lanka. Ecol Econ 185:107043. https://doi.org/10.1016/j.ecolecon.2021.107043
WHO (2008) Flash Floods - June 2008 - Sri Lanka. ReliefWeb. Accessed 13 June 2022, from https://reliefweb.int/report/sri-lanka/flash-floods-june-2008-sri-lanka
Yu M, Deng Y, Shi P (2015) Mapping forest wildfire risk of the world. In: IHDP/Future earth-integrated risk governance project series, pp 261–275. https://doi.org/10.1007/978-3-662-45430-5_14

Chapter 18
Disaster Management Law in Pakistan

Muneeb-ur Rahman, Haseeb-ur Rahman, Atta-ur Rahman, and Rajib Shaw

Abstract In Pakistan, the devastating 2005 Kashmir earthquake was a paradigm shift in Disaster Management system and legislation. After 2005 Kashmir Earthquake, the then Government has realized to transfer the mechanism of addressing Disasters from reactive to proactive approach. Prior to Kashmir earthquake, the Disaster Management system was run under the reactive approach dominated by Prevention and Relief Act, 1958. As Pakistan is prone to diverse nature of disasters and in post-Kashmir Earthquake, the Government has realized the significance of Disaster Management. As a result, the National Disaster Management Commission (NDMC) was established in 2006. Subsequently, the National Disaster Management Authority (NDMA) a focal body was also established to devise policies as well as to materialize plans and strategies for minimizing risk and increasing community resilience. As a consequence, in 2007 the National Disaster Risk Management Framework was prepared followed by National Disaster Management Act 2010. This has led to establishment of dedicated Ministry of Climate Change and Environmental Coordination, National Disaster Risk Reduction Policy in 2013 and Pakistan Climate Change Act 2017. Likewise, the Disaster Management System was decentralized and Provincial Disaster Management Authorities and further transmitted to local level in the form of District Disaster Management Authority. In Pakistan, thc Disaster Management Law and legislations are gradually gaining significance in Government set-up and currently, DRR is part and parcel of the planning process.

Keywords Disaster · Legislation · NDMA · Disaster management act

---

M. Rahman
Law College, University of Peshawar, Peshawar, Pakistan

H. Rahman
Institute of Space Technology, Islamabad, Pakistan

A. Rahman (✉)
Department of Geography and Geomatics, University of Peshawar, Peshawar, Pakistan
e-mail: atta-ur-rehman@uop.edu.pk

R. Shaw
Graduate School of Media and Governance, Keio Unioversity, Minato, Japan

Y. Cui and R. Shaw (eds.), *Disaster Law*, Disaster Risk Reduction,
https://doi.org/10.1007/978-981-97-7374-9_18

18.1 Introduction

Pakistan, a country located at the cross road of South Asia. The country is exposed to multiple and complex human induced and natural disasters, which require an effective legal structure for disaster management. Pakistan is vulnerable to several natural disasters such as floods, earthquakes, cyclones, and landslides due to its diverse physical terrain (Rahman et al. 2015; Mahmood et al. 2019). The complexity of the catastrophe landscape is further increased by urbanization, accidents in industry, and climate change, in addition to these natural obstacles. Pakistan has made efforts to create a Disaster Management comprehensive Law that includes policies, laws, and institutional structures in recognition of the necessity of addressing these complex threats methodically (Malik et al. 2020).

The Disaster Management Law of Pakistan is based on the understanding that preventing catastrophes from hurting property, people and ecosystems requires proactive actions (Khan and Rahman 2022). The legal environment has changed throughout time to take into account the growing frequency of disasters and the shifting nature of hazards. Acts like the National Disaster Management Act, which outline the duties and obligations of different parties, including municipalities, nonprofit organizations, and federal and provincial governments, are part of the legislative framework. These legal tools are intended to encourage risk mitigation, readiness, and community resilience in addition to facilitating efficient response to disasters (Norris et al. 2008).

The National Disaster Management Authority (NDMA) and its provincial equivalents are important components of Disaster Management Law of Pakistan. These establishments function as the central nervous systems for disaster management, arranging activities, distributing alerts in advance, and developing guidelines to improve the nation's overall readiness. The legislative system also recognizes society's common duty to reduce and manage catastrophes, emphasizing the value of cooperation between public and private entities (Allen 2006). The aforementioned regulation also stipulates the establishment of contingency funds, guaranteeing the accessibility of monetary resources for prompt reaction and rehabilitation endeavors (Goniewicz 2023).

Pakistan has created an extensive legal framework for disaster management in order to mitigate this risk. This framework is intended to assist the nation in anticipating, responding to, and recovering from calamities. The National Disaster Response Plan, the National Disaster Management Act (2010), the National Disaster Risk Management Framework (2007), and the National Calamities (Prevention and Relief Act) (1958) are all included in the framework. A number of organizations are also established by the framework, including the National Institute of Disaster Management, the National Disaster Management Commission, the National Disaster Management Authority, and the Earthquake Rehabilitation and Reconstruction Authority (Ahmed 2013).

Nonetheless, there are several difficulties in implementing Disaster Management Law of Pakistan into practice. Persistent challenges include things like limited resources, red tape, and the requirement for more community involvement. Notwithstanding these obstacles, the government's dedication to enhancing catastrophe resilience and promoting a preparation culture is reflected in the changing legislative environment. The legal complexities of disaster management in Pakistan are thoroughly explored in this introduction, which also looks at the country's problems, achievements, and future innovations that might help make it a safer and more resilient place to live in times of crisis (Khan et al. 2021).

18.2 The Study Area

Geographically, Pakistan is located from 23° 36 min to 38° 03 min North latitude and 61° 02 min to 78° 01 min East Longitude. It is bordered by the mountains of Hindukush to the north and stretches from the Pamirs to the Arabian Sea in the South. With a total area of 881,913 km^2, the country is about four times the size of the United Kingdom. Its topography is diversified, including western Himalayan offshoots, the hilly terrain of Baluchistan province, Potwar Plateau and the lush green fertile Indus Plain (Rahman et al. 2014).

Pakistan has a diverse range of climatic conditions. The Indus valley has scorching summers, whereas the high mountains in the North have mild-warm summer, the northern and northwestern high mountainous regions have cold to very cold winters, and the southern coastal strip has a temperate climate. In Pakistan, rainfall varies from a minimum of 160 mm in the northern regions of the lower Indus plain and western part of Baluchistan Province to 1200 mm in the Himalayan area. On the one hand, humid condition is a source of fresh water and large-scale population depends on, while on the other hand, intense and heavy rainfall poses serious hazards of flash flood in the small catchment areas and mountainous areas, whereas pluvial floods occur in the urban areas, riverine floods in the floodplains of River Indus and its tributaries and Glacial Lake Outburst Floods (GLOF) in the Himalayas-Karakorum and Hindukush region (Khan et al. 2022; Siddique and Rahman 2023). High humidity is limited to the lesser and sub-Himalayas and coastal strip in the south, and monsoonal rains usually occur late in the summer (Malik et al. 2012) (Fig. 18.1).

18.3 Pakistan: History and Development of Disaster Management Law

The National Calamities (Prevention and Relief) Act of 1958 served as Pakistan's primary legal framework for emergency response operations. For almost half a century, the country was run under the reactive approach of Relief and compensation. This means that annually budget was allocated for disasters and they were waiting for disasters to come rather than investing on preparedness and disaster mitigation.

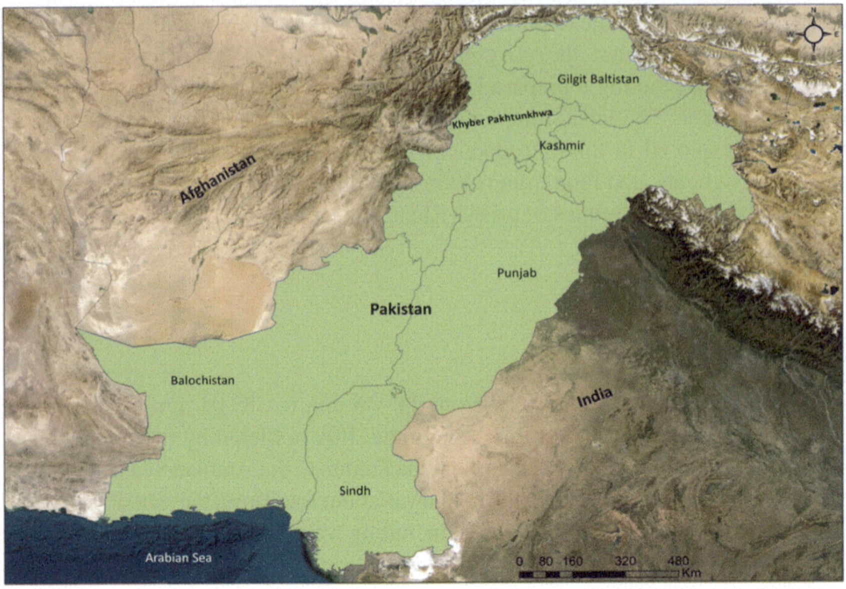

Fig. 18.1 Location of the study area, Pakistan

However, following the Kashmir 2005 earthquake, there was a paradigm shift from reactive to proactive approach. And as a result, the National Disaster Management Ordinance (NDMO) was promulgated to offer a thorough National Disaster Risk Management (DRM) framework. With the intention of reducing risks and effectively and efficiently managing future catastrophes, the NDMO was finally enacted by the parliament and renamed the National Disaster Management Act (NDM Act 2010). The Disaster Management System was formed by the legislation procedure at three levels: District, Province and the National. The National Calamities (Prevention and Relief Act 1958), the National Disaster Response Plan, and the National Disaster Risk Management Framework (2007) make up the framework. The framework also creates various entities, including the National Disaster Management Commission, the National Disaster Management Authority, the Earthquake Rehabilitation and Reconstruction Authority, and the National Institute of Disaster Management (Ali and Iqbal 2021).

18.4 Pakistan: Nexus of Disasters and Disaster Management Legislations

Disasters, whether caused by natural processes or human-induced, can cause enormous devastation to communities, resulting into physical ruin, economic hardships and incalculable human suffering. Nonetheless, strong and effective laws can considerably reduce the extent of these extreme events and incidents. Disaster law goes beyond simply responding to events after they occur; it is about constructing a safer and more resilient future. In this regard, the interventions may reduce the effect of disasters, assist impacted communities, and strengthen our ability to endure future crises by adopting and executing appropriate legislation. In response to the earthquake that struck Azad Jammu and Kashmir in 2005, which claimed over 73,000 lives, and the floods that hit Pakistan in 2010 that affected over 20 million people, the government passed a number of laws designed to minimize the effects of natural disasters. Parallel to this, a landmark but important step was taken in 2006 in the form of National Disaster Management Ordinance and as a consequence the National Disaster Management Authority (NDMA) was instituted to oversee the national disaster management initiatives, devise mitigation strategies and supervise overall disaster resilience process.

The National Disaster Management Authority (NDMA) is a key institution. In addition to working and coordinating with the authorities of provincial/ regional and districts to guarantee an efficient response to extreme events and catastrophes. Likewise, the NDMA is in charge of preparing disaster management guidelines, disaster management policies, plans and formulate strategies. Under the legal coverage, the disaster management at the provincial level is further addressed by the creation of Provincial Disaster Management Authorities (PDMAs). To enable a successful disaster response, the PDMAs are in charge of creating disaster management plans, carrying out risk assessments, and working with district authorities. In order to provide financial assistance for initiatives linked to disaster risk reduction and management, the Government of Pakistan has also established the National Disaster Risk Management Fund (NDRMF). The funds, which are allocated by the NDRMF are primarily to initiate and emphasize the research and development, capacity building, and disaster risk reduction. The goal of these legislative efforts and policies is to lessen the effects of disastrous events in Pakistan and enhance community resilience against the unforeseen events (Hussain et al. 2020).

18.5 Pakistan: Disaster Management Law

The National Disaster Management Act of 2010 (NDMA 2010) is the foundation of Pakistan's disaster management legislative framework. The Disaster management law specifically focuses on key disasters that face Pakistan including Extreme weather events, environmental degradations, floods, drought, tsunamis, landsliding, earthquakes, nuclear and chemical emergencies, heatwaves, storms and cyclones, fire events, etc. These are some of the hazards highlighted in the legislations.

In Pakistan under this legislation, a multi-tiered structure was established, where national, provincial, and district-level authorities are responsible for disaster preparedness, emergency response, and early recovery (NDMA 2010, Sect. 3). The Prime Minister heads the National Disaster Management Authority (NDMA), which develops policies, strategies, and recommendations for disaster risk reduction, preparedness, mitigation, response, and recovery (NDMA 2010, Sect. 4). The statutory structure additionally encompasses the National Disaster Risk Management structure (2007), the National Disaster Response Plan, and the National Calamities (Prevention and Relief Act) of 1958. The framework also creates various entities, including the National Disaster Management Commission, the Earthquake Rehabilitation and Reconstruction Authority (ERRA), and the National Institute of Disaster Management (NIDM). The legislative framework is intended to assist the country prepare for, respond to, and recover from catastrophes.

The Disaster Risk Reduction (DRR) is emphasized by the National Disaster Management Act, 2010 (NDMA 2010) as a crucial component of disaster management. The act requires the integration of disaster risk reduction (DRR) into development plans, the inclusion of risk assessments in public policy choices, and the promotion of public education and awareness (NDMA 2010, Sect. 9). This emphasis on prevention is indicative of a move away from purely reactive approaches. The Act requires risk assessments to be included into public policy choices, mainstreaming disaster risk reduction into development plans, and encouraging public awareness and education (NDMA 2010, Sect. 9). This emphasis on prevention represents a shift away from reactive exclusively method. When a natural disaster occurs, the NDMA 2010 authorizes the authorities to respond quickly and firmly. The NDMA 2010 gives authorities the authority to respond quickly and forcefully in the event of a disaster. To enable efficient reaction measures, the Act permits the requisition of resources, the activation of military forces, and the proclamation of state emergencies (NDMA 2010, Sects. 15–16).

The National Disaster Management Act of 2010, which forms the backbone of Pakistan's disaster management legal framework, provides a strong foundation for mitigating the impact of disasters. However, the Act faces certain challenges, such as implementation gaps that hinder its effectiveness at the local level. Inadequate resources, lack of skilled personnel, and weak coordination between different tiers of government can impede effective disaster response (IFRC 2021). To build a more resilient future for its citizens in the face of natural hazards, Pakistan must continue to bridge the gap between policy and practice, enhance local capacity, and ensure transparent and accountable disaster management. Section three of the Act establishes a Provincial Disaster Management Commission for each province, which is responsible for laying down policies and plans for disaster management in the province. The Provincial Commission has the authority to create a disaster management policy at the provincial level and develop a corresponding plan, aligning it with the guidelines set by the National Commission. It is authorized to approve disaster management plans formulated by departments within the Provincial Government, evaluate the execution of these plans, supervise the allocation of funds for initiatives related to mitigation and preparedness, assess the integration of preventive and mitigate measures into the development plans of various provincial departments, scrutinize actions related to mitigation, capacity-building, and preparedness carried out by Provincial Government departments, and issue necessary guidelines or directives when deemed necessary (Van 2006).

According to the National Disaster Management Act of 2010, the Provincial Disaster Management Commission is responsible for formulating disaster management policies and strategies for the province. The Commission, led by a Chairperson and made up of numerous members, has the ability to exercise all or specified functions of the Provincial Commission during emergency situations (Khan 2007).

Section four of the Disaster Management Act of 2010 requires each district to establish a District Disaster Management Authority, outlining the entity's functions and organizational structure. The law emphasizes the need of establishing a district-level body in charge of planning, coordinating, and carrying out disaster management measures. This body must follow the requirements defined by the government in order to carry out all disaster management actions within the district. It provides more clarification on the establishment of a disaster management plan, which includes a district response plan for the district, as well as the coordination and oversight of the district and provincial plans' implementation to guarantee that the districts' most disaster-prone areas are identified and that both local authorities and government departments are taking action to prevent disasters and lessen their effects. The legislation requires all district-level government agencies as well as local district authorities to adhere to the authority's established criteria for preventive, mitigation, readiness, and response actions (DDMA 2014).

18.6 Pakistan: Disasters and Climate Change Related Legislations

Pakistan is one of the top ten nations in the world facing significant climate change consequences. Over the last century, the nation has seen a yearly mean temperature rise of roughly 0.63 °C and a sea-level rise of about 1.1 mm per year along the Karachi coast. However, between 2006 and 2015, the reported sea-level rise increased to 3.6 mm per year (IFRC 2021). Pakistan's precipitation pattern has been complicated over history. Annual rainfall decreased for a long time in the early twentieth century, although a minor increase has been observed after 1960. Despite the overall tendency, there are significant regional differences. Particularly, Pakistan's dry plains and coastal belt have seen a 10–15% decline in mean rainfall on average since 1960, which has led to the continued destruction of mangrove ecosystems and wetlands of the nation (Rahman and Shakir 2023). Parallel to this, Pakistan has experienced more heat wave days annually as well as more instances of intense rainfall (IFRC 2021).

The Pakistani Government has addressed climate change by enacting the Climate Change Act 2017. This comprehensive federal legislation aims to tackle the increasing environmental and climate challenges across the nation. The act promotes climate resilience, mitigation, and sustainable development by establishing a legal and institutional framework for managing climate change issues. It creates the Climate Change Council and the Climate Change Authority, which are responsible for developing and implementing climate policies, strategies, and plans (Rahman et al. 2019). The act highlights the importance of climate adaptation, reducing greenhouse gas emissions, and integrating climate considerations into various sectors, including agriculture, water resources, and energy. Additionally, the Pakistan Climate Change Act, 2017 provides a legal foundation for mitigating climate change impacts, enhancing national resilience to climate-related challenges, and fostering sustainable development practices (GoP 2022).

18.7 Case Study: Provincial/Regional Disaster Management Law

The Khyber Pakhtunkhwa (KP) Climate Change Act is a significant piece of legislation aimed at addressing the pressing issues caused by climate change in the region. Acting to lessen the negative effects of climate change, this law lays the groundwork for an extensive and proactive approach to catastrophe management (Hamzah 2013). The Act outlines strategies for sustainable development and highlights how important it is to understand and adapt to the shifting climatic dynamics within KP. It emphasizes the importance of developing disaster management activities with climate resilience in mind.

The purpose of this legislative framework is to foster cooperation amongst relevant parties to lay the groundwork for effective teamwork while tackling climate change-related disasters. To improve the province's resilience, the Act outlines protocols for risk assessment, the creation of early warning systems, and the implementation of adaptable measures. Moreover, it emphasizes how vital it is to involve and engage communities, realizing the vital part that local communities play in both anticipating and responding to catastrophes (Gil and Kilmer 2016).

Moreover, the KP Climate Change Act is governed by both national and international commitments, ensuring a consistent approach to climate action. The Act positions Khyber Pakhtunkhwa at the forefront of proactive and long-term catastrophe risk reduction initiatives by incorporating climate change considerations into disaster management regulations. This legislative initiative serves as a core component in the development of a resilient and adaptive framework to protect the province's residents and ecosystems in the face of an increasingly unpredictable climate (Ahmed et al. 2020).

18.8 Pakistan: Strength, Challenges and Potentials of Disaster Management Legislations

Disaster Legislations are critical for reducing the effects of increasing disasters. The reliance on a centralized institutional architecture in disaster laws might potentially impede an effective response to disasters (Deen 2015). This demonstrates that the huge problem of decreasing losses and damages caused by disasters continues (Smith 2013). However, in Pakistan, various issues must be addressed to ensure their efficiency. In Pakistan, the main disaster prevention and enhancing resilience strategies, which are specifically highlighted in the legislations, policies and plans include assessment of disaster risk, community-based disaster risk reduction, building bye-laws, building codes revision and its compliance, disaster mitigation, horizontal coordination and linkages between line agencies as well as mainstreaming disaster risk reduction in policies, frameworks, legislations and plans. However, there are challenges and weaknesses in disaster law such as weaknesses in strict implementations of disaster law, local and micro level risk assessment and zonation mapping, safety and resilience of critical infrastructure, periodic revision of plans and policy framework, challenges and increasing impact of climate change, its mitigation and adaptations strategies, etc. Furthermore, some of the key difficulties are insufficient resource allocation and low engagement from affected populations in planning and decision-making process. Addressing these challenges and weaknesses may further boost-up the disaster resilience in the country.

Pakistan's disaster legislation offers a number of advantages and opportunities. They can draw attention to the conflicts and difficulties that arise when the emphasis is shifted from the hazard occurrence to the processes that lead to vulnerability and a reduction in disaster resistance. A national-wide, coordinated, capabilities-based approach to preparedness that maximizes the utilization of available resources can also be facilitated by disaster law. The purpose of the National Disaster Management Authority (NDMA) and Provincial Disaster Management Authorities (PDMAs) is to manage catastrophes at the federal and local levels, respectively. Along with collaborating with authorities of provincial and district to guarantee efficient disaster response, the NDMA is in charge of creating policies, strategies, and for disaster management guidelines. To guarantee efficient disaster response, it is the PDMAs' responsibility to create disaster management plans, carry out risk assessments, and work in tandem with district authorities (Azhar 2022). The National Disaster Risk Management Fund (NDRMF) was also founded by the Government of Pakistan to offer funding for initiatives aimed at mitigating disaster risk. Funding for capacity building, research and development, and disaster risk reduction initiatives is provided by the NDRMF. These initiatives and legislations attempt to mitigate the effects of natural disaster on the environment and the people of Pakistan.

In Pakistan, the disaster's prediction, forecasting and early warning system is another challenging and weak area and needs to be addressed in the disaster law and legislations. At the regional level, the system of forecasting extreme weather event does exist, but there are a list of unserved areas specifically in the north, north-western and western part of the country as these are areas located beyond the reach of existing forecasting network. And it is these areas, which has rough and uneven topography and most often it pose serious threats of extreme weather events. Parallel to this, detailed micro-level analysis, and installation of latest-state-of-the-art standard equipment are required to effectively forecast the unforeseen events. Similarly, after forecasting and event prediction, there is a need for effective mechanism of early warning system, awareness of communities, training of professionals in disseminating the early warning to vulnerable communities, evacuation and emergency response.

In Pakistan, the disaster law and legislation has discerned the emergency response mechanism. During the disaster situation, the legislation has also focused on the search and rescuing the vulnerable communities, first aid, psycho-social therapy, shelter during emergency, food, water and sanitation. In Pakistan, after thorough evaluation of emergency response system, there are weaknesses, which include emergency power, micro-level analysis of different level of emergencies, relief and on-spot cash compensation and management of camps, etc. In Pakistan, the disaster-related legislation has not been significantly shifted its focus from managing risks to stressing vulnerability and enhancing resilience.

In Pakistan, the disaster law and related legislations on disaster preparedness have highlighted the disaster preparedness plans, preparation of monsoon and other contingency plans, allocation of funds for disaster preparedness activities, stockpiling of non-perishable food items and materials, simulations, awareness and training exercises. However, in disaster preparedness strategies, the missing links and areas include emergency response planning, disaster-specific emergency evacuation plans, emergency response training and first aid.

In Pakistan, the structure of disaster risk management is highlighted in disaster legislations and the role and responsibilities of government institutions. The governing structure and administrative bodies are available at federal, provincial and to some extent at district level with a prescribed roles and responsibilities. The challenges and weaknesses in institutional arrangements at provincial level are a gray area in disaster law and include the absence of forecasting and early warning system. Similarly, at local level the disaster-related governing body is not available and hence one of the areas need to be addressed in disaster-related legislations. Furthermore, the missing and gray areas call for the decision makers and politicians to address the areas and mechanism for accountability of financial assistance provided to affected communities and individuals, devise quality standard for assistance, ensure access to data and information, community participation in planning and decision-making process and provisions of priority to vulnerable groups.

In post-disaster phase, the most important sector is early recovery, rehabilitation and reconstruction with the intention to build back better. In Pakistan, the funds are allocated for early recovery and reconstruction activities of critical infrastructure and housing sectors. However, the weakness and poorly addressed areas include standards for shelter reconstruction, issues related to private sector compensation and reconstruction and sources of livelihoods earnings.

18.9 Discussions

The study of disaster management law in Pakistan provides a nuanced perspective on the nation's preparedness, response, and recovery mechanisms in light of both natural and man-made disasters. Pakistan has made notable advancements in establishing a robust legal infrastructure aimed at tackling the diverse challenges posed by such calamities, exemplified by the establishment of the National Disaster Management Authority (NDMA) and Provincial Disaster Management Authorities (PDMAs) pursuant to the National Disaster Management Ordinance of 2006. These institutional structures were crafted with the intent of enhancing coordination, optimizing resource allocation, and streamlining disaster response efforts nationwide.

Despite these legislative accomplishments, numerous challenges persist in effectively implementing and enforcing disaster management legislation. Insufficient resources and capabilities at both the national and provincial levels hinder the execution of comprehensive disaster planning and response strategies. Additionally, organizational inefficiencies, overlapping responsibilities among various government entities, and a fragmented approach to disaster management can frequently obstruct the seamless coordination needed for an efficient crisis response.

To foster a culture of preparedness and enhance the resilience of communities susceptible to disasters, active community involvement and participation are integral elements. Despite certain initiatives aimed at integrating local populations into disaster risk reduction, there remains a requirement for more structured and sustained grassroots engagement. By providing communities with pertinent information, comprehensive training, and opportunities for collaborative decision-making, they can be empowered to effectively mitigate risks, respond adeptly to catastrophes, and contribute to long-term recovery endeavors.

Moreover, the utilization of technological advancements holds promise for enhancing the efficiency and effectiveness of disaster management practices in Pakistan. Satellite imaging, geographic information systems (GIS), and mobile applications can all contribute to enhancing early warning systems, expediting communication during emergencies, and facilitating data-driven decision-making. However, challenges such as limited technology access, disparities in digital literacy, and infrastructural constraints need to be addressed to fully harness the advantages of technological advancements in disaster management.

The legal framework of disaster management in Pakistan highlights the pressing requirement for climate change adaptation. The necessity of incorporating climate resilience measures into disaster management policies and practices is imperative, given the growing frequency and intensity of climate-related catastrophes such as heatwaves, droughts, and floods. A comprehensive strategy to handle the changing threat landscape must prioritize strengthening infrastructure, encouraging sustainable land-use planning, and boosting community resilience to climate effects.

Finally, despite notable advancements in constructing a legislative structure for disaster management, Pakistan needs to prioritize key sectors necessitating reform and enhancement. Overcoming challenges such as resource limitations, bureaucratic impediments, and fragmented coordination mechanisms, while emphasizing community engagement, technological progress, and climate resilience, is crucial for fostering a more resilient and flexible nation capable of efficiently addressing, responding to, and recuperating from disasters in contemporary times. Persistent endeavors to refine disaster management regulations and protocols will be essential in safeguarding the well-being and prosperity of Pakistan's population amid an increasingly unpredictable future.

18.10 Conclusion

The narrative surrounding disaster management legislation in Pakistan reflects both commendable progress and enduring challenges. The establishment of a comprehensive legal framework aimed at addressing disaster preparedness, response, and recovery represents a significant milestone in the nation's efforts to mitigate the impact of disasters. The formation of institutions like the National Disaster Management Authority (NDMA) and Provincial Disaster Management Authorities (PDMAs) under the National Disaster Management Ordinance of 2006 underscores a proactive approach to enhancing coordination and streamlining response mechanisms. However, the effectiveness of these regulations is hindered by various obstacles that impede their efficient implementation. Critical issues such as resource allocation, inter-agency cooperation, and the imperative need for continuous adaptation to emerging threats remain focal points that demand urgent attention.

Looking ahead, it is evident that the evolving nature of disasters, especially those worsened by climate change, necessitates a review of existing legal and regulatory frameworks. The future advancement of disaster management legislation in Pakistan greatly relies on boosting community engagement, harnessing technological progress, and integrating scientific insights into disaster response strategies. Additionally, achieving a nuanced equilibrium between safeguarding individual rights and ensuring timely interventions, particularly for vulnerable communities, becomes crucial. Furthermore, instituting mechanisms for accountability and allocating annual budgets to support disaster management initiatives are fundamental aspects of a robust legislative framework.

Ensuring the resilience of the legal framework and, consequently, Pakistan's ability to mitigate, respond to, and recuperate from disasters requires ongoing evaluation, adaptation, and capacity-building endeavors. It is through these cooperative initiatives that Pakistan can strengthen its disaster management infrastructure, enhance its readiness, and ensure the safety and welfare of its citizens amidst a progressively uncertain and perilous environment.

References

Ahmed Z (2013) Disaster risks and disaster management policies and practices in Pakistan: a critical analysis of disaster management act 2010 of Pakistan. Int J Disaster Risk Reduct 4:15–20

Ahmed W, Tan Q, Shaikh GM, Waqas H, Kanasro NA, Ali S, Solangi YA (2020) Assessing and prioritizing the climate change policy objectives for sustainable development in Pakistan. Symmetry 12(8):1203

Ali A, Iqbal MJ (2021) National disaster management act, 2010 of Pakistan: a review. J Disaster Emerg Res 4(1):52–59

Allen KM (2006) Community-based disaster preparedness and climate adaptation: local capacity-building in the Philippines. Disasters 30(1):81–101

Azhar A (2022) Disaster management reforms in Pakistan. Public sector reforms in Pakistan: Hierarchies, markets and networks. Springer International Publishing, Cham, pp 329–348

Climate Risk Country Profile: Pakistan (2021) The World Bank Group and the Asian Development Bank

DDMA (2014) District Disaster Management Act, 2014. https://pdma.punjab.gov.pk/system/files/Muzaffargarh.pdf. Accessed 07 January 2024

Deen S (2015) Pakistan 2010 floods. policy gaps in disaster preparedness and response. Int J Disaster Risk Reduct 12:341–349

Gil-Rivas V, Kilmer RP (2016) Building community capacity and fostering disaster resilience. J Clin Psychol 72(12):1318–1332

Government of Pakistan (GoP) (2022) Ministry of climate change. Pakistan's first biennial update report (bur-1) to the United Nations framework convention on climate change (UNFCCC)

Hamzah WP (2013) Moving forward in the climate change policies and practices. In: Post-2020 climate change regime formation. Routledge, pp 131–165

Hussain M, Butt AR, Uzma F, Ahmed R, Irshad S, Rehman A, Yousaf B (2020) A comprehensive review of climate change impacts, adaptation, and mitigation on environmental and natural calamities in Pakistan. Environ Monit Assess 192:1–20

IFRC (2021) Climate change impacts on health and livelihoods: Pakistan assessment

Khan MA (2007) Disaster preparedness for natural hazards: current status in Pakistan. In: International centre for integrated mountain development (ICIMOD)

Khan MBA, Rahman A, Shaw R (2021) Evaluation of ecosystem-based approaches for disaster and climate risk resilience and policy perspectives in Pakistan. In: Mukherjee M, Shaw R (eds) ecosystem-based disaster and climate resilience. Disaster and risk research: GADRI Book Series. Springer, Singapore

Khan A, Rahman A, Samiullah, Ayub M (2022) Impact of soil sealing on the genesis of pluvial flood in Peshawar, Pakistan. Arab J Geosci 15(7):1–15

Khan MBA, Rahman R (2022) Extent and evaluation of flash flood resilience in mountainous communities of daral and chail valleys, district swat, Pakistan. Proc Pak Acad Sci: Part A (Phys Comput Sci) 59(1):1–13

Mahmood S, Rahman A, Sajjad A (2019) Assessment of 2010 flood disaster causes and damages in district Muzaffargarh, Central Indus Basin, Pakistan. Environ Earth Sci 78(3):1–5

Malik S, Roosli R, Tariq F, Yusof NA (2020) Policy framework and institutional arrangements: case of affordable housing delivery for low-income groups in Punjab, Pakistan. Hous Policy Debate 30(2):243–268

Malik SM, Awan H, Khan N (2012) Mapping vulnerability to climate change and its repercussions on human health in Pakistan. Glob Health 8(1):1–10

NDMA (2010) National Disaster Management Act, 2010. http://ndma.gov.pk/Flood%20Mitigation%20Course.html. Accessed 07 January 2024

Norris FH, Stevens SP, Pfefferbaum B, Wyche KF, Pfefferbaum RL (2008) Community resilience as a metaphor, theory, set of capacities, and strategy for disaster readiness. Am J Commun Psychol 41:127–150

Rahman A, Khan AN, Collins AE (2014) Analysis of landslide causes and associated damages in the Kashmir Himalayas of Pakistan. Nat Hazards 71(1):803–821
Rahman A, Khan AN, Shaw R (2015) Disaster risk reduction approaches in Pakistan. Springer, Tokyo
Rahman A, Mahmood S, Dawood M, Rahman G, Chen F (2019) Impact of climate change on flood factors and extent of damages in the hindu kush region. Oxford research encyclopedia of natural hazard science
Rahman HU, Shakir M (2023) Nexus of land use land cover dynamics and extent of soil loss in the Panjkora River Basin of eastern Hindu Kush. J Water Clim Chang 14(12):4669–4688
Siddique F, Rahman A (2023) Genesis and spatio-temporal analysis of glacial lakes in the peri-glacial environment of Western Himalayas. Int J Eng Geosci 8(2):154–164
Smith K (2013) Environmental hazards: assessing risk and reducing disaster. Routledge
Van ND (2006) Disaster risk management in South Africa: the function and the activity-towards an integrated approach. Politeia 25(2):96–116

Chapter 19
Water Scarcity: Judicial Responses to the Disaster in Making

Priya A. Sondhi and Anoop Kumar

"Thousands have lived without love, not one without water."
—W. H. Auden

Abstract India is a country with great dependency on monsoon and rivers for water supply. Rains are crucial to almost 60% of India's rain-fed agriculture. Hence, the timely arrival and adequacy of monsoon winds plays a vital role in our farming practices. We have been a witness to monsoon variability in the last decade resulting into droughts. Continuous droughts, rising pollution of waterbodies, and overexploitation of groundwater have resulted in a critical scenario of water scarcity. Majority of our population does not have a trustworthy and steady means of getting water for their daily needs. As per NITI Aayog estimates "21 major cities, including Delhi, would run out of groundwater by 2030." 12% of India's population is already living the "Day Zero' scenario." It is very essential to study the reasons of water scarcity which include climate change and infrastructure issues like groundwater extraction and wastage of water. Consequently, it is essential to study the initiatives of the government and judicial discourses on water scarcity. This leads us to the precedents like the famous drought case, *Swaraj Abhiyan vs UoI*. There are certain substantial questions to answer—What is right to water? Is right to water a statutory right or a fundamental right? Whether ground water can be treated as a private property? Is right to water more important than right to occupation? Is there any right to draw ground water for personal and commercial uses? Whether state governments have right to approach the Supreme Court for uninterrupted supply of water from another state? What is the solution to issues like *Plachimada* issue? What is the solution to issues like *Span Motel* case? Is water a trust for future generations? Though a green jurisprudence is being involved, awareness and implementation of law are critical areas of concern. Awareness of evolution of this green jurisprudence is key to bringing change in the current scenario wherein environmental is a matter of

P. A. Sondhi (✉)
4 Y 703, AWHO, Gurjinder Vihar, Greater Noida, UP, India
e-mail: priyasondhi03@gmail.com

A. Kumar
Buxar, Bihar, India

Y. Cui and R. Shaw (eds.), *Disaster Law*, Disaster Risk Reduction,
https://doi.org/10.1007/978-981-97-7374-9_19

urgent concern. Lack of awareness of these precedents can result into injustice to mother earth and its living beings and multiplicity of cases. It is pertinent to investigate the level of awareness of law students, lawyers, judges of lower judiciary, and law teachers about this evolving jurisprudence. Hence, this article will address all the above-mentioned issues addressed by judiciary and also investigate the level of awareness of law students, lawyers, judges of lower judiciary, and law teachers about this evolving jurisprudence.

Keywords Green jurisprudence · Water scarcity · Judiciary · Supreme court

19.1 Introduction

Water is an essential ingredient for human existence. The existence of life in any form depends on the presence or absence of it. Down the years of existence of mankind on earth, civilizations developed around the rivers. Civilizations were nourished by rivers, through their abundance, providing fertility to the soil and life processes; water has always been the essence for growth in any civilization.

There is an unequivocal linkage between water and human environment. It is speculative to comment on the need for water at the hunting and gathering stage of human existence. Probably we can link the requirement for water with the increase in population in the human environment. One can comment with clarity about the need for water in the agricultural societies. Nevertheless, human environment depended on water for people, for chattels, for agriculture, etc. To all probabilities, the link between water and sanitation started establishing here.

The four major ancient civilizations of the world, the Harappa (Indus river), Egypt (Nile river), Mesopotamia (Euphrates and Tigris), and China (the yellow river) developed around rivers. During excavations, there were remnants of wells in Egypt, wells, waterpipes, and toilets in Indus civilization. It seems from the very beginning mankind preferred to give lot of importance to wells and springs, probably as a source of drinking water (IWA 2020). As civilization progressed, humanity flourished near rivers.

During Rigvedic times, several gods have been attributed to water in Rig Veda. Apas, who is mentioned in four Suktas, is the God of waters (Saxena 2012). Further, Indra, Varun, and Parjanya are some of the other gods who, apart from having their own independent portfolios, are also in some direct or indirect way related to some or the other form of water (Saxena 2012).

In general, the cities with economic prosperity also saw abundance of water. For ex. *Kannauj.* In fact, *Kannauj's* water resources and prosperity were also responsible for the historical tripartite conflict of *Pratihar-Pal- Rashtrakuta.* Thus, history teaches us that lot of cities were made, lot of capitals were shifted because of abundance or scarcity of water as a source of civilization (Jagran Josh 2015).[1]

[1] https://www.jagranjosh.com/general-knowledge/tripartite-struggle-for-kannauj-1437459496-1

Lack of access to water resources poses a big threat to the humanity. It has emerged as a disaster which needs urgent attention of global community. In the Indian context, Niti Aayog in its report in 2018 confirmed that India is facing the "worst water crisis in its history" (The Hindu 2018). What adds to the fear of water crisis is the lack of efficient water governance in India. In this article we will address the issues in the following chapters: Part I—Water Scarcity: A Disaster in Making, Part II—Water: The Legal Regime; Part III: Water Scarcity: Judicial Responses and Part IV: Analysis of Data followed by Conclusion.

19.2 Part I: Water Scarcity: Disaster in Making

In simple terms water scarcity can be defined as lack of sufficient available water resources to meet the demands of water usage within a region (Science daily, n.d). UN Water (n.d.) defines water scarcity as "*scarcity in availability of water due to physical shortage, or scarcity in access due to the failure of institutions to ensure a regular supply or due to a lack of adequate infrastructure*".

Water scarcity broadly means scarcity in availability due to any of the following three reasons; Firstly due to physical shortage, secondly due to scarcity in access which might be due to the failure of institutions to guarantee a continuous supply, and thirdly due to a lack of adequate infrastructure. In fact, water scarcity has affected every continent. We must not be oblivious to the fact that water use has been growing globally due to increase in population. Thus, the simple concept of demand and supply comes into operation here. The fact remains that we need to have efficient policies to reduce the challenges due to water stress (UN Water, 2020).

Water scarcity is divided into two parts—surface water and ground water.

It is very essential to study water scarcity to be able to arrive at the larger concept of water security. Water security or lack of water scarcity will provide us with six related securities—human community security, water resources security, food security, energy security, climate security, and national security (Bruce Lankford et al. 2013) the concern is to arrive at water resource consumption in such a manner that all the human requirements are met without compromising on the natural reserve. This would lead to water security and aid other related securities.

In so far as causes of water scarcity are concerned, following are the major ones;

1. ***Pollution***. Water pollution is majorly caused by "pesticides and fertilizers that flow away from farms, untreated human wastewater, and industrial waste." Many pollutants that leach into underground aquifers also render groundwater unfit for use.
2. ***Agriculture***. Agriculture is the backbone of Indian economy and society. Globally, agriculture uses 70% of available water. But 60% of this gets wasted as a result of "leaky irrigation systems, inefficient application methods as well as the cultivation of crops that demand huge amount of water." As a result of this, rivers, lakes, and underground aquifers are drying out (World Wildlife Fund n.d.).

3. ***Population growth***. Rapid growth of population coupled with economic development and industrialization has led to a massive loss of biodiversity. The same has adversely affected water availability globally.
4. ***Climate change***. Climate change has led to Hadley Cell expansion, a phenomenon given birth by climate change. This has led to deficiency of rainwater in the equatorial regions like sub-Saharan Africa, the Middle East and Central America. As of now, river flooding has put lives of at least 21 million people worldwide at risk every year, which could touch 54 million by 2030 (World Resources Institute n.d.).
5. ***Dismal water infrastructure***. Globally, water infrastructure right from treatment plants, pipes, to sewer systems is in a pathetic state.

The reasons are many, but the resultant data on water availability/scarcity is as follows:

1. Of the total available water, 72% is used in agriculture, 16% for households and services, and remaining 12% by industries (UN Water 2021).
2. Globally, 2.3 billion population people live in water-stressed countries. Of this, 733 million are inhabitants of critically water-stressed countries (UN Water 2021).
3. Approximately, two-thirds of the world population faces the problem of severe water scarcity in least one month of the entire year (UN Water n.d).
4. 700 million people worldwide face the threat of being displaced by intense water scarcity by 2030 (UN Water n.d).

The data is certainly not very encouraging. As per recent UNICEF Report, "more than 450 million, or one in five children, worldwide reside in areas which experience high or extremely high-water challenges. Eastern and southern Africa had the highest proportion of children living in such areas. More than 155 million children in South Asia live in areas with high or even extremely high water vulnerability" (Down to Earth n.d.).

Even though India comprises 16% of the population around the world, it has merely four percent of the total freshwater resources around the world. With the changing weather patterns and recurring droughts, India is water stressed (Down to Earth n.d.). A NITI Aayog report in 2018, "around 600 million people, or nearly half of India's population, face extreme water stress. That three-fourths of India's rural households do not have piped, potable water and rely on sources that pose a serious health risk. India has become the world's largest extractor of groundwater, accounting for 25% of the total. That 70% of our sources are contaminated and our major rivers are dying because of pollution. Its conclusion needs urgent attention. 'India is suffering from its worst water crisis in its history'" (India Today 2020).

Thus, we need to take some serious steps in terms of implementation of law at normative level to be able to rescue ourselves from the impending water crisis.

19.3 Part II—Water: The Legal Regime

It is very important to understand the law at normative level regarding water in India. It is essential to analyze the constitutional law, statutory law, policy initiatives, and international developments. The judicial precedents can only be studied well on a strong grounding of the understanding of law and policy because they reflect its spirit and word.

It is pertinent to note that the right of access to water places two interrelated but distinct obligations on the State (Visser 2002):

1. Obligation to ensure that all people have physical access to water.
2. Obligation to ensure economic access to water by all.

Considering the role of India as the welfare state, both the obligations are very significant. The major laws in India that ensure access to water and water conservation can be studied under the following heads:

1. **Constitution of India**

The Constitution of India is the supreme law of the land. Under this head, we need to study Article 51-A, Schedule VII and Article 262 and the Constitution (73rd) Amendment Act, 1992.

A. ***Article 51-A(g)***, "every citizen of India is under a fundamental duty to protect and improve the natural environment including forests, lakes, rivers, wild life and to have compassion for living creatures."
B. ***Seventh Schedule***: Subject of "water" finds place under "Entry 17 of List–II (State List)" of 7th Schedule. It is also subject to the provisions of "Entry 56 of List–I (Union List)."

   Thus, state has power to regulate water supplies, irrigation, canals drainage, water storage, and water powers. However, the Union government has exclusive right regarding regulation and development of inter-state rivers and river valleys.
C. ***Article 262***: Under Article 262 of the Constitution the Parliament has been empowered to "provide for the adjudication of any dispute or complaint with respect to the use, distribution or control of the waters of, or in, any inter-State river or river valley. Further it empowers Parliament to provide that neither the Supreme Court nor any other court shall exercise jurisdiction in respect of any such dispute or complaint" (Article 262(2)).

   So far, the Parliament has passed 4 Acts, three under Entry 56 of List–I and one under Article 262. These are: "River Boards Act 1956; Betwa River Board Act 1976; Brahmaputra Board Act 1980; and The Inter-State River Water Disputes Act, 1956."
D. ***The Constitution (73rd) Amendment Act, 1992***: By the Constitution (73rd) Amendment Act, 1992 the dream of a decentralized structure of governance at the level of panchayats was fulfilled. Panchayat was established as an institution of self-government, comprised of elected members. The Amendment Act added Part IX-A. Under Article 243G, the legislature of a State has been empowered

to "make a law to empower the panchayat to prepare plans for economic development and social justice apart from other matters specified in the Eleventh Schedule to the Constitution."

The relevant subjects in the Eleventh Schedule are as follows:

"Minor irrigation, water management and watershed development (Entry 3), fisheries (Entry 5); drinking water (Entry 11); waterways (Entry 13); health and sanitation (Entry 23); public distribution system (Entry 28) and Maintenance of community assets (Entry 29)."

2. **The Easement Act, 1882**. Under the Act, the government has exclusive right pertaining to regulating the collection, detention, and distribution of the waters derived from rivers and streams flowing in natural channels or natural lakes or ponds or the water flowing, collected, detained, or distributed in/or by any channel constructed at the public expense for purpose of irrigation (Section 2).

Further, the Act confers the right on the owner of the land, pertaining to collection and disposal, within his own limits, all water under the land which does not pass in a defined channel (Section 7).

3. **The Water (Prevention and Control of Pollution) Act, 1974**. The Act was enacted "for prevention and control of water pollution." It was amended in 1988. Salient features of the Act are:

    a. Under the Act, pollution control boards were created for implementation of its provisions.
    b. Act has object of maintaining and restoring the "wholesomeness" of aquatic resources.
    c. The Act prohibits discharging of sewage or pollutants into water bodies including lakes. Further, the state pollution control boards are bound to intervene and stop such activity.
    d. Under Section 42, it also lays down penalties and fines for certain acts "including pulling down pillars, obstructing any person acting under the orders or direction of the Board, damaging any works or property belonging to the Board and Failure to furnish any officer other employee of the Board any information required."
    e. The Act provides for "the levy and collection of cess or fees from industries consuming water and local authorities—to provide for the prevention of water pollution and cater to the maintenance of the water bodies and carry out activities to promote restoration of water."
    f. The Central Pollution Control Board promotes the cleanliness of streams and wells in different areas of the state.

4. **The Environment (Protection) Act, 1986**. Under Section 3(3) of the Act, The Government of India has also set up the Central Ground Water Authority for regulating the indiscriminate use of ground water in various parts of the country and particularly in the major urban metropolises (CGWB n.d.). The Authority has following powers and functions:

"Under Section 5 of the Act, it may issue directions and taking such measures in respect of all the matters referred to in Section 3 of the Act. To resort to penal provisions contained in Sections 15 to 21 of the Act. To regulate and control, management and development of ground water in the country and to issue necessary regulatory directions for the purpose. Exercising powers under Section 4 of the Act for the appointment of officers."

5. **The Indian Penal Code 1860**

   - Section 277 of the Code provides for "the punishment to be given to the person who commits an offence of fouling of a public reservoir or a public spring voluntarily shall be liable to be punished with imprisonment of three months or with a fine of 500 Rupees or with both." Illustration A to the section seeks to explain the situation well.

6. **Relevant State Legislations**. Various state legislations of the different States touch upon the various aspects of the control, regulation, and distribution of water. Some of the relevant legislations are as follows:

Laws relating to canals and irrigation.	• The Northern India Canal and Draining Act, 1873. • The Bombay Irrigation Act, 1879. • The Rajasthan Irrigation and Drainage Act, 1954. • Karnataka Irrigation Act, 1965.
Use of water sources.	• The Kumaon and Garhwal Water (Collection, Retention and Distribution) Act, 1975.
Water sewerage and drainage.	• The Uttar Pradesh Water Supply and Sewerage Act, 1975.
Ground water.	• Madras Metropolitan Area Ground Water (Regulation) Act, 1987. • Kerala Ground Water (Control and Regulation) Act, 2002. • Karnataka Ground Water (Protection and Regulation for Drinking Water) Act, 2003.

7. **The Coastal Regulation Zone (CRZ) Notification**. The CRZ notification was first issued in 1991 by the Ministry of Environment, Forest and Climate Change (MoEFCC) under the Environment (Protection) Act, 1986. Its object was to protect and conserve coastal environment. By restricting various activities, including construction, it gives some protection to the backwaters and estuaries.

It was amended and consolidated and issued in the CRZ 2011 notification. It was replaced in 2018, by the Coastal Regulation Zone (CRZ) Notification, 2018 based on the recommendation of Shailesh Nayak committee constituted by the MoEFCC in 2014 for comprehensive evaluation of CRZ 2011 notification (PIB 2018).

All the above-mentioned legal norms aim at maintaining the water resources properly for the livelihood concerns of human beings. Somehow even after understanding the necessity of water we have been negligent in water resource management. This resulted into water stress first and then water scarcity.

8. **Policy Initiatives**

In modern, post-independence India, the first National Water Policy was adopted in 1987, reviewed and updated in 2002 and later in 2012. We are currently governed by the National Water Policy 2012. As per the basic principles of the policy, "access to safe and clean drinking water and sanitation should be regarded as a right to life" (Singh et al. n.d.). Also "safe drinking water and sanitation, should be treated as an economic good so as to promote its conservation and efficient use." One more document worth mention is the Water Policy and Action Plan 2020. There are a number of policy initiatives taken by the government for water resources. In addition to this, different states have different norms relating to rainwater harvesting.

9. **Model Groundwater (Sustainable Management) Bill, 2017**

The Groundwater (Sustainable Management) Bill, 2017 has been drafted by the Ministry of Water Resources, River Development and Ganga Rejuvenation. It provides a template for the states to further legislate on water scarcity. The bill reflects the legal developments since the 1970s (Cullet 2019).

10. **International Developments**

At international level the year 2000 is significant in the world history of planned and goal-oriented development. Eight Millennium Development Goals (MDGs) were adopted by the UN Millennium Declaration. 191 UN Members and 22 International Organization's committed toward them till 2015. Under MDG 7, i.e., ensuring environmental sustainability, target 10 India's performance was comparatively good. As per the report submitted by India, "while 86.9% households in rural and 90.1% households in urban area had access to improved source of drinking water. Thus, the target of halving the proportion of households without access to safe drinking water sources from its 1990 level to be reached by 2015, was achieved in rural areas and reported as likely to be achieved in urban areas." At all India level also, the target for access to improved source of drinking water was found to be achieved. Tap water from treated and untreated source, hand pump, tube well, well covered or uncovered can be the different sources (MoSPI 2017).

In the year 2015, the 2030 Agenda for Sustainable Development was adopted by all United Nations Member States. Out of the seventeen goals, SDG Goal 6 relates to clean water and sanitation; to ensure availability and sustainable management of water and sanitation for all. Target 1 aims at safe and affordable drinking water. As per the 2018 report, "while the national target is to provide safe and adequate drinking water to all, currently only 71.8% of the rural population in India has access to safe and adequate drinking water. Goa, Gujarat and Madhya Pradesh are close to achieving universal coverage in rural areas. Uttar Pradesh follows with a coverage of about 98%. As per 2011 Census data, 85.5% population had access to safe drinking water."

It may be noted here that international law, both customary and modern norms, emphasizes upon equitable utilization of water is ensured by the customary international law for transboundary fresh water resources.

A. The Madrid Declaration of 1911 in explicit terms prevents any alteration in the regime of rivers and lakes, contiguous or successive to the detriment of a co-riparian without the consent of the other.
B. Declaration of Montevideo 1933 prohibits any state, without the consent of the other riparian state, from introducing into water courses of an international character, for industrial or agricultural exploitation of their waters, any alterations which may prove injurious to other interested states (Article 2).
C. International Law Association's (ILA) Helsinki Rules 1966 on the Uses of the Waters of International Rivers provides that, *every basin State is entitled, within its territory, to a reasonable and equitable share in the beneficial uses of the waters of an international drainage basin* (Article 4).
D. UN Convention on the Law of the Non-navigational Uses of International Watercourses was adopted by the UN General Assembly in 1997, which governs shared freshwater resources, and is universally applicable to all member states. Article 5 lays down a widely accepted principle, "It requires that a State sharing an international watercourse with other States utilise the watercourse, in its territory, in a manner that is equitable and reasonable vis-à-vis the other States sharing it."

Thus, there is no dearth of law at normative level. We need to start taking constructive steps for implementation.

19.4 Part III: Water Scarcity: Judicial Responses

The analysis of judicial responses begins with a few essential questions. Is right to water a statutory right or a fundamental right? What are the basic principles for water conservation? Is groundwater a private property? Is there a guaranteed right to continue to draw ground water for commercial purposes? Is public trust doctrine applicable to ground water? Is water a right of future generation? What are the cases relating to drought or water scarcity? It is important to note that the important cases relating to water pollution cover a very important aspect of water scarcity—right to clean water. Water jurisprudence has developed much more than the commonly understood M.C Mehta Ganges cases.

The questions can be answered with the help of the following cases.

1. **Narmada Bachao Andolan v. Union of India (2000)** In this case, it was observed that "Water is the basic need for the survival of human beings and is part of the

right to life and human rights as enshrined in Article 21 of the Constitution of India and the right to healthy environment and to sustainable development are fundamental human rights implicit in the right to life."

Thus, right to water is a fundamental right. This precedent was followed in other cases like **Hinch Lal Tiwari v. Kamala Devi (2001)**, wherein direction was given to the state to restore a pond and **A.P. Pollution Control Board II v. Prof. M.V. Nayudu (2001)**, the honorable apex court struck down the exemption granted by the Andhra Pradesh government to a polluting industry, which allowed it to be set up near the Himayat Sagar lake and the Osman Sagar lake, in violation of the Environment Protection Act 1986. It was also observed that the order has been carelessly passed and ignored the "precautionary principle."

2. **Vellore Citizens Welfare Forum v. Union of India (1996)** gave relief to the victims of water pollution caused by tanneries. "The 'precautionary principle' when applied by the courts to Indian condition means: (i) that environmental measures taken by the state and the statutory authorities must anticipate, prevent and attack the causes of environmental degradation; (ii) that where there are threats of serious and irreversible damage, lack of scientific certainty should not be used as a reason for posting measures to prevent environmental degradation; and (iii) that the 'onus of proof' is on the actor or the developer/industrialist to show that his action is environmentally benign."

It was observed that "the constitutional and statutory provisions protect a person's right to fresh air, clean water and pollution-free environment, but the source of the right is the inalienable common law right of clean environment."

Thus, "the precautionary principle" and the "polluter pays principle are now the preemptory norms of water jurisprudence."

3. **Hindustan Coca-Cola Beverages (P) Ltd. vs Perumatty Grama Panchayat (2005) also called as Plachimada coco cola case**[2]: This is the classic case relating to the extent to which a person/party can draw groundwater. The issue started when the villages around Hindustan Coca-Cola Beverages Private Limited (HCCBPL), bottling plant at Plachimada, Kerala started observing within six months, that water was turning milky white or blackish, complaints of unusual stomachaches, wells emptying unusually fast and crop yields decreasing. After a long struggle in 2005, the Supreme Court issued a notice based on an application by the Perumatty panchayat. It sought a stay on the decision of the Kerala high court division bench "allowing the plant the use of five lakh litres of groundwater daily." Interestingly, the Perumatty panchayat was asserting its right to clean water for potable as well as agricultural purposes; and, on the other hand, the MNC, in this case, a private owner, was speaking about its right to extract groundwater for the purpose of manufacturing aerated soft drinks. In July 2017, Coca-Cola's Indian subsidiary, Hindustan Coca-Cola Beverages Limited, informed the Supreme Court that it had no plans whatsoever to restart operations in its bottling plant in Plachimada, Kerala

[2] https://thewire.in/law/coca-cola-plachimada-kerala-water

Similar question arose in **Shailesh Singh vs Hotel Holiday Regency, Moradabad (Plumber, 2019)** wherein Principal Bench of National Green Tribunal held that "no groundwater extraction will be allowed by Industries for commercial purpose in area developed by Uttar Pradesh State Industrial Corporation (UPSIC), area at Ghaziabad. It was observed that since the OCS areas have been found to be seriously affected by over-drawal of groundwater, regulation of such drawal for commercial purposes cannot be dispensed with for any industry even in the industrial area. It was also observed that the availability of water for drinking is a first priority." A similar view was taken in **M/s India Glycols Limited vs Central Ground Water Authority (Plumber, 2019)**. **In Bhim Singh vs M/S Uni product (Pvt. Ltd.) (Plumber, 2020)**. The Principal Bench of National Green Tribunal directed "ground water being extracted without NOC and without any safeguards, by two carpet manufacturing units, in Rewari, Haryana, be discontinued, till NOC is given."

Thus, groundwater withdrawal can be regulated, because there is no guaranteed right to continue to draw ground water for commercial purposes without any permission. Nevertheless, but the existence of landownership-groundwater nexus needs to be broken and the doctrine of public trust needs to be extended to groundwater in a crystal clear manner.

4. **M.C Mehta vs Kamal Nath (1997)**: This case is commonly known as the Spam motel case. The facts of the case are that the Indian Express published an article, which reported that a private company, Span Motels Private Ltd., owner of Span Resorts, had floated an ambitious project called Span Club. Kamal Nath, the then Minister of Environment and Forests had direct links with this company. The company encroached upon land including forest land, impacting the course of river Beas. In 1993, these activities by the company caused floods in the river and a property worth hundreds of crores was destroyed. The apex court declared the State to be the trustee of all natural resources, meant for public use and enjoyment. As a trustee it is under a legal duty to protect the natural resources of the seashore, running waters, air, forests, and ecologically fragile lands. Public at large is the beneficiary of these resources, which cannot be converted into private ownership.

Thus, the doctrine of public trust initiated by Joseph Sax, was made applicable in India. The Supreme Court has recognized that water is a community resource to be held by the State in public trust. This understanding for protection for water bodies resulted in fines being imposed in many cases. In, **National Institute of Medical Science University Rajasthan and Others v. State of Rajasthan and Others (2017)** concerning water shortage in Jaipur city and the drying up of Ramgarh Lake due to massive encroachments in the catchment areas of Ramgarh Dam especially by the National Institute of Medical Sciences University or NIMS, the apex court-imposed costs of Rs. 10 lakhs per petition for the encroachment by NIMS. Court also directed the demolition of the unauthorized construction by or on behalf of NIMS at the expense of NIMS. Similarly, in **Jitendra Singh v. Ministry of**

Environment (2019), it was observed that waterbodies, specifically, are an important source of fishery and much needed potable water. Allowing such invaluable community resources to be taken over by a few is hence grossly illegal."

5. **State of T.N. V. Hind Stone, (1981) 2 SCC 205, at page 212**:

"Rivers, Forests, Minerals and such other resources constitute a nation's natural wealth. These resources are not to be frittered away and exhausted by any one generation. Every generation owes a duty to all succeeding generations to develop and conserve the natural resources of the nation in the best possible way. It is in the interest of mankind. It is in the interest of the nation." **Thus, water is a trust of future generation**.

6. **Drought/Water scarcity cases**: The most important drought case is **Swaraj Abhiyan vs Union of India (2017)**. In fact, this case is called the drought case of India. The apex court has issued significant guidelines on disaster/drought management in this landmark case. In this case, a writ petition was filed by the petitioner in the backdrop of a declaration of drought in some districts in Uttar Pradesh, Madhya Pradesh, Karnataka, Andhra Pradesh, Telangana, Maharashtra, Odisha, Jharkhand and Chhattisgarh in 2016. According to Swaraj Abhiyan drought ought to be declared in most parts of the respondent States of Bihar, Gujarat, and Haryana. The petitioner, therefore, sought a direction to these 3 states to declare a drought and provide essential relief and compensation to people affected by the drought.

The Court issued guidelines relating to **constitution of National Disaster Response Force with regular specialist cadre**, **establishment of a National Disaster Mitigation Fund, formulation of a National Planand revision of the Drought Management Manual**. In a significant move for water rights of the drought hit, the appeal filed by Maharashtra Cricket Association against Bombay High Court order directing the BCCI to shift all the IPL matches scheduled after 30th April 2016 to venues outside Maharashtra, did not bear fruit as the Supreme Court refused to interfere (KM Ashok 2016).[3] In one of the cases relating to water scarcity in Thane, **Mangesh Shelar vs State of Maharashtra**, the Bombay High Court directed the Thane Municipal Corporation (TMC) to stop issuing any fresh occupancy and commencement certificate in the Ghodbunder Road area of Thane till 9 June 2017, due to the problem of water scarcity (Kashyap 2017).[4]

Nevertheless, court has refrained from interfering in policy decisions of government. One more significant case here is **Sanjay Kale vs State of Maharashtra (Hindu** 2016) wherein, the Supreme Court refused to direct the Maharashtra government to completely cut the water supply to the distilleries and breweries in the state and divert drinking water to drought-hit regions. The Bombay High Court had allowed a 60% cut since drinking water is a priority. The court refused to interfere

[3] https://www.livelaw.in/sc-refuses-allow-ipl-matches-drought-hit-maharashtra-may/

[4] https://www.livelaw.in/bombay-hc-bars-issuance-occupancy-certificate-light-severe-water-scarcity-thane-read-order/

on the ground that these are all policy decisions and there must be a balance. The court's interference will be like taking over governance. Similarly, Supreme Court slammed the Delhi government over the controversy surrounding Munak canal row in 2016 and expressed strong displeasure toward Delhi state government for bringing each and every case before the judiciary to gain limelight (Shaikh 2016).[5]

7. **Nodal Agency**: In **Lt. Col. Sarvadaman Singh Oberoi v. Union of India (2020)**, It was held that "all States/UTs may designate a nodal agency for the restoration of water bodies, wherever no such agency has so far been designated. Under the oversight of the Chief Secretaries of the States/UTs, the designated nodal agency may hold its meeting not later than 31-01-2021 to take stock of the situation and plan further steps, including directions to District authorities for further course of action up to Panchayat levels and to evolve further monitoring mechanism as well as Grievance Redressal Mechanism."

Therefore, Judicial verdicts have played the most crucial role in preventing water scarcity and enhancing water conservation in India. Widening the ambit of Article 21 of the Constitution, the Supreme Court has recognized right to water as a fundamental human right as part of the Right to Life guaranteed under Article 21. The ambit of right to life has been expanded over the last three decades to such an extent that it includes the right to health and the right to a clean environment, thereby taking right to clean drinking water under its ambit (Kothari n.d.).

19.5 Part IV: Analysis of Data

As stated earlier, a green jurisprudence is being involved. However, awareness and implementation of law are critical areas of concern. Awareness of evolution of this green jurisprudence is key to bringing change in the current scenario wherein environmental is a matter of urgent concern. Lack of awareness of these precedents can result into injustice to mother earth and its living beings and multiplicity of cases. It is pertinent to investigate the level of awareness of law students, lawyers, judges of lower judiciary, and law teachers about this evolving jurisprudence.

Hence, this part addresses the data collection wherein questions were asked to equal number of judges of lower judiciary, lawyers, law teachers, and law students in Bareilly, Pilibhit, Rampur, and Amroha districts of Uttar Pradesh, India, about all the above-mentioned issues relating to water scarcity and current green jurisprudence.

Analysis of Responses:

1. As regards the implication of "water scarcity" a vast majority of judges, lawyers, law teachers, and law students think that it broadly refers to scarcity in the availability of water due to all the reasons viz., physical shortage; scarcity in

[5] https://www.india.com/news/cities/delhi-water-crisis-supreme-court-slams-aap-government-over-munak-canal-row-968580/

access which might be due to the failure of institutions to ensure a regular supply; and a lack of adequate infrastructure.

It may be noted that it is important to have awareness about water scarcity which can have its impact not only on drinking but also on sanitation. When sewage systems fail, threat of diseases also surges.

2. 25% of judges think that pollution is the main cause of water scarcity, while another 25% of them blame "agriculture and population growth" for it. Most of the law teachers blame "climate change" for this. Lawyers blame "pollution" and "climate change," while law students blame "agriculture and population."

   It may be noted that in India we are facing water scarcity issues in all the river basins and all the above mentioned causes have contributed to it in varying degrees in different river basins.
3. While judges and law teachers totally agree to "study water scarcity for larger concept of water security," except few lawyers and law students, they also agree to study it.

   It is very necessary for the lawyers and law students to understand that water security includes access to safe drinking water, managing water resources effectively and reducing the risk of water-borne diseases.
4. While most of the judges, lawyers, and law students are not certain about the year of report by when Niti Aayog, most of the teachers think it to be 2018. Dissemination of information relating to the Niti Aayog report is very necessary for public at large.
5. Most of the judges and lawyers had no idea about the percent of world's total groundwater extracted by India. Most of the law teachers are either not certain or think it to be 25%. Most of the law students think it to be 22%.
6. Most of the judges and lawyers had no idea about the percent of world's total groundwater extracted by India. Most of the law teachers are either not certain or think it to be 25%. Most of the law students think it to be 22%.
7. Most of the judges and lawyers think that 50% of water resources of India are contaminated and dying because of pollution. While most law teachers and law students are not certain.

   Here, the responses seem to have a clear challenge. The assessment of all the four groups is far lesser than the real picture. This means that we need to sensitize people about cases like Plachimada case, contamination of water in Coorg foothills, etc., and their impact on the overall ecological balance of a locality.
8. A vast majority of judges, lawyers, law teachers, and law students think that the Ganga is the most polluted river of India, followed by the Yamuna. This is also surprising considering the number of researches of extreme pollution in Yamuna river, specially in Delhi NCR region.

   We need to have more empirical researches on all the river basins and dissemination of information about the same.
9. Barring some disagreements, a vast majority of judges, lawyers, law teachers, and law students consider that the state to be duty-bound to provide access to water to people.

10. Most of the judges, lawyers, law teachers, and law students think that the State, the Judiciary, and the people, all of them play the most crucial role in protecting water bodies in India.
11. Majority of the judges, lawyers, law teachers, and law students think that the judiciary is playing its role to protect water resources in India.
12. Majority of the judges, lawyers, law teachers, and law students consider "right to water" a fundamental right.
13. A vast majority of judges, lawyers, law teachers, and law students think that granting legal personality to water bodies is effective in protecting them.
14. Most of the judges, lawyers, and law students think that a special court or tribunal exist in India to protect water resources. Most of law teachers don't agree on such existence. Currently NGT looks into such cases but we don't have a specific court or tribunal for water resources.
15. Majority of the judges, lawyers, law teachers, and law students think that there should be special courts for protection of water resources.
16. A vast majority of the judges, lawyers, law teachers, and law students think that groundwater withdrawal can be regulated by the judiciary.
17. All the judges and majority of the lawyers, law teachers, and law students think that the doctrine of public trust initiated by Joseph Sax is applicable in India.
18. All the judges and law students and a vast majority of the lawyers and law teachers and think that water resources are a trust for future generation.
19. A vast majority of judges, lawyers, law teachers, and law students think that all States/UTs should designate a nodal agency for the restoration of water bodies.
20. Majority of the judges, lawyers, law teachers, and law students think that State is the trustee of all natural resources, meant for public use and enjoyment, which includes water resources.

    It may be noted that the responses are mostly correct when the questions relate to the law at normative level (Tables 19.1 and 19.2).

19.6 Conclusions

Water scarcity is a complex issue. It needs a multipronged approach. At the domestic level, there is a clear reflection of SDG 6 in current law and policy of India. The following conclusions can be drawn. Firstly, sustainable development has a strong constitutional basis. Right to clean water is a right under Article 21 of Constitution of India due to right to clean and healthy environment. Secondly, it is essentially a negative right, i.e., the right not to have water sources polluted. Thirdly, we certainly have law at normative level, but implementation is not very appreciable. The judiciary has been playing important role in prevention of water scarcity. Nevertheless, certain more constructive steps are required.

A solution to water scarcity requires multiple efforts at various levels. Every stakeholder needs to contribute by way of preventive measures.

Table 19.1 Responses to questions on water scarcity

Question no	Judges	Law teachers	Lawyers	Law students
1	a. 0	a. 0	a. 10%	a. 10%
	b. 5%	b. 10%	b. 0	b. 20%
	c. 20%	c. 25%	c. 20%	c. 10%
	d. 75%	d. 65%	d. 70%	d. 60%
2	a. 25%	a. 25%	a. 35%	a. 20%
	b. 25%	b. 30%	b. 20%	b. 50%
	c. 35%	c. 35%	c. 35%	c. 20%
	d. 15%	d. 10%	d. 10%	d. 10%
3	a. 100%	a. 100%	a. 95%	a. 90%
	b. 0	b. 0	b. 5%	b. 10%
4	a. 5%	a. 20%	a. 10%	a. 5%
	b. 30%	b. 30%	b. 25%	b. 30%
	c. 25%	c. 25%	c. 20%	c. 20%
	d. 40%	d. 25%	d. 45%	d. 45%
5	a. 10%	a. 5%	a. 5%	a. 5%
	b. 30%	b. 50%	b. 25%	b. 50%
	c. 35%	c. 20%	c. 40%	c. 30%
	d. 25%	d. 25%	d. 30%	d. 15%
6	a. 10%	a. 25%	a. 5%	a. 15%
	b. 15%	b. 15%	b. 30%	b. 40%
	c. 30%	c. 30%	c. 25%	c. 20%
	d. 45%	d. 30%	d. 40%	d. 25%
7	a. 45%	a. 25%	a. 40%	a. 20%
	b. 0	b. 5%	b. 5%	b. 20%
	c. 15%	c. 25%	c. 20%	c. 20%
	d. 40%	d. 45%	d. 35%	d. 40%
8	a. 85%	a. 90%	a. 65%	a. 90%
	b. 15%	b. 5%	b. 35%	b. 5%
	c. 0	c. 0	c. 0	c. 5%
	d. 0	d. 5%	d. 0	d. 0
9	a. 80%	a. 80%	a. 85%	a. 70%
	b. 10%	b. 5%	b. 10%	b. 20%
	c. 10%	c. 15%	c. 5%	c. 10%
10	a. 35%	a. 15%	a. 15%	a. 35%
	b. 15%	b. 5%	b. 5%	b. 10%
	c. 10%	c. 15%	c. 15%	c. 10%
	d. 40%	d. 65%	d. 65%	d. 45%

Table 19.2 Responses to questions on judicial precedents

Question no	Judges	Law teachers	Lawyers	Law students
1	a. 75%	a. 65%	a. 60%	a. 55%
	b. 25%	b. 30%	b. 40%	b. 45%
	c. 0	c. 5%	c. 0	c. 0
2	a. 95%	a. 85	a. 95%	a. 60%
	b. 5%	b. 10%	b. 5%	b. 30%
	c. 0	c. 5%	c. 0	c. 10%
3	a. 80%	a. 75%	a. 85%	a. 70%
	b. 20%	b. 15%	b. 15%	b. 30%
	c. 0	c. 10%	c. 0	c. 0
4	a. 65%	a. 45%	a. 50%	a. 65%
	b. 35%	b. 50%	b. 45%	b. 35%
	c. 0	c. 5%	c. 5%	c. 0
5	a. 80%	a. 95%	a. 65%	a. 60%
	b. 15%	b. 0	b. 30%	b. 35%
	c. 5%	c. 5%	c. 5%	c. 5%
6	a. 90%	a. 90%	a. 70%	a. 70%
	b. 10%	b. 0	b. 20%	b. 20%
	c. 0	c. 10%	c. 10%	c. 10%
7	a. 100%	a. 80%	a. 75%	a. 85%
	b. 0	b. 10%	b. 10%	b. 10%
	c. 0	c. 10%	c. 15%	c. 5%
8	a. 100%	a. 85%	a. 85%	a. 100%
	b. 0	b. 5%	b. 10%	b. 0
	c. 0	c. 10%	c. 5%	c. 0
9	a. 90%	a. 85%	a. 95%	a. 95%
	b. 10%	b. 10%	b. 5%	b. 5%
	c. 0	c. 5%	c. 0	c. 0
10	a. 85%	a. 65%	a. 90%	a. 80%
	b. 15%	b. 30%	b. 10%	b. 20%
	c. 0	c. 5%	c. 0	c. 0

1. It is very important to engage citizens in water-related issues in a multi-pronged manner. We need to sensitize people about healthy practices of daily water usage. Both direct usage such as drinking, washing, etc., and indirect usage in manufacturing activities need to be considered. This would result in environmentally responsible behavior. Home water conservation, landscaping and garden practices and community education can bring good results.

2. A strong focus on rainwater harvesting is required. We need to study both ancient practices and new technology for arriving at best model. The hill areas need these strategies the most.
3. We need to systematically plan water demand management strategies. Using "block rates" or conservation rates, whereby as households increase the amount of water they consume, they are charged higher; encourages conservation and needs to be promoted
4. Every state has its own unique challenges and needs considerable freedom to formulate its own policies under an umbrella policy on water scarcity. For ex, Himachal Pradesh; the snow laden place; the home of perineal rivers Ravi, Chenab, Beas, and Sutlej is also facing water scarcity.
5. Traditional water harvesting structures like *Baories*, dug wells, step wells, *khatries* and springs are the traditional water harvesting structures have been used as source of drinking water for centuries. They need to be restored.
6. We must inculcate the culture of treating water as a community property and trust for future generation. Thus, not a private property.
7. The data clearly shows that most of the respondents have considerable information about the issue, but the authors believe that we need to continue uninterrupted dissemination of information about water scarcity and judicial precedents, since the information needs to be converted into serious action.
8. Water scarcity needs to be taught as a part of curriculum in schools as citizen science.
9. Children need to be sensitized about water scarcity with the help of awareness activities. This will help in developing a sense of responsibility for personal water usage and agony of people affected by water scarcity. Restricted water usage exercises for students can be of great help.
10. All the governmental schemes relating to fresh water supply, sanitation, etc., need proper dissemination of information to public at large.
11. Factors like public acceptance, regional culture, historical issues, investments in water infrastructure, developing techniques, etc., need to be considered while forming policies relating to water scarcity. Policy and pricing reforms need proper pre-analysis.

It is pertinent to note that water scarcity will also have severe impact on vulnerable groups especially women and female children who have the duty for collection of water. This can further result into security issues and school dropouts in rural areas. Children living in high water stress regions will get affected the most.

The issues relating to displacement have also been identified by UN and other international agencies.

References

A Brief History of Water and Health from Ancient Civilizations to Modern Times. IWA. www.iwapublishing.com/news/brief-history-water-and-health-ancient-civilizations-modern-times. Accessed 19 April 2020

A.P. Pollution Control Board II vs. Prof. M. V. Nayudu (Retd.) & Ors., (2001) 2 SCC 62

Agarwal A, Narain S (1997) Dying wisdom. Centre for Science and Environment, New Delhi, pp 42–43

A.P. Pollution Control Board II vs. Prof.M. V. Nayudu (Retd.) &Ors., (2001) 2 SCC 62

Anil Agarwal and Sunita Narain, Dying wisdom (New Delhi: Centre for Science and Environment 1997), 42–43

Bruce Lankford, Karen Bakker, Mark Zeitoun, Declan Conway "The web of sustainable water security" in Water Security Principles, Perspectives and Practices, eds Bruce Lankford, Karen Bakker, Mark Zeitoun, Declan Conway (London: Routledge 2013)

Central Ground Water Board (CGWB). http://cgwb.gov.in/aboutcgwa.html

Cullet Philippe (2019, March 8) Model Groundwater (Sustainable Management) Bill, 2017: A New Paradigm for Groundwater Regulation. Centre for Policy Research. https://www.cprindia.org/articles/model-groundwater-sustainable-management-bill-2017-new-paradigm-groundwater-regulation

Central Ground Water Board (CGWB). http://cgwb.gov.in/aboutcgwa.html

Hari Pal Singh, M.R. Sharma, Quamural Hassan, Naved Ahsan "Impact of drought on drinking water resources in Himanchal Pradesh' Biological Forum—An International Journal, 2(1) (2010):73

Hinch Lal Tiwari vs Kamala Devi, (2001) 6 SCC 496

Hindu PTI (2016, May 24). SC refuses to ask Maharashtra to cut water supply to liquor industry Hindu. https://www.thehindu.com/news/cities/mumbai/SC-refuses-to-ask-Maharashtra-to-cut-water-supply-to-liquor-industry/article14336931.ece

Hindustan Coca-Cola Beverages (P) Ltd. vs Perumatty Grama Panchayat. 2005(2)KLT554

https://www.downtoearth.org.in/blog/water/india-s-water-crisis-the-seen-and-unseen-76049

https://www.downtoearth.org.in/news/water/every-fifth-child-faces-water-scarcity-globally-unicef-report-76048

https://www.indiatoday.in/magazine/cover-story/story/20210329-the-great-indian-thirst-1781280-2021-03-20

Jagran Josh (2015, July 15). Tripartite Struggle for Kannauj. Jagran Josh. https://www.jagranjosh.com/general-knowledge/tripartite-struggle-for-kannauj-1437459496-1

Jayna Kothari. http://www.ielrc.org/activities/workshop_0612/content/d0607.pdf

Jitendra Singh v. Ministry of Environment, 2019 SCC Online 1510 pr 20

Kashyap (2017, May 8) Bombay HC Bars Issuance Of Occupancy Certificate In Light Of Severe Water Scarcity In Thane. Livelaw. https://www.livelaw.in/bombay-hc-bars-issuance-occupancy-certificate-light-severe-water-scarcity-thane-read-order

KM Ashok (2016, April 27) SC refuses to allow IPL matches in drought hit Maharashtra in May, Livelaw. https://www.livelaw.in/sc-refuses-allow-ipl-matches-drought-hit-maharashtra-may/

Lankford B, Bakker K, Zeitoun M, Conway D (2013) The web of sustainable water security. In: Lankford B, Bakker K, Zeitoun M, Conway D (eds) Water security principles, perspectives and practices. Routledge, London

Millennium Development Goals, Final Report of India' Ministry of Statistics and Programme Implementation, Government of India. http://www.mospi.gov.in/sites/default/files/publication_reports/MDG_Final_Country_report_of_India_27nov17.pdf. Accessed 2 May 2020

M.C Mehta vs Kamal Nath, (1997) 1 Suppl. S.C.C. 388

Narmada Bachao Andolan vs Union of India, (2000) 10 SCC 664

Nodal Agency: InLt. Col. Sarvadaman Singh Oberoi v. Union of India (2020) 2020 SCC OnLine NGT 862

Plumber Mustafa (2019, December 6) There Is No Guaranteed Right To Continue To Draw Ground Water For Commercial Purposes : NGT, Livelaw, https://www.livelaw.in/environment/ngt-groundwater-is-scarce-and-not-unlimited-150536

Plumber Mustafa (2019, October 22) NGT Bars Groundwater Extraction For Commercial Purpose By Industries In Ghaziabad Area, Livelaw. https://www.livelaw.in/environment/ngt-groundwater-is-scarce-and-not-unlimited-150536

Plumber Mustafa (2020, January 9) NGT Directs Discontinuation Of Groundwater Extraction By Two Carpet Manufacturing Units In Rewari, Livelaw. https://www.livelaw.in/environment/ngt-directs-discontinuation-of-groundwater-extraction-by-two-carpet-manufacturing-units-in-rewari-151443

Press Information Bureau. https://pib.gov.in/PressReleasePage.aspx?PRID=1557592

Saxena C (2012) The concept of water in Rig Veda. Int J Soc Sci Interdiscipl Res 1(8). http://www.indianresearchjournals.com/pdf/IJSSIR/2012/August/11.pdf

Science daily. https://www.sciencedaily.com/terms/water_scarcity.htm

Shaikh M (2016, February 22) Delhi Water crisis: Supreme Court slams AAP Government over Munak canal row. India.com. https://www.india.com/news/cities/delhi-water-crisis-supreme-court-slams-aap-government-over-munak-canal-row-968580/

Singh HP, Sharma MR, Hassan Q, Ahsan N (2010) Impact of drought on drinking water resources in Himanchal Pradesh. Biol Forum Int J 2(1):73

Swaraj Abhiyan vs Union of India, 2017 SCCOnLine SC1589

The Hindu, India faces worst water crisis: NITI Aayog. https://www.thehindu.com/sci-tech/energy-and-environment/india-faces-worst-water-crisis-niti-aayog/article24165708.ece

UN World Water Development Report 2020: Water and Climate Change. https://unesdoc.unesco.org/ark:/48223/pf0000372985.locale=en

UN Water (2021) Summary Progress Update 2021: SDG 6—water and sanitation for all. https://www.unwater.org/publications/summary-progress-update-2021-sdg-6-water-and-sanitation-for-all/

UN Water (nd). https://www.unwater.org/water-facts/scarcity/

Vellore Citizens Welfare Forum vs Union of India, (1996) 5 SCC 647

Visser J, Cottle E, Mettler J (2002) The free basic water supply policy: how effective is it in realising the right? ESR Rev 3(1), July 2002. http://www.communitylawcentre.org.za/ser/esr2002/2002july_water.php

'Water crisis in Himanchal Pradesh' Peoples democracy. https://peoplesdemocracy.in/2018/0603_pd/water-crisis-himachal-pradesh. Accessed 21 April 2020

'Water crisis in Himanchal Pradesh' Peoples democracy. Accessed April 21, 2020. https://peoplesdemocracy.in/2018/0603_pd/water-crisis-himachal-pradesh

Water Crisis in Himanchal' India Environment Portal. http://www.indiaenvironmentportal.org.in/content/145805/water-crisis-in-himachal. Accessed 21 April 2020

Water policy in India: a review. Research gate. https://www.researchgate.net/publication/235919642_Water_Policy_in_India_A_Review. Accessed 2 May 2020

World Resources Institute. https://www.wri.org/insights/7-reasons-were-facing-global-water-crisis

World Wilflife Fund. https://www.worldwildlife.org/threats/water-scarcity

The manufacturer's authorised representative in the EU is Springer Nature Customer Service Centre GmbH, Europaplatz 3, 69115 Heidelberg, Germany. If you have any concerns regarding our products, please contact ProductSafety@springernature.com

Printed and bound by CPI Group (UK) Ltd, Croydon, CR0 4YY
01/10/2026
02225930-0008